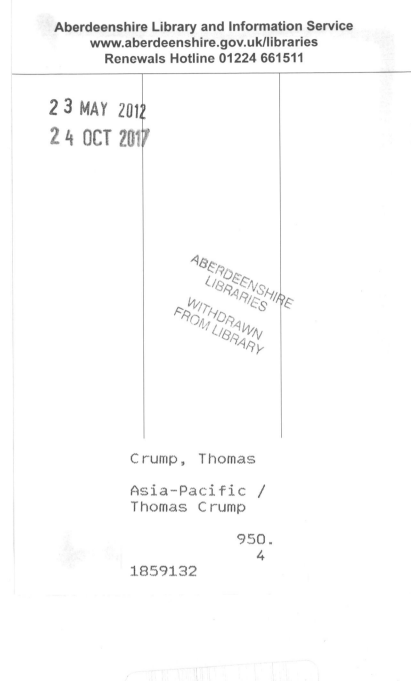

Asia-Pacific

Thomas Crump

hambledon
continuum

Hambledon Continuum is an imprint of Continuum Books
Continuum UK, The Tower Building, 11 York Road, London SE1 7NX
Continuum US, 80 Maiden Lane, Suite 704, New York, NY 10038

www.continuumbooks.com

First published 2007

British Library Cataloguing-in-Publication Data
A catalogue record for this book is available from the British Library.

ISBN 978 1 85285 518 5

Typeset by Egan Reid, Auckland, New Zealand
Printed and bound by MPG Books Ltd, Cornwall, Great Britain

Contents

Table 1: Book Structure

	Old Pacific		New Pacific		
Chapters	2–5	6–12	13	16	17
Region	East Asia	Southeast Asia	Russian Far East	North America	Australasia
Area (1,000 sq. km)	10,196	4,224	5,000 (17,075[1])	3,305 (19,131)	7,961
Population (millions)	1,473	482	8 (146)	47 (306)	23
Main Languages	Chinese, Japanese, Korean	Chinese,[2] English, Khmer, Indo-Malay,[3] Thai, Vietnamese	Russian	English[4]	English
Separate States (number in square brackets)	China, Japan, North Korea, South Korea (Taiwan[5]) [4]	Indonesia, Cambodia, Malaysia, Philippines, Papua-New Guinea (PNG), Singapore, Thailand, Vietnam [8]	Russia [1]	Canada US [2]	Australia, New Zealand [2]

1 The figures given in brackets for area and population relate to the totals for the countries listed: so that, for instance, the total area of North America is 19,131,000 sq. km while the total population is 306,000,000. The smaller numbers, respectively 3,305,000 and 47,000,000 sq. km, are for the states and provinces – Alaska, British Columbia, California, Oregon and Washington – actually on the Pacific. A similar rule explains the figures given for Latin America and Russia.

2 Chinese only has official status in Singapore, but is widely spoken throughout all the other states of Southeast Asia.

3 This comprises two official languages, Malay, spoken in Malaysia and Bahasi Indonesia, spoken in Indonesia: the distinction between the two follows a decision of the Indonesian government made at the time independence was granted in 1949.

4 The North American west coast is noted for its ethnic diversity: Spanish, in particular, is widely spoken among the Latino population of California.

5 Although the PRC has, sincc its foundation in 1949, consistently claimed Taiwan as a province, it has never been able to enforce its rule over the island.

East Asia

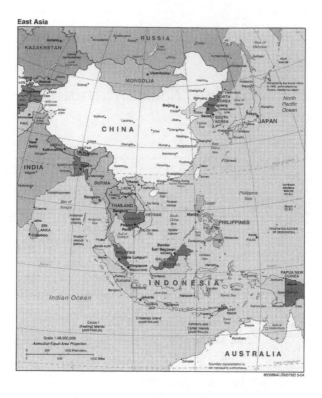

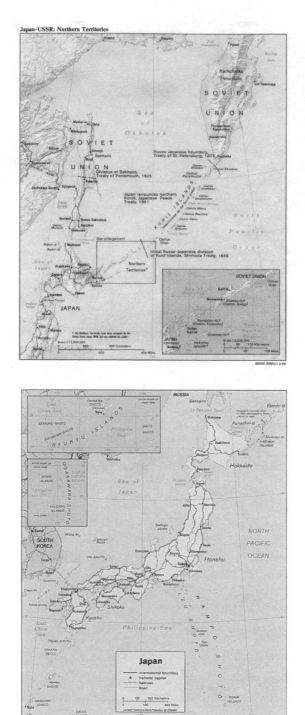

Japan-USSR: Northern Territories

Japan

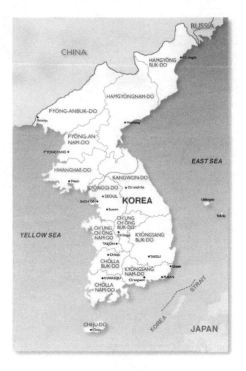

Abbreviations

ABIM	Islam Youth Movement of Malaya
ABRI	Armed Forces of Republic of Indonesia
ANZUS	Australia, New Zealand and United States
APEC	Asia-Pacific Economic Community
Apodeti	Timorese Popular Democratic Association.
ASEAN	Association of Southeast Asian Nation
ASG	Abu Sayyef group
BLDP	Buddhist Liberal Democratic Party
CGDK	Coalition Government of Democratic Kampuchea
CIA	Central Intelligence Agency
COMECON	Council for Mutual Economic Assistance
CPP	Cambodian Peoples Party
DMZ	Demilitarized zone
DRP	Democratic Republican Party
DRV	Democratic Republic of Vietnam
EEC	European Economic Community (now EU)
EU	European Union
FAO	Food and Agriculture Organisation
FDI	foreign direct investment
FIDF	Financial Institutions Development Fund
Fretilin	Revolutionary Front of Independent East Timor.
Funcinpec	Front uni national pour un Cambodge indépendent , neutre, pacifique et cooperative
GAM	Independent Aceh movement
GATT	General Agreement on Trade and Tariffs
GDP	Gross Domestic Product
gestapu	September 30 Movement
GULAG	
GVN	Government of Vietnam
IAEA	International Atomic Energy Authority
IAIN	State Institute for Islamic Studies
ICMI	All-Indonesian Union of Muslim Intellectuals
IGGI	Inter-governmental Group on Indonesia

IMF	International Monetary Fund
IOC	International Olympic Committee
IPTN	Indonesian air-craft industry
ISA	Internal Security Act
ISPS	International ship and port facility security code_
ITTO	International Tropical Timber Organization
JAL	Japan Airlines
KAMI	Indonesian Students Action Front
KCIA	Korean Central Intelligence Agency
KEDO	Korean Peninsular Energy Development Organization
KNUFNS	Kampuchean National United Front for National Salvation
Kostrad	Army Strategic Reserve Command
KPDR	Korean People's Democratic Republic
KPM	Royal Steam Packet Company
KPNLF	Khmer People's National Liberation Front
KPPR	Khmer People's Revolutionary Party
KWP	Khmer Workers' Party
LDP	Liberal Democratic Party
LNG	liquefied natural gas
MCA	Malayan Chinese Association
MCP	Malayan Communist Party
METI	Ministry of Economics Trade and Industry
MITI	Ministry of International Trade and Industry
MNLA	Malayan National Liberation Army
MNLF	Moro National Liberation Front
MPRS	Provincial People's Consultative Assembly
MSC	Malaysian Solidarity Convention
NAFTA	North-American Free Trade Association.
NCNP	National Congress for New Politics
NCPO	National Council for Public Order
NLF	National Liberation Front
NOC	National Operations Council
NU	Nadhlatul Ulama
OECD	Organization for Economic Cooperation and Development
OPEC	Organisation of Petrol-Exporting Countries
OPM	Free Papua Organisation
PAP	People's Action Party
PAS	Pan-Malayan Islamic Party
PDA	People's Democratic Army
PDI	Indonesian Democratic Party
PKI	Indonesian Communist Party

PMIP	Pan-Malayan Islamic Party
PNG	Papua-New Guinea
PNI	Indonesian Nationalist Party
PRRI	Revolutionary Government of the Indonesian Republic
PSI	Indonesian Socialist Party
PRPK	People's Revolutionary Party of Kampuchea
ROK	Republic of Korea
RUSI	Republic of the United States of Indonesia
SAS	Special Air Services
SCAP	Supreme Command[er] Allies Pacific
SEATO	South East Asia Treaty Organization
SNC	Supreme National Council
SPP	Singapore Progressive Party
Supersemar	11th March letter of instruction
TBT	Tributyl phosphate
TEU	twenty-feet equivalent unit
UDT	Timor Democratic Union
UMNO	United Malay National Organization
UNTAC	United Nations Transitional Authority in Cambodia
USAF	United States Air Force
VWP	Vietnamese Workers' Party
WTO	World Trade Organisation

1

Introduction: the world of Asia-Pacific

ESSENTIAL GEOGRAPHY

Asia-Pacific may suggest an ungainly beast, but it is still one which has half the world as its domain. The problem for Europeans and East-coast Americans is that it is far from their *Atlantic* half of the world, which is also safely beyond reach of any rockets that Kim Jong Il may decide to launch from North Korea. Kim's sights, from his Asian base, are on the American west coast – the other side of his ocean, the Pacific. San Francisco may be at risk; Washington is safe. Quite consistently, Asia-Pacific, on any terms – economic, political, cultural – is where the action has been for most of the last sixty-odd years since the end of World War II. This is not just my conviction: it is also that of almost all those who have ventured into this region. The title of an exhaustive recent study, Niall Ferguson's *The Way of the World: Twentieth-Century Conflict and the Descent of the West* [1] – which concludes with the thesis that 'Asia was the winner' [2] – says it all. By surveying in some detail the part of the world, Asia-Pacific, which counts for more than any other in this process of conflict and decline, my book is designed to help understand it. The inherent fascination – and all too often horror – of the events it records are in any case compelling.

Asia-Pacific is a geographical concept that has emerged from the way the region it designates has developed in the years following the end of World War II in 1945. Its hard core is defined by the Asian nations with a Pacific coastline: these, in turn, are either 'continental' or 'insular'. Going from north to south, the *continental* nations – all part of the great Asian land-mass – are Russia, Korea, China, Vietnam, Cambodia, Thailand and mainland Malaysia. The *insular* nations are Japan, the Philippines, North Borneo, Singapore and Indonesia. The region shown by the map on page x extends beyond Asia – in the eastern Pacific, to include Canada and the United States (not shown), and in the southern Pacific to include Australia, and somewhat marginally Timor Leste and Papua New-Guinea. Asia-Pacific, according to this extended definition, is then presented in terms of the five regions of Table 1, of which the first two, East and Southeast Asia, belong to what I call – for good historical reasons – 'old Pacific' and the last three, the Russian Far East, North America and Australasia, to the 'new Pacific'.

This world was transformed World War II, in which, unlike the first, key battles were fought in the Pacific theatre – at great costs in men, material and territory, to both sides. Losses were not confined to the armed forces: the civilian populations of the old Pacific overrun by Japanese armies endured the horrors of occupation, while in Japan itself cities were reduced to ruins by American bombing. While most of the tens of millions who died were Asians, hundreds of thousands of Europeans and Americans, both soldiers and civilians, also lost their lives, to say nothing of those who suffered as prisoners of the Japanese. The Europeans, in particular, if asked what they were fighting for, would simply have answered 'the restoration of the world lost to the Japanese'. After 1945 it took many of them a long time to realize that this was not what history had in store for them. Far too many of the ordinary people on the ground wanted a new and different world, and critically they almost always had American support when it counted. Even so, for some thirty years after 1945 the historical process was nearly derailed by the threat of a communist takeover.

This first chapter, looking in turn at each of the five regions of Table 1, provides short historical summaries of the period before the end of the Pacific War. First, however, it is useful to note, as significant background, some general characteristics specific to the region – or at least the greater part of it. On the geophysical side, there are extremes of weather, with cold winters and hot, steamy summers in the temperate zone, and hurricanes – particularly in late summer – in the tropical and the subtropical regions. Extreme seismic activity – earthquakes, volcanic eruptions and tsunamis – are the product of a 'ring of fire' around the Pacific Rim. As for cultural geography, Asia-Pacific is to be noted both for the diversity of its major languages[3] – English, Russian, Chinese, Korean, Japanese, Vietnamese, Thai and Bahai Indonesia belong mostly to quite separate language groups[4] – and for the presence of countless secondary languages, many without any written form and almost all unknown outside local communities. On the human side, also, urban populations counted in tens of millions are to be found on both sides of the Pacific, particularly in coastal areas – in some cases, such as notably Australia, China, Russia and the United States, in countries with vast unpopulated areas inland.

Returning to the five regions, it is useful to look first at the two regions, East and Southeast Asia, of the old Pacific, which, in contrast to the three regions of the new Pacific, comprise states with a recorded history going back hundreds, if not thousands, of years – noting that the impact of the Western world was at best marginal until the great sixteenth-century voyages of discovery. What is more every one of the states of the old Pacific evolved around a core culture, each with its dominant written language:[5] at the same time, however, other aspects of culture, such as the Buddhist religion, extended across the regions – an early instance of globalization.

The key historical distinction between East and Southeast Asia – the key regions of the 'western' Pacific[6] – is defined by European nineteenth-century colonial history. In spite of the success of European powers – joined later by the US – in establishing a dominant commercial presence in East Asia, none of the four states in this region ever became part of a European[7] colonial empire. Of the eight states of Southeast Asia only Thailand escaped this fate. Although the Southeast Asian colonial empires were seemingly indestructible at the turn of the twentieth century, no part of them long survived the devastation of the Pacific War (1941–45), in which almost all their territory was lost to Japan. The basic framework, as of the beginning of the twenty-first century (shown by Table 1 on page vii), began to acquire its present structure almost immediately after World War II as a result of a many-stranded historical process which defines the substance of this book. Table 1 lists 17 separate states, allocated to five separate regions, providing the subject matter of chapters 2 to 13, and of chapters 16 and 17. Each of the five regions has its own identity defined by certain shared characteristics, the result of a significant level of historical interaction. This in turn underlies the distinction, apparent in the first row of headings, between the old and new Pacific.

In the fifty-odd years up to 1940 almost the only events that counted internationally in the Asia-Pacific theatre derived from the violent interaction, orchestrated at every stage by Japan, between that country and China. Because the key events mostly took part in the years of the world economic depression, which followed the great stock market crash of 1929, the other Asia-Pacific countries listed in Table 1 – including the colonial empires in Southeast Asia – were almost completely tied up with domestic issues. The problem, at every level, was simply to make ends meet, when commodity exports – the mainstay of every national and colonial economy – fetched record low prices. Inevitably, poor rural communities lost the most. Japan itself suffered no less from the depression: its powerful military establishment's reaction to it led, however, to its following a path of conquest in China that led, in the end, to World War II. For this reason a disproportionate part of this first chapter is devoted to East Asia, where the trouble all started. If the events recorded in the following section had never taken place, world history would have been a quite different story.

CHINA AND JAPAN

The key to East Asian history in the early twentieth century was the gradual collapse of Imperial China, a process which finally came to an end in 1911, following nearly a century of incursions by foreign powers, each intent on establishing its own privileges – if necessary by force of arms – as an instrument of economic exploitation. Whatever the contributions of, among others, the British, French, Germans, Japanese, Russians and Americans – each with their own *treaty ports* along the coasts and rivers of China – to the development of a modern economy, the *foreign devils* were unwelcome not only to the majority of the population, but also to the Imperial Court, presided over almost to the end of its days by the renowned Dowager Empress, Ci-Xi. The climax came with the Boxer Rebellion of 1900,[8] when a fanatical religious movement, which Ci-Xi did little to restrain, rose up against the foreigners, creating considerable terror but in the end failing to dislodge them.

The empire, when it finally collapsed in 1911, yielded to the first Chinese republic: this was led by Sun Yatsen – still remembered as the 'Father of the Nation' – after he had succeeded in merging a number of pre-existing revolutionary groups into a single party, the Guomindang. The state soon disintegrated, after a key commander, General Yuan Shikai, turned on Sun Yatsen, while, at the same time, imperial Japan – which had joined the allied powers at the beginning of World War I – extended its hold on the mainland by taking over German territorial interests. Where Yuan had led in betraying the new republic, others followed. By 1916 China had become a battle-ground contested by local warlords, some of whom – such as Zhang Zuolin in Manchuria – became extremely powerful.

Sun Yatsen, forced into exile, sought foreign contacts useful to his cause, which was simply to restore the republic under the Guomindang. Through a Dutch trade union activist, Hendrik Sneevliet,[9] he came in contact with the Communist International – Lenin's 'Comintern' – which had taken the first steps to organize the party in China. In Shanghai, its first congress, in July 1921, was attended by 60 delegates – one of whom happened to be called Mao Zedong. At the party's third congress in 1923 Sneevliet persuaded its members to work within the Guomindang, having already prepared the ground with Sun Yatsen. The communists were acceptable to Sun because the aim of both sides was to end Western imperialism, in other words, to ring down the curtain on 'treaty-port China'. At the same time the alliance would face down the warlords, who, to many in the new Chinese Communist Party (CCP), were the main enemy.

Sun found a powerful new ally in Jiang Jieshi,[10] who soon attained a dominant position in the party, at the same time organizing a well-disciplined military force known as the National Revolutionary Army. Then, after Sun died in 1925, Jiang was the strong man who took over the party. Starting in Guangzhou in June 1926, Jiang led his new army on a path of conquest: by the end of the year he had taken several important cities along both the Yangze and the coast of Fukien, defeating the warlords who stood in his way.

Jiang continued his advance and in March 1927, captured first Shanghai and then Nanjing. A month later, as his forces tightened their hold on Shanghai, a communist-led mass-uprising, after disarming the police, took over much of the city. The foreign business community had already had its fill of communist-led strikes, and the Western powers organized the defence of the foreign settlements with their own troops. Jiang then ordered the irregular forces to surrender their arms, but a hardcore numbering some three thousand held out. By a clever subterfuge Jiang captured its leaders, who were sent off to summary execution; that was the end not only of the Chinese Communist Party in Shanghai but also of its alliance with the Guomindang. One captured leader did, however, escape: his name, Zhou Enlai, would become well known in the subsequent history of China. Another, Mao Zedong – whose day was yet to come – was conveniently absent from Shanghai at the critical time.

Jiang had cost his lot with the West. In the summer of 1927 the general commanding the hardcore of the communist militia decided to join him. Jiang then purged the combined forces of all communists. Stalin, informed of this move, ordered a series of communist revolts against Jiang's army: although at this early stage they had little success, these were the opening moves in a revolution that would not end until Mao's decisive victory in 1949. A year later the consolidated Guomindang forces advanced to occupy northern China. Zhang Zuolin, the Manchurian warlord, abandoned Beijing, which fell to Jiang's army on 8 June 1928. With warlords no longer dividing up China into their own domains, the country was united under one government for the first time since the fall of the empire in 1911.

Jiang still faced two considerable long-term problems: on one side the communists, if down, were by no means out; on the other, the Japanese, always ready to fish in the troubled waters, were only too ready to resort to armed force, in any confrontation with China. For three years, however, from 1928 to 1931, he had something of a respite. Then Japan occupied Manchuria in 1931 going on, in 1933, to take over the whole of China north of the Great Wall, with a demilitarized zone embracing Beijing and Tianjin established to the south of it. The result was that in a large and important part of the country Jiang's government, and particularly his armed forces, could only operate within the limits imposed by local Japanese commanders. At the same time the communists had established a strong base in Jiangshi province in south China, where, in January 1931, their 'Fourth Army' successfully held out in the face of encirclement by a strong Guomindang force.

Although communist guerrillas avoided direct confrontation with Guomindang forces, the Jiangshi Soviet Republic, set up in 1931, still provided an indispensable territorial base for deployment and supply. The province of Jiangshi was, however, too close for comfort to the main power base of the Guomindang, as counter-attacks made by Jiang's generals made clear in the years 1931 to 1934. By the end of the summer of 1934 the Communist Red Army, following defeat in a key battle at Guangchang, was completely encircled by some 400,000 Guomindang troops.

The only possible salvation lay in a break-out towards the west, away from the main power base of the Guomindang. In October 1934 some 87,000 communists, with a heavily overloaded baggage train, managed to get through the block-houses surrounding Jiangxi, only to find themselves confronting Guomindang forces across the Xiang, the widest river in Hunan province. Instead of finding hoped-for reinforcements they were forced into a battle with the Guomindang in which they lost more than half their numbers. Even so Jiang still allowed the survivors to escape across the river. This was not just carelessness, but part of a grand strategy designed to lead the communists into confronting warlords in western China who were still holding out against the Guomindang.

Such, at all events, was the beginning of the epic journey known to history as the 'Long March'. Although at first absent, Mao Zedong rejoined the Red Army later in the year, and supported by Zhou Enlai, persuaded the soldiers not to move north, where the Guomindang would be waiting for them, but far inland to the west. There they could consolidate their forces – to live to fight another day. Following the tactics laid down by Mao, the soldiers moved, with a minimum of equipment and remarkable speed, across appalling difficult country – as they would continue to do for most of 1935. In the middle of January the party's Central Committee, after meeting for three days in the remote city of Zunyi, accepted Mao's strategy, at the same time voting for a major reform of the party hierarchy. At the end of the day Mao had gained control of the Red Army, with Zhou Enlai as his second in command. This was a very strong team, better able that any of its predecessors to take a party line independent of the Comintern. What is more, Mao, from the early days of the 1920s, had built up a carefully constructed claim to represent the interests of the millions of Chinese peasants[11] – promising the overthrow of local tyrants and the expulsion of foreigners, while Zhou – who, with Deng Xiaoping, had spent two years (1920–22) working with the Comintern in France – knew how to deal with the outside world. Although no written reports of what happened during the Zunyi conference ever surfaced, the decisions then made were to change the course of history. Mao was chairman of the Chinese Communist Party (CCP) until his death in 1976, becoming the first president of People's Republic of China in 1949, while Zhou became the first prime minister and foreign secretary.

Sooner or later, the Long March would have to change direction and turn north – otherwise the Red Army would have ended up in the jungles of northern Burma. In the spring of 1935, Mao set his sights on the northwest province of Shaanshi, which proved to be the end-point of the Long March. There, in

October 1936, Mao established his headquarters in the town of Yan'an. Although only 20,000 survived the Long March, Shaanshi was a good base for the CCP both to consolidate and recruit new members – which, over the course of time, it did with considerable success. The greatest problem, shortage of food in a poor agricultural area, was in part solved by Mao's unprecedentedly effective mobilization of the peasants. Even so it could have proved fatal had it not been for the outbreak of full-scale war between Japan and China in July 1937.

Although Jiang was still intent on winning the war against the Red Army, locally recruited Guomindang troops in northern China – by capturing and holding him to ransom on a visit to their front – secured his commitment to a united front to fight the Japanese. On the other side Mao received a directive from the Comintern to collaborate with Jiang. The alliance, therefore, was sealed, even though both parties were in their hearts against it. Its result was immediately advantageous to Mao, who was free to build up the Yan'an Soviet without fearing any interference from Guomindang forces. It was to remain his operational base for nearly ten years, with neither the Japanese nor the Guomindang able to dislodge him.

Inevitably the balance of power changed drastically as a result of the full-scale war with Japan. By the end of 1937, China had lost its economic heartland, including Shanghai and the capital, Nanjing. Although about half of the population fell under Japanese rule, to suffer the appalling hardships that went with it, only a small fraction of Chinese territory was actually surrendered – there were even parts of the coastline which the Japanese never occupied. Holding on to territory, at any cost, was never the Guomindang strategy. On the contrary, Guomindang defence was based on 'trading space for time' – much the same strategy as Mao had used against Jiang in the period before he finally ended up in Yan'an. The result, also, for Jiang, was much the same. With Nanjing lost, he had been forced, by the end of 1938, to move his capital to Chongqing, far inland on the Yangze river – to remain there until the end of the Pacific War. The result was a sort of strategic triangle, with Jiang in Chongqing, Mao in Yan'an, and the Japanese in the main cities and harbours.

By this time events in China were making considerable impact on the outside world, particularly in the US. In August 1937 President Franklin D. Roosevelt increased the American garrison in Shanghai, while urging US civilians to leave China. In September US merchant ships were forbidden to transport war material to either side, a move calculated to hinder Japan's war effort. More important in the long run was a doom-laden speech by Roosevelt on 5 October 1937, in which he told the American people, how, 'without a declaration of war … civilians … are being ruthlessly murdered by bombs from the air … ships are being attacked and sunk by submarines without cause or notice', going on to add, 'Let no one imagine that America will escape … that this Western hemisphere will not be attacked ... the peace-loving nations must make a concerted effort to uphold laws and principles on which peace alone can rest secure'.[12]

Roosevelt's words were directed not only to Japan, but also to Nazi Germany, which was actively supporting General Franco in the Spanish Civil War. In both cases the majority of Americans – whose views were shared emphatically by the Congress – were opposed to sanctions. Even so the line-up of forces in the world conflict predicted by Roosevelt was becoming clear, with Italy, in November, 1937, joining Germany and Japan in the anti-Comintern pact.

Jiang's position, as declared from Chongqing, was simple: 'the time must come when Japan's military strength will be exhausted thus giving China the ultimate victory'.[13] Jiang, however, contributed little to the process of exhaustion. His forces, such as they were, had only two supply routes from the outside world: the shorter started at Haiphong in French Indochina, while the longer, developed in the course of 1938, was the Burma Road starting at Rangoon on the Indian Ocean. Essential supplies did reach Chongqing over both routes, but Jiang made poor use of them. Two American officers built up the only effective arms of the Guomindang military: one, Claire Chennault, helped by American mercenary pilots, built up the air-force, and the other, Joseph Stilwell, the US Military Attaché, did his best to train the Guomindang army to fight the Japanese. Here he was continuously frustrated by Jiang, who was far more concerned to hold Guomindang forces back for future deployment against the communists. Jiang's essential strategy, as Stilwell saw it, was to rely on the US for defeating the Japanese.

If, in the early years of World War II, this was quite unrealistic, the position changed radically after the Nazi blitzkrieg overran Western Europe in the early summer of 1940. Then the US government intervened actively on the side of China. A series of trade embargoes on the export of essential war material – of which the first was imposed on 25 July 1940 – culminated, on 1 August 1941, with a complete oil embargo combined with all Japanese assets being frozen by the US, the UK and the Netherlands. The course was set for war, and with the Japanese attack on Pearl Harbor on 7 December, Jiang's American strategy became entirely realistic – at least as seen from Chongqing.

For Jiang the pay-off came with the defeat of Japan in August 1945. His own forces had contributed relatively little – although few in the West were willing to give him away. In reality the Guomindang, with a corrupt regime based on forced labour and indifferent to starvation among millions of Chinese peasants, had relied on local warlords and the military to remain in power, while radical intellectuals, if they remained in Chongqing, did their best to subvert it, and if they did not, found their way to join Mao in Yan'an. Inevitably, with the end of the war in 1945, the Guomindang, with its history of corruption and intrigue during the years in Chongqing, was poorly equipped to meet the challenge of rebuilding

China after eight years of devastation and occupation by the Japanese.

All the while Mao was in Yan'an biding his time. With the recruitment of poor peasants, the numbers in his forces increased tenfold from 90,000 to 900,000 over the war years, 1937–45. Although Mao was ruthless in his demands for individual sacrifice, he successfully promoted his regime as offering something better than subordination to money-lenders, absentee landlords and non-local officials. In Yan'an Mao paid much attention to establishing the theoretical basis for his future government of China. Known as 'Mao Zedong thought', its focus was on *wuchan jieji*, or the 'property-less class', which included both peasants and the urban proletariat. The Chinese challenge to Marxist-Leninism was that it had to reckon with over two thousand years of feudalism and only forty of capitalism – at a time when Mao was still cooperating with the Comintern. In the critical midwar years, 1942–44, Mao's programme of 'thought reform', with its focus of non-complying individuals, such as anti-Guomindang exiles in Yan'an, consolidated his leadership of the CCP.

From 1943, as US forces gained the upper hand in the Pacific War, the Japanese hold on north China weakened, much to the advantage of Mao in Yan'an. Then, in 1944, Jiang lost many of his best soldiers to the Japanese 'Ichigo offensive' south of the Yangze. By this time Washington, finally realizing that the CCP could be an important factor in post-war Chinese politics, sent the 'Dixie Mission'[14] to talk with Mao in Yan'an. Jiang was furious, but given his dependence on US supplies, did his best to conceal his feelings. Even so he refused to contemplate Mao's proposal – communicating to him by the Dixie Mission – for a coalition government with equal representation for the CCP and the Guomindang. The Americans, observing the CCP in Yan'an, were impressed by its buoyant mood: early in 1945, it went on to organize the seventh Party Congress, which confirmed that Mao had no rivals as leader of the party.

Where, in the late nineteenth century, China turned its back on the world, Japan opened up to assimilate and adapt not only the technology of the Western industrial powers, but also their legal systems and government institutions. Although this process is associated with the emperor Meiji (1858–1912), he was hardly more than a figurehead, content to take credit for the considerable achievements of the governments acting in his name. In the twenty or so years before World War I these included the establishment of a considerable Japanese presence on the mainland of East Asia, acquired not only in competition with leading European powers, but also at the cost of fighting two wars, the first against China in 1894, and the second against Russia, in 1904–05. Although both were won decisively by Japan, in 1895 France, Germany and Italy – in the so-called 'triple intervention' – combined to prevent Japan from retaining all the mainland territory conquered in China, while, in 1905, President Theodore Roosevelt of the United States, concerned that Japan was becoming too powerful, dictated terms of peace which denied it almost all mainland territory conquered from Russia. Rioters in Tokyo protested against the poor terms of the treaty, but, for the second time in ten years, Japan had lost out in the game of diplomacy.

Japan's gains were still considerable: after 1895 it was allowed to retain the island of Taiwan (which had belonged to China since the seventeenth century), and after 1905, the Kuril Islands and the southern half of Sakhalin in the seas off the north coast of Hokkaido. Russia also had to withdraw its troops from Manchuria and accept unrestricted freedom of action for the Japanese in Korea, which, as a result, was the real loser from both wars. After 1905 neither Russia nor China was in a position to guarantee the territorial integrity of an ancient kingdom almost unknown to the outside world. This was an unmistakable invitation for a Japanese takeover, which was finally completed in 1910. Then, in 1914, Japan, having joined the allies in World War I, acquired the German territories on the Chinese mainland. Three years later, in 1917, the success of Lenin's October revolution in Russia, led to a large allied force being sent to Vladivostok. When the British and Americans withdrew after the end of World War I, the Japanese remained until 1922 with some 50,000 troops on the mainland. When they finally withdrew they allowed the Chinese warlord, Zhang Zuolin, whose fief included most of Manchuria, to help himself to the vast stockpile of munitions built up by the combined allied forces. With their sights still set on Manchuria the Japanese had acquired a valuable potential ally. They had, however, to bide their time, but when it came, events on the ground – which included blowing up two trains – orchestrated by the Japanese military, eventually led to China losing Manchuria, which in 1932 was set up by Tokyo as the vassal state of Manchukuo. Its emperor was Pu-yi, who, two years old when the Dowager Empress Ci-Xi died in 1908, was then heir to the throne. The world was horrified: on 24 February 1933 the Japanese delegates, quite unrepentant, walked out of the League of Nations, set up in 1919 by the Treaty of Versailles to guarantee international peace.

Three factors, not directly related to each other, explain the course of war followed by Japan in China in the 1930s. First, too many generals could – or would not – accept the authority of a cabinet government, responsible to parliament. Their position was enhanced by the rule that only high-ranking officers could be cabinet ministers in the service departments. In the 1930s the generals, more than ever before, insisted on their own agenda – often with large-scale public support.

The second factor was that – as seen from Tokyo – Japan, since the days of the triple intervention, had suffered a series of diplomatic defeats. The Japanese were consistently denied the spoils of every victory won in the field – whether over Chinese, Russians or Germans. Unmistakably they were second-class citizens in the world of the great powers – a position consistently taken by Prince Konoye, prime minister during much of the five years (1937–41) immediately preceding the Pacific War.

The third factor, in the 1930s, was the world-wide economic depression. In Japan – where welfare benefits were almost unknown – a job in an armaments factory or naval shipyard offered an escape from unemployment. The tradition of mutual support in rural Japan lost ground as many victims of the world-wide agricultural depression migrated to the cities. The popularity of Japan's expansionist policies led people at grass-roots level to accept the material hardship resulting from their country investing, disproportionately, in armaments and military operations.

The emperor was mainly important for being a stabilizing factor in a chaotic course of political events. He ruled, not by giving any explicit directions, but simply by virtue of the fact that he somehow stood above actual events. This was the essence of the official cult, which, in everyday life, meant displaying endless signs of respect for the emperor. It hardly mattered that Court Japanese was unintelligible to ordinary people, because there was never any occasion for the emperor actually to speak to them. If the emperor appeared at all, it was as a remote figure, riding on a white horse in a resplendent uniform, on ceremonial occasions staged by the military. The vast imperial establishment, known as the *kunaishō*, which was headed by its own minister in the cabinet, served to keep the emperor at a distance. In no sense was it an alternative cabinet or military high command. Its function was rather to dissimulate, to ensure that whatever intelligence did get through to the emperor was appropriately sanitized. As Saionji, one of Japan's most respected elder statesmen, noted, 'It is not necessary to lie but tell the emperor things that will please him in order to ease his mind.'[15]

From the early 1930s the emperor, to make sense of his position as a constitutional monarch, had to ride two horses at once, one representing the civil government, and other the military. With the setting up of the puppet state of Manchukuo in 1932, Japan passed a critical watershed. The emperor had proved powerless in dealing with the Manchurian crisis. Worse still, the Japanese people, completely unaware of his own views, rejoiced in the success of the 'Emperor's Army' in Manchuria, fully believing that the emperor himself shared their feelings. Civilian prime ministers bowed to the military.

The war in China escalated when, following a skirmish between Japanese and Chinese troops at the Marco Polo Bridge, close to Beijing, on 7 July 1937, Jiang Jieshi mobilized the Chinese army, while demanding direct negotiations with Tokyo. Then, on 14 August, Chinese planes bombed Japanese naval installations in Shanghai, provoking massive retaliation by local Japanese commanders who communicated next to nothing about their military operations to Prince Konoye's government in Tokyo.

In December, Konoye ordered the capture of Nanking, where Jiang Jieshi's government had taken refuge. While capturing the city, Japanese troops were responsible for 'the spontaneous and indiscriminate slaughter and torture … of … as many as 200,000 Chinese, including civilians and soldiers'. The 'Rape of Nanking' was reported world-wide and regarded as an unspeakable atrocity.

An imperial conference on 11 January 1938, orchestrated by Konoye – possibly as an attempt to pre-empt the military – ratified his government's policy to annihilate China. There was no quick victory. Jiang, having moved his government to Chongjing, was out of reach of the Japanese forces. Konoye finally talked of peace, but the generals insisted on continuing the war, leading him to resign in January 1939. His successors did no better; the generals called the shots. With the escalation of the war, on 16 July 1939 the United States gave six months' advance notice that it would abrogate the Treaty of Commerce and Navigation, agreed with Japan in 1911, leaving the way open to follow up with economic sanctions. The Japanese were unmoved.

Even before the beginning of World War II in Europe in September 1939 Japan was committed to establishing its 'Greater East Asia Co-Prosperity Sphere' and it was certainly noted in Tokyo that France and Britain, the two great powers threatening war with Germany, both had substantial empires in Southeast Asia – to say nothing of the Netherlands.

The fall of Western Europe in the summer of 1940 changed the balance of power radically in favour of Japan, while at the same time Japanese attempts to turn the United States away from economic sanctions were getting nowhere. The Army Minister, General Hata, anxious for a military alliance with Germany and Italy, brought down the weak government in Tokyo: on 22 July Konoye became prime minister for the second time. He had already, on 19 July, privately agreed a policy in which top priority would be given to the German alliance coupled with a non-aggression pact with the Soviet Union. The underlying rationale was that Japan could then move south from China to appropriate the European colonies in Southeast Asia. It was assumed that Britain would soon fall to a German invasion, while the United States, confronted by an alliance between Germany and Japan, would prefer to stay neutral.

This was a considerable miscalculation. True enough, in Vietnam, France's Vichy government, pressed by Germany, consented to Japanese troops being deployed along a new southern front in the war with China. On the other hand, Britain did not fall to a German invasion, and made clear that any Japanese claims to its colonies in Asia would be resisted. The Japanese did no better with the Netherlands, whose government, which had escaped to exile in London, made clear that it would resist Japanese claims to the Dutch East Indies. To add insult to injury, on 25 July the United States embargoed the export to Japan of oil and scrap iron, adding aviation fuel to the list on 31 July. On 7 August Washington protested against deploying Japanese troops in northern Vietnam, but even so this became a *fait accompli* on 26 September.

Finally, on 27 September, the Tripartite Pact, signed in Berlin between Germany, Italy and Japan, established the so-called 'Axis Powers'. At the same time it was agreed that if any one of them were involved in war with the United States, the others would join as allies. By this time the naval chief of staff in Tokyo, Admiral Fushimi, had already discussed with the emperor the strategic preparations necessary for a Japanese-American war.[16] The prospect of war against Britain and the United States also dominated the imperial conference on 19 September, which gave formal approval to the terms negotiated for the Tripartite Pact.

Japan, urged on by its foreign minister, Yōsuke Matsuoka, was now set on a course that could easily lead to war. Matsuoka's case was that when it came to a clash of arms Japan never lost a battle, whereas, when it came to diplomacy, it consistently got the worst of the bargain. He was convinced that the US, confronted by the Tripartite Pact, would climb down in its policy of sanctions. In March 1941, Matsuoka visited Berlin, noting Hitler's frustration at his failure to defeat Britain, and then called in on Moscow to sign a neutrality pact with Stalin.

While Matsuoka was booking one success after another in Berlin and Moscow, he did nothing to prevent the deterioration of relations with Washington – which, if anything, he welcomed. Finally, on 21 June 1941, the US Secretary of State, Cordell Hull, insisted that Japan should abandon the Tripartite Pact and withdraw its troops from China.

The German invasion of the Soviet Union on 22 June 1941 radically changed the line-up in World War II, with two great powers now allied in the war against Germany and Italy. For Matsuoka, the opportunity was not one to be missed. Japan should declare war on the Soviet Union, for, in his own words, 'We can't simply share in the spoils of victory unless we've done something'. What is more, 'If we hit the Soviets without delay, the United States won't enter the war' – on which matter Matsuoka could well have been right.

It was never, however, put to the test. The Japanese Supreme Command, clearly set on a course leading to war, decided to go south, rather than north. This decision, accepted at a meeting on 2 July at which the emperor presided, also provided the occasion for getting rid of Matsuoka, whose machinations had become intolerable – particularly to the army commander, General Tōjō. Konoye's whole cabinet resigned on 16 July, to be replaced by his third and final administration, with a new foreign minister.

A week later, on 24 July, the Japanese Army – as agreed at the last minute with France's Vichy government – occupied the whole of Indochina. In Washington, Roosevelt, at the express wish of Jiang Jieshi, ordered all Japanese assets to be frozen, with Britain and the Netherlands doing likewise. With the complete oil embargo on 1 August, Japanese trade was effectively confined to Manchuria, Indochina and Thailand, none of which could supply oil.

This was the point of no return. The decision to extend military operations south, rather than north, inevitably involved the Japanese Navy. The island empire of the Netherlands East Indies, with its vast resources in oil and rubber, could only be acquired with a seaborne invasion. The naval chief of staff, Admiral Nagano, made the point in a meeting with the emperor: 'in the circumstances we had better take the initiative. We will win'.

A secret deadline of 10 October 1941 was set for a diplomatic solution, but inevitably Washington maintained its economic sanctions after Tokyo had made clear that any concession requiring troops to be withdrawn from China would be refused. In General Tōjō's words this would mean 'defeat of Japan by the United States – a stain on the history of the Japanese empire'. Konoye, driven into a corner, resigned, to be succeeded by Tōjō, the only member of the cabinet who could rely on complete loyalty from the military.

By this time plans for war had already been made, with 30 November chosen as the deadline for putting them into effect. With the American people solidly behind Cordell Hull and Roosevelt, no new concession came from Washington, and on that day the order for war was given in Tokyo.

China was always the key to the crisis. Jiang Jieshi, helped by his calculating and charming wife,[17] projected an image of China as one of the great democracies. General 'vinegar' Joe Stilwell, who represented the US in China, saw him as 'the most astute politician of the twentieth century ... he must be or he wouldn't be alive'. Stilwell was one of the few who realized that Jiang was just as anxious about Mao Zedong's communists in his own backyard as about the Japanese – whom he could leave America and its allies to take care of. (He was right on both points.)

American journalists in China, at one and the same time anxious neither to lose their accreditation nor support the Japanese, accepted Jiang on his own terms, and what they wrote determined American public opinion. But there was more to it than that: 'the rise of international Fascism shaped America's view of China and the fervent syllogism at its core: democracy was threatened by the aggressor nations; China was under attack by an aggressor nation; therefore China was a democracy and her battle was the battle of world democracy'. Given that 'Japan could not consent to a settlement that did not recognize her colonial control of China [while] the United States could not consent to one that did ... at bottom there was no area for bargaining'.[18]

Japan began the Pacific War with the attack on Pearl Harbor on 7 December 1941 orchestrated by Admiral Yamamoto, its naval commander-in-chief. The

Philippines, Guam, Midway, and two British colonies, Hong Kong and Malaya (including Singapore), were attacked on the same day (which in the Far East – including Japan – was already 8 December). On 8 December in Washington, Roosevelt, referring to the previous day as 'one which will live in infamy' asked the Congress to declare war on Japan – in both houses together there was only one dissenting vote. The United States was at war with Japan.

In Bangkok, the government's first reaction was to refuse the Japanese permission to send their troops through Thailand. No matter – Japan simply invaded Thailand: Phibun,[19] the prime minister, realizing only too well the consequences of resisting the Japanese, ordered immediate surrender. He was in any case indebted to the Japanese, for in September 1940 they had intervened in Indochina to force a settlement by which Thailand recovered all of Laos west of the Mekong River, together with two Cambodian provinces, lost to France in the nineteenth century. Following the Thai surrender Phibun, on 12 December, concluded a military alliance with Japan, and on 25 January 1942 declared war on the US and Britain. For this the Japanese rewarded him by restoring to Thailand three Malaysian provinces lost to Britain in the nineteenth century. In Washington, however, the Thai minister, Seni Pramoj, having declared his allegiance to the allies, held back from delivering the formal note to the State Department.

In London, on 8 December, Winston Churchill declared war on Japan after consulting with his war cabinet, and then announced his decision to Parliament, where both houses accepted it unanimously. The Dutch government in exile followed the same day. In Germany Hitler, on the morning of 8 December, gave orders to the German Navy to attack American ships wherever found. The declaration of war on Britain and the United States, to which Germany was committed by the Tripartite Pact, followed on 11 December.

There has been endless debate about why Britain and the United States allowed themselves to be taken by surprise, when the events recounted in this chapter, most of which were already known at the time, pointed unmistakably to war with Japan. Churchill, long after the event, explained why this was so. 'A declaration of war could not be reconciled with reason … however sincerely we try to put ourselves in another person's position, we cannot allow for processes of the human mind to which reason offers no key', and he went on to add, 'madness is an affliction which in war carries with it the advantage of surprise'.[20] Within a few months that advantage carried Japan to the conquest of great empires in the Far East, belonging to Britain, the Netherlands and the United States. (Indochina, France's only Far Eastern colony, was already in its hands.)

THE OLD COLONIES OF SOUTHEAST ASIA

What was lost to Japan in the critical months after Pearl Harbor were four great empires in Southeast Asia, established by the Netherlands, the United Kingdom, France and the United States, over a period of nearly three and a half centuries. Each of these four states went its own way in exploiting local economic potential and enforcing law and order. If in the Dutch East Indies, British Malaya, Singapore and North Borneo, French Indochina and the American Philippines rule by an outside power defined a certain congruence in forms of government, there were also significant local variations – the result of both geophysical and demographic factors and distinctive European and American principles relating to the government of subject peoples. There was in any case little coordination among the imperial powers, accompanied by an implicit policy of non-interference. To visitors from outside the metropolitan state – and they were few in number – Indochina, for example, had a distinctive French colonial style, and the same was true, *mutatis mutandis*, of the worlds created by the Dutch, the British and the Americans in Southeast Asia. The expatriate cultures shared by the planters, mine-overseers, local administrators, professional men and soldiers, were in many ways more distinctively French, Dutch, British or American – as the case required – than those to be found at home. Indeed, by the twentieth century, an increasing number of people, born to established colonial families, knew little else.[21]

British involvement in the Far East went further than that of either France or the Netherlands. Britain's interests were not confined to its colonies in what is now Malaysia. For one thing, it was deeply committed, both economically and strategically, to Australia and New Zealand. For another, the colony of Hong Kong[22] meant a high-level involvement in China, the more so given the very strong British presence in Shanghai. Finally, the naval base of Singapore, commanding the principal sea-lanes from Europe to the Pacific, represented a high-level strategic commitment to the Pacific – equalled only by that of the US. The position of the Unites States was also somewhat special in that its interests in the Philippines related to an overall Pacific strategy anchored to the American west coast (with San Diego as the principal base of the USN Pacific fleet), Hawaii and the Panama Canal Zone. Significantly, the factors outlined in this paragraph combined to ensure that – except for China – those who actually fought the battles of the Pacific War, whether on land, at sea or in the air, on one side spoke Japanese, and on the other, English.

RUSSIA

The historical record of the new Pacific starts with European discovery and exploitation, a process that began in the early sixteenth century. For obvious geographical reasons,[23] the development of the Russian Far East, with thousands of kilometres of Pacific coastline, took place overland until, in the eighteenth century, it extended across the Bering Strait, to the North American mainland, to incorporate Alaska – a vast area of land ultimately sold to the US in 1868. The Russian position was unique for the fact that its Far East and Pacific regions were simply an overland extension, however tenuous, of the metropolis. Policy was made first in St Petersburg, and then, after 1917, in Moscow. The long process, starting in the seventeenth century, by which Russia came to incorporate Siberia, inevitably involved confrontation with imperial China, which, in turn, had to come to terms with the existence of a neighbouring state that would not become a vassal. Once established along its long Pacific coastline – with the rail link to Vladivostok completed at the beginning of the twentieth century – Russia's involvement in the ocean itself was extremely limited, and in the Russo-Japanese war (1904–05) absolutely disastrous. Effectively it was no more a Pacific power than France or the Netherlands, and in the years between the two world wars the policies enforced by Stalin effectively withdrew the Soviet Pacific from the world stage – a position maintained so long as the Soviet Union remained neutral in the Pacific War. Then by joining the allies, on 12 August 1945, for the last three days of hostilities, its position changed completely, so that in the post-war world, as described in Chapter 13, the Soviet Union became a major actor.

NORTH AMERICA

The role of the United States – consistently supported by Canada, its North American neighbour – is the subject matter of Chapter 16. In contrast the 11 Spanish speaking states[24] with a Pacific coastline have only been marginally involved in Asia-Pacific affairs, with their governments accepting, however reluctantly, that Washington – if not always listened to – calls the shots. The only exception here is Panama: this is the result of the construction, at the beginning of the twentieth century, of the Panama Canal and its subsequent operation by the United States.

The American west coast changed radically as a result of the Pacific War. Although the foundations had already been laid, what was built upon them in the years 1941–45 was altogether remarkable. Following the start of production in 1892, California had by 1941 become the US's largest producer of oil, with oil-refining the state's largest industry, and Los Angeles the world's largest oil terminal – as well as being the west coast's busiest seaport and the home to shipyards employing some 20,000 workers.

The American west coast had also become the centre of the aircraft industry, with Boeing operating in Washington state and Douglas, Lockheed and McDonnell in California. During the Pacific War both the manufacture of aircraft and shipbuilding – accounting for nearly 50 per cent of all wartime production – expanded at a rate that transformed the character of the Pacific coast. With countless men leaving home to serve in the armed forces, there were new employment opportunities for ethnic minorities and all those who had fled the dust bowl states in the 1930s – and above all, women. By 1943 unemployment was no longer a problem: on the contrary the demands of the military could only be met by the defence industries working ten-hour shifts. In aircraft manufacture in California the workforce grew from 25,000 to 300,000 between 1940 and 1943, with Douglas as the largest single employer. By early 1944 Boeing, mainly in Washington state, had increased production above 300 planes a month, from 60 two years earlier – to reach a peak of sixteen every day. Among these were the giant B29 Superfortresses, produced in conjunction with other west-coast aircraft companies, and used, from late 1944 onwards, to bomb targets in Japan – including, finally, Hiroshima and Nagasaki, in August 1945.

Wartime shipbuilding was equally spectacular. Henry J. Kaiser, a leading American industrialist, reacted to Pearl Harbor by promising to build merchant ships on the west coast on a scale so extravagant that his name quickly became known nationwide. All down the west coast, where there was little history of large-scale shipbuilding, he – and others who followed him – opened new shipyards. One new yard at Richmond, on San Francisco Bay, employed 90,000 workers, mostly women, adding considerably to the city's population – and the demand for housing. The population of the whole bay area increased by more than half a million; the number of those working in the shipyards increased sixtyfold, to reach 244,000 in 1944 – more than six times as many as were employed in the whole country in 1939. In just over three years, with construction time brought down to as little as ten days, it produced 747 ships – a number that included some warships. Kaiser was more than making good on his promises. At the peak of production a ship was launched every day, to say nothing of the other yards up and down the coast – particularly in the Los Angeles area. Unquestionably, wartime shipbuilding on the west coast rivalled aircraft construction – although the technological advances were far less significant. At the same time both industries supported a whole range of local suppliers. Much more important in the long term, they established the west coast's claim to a lion's share of defence industry in the second half of the twentieth century.

While millions benefited from the booming west-coast war economy, some 120,000 Japanese residents, a term broadly defined to include those of the second generation – the so-called 'nisei' – lost both their freedom and livelihood as a result of a presidential order of February 1942. They were held in internment camps hastily set up in a number of different states. This was a response to public opinion, at a time when the Japanese, like the Chinese, had long been unpopular, and their success resented by their white neighbours. Although there was no evidence whatever that they were disloyal, let alone a security risk, Washington decided otherwise – leaving the way open for their property to be expropriated without compensation, to the considerable profit of those who then acquired it. Judicial remedies failed the Japanese, right up to the US Supreme Court.

In spite of all the hostility, a way out of the internment camps was provided by the opportunity for young Japanese to serve in the US Army. The 100th Infantry Division, set up with considerable official resistance, led the way in June 1942, and on 1 February 1943 President Roosevelt announced the formation of the 442nd Regimental Combat Team, in which volunteers from both Hawaii and the continental US would be part of US combat forces. By the end of the war in Europe, this unit, fighting mainly in Italy, had won more medals than any other in the US Army – much to the honour of the American Japanese community. Although peace did not lead to their property being restored, the American public soon recognized that their internment was a monstrous injustice.

AUSTRALIA

In 1901, the new independent commonwealth of Australia took over the administration of five separate British colonies, of which the three along the Pacific coast – Queensland, New South Wales and Victoria – were much the more important.[25] In every dimension, social, economic or political, these colonies were not a home-grown product, but an adaptation of British ways of life to an entirely new environment. This remained true of the new commonwealth, particularly in the years before the Pacific War. The point has been well made by an American scholar, Jared Diamond:

> White English colonists did not create a literate, food-producing, industrial democracy in Australia. Instead they imported all the elements from outside Australia: the livestock, all the crops (except macadamia nuts), the metallurgical knowledge, the steam engines, the guns, the alphabet, the political institutions, even the germs ... By an accident of geography, the colonists who landed at Sydney in 1788 inherited those elements. Europeans have never learned to survive in Australia ... without their inherited Eurasian technology.[26]

The successful Australian agriculture was based almost entirely on non-native crops and animals, to which the native inhabitants could contribute very little. Although when the English first arrived in 1788 the largest aboriginal populations were in the parts of the continent most suited for European settlement, their distinctive way of life was only able to survive in the vast barren areas which, with the exception of minerals and fossil fuels found in certain localities, offered nothing to a modern economy. Even so, they were the only people who 'did create a society in Australia',[27] as the mainstream of modern Australian society is beginning to realize.[28] In 1901, however, there was little enlightened thinking about the new commonwealth's aboriginal inhabitants.

Until World War I Australian foreign relations remained an imperial prerogative, and the Commonwealth was little inclined to bypass Whitehall. There was still local concern for particular foreign policy issues. Of these the most important was to counter the influence of China, which had sent many immigrants to Australia. The Anglo-Japanese naval treaty of 1902 was therefore welcomed, as was US President Theodore Roosevelt's 'Great White Fleet' when it visited Australia in 1908, impressing upon Australians the strategic importance of the US Navy, as a rival to Britain's Royal Navy.

World War I radically changed the status of Australia both at home and in the world at large. The people were solidly behind the British. In the fight against Turkey, which brought the war to almost every home in the country, a separate Australia and New Zealand Army Corps, known simply as ANZAC – an acronym that still resonates in both countries – landed on their own eponymous beach on 25 April 1915; these volunteer soldiers were immediately involved in bitter fighting, which ended, without any gains being achieved, in a single night in January 1916; ANZAC returned to Egypt, leaving more than ten thousand dead behind in Turkey. For the families back home this was an appalling trauma, and on 25 April, the first anniversary of the ANZAC landings, was commemorated as a day of national remembrance. ANZAC Day is still a public holiday in Australia and New Zealand. In the final two years of the war Australia fought equally hard on the western front.

In May 1918, the prime minister, Billy Hughes, tried unsuccessfully to win the support of President Woodrow Wilson for Australia's claim to the German colonies occupied by Japan, while outside the White House the idea of an Australian Monroe doctrine was well received. Going on to the Imperial Conference in London, Hughes gained the support of the other delegates for equal status for the British dominions in the councils of empire so that each separate government could deal directly with London, leaving the governor-general as no more than the king's formal representative.

Australia was then granted two seats at the Versailles Peace Conference in 1919. There Hughes not only won recognition of Australia's claim to the German colonies in New Guinea and the offshore islands, but successfully blocked a clause proposed for the new League of Nations Charter providing for equal treatment for all, 'without making any distinction on account of their race or nationality'. Although on both points Hughes got his way in face of opposition from Woodrow Wilson, there would be a high price to pay for a political stance dictated entirely by Hughes' need to allow the White Australia policy, which had massive support within the country, to prevail over the interests of the world community. In Hughes' own judgement, put before the Australian people when he returned home from Versailles in September, 1919, 'Australia became a nation, and entered into a family of nations on a footing of equality ... Australia had to press her views, and to endeavour to insist upon their acceptance by other nations.'[29] He did not give away that his stance on race had humiliated Japan in a way which would not be forgotten.

Internationally things were not going well for Australia, and in the years leading up to World War II little would change its fortunes. For many years Australia failed to appoint its own diplomatic missions abroad, a privilege agreed by the Imperial Conference of 1923, nor, after 1931, did it show any enthusiasm for the enhanced status granted by the British Statute of Westminster – which Canberra only adopted formally in 1942. Australia, as a result of British initiative at the 1926 Imperial Conference, which led to a pre-emptive claim to some two-thirds of Antarctica, acquired the largest single part, after a share-out with Britain and New Zealand. None of this made much impact inside the country, where the economy had to adjust to the world-wide depression. In the long term the most significant change was the development of long-distance air-links first with Britain, and then with Pacific Asia and the United States. Except for the ties with Britain, based both on sentiment and economic factors, such as imperial preference, the prevailing mood was isolationist. Assisted immigration from Britain continued in an economy which still had considerable room for expansion, but newcomers could not expect to find streets paved with gold.

Everything changed with World War II. By an accident of history, in April 1939 Australia acquired a new prime minister, Robert Menzies, who, contemplating the threat of war in Europe, declared within days that 'Britain's peace is precious to us because her peace is ours'. When, on 3 September, Britain declared war on Germany, Menzies announced, the same day, that 'as a result, Australia is also at war'.[30]

The country was poorly equipped for war, and its small navy, with no more than six cruisers, could not on its own guarantee open communications with Britain. The Royal Navy, with its key base in Singapore, was essential for Australia's defence, the more so after the German occupation of France and the Netherlands in the summer of 1940. On the other side of the world, although there was never any question of Australian or New Zealand troops fighting in

Europe, three divisions were sent to Egypt. When Germany, having overrun the Greek mainland in April 1941, invaded Crete, these divisions were part of the allied force sent to defend the island. The defence failed, with heavy losses, which included several thousand Australians and New Zealanders.

The trauma, in Australia, was far less than that following the evacuation of Gallipoli in 1916. Even so, Menzies, who had been in England in the early months of 1941, lost his job. This, however, was the result of revolt within his own United Australia Party – which had never shown much talent for unity. The result, after an interregnum in the late summer, was that the Labour Party leader, John Curtin, became prime minister on 3 October. Before the end of the year he had to lead Australia in a war which, following the Japanese attack on Pearl Harbor, on 7 December, had become far closer to home. The only advantage – which in the end was to prove decisive – was that the US was now an ally.

In the short term the war went disastrously for the new allied powers. Within a matter of months almost the whole of Southeast Asia, including Singapore – which Churchill had promised Australia to defend at any cost – was lost to the Japanese. Several thousand Australian soldiers, sent at the last minute to help defend Singapore and the Dutch island of Java, were taken prisoner.

The Australians, however, did hold out in a small enclave on the south coast of New Guinea (including the capital, Port Moresby), and in May 1942, a Japanese attempt to invade from the sea was checked by a decisive battle between American and Japanese fleets in the Coral Sea. Less than a month later, another great sea battle thwarted a Japanese invasion of the American Midway Island. Although Coral Sea and Midway meant heavy losses for both sides, the allied navies could recover, while the Japanese could not. At Midway Japan lost its command of the seas, and with it went any threat of an invasion of Australia.

By this time, however, plans had been made to defend the country, while the American commander in the Pacific, General MacArthur, chose Brisbane as the site of his military headquarters for the reconquest of Southeast Asia and the eventual defeat of Japan. Already, on 27 December 1941, Curtin, writing in the Melbourne Herald, had stated that

> The Australian government ... regards the Pacific struggle as primarily one in which the United States and Australia must have the fullest say in the direction of the democracies' fighting plan. Without any inhibitions of any kind, I make it quite clear that Australia looks to America, free of any pangs as to our traditional links or kinship with the United Kingdom.

Both Churchill and Roosevelt, who were planning to make the defeat of Germany in Europe their first priority, regarded this statement as extremely disloyal: it did, on the other hand, express the war policy favoured by General MacArthur, who, as supreme commander in the Pacific, also commanded the Australian forces.

While Australia, strategically, was indispensable for MacArthur as a base for tens of thousands of American troops, he did little to involve Australian forces in his plans, even though Curtin had insisted – in face of Churchill's protests – on the repatriation of two Australian divisions in Egypt. Nonetheless, Australia fought very effectively in New Guinea, so that, by the end of 1943, the Japanese, reduced to a third of their original number, were pent up in a small enclave on the north coast. Even so, in June 1944, Curtin's government began to demobilize, as if to tell his people 'we know when we're not wanted'. A year later, however, as the Pacific War entered its final phase, MacArthur, with an eye to its strategic oil-wells, did commit two Australian divisions to an invasion of Borneo, where several hundred soldiers needlessly lost their lives. By August, however, much of the island had been liberated, and with the defeat of Japan there were still some 50,000 Australian troops in the region. These – as recorded in Chapter 11 – then played an important part in re-establishing law and order in the eastern islands of what is now Indonesia.

All in all, Australia, did not have a glorious war. Only the successful New Guinea campaign brought it some renown. Except for the small population of Darwin, which was bombed several times by the Japanese, civilians in Australia had no direct experience of war; instead it was a major boost to their country's economy. In contrast to Britain and the US, military expenditure decreased significantly as the war went on,[31] while the American military presence brought millions of dollars into local economies. An economy based largely on agricultural exports benefited considerably from the wartime devastation of Europe and Asia: wheat prices went up threefold and export volume eightfold, with meat, wool and other agricultural commodities not far behind.

Although by the end of the war the population had increased to 7.5 million, new immigrants – still strictly selected according to ethnic criteria – were essential. In international politics, for all that Curtin had said about America and Britain in December 1941, Washington placed Australia on the same level as the Philippines or New Zealand, while Britain, despite its failures in the Pacific theatre of war, remained close to the hearts of most Australians. After all that was where most of them had their roots, while being, at the same time, the much preferred source of new immigrants.

2

Revolutionary China

THE DEFEAT OF THE GUOMINDANG

At the end of the Pacific War Americans still saw Jiang's China as an outpost of modern civilization, a bulwark of democracy, fully capable to moving effectively into the power vacuum which would follow the Japanese surrender in August 1945. In spite of the intelligence provided by the Dixie Mission, there was little concern about what Mao Zedong might be planning from his base in Yan'an. For the Chinese the defeat of Japan came much sooner than anyone had anticipated. Even so Mao was able to ensure that most of the Japanese in north China surrendered to his forces, while the Guomindang strategy was to enlist the support of local Japanese forces in resisting a communist takeover. By this time also, the impending arrival of Soviet Forces was also a key factor in the equation, since – as agreed at the Yalta Conference in February 1945 – their soldiers would be part of the occupying force in northeast China for the three months immediately following the defeat of Japan. Such, however, was Washington's mistrust of Moscow, that 53,000 US Marines were sent to prevent any Soviet takeover in Beijing and Tianjin. At the same time the US provided the air and sea transport necessary for bringing Guomindang forces to north China and Manchuria.

On the other hand Yalta – in exchange for a Soviet commitment to recognize the Guomindang as China's only legitimate government – restored to the Soviet Union the rights, acquired by Russia in Tsarist times, to the railways in northeast China. Manchuria – a Japanese puppet state since 1931 and before that year the fief of the warlord Zhang Zuolin – was up for grabs, with both the Guomindang (helped by the Americans) and Chinese Communist Party (CCP) forces rushing to occupy it: in the result Jiang took over in the large cities and along the railways, while Mao became dominant in the countryside. Their relative positions then reflected those in much of the rest of China.

The Guomindang, with armed forces twice as large as those of the CCP, was, however, much stronger – at least on paper. Holding much more territory, and almost all the major cities, it also enjoyed the prospect of continuing US backing. Washington, intent on preventing civil war at all costs, recognized the need for some form of coalition government, in spite of the irrevocable commitments made to Jiang. In January 1946 – following an initiative by General George C. Marshall – this led to a joint political consultative committee meeting in Beijing, to discuss the possibility of Guomindang and CCP forces being combined, a proposal to which Jiang's consent would be obtained in exchange for a vast new loan from the US. Although Jiang and Mao met on this occasion, neither was intent on honouring any promises made – given the right circumstances, either side would double-cross the other. One immediate result of the meeting was an end to fighting in north China, Mao's own heartland, but neither side controlled the situation in north-east China, which was politically and economically much more important.

There Jiang, to save his position, had already asked that the Soviet Forces should stay after the due date for their departure, 15 November 1945 – a move which effectively, if somewhat ironically, held Mao at bay. In the event the Soviet forces only left in May 1946, having used the extra time granted to dismantle the industry established by the Japanese, and take back to the Soviet Union all usable equipment – together with some 500,000 Japanese prisoners-of-war to work in the Siberian *gulags*. At the same time the armaments left behind by the Japanese came mainly into the welcoming hands of the Mao's Red Army.[1]

In 1946 Jiang's mission, as he saw it, was simply to enforce the rule by the Guomindang over the whole of China: in this, as Mao later conceded,[2] he would certainly have succeeded at a much earlier stage if China had been left alone by Japan – but then a lot of history would have had to be rewritten. There would, for one thing, have been no Pacific War. Even so Jiang largely dug his own grave, and that of a China ruled by the Guomindang.

He failed in almost every possible way. As for strategy, his first challenge – which was immense – was to make the Guomindang writ run in all the areas that had been under Japanese occupation. This inevitably meant war with Mao, particularly in north-east China after the Soviet forces had departed. Everywhere Jiang concentrated too much on the control of the cities and lines of communication, without taking into account the fact that Mao's strength had always been in the countryside. He made little attempt to secure north China, a poor under-developed agricultural area, even though it was the centre of Mao's power.

Continuing his style of government, as it had been during the war years in Chongqing, Jiang imposed new taxes on the poor, while doing nothing to curb profiteers and corrupt officials; he relied almost exclusively on the generals who had been with him in Chongqing, treating local leaders in the areas freed from Japanese occupation as former collaborators. His economic policies led to massive inflation, hurting particularly the urban middle classes and industrial capitalists.

While Jiang's policies lost him popular support, Mao's whole strategy was to mobilize it, particularly in the areas and among the classes that Jiang left out of account. From his heartland in north China Mao, with the support of poor peasant leaders, enforced widespread land reform, which then snowballed to further radical reform in other sectors. He was not afraid of antagonizing landlords, nor carpet-baggers from south China who, bent on exploiting the local communities freed from Japanese occupation, had followed in the wake of Guomindang forces. Jiang, on the other hand, failed to take into account that much of north China – which in the previous twenty-odd years had known only the rule of warlords or the Japanese military – was not likely, once freed from tyranny, to welcome a government whose base was in the south.

Throughout 1946 Mao bided his time. Then, in 1947, after the winter – almost always severe in north China – was over, he began to counter-attack the Guomindang forces. The ground had been well prepared. Mao, after first taking the Shandong peninsula, went on to take the whole key area between the Yellow and Yangze Rivers, recruiting new troops along the way and supplying the captured US equipment. At this stage, George Marshall – who had become US Secretary of State – correctly read the writing on the wall, and ordered the withdrawal of the US troops who had been sent to China to defend it against Soviet forces. Jiang's tactics, which required the defence of almost every city even after its lines of communication had been cut off, meant that one after the other, the cities, following months of siege, had no option but to surrender – providing Mao not only with new arms and equipment, but also with the possibility of recruiting the survivors to his side.

The process, whereby Mao increased his strength at the cost of Jiang, was cumulative. Finally, in January 1949, it culminated in Beijing, with the Guomindang commander transferring all his troops to Mao's Red Army, where he was himself rewarded with a major command. With this increase in numbers, together with a massive arsenal of American trucks and tanks, the Red Army became a force that Jiang was powerless to resist. In June 1949 the loss of Shanghai and Nanjing – his old capital city – convinced him that China, south of the Yangze, was no longer defensible. Already, in 1948, Stalin had advised Mao against proceeding beyond the Yangze, fearing that to do so would provoke the US into supporting Jiang on such a scale that the Guomindang, in spite of its losses, would be able to hold out indefinitely. Stalin's assessment of US policy was mistaken, and Mao deliberately ignored his advice. In September Jiang and his Guomindang government fled to Taiwan, accompanied by several thousands of soldiers and as much bullion as they could carry. On 1 October 1949, Mao, with his generals beside him, stood on the balcony of the Tiananmen Gate in Beijing, and proclaimed to a crowd of some 300,000, 'The Central People's Government of the People's Republic of China is founded today'. He had become the ruler of a quarter of the world's population.

MAO'S PEOPLE'S REPUBLIC

Proclaimed head of state on 1 October 1949, Mao had to deal with unfinished business on two sides. First, he needed to come to terms with the fact that Jiang's Guomindang was still claiming to rule China from the island of Taiwan, while, at the same time, there were still two European colonies, British Hong Kong and Portuguese Macao, on China's south coast. Second, Mao needed to establish a relationship with the Soviet Union which took into account the fact that his government ruled China.

Taiwan's status as an integral part of China was always problematic. Before the Qing dynasty (1644–1911) Taiwan was a little-known offshore island, with a small, but long-established indigenous Austronesian population, whose descendants became the first inhabitants of many of the islands of Oceania.[3] With a steadily increasing number of Chinese settlers it was formally incorporated as a prefecture of the province of Fukien in 1685. Only in 1885 did it become a separate province, but even then its population was only three million, of whom some 120,000 were Austronesian aborigines.[4] Then, in 1895, Japan, following its victory in the Sino-Japanese war, acquired Taiwan as its first colony. During fifty years of Japanese rule Chinese banditry was suppressed, law and order established, roads and railways constructed and a modern agricultural economy – based on the production of sugar cane and rice for the Japanese market – was established.

Although local Chinese resistance to Japanese rule was on occasion brutally suppressed, this was as nothing compared to what the Taiwanese suffered after the defeat of Japan in 1945. Mainland Chinese effectively conquered the island in the name of the Guomindang, treating the local Chinese as former enemy collaborators and confiscating much of their property. In 1947 protest by local Chinese against Guomindang corruption led to a pogrom in which some 20,000 were killed.

When, on 10 December 1949, Jiang arrived in Taiwan, he found an island in a state of economic and political collapse, exacerbated by the presence of more than a million refugees from the mainland. Two weeks later a US State Department policy guidance paper advised American diplomats to prepare for the fall of Taiwan to the Chinese Communists.

In fact the tide had already turned against the communists in October. After Mao's victory on the mainland Guomindang forces still occupied Jinmen and Mazu,[5] small islands only a few kilometres off the south China coast. On 25 October 17,000 communist troops landed on Jinmen, expecting an easy victory over the entrenched Guomindang forces. It was not to be. In a last-ditch stand the local garrison routed the invaders, inflicting more than 8,000 casualties and taking some 6,000 prisoners. The long-term result was that Jinmen and Mazu remain to this day subject to rule from Taiwan.

His occupation and government of Taiwan allowed Jiang to make good his claim to be the legitimate ruler of China – it just happened that the greater part of the country had fallen to insurgents. Although this was not how the world saw things – Britain recognized Mao's new government on 6 January 1950 – Jiang, critically, retained the support of the US, and as a result the right of the Guomindang to represent China in the UN, and occupy its permanent seat on the Security Council. This was completely unacceptable to Mao, but he was powerless to change the position; indeed, by the end of 1949, his most urgent problem was to regularize the relationship between his new People's Republic of China (PRC) and Soviet Russia.

This required Mao to visit Moscow – making his first journey ever outside China – to confront Stalin. Mao arrived in Moscow just before the end of 1949. Although, in the perception of the West, the only purpose of the meeting was to create 'a monolithic Red bloc'[6] stretching from Eastern Europe to the Pacific, Mao looked forward to it with considerable foreboding. He had good reason to doubt whether Stalin ever understood his version of communism. Mao's doubts, which went back to the late 1920s, about the wisdom of following the line laid down by the Comintern – Stalin's instrument for establishing communism internationally – were confirmed when it opposed the Long March[7] in 1934. His unforeseen ascent within the CCP in 1935 added to the Comintern's hostility, which became only too clear when Stalin chose to support the Guomindang right up to the end of the Pacific War. When Soviet forces went on to occupy Manchuria they barred entry to Mao's People's Liberation Army (PLA),[8] and allowed the US to airlift Guomindang forces to accept the Japanese surrender. Even Mao's final victory in September 1949 was accepted with an ill grace by the Soviet leaders.

Mao spent ten weeks in Moscow, accompanied by his foreign secretary, Zhou Enlai, who was much more at home in the world outside China. Stalin's reluctant acceptance of Zhou as chief Chinese negotiator was seen by Mao as a statement that the Soviet Union would abandon all connection with the Guomindang, to which – according to Stalin – it was committed by the Yalta agreement of 1945. Stalin only relented on learning that the UK was about to grant diplomatic recognition to the PRC.[9] The way was open for Zhou, representing the PRC, to sign, together with Andrei Vyshinsky, his Soviet opposite number, the Sino-Soviet Treaty of Alliance on 14 February 1950; both Mao and Stalin were present. The treaty provided for a $300 million credit, spread over five years, to be allocated entirely to military purchases – with half allocated to the navy.[10] The PRC had to pay a high price – which included entrusting to the Soviets a substantial part of its bullion stocks. Throughout the 1950s the influence of the Soviet Union over China was mainly to be seen in the large cities, with politically correct architecture prominent in new government buildings. The treaty was not a good bargain for China, and Nikita Khrushchev later described it as 'an insult to the

Chinese people'. Even so it remained in force, for what it was worth, for the entire thirty-year period designated in its clause 6.

WAR IN KOREA

Mao returned home in March 1950. Unknown to him, Kim Il Sung in North Korea was already planning the invasion of South Korea, which was then launched on 25 June.[11] The US immediately rallied to support South Korea, which lost almost all its territory in the first few weeks of fighting. After a whole US division had landed in the first week of July, on 7 July a Security Council resolution committed the UN to support South Korea, so that the US forces were soon joined by those of several other nations, notably Britain. With the tide turning strongly in their favour in September, by the end of the month the UN forces, having recovered all the territory lost in South Korea, went on to advance into North Korea.

This presented Mao with a formidable crisis. It is doubtful whether he ever welcomed Kim Il Sung's invasion, and his first reaction when Stalin suggested that soldiers from the PRC should support the North Korean forces was to hold back.[12] On the other hand, from Mao's perspective, a US conquest of North Korea could well be no more than the first stage of an operation planned to recover China for the Guomindang. Mao, like the old Chinese emperors, saw Korea essentially as a Chinese vassal state, and with a communist government in North Korea it fulfilled, to a degree, this traditional role. It was regrettable that Kim's rule did not extend to the southern half of the peninsula, but all the evidence is that Mao never encouraged Kim to attempt a takeover: the risks were far too great. What is more Kim was always in Stalin's camp rather than Mao's: during the war years he had been trained as a guerrilla commander in the Soviet Union, and when the war ended and Soviet forces pre-empted Mao's PLA in the occupation of Manchuria, they provided North Korea's only link with the outside world. In the five years after 1945 North Korea's armed forces were equipped and trained by the Soviet military. Mao, still fighting the Guomindang inside China, was nowhere.

Finally, on 14 October 1950, Mao notified Stalin that the Chinese army would participate in the defence of North Korea,[13] and before the end of the month Chinese troops effectively took over the whole of the front line. Although Article 1 of the Sino-Soviet treaty agreed in February committed the Soviet Union 'to immediately render military and other assistance'[14] to the PRC if it were attacked by the US, Stalin held back, claiming that the attacking forces were those of the UN.[15] It did not matter that Zhou Enlai presented the war to the Chinese people as a crusade against US imperialism: the fact that this is not how Stalin chose to see it does not mean that the war, with the vast losses suffered by both sides, did not suit his book. After all the 1953 armistice was only agreed after he died.[16]

Three years of war in Korea cost the PRC some half million dead and the same number of wounded. Among the dead was Mao's oldest son, Anying, and the trauma suffered by his loss made Mao, more than ever, a man without ordinary feelings, impervious to the human suffering involved in pursuing his ends.

With hindsight, it is easy to say that Mao, in rescuing Kim Il Sung in 1950, made the most grievous political error of his entire career. As abundant official documentation makes clear, Syngman Rhee's Republic of Korea, if extended north to the Yalu River to become a state bordering China, would never have been used as a base for an US attack on the PRC. If anything it would, in the course of time, have become a commercial outlet for China, even at a level rivalling Hong Kong. By preventing this happening Mao ensured that the US, with its overwhelming power, would defend every bit of land in East and Southeast Asia, not already in communist hands – as later proved to be the case. For the PRC, any chance of recovering Taiwan was lost. Moreover, North Korea, particularly after it was left out in the cold following the collapse of the Soviet Union in 1991, survived to become an almost insoluble problem for the PRC.[17] It is little consolation that the original fault lay not with Mao, but with Kim Il Sung and his master, Stalin.

MAO'S CONTINENTAL EMPIRE AND THE BREAK WITH THE SOVIET UNION

Apart from the Korean War, the PRC in the 1950s hardly had a significant Pacific history. Mao's China (see map on page ix) during the years of struggle against the Guomindang was far inland: until 1945 almost the entire coastline was occupied by the Japanese. Mao's experiences of both Americans and Russians confirmed his fundamental conviction that the world outside China was to be mistrusted. As far as possible China, in accordance with its long history as the central state, should move its land frontiers to extend inland as far as possible, and neutralize threats from the outside world. To Mao this justified the annexation of Tibet in 1950–51, a move so widely condemned that it only increased his isolation.

But little of this mattered: there was plenty to be done in the way of transforming China, a process epitomized by the 'Hundred Flowers' campaign (1956–57) and the 'Great Leap Forward' (1957–62) that followed it. The Korean War provided a pretext for tighter political control, essential for the collectivization of the peasants – almost complete by 1957 – and an intensive industrialization programme which almost doubled the urban population. In practical terms these policies had little success – so much so that for four years (1958–62) there was widespread famine. Mao's conviction that China must go it alone, and that he was the only man to lead his people along a 'Chinese Road',[18] was reinforced in November 1957, when, on the invitation of Khrushchev, he went to Moscow for the Congress of Communist Parties in Communist Countries – his last ever visit abroad. He particularly mistrusted Khrushchev's policy of co-existence with the West; nor – given the way he was presenting himself in China – was he happy with Khrushchev's denunciation of Stalin's cult of personality. In Beijing he was busy with the construction of the Tiananmen Square, facing the old Forbidden City, and designed to be grander than Moscow's Red Square.

Early in 1958, Khrushchev, taking a positive view of the Moscow Conference – where Mao had backed Moscow's bloc leadership and accepted a Soviet offer of help in developing nuclear weapons and missiles – decided to ask for Mao's cooperation in setting up long-wave radio stations along the Chinese coast for communication with new submarines planned for the Soviet Pacific fleet. The whole operation would be a joint venture, opening, also, the Soviet Arctic coast to China.

When the Soviet Ambassador, Pavel Yudin, presented the plan to Mao on 22 July it was received with scorn: Mao insisted that he deal directly with Khrushchev, who was left with no choice but to go to Beijing without delay. Once there, Mao did everything to make him feel uncomfortable, and refused to listen when he insisted that 'a common fleet' was necessary to contend with the US Seventh Fleet. Mao, regarding the whole plan as an attack on Chinese sovereignty, retorted by saying 'the British, Japanese and other foreigners who stayed in our country a long time have already been driven away from us, Comrade Khrushchev … We do not want anyone to use our land to achieve their own purposes any more'.[19]

The Soviet delegation went home early, immensely frustrated by their failure to achieve anything. A month later, on 23 August, Mao – without consulting Moscow – bombarded both Jinmen and Mazu. There was an immediate international crisis, as the US mounted a massive show of force in the Taiwan Strait. Khrushchev was committed to declare his support for Beijing, and on 4 September, US Secretary of State Dulles threatened war to defend the islands occupied by the Guomindang. Gromyko, his Soviet opposite number, was in Beijing the next day, to hear Mao outline his strategy in the event of nuclear war – which, under the 1950 Sino-Soviet Treaty of Alliance, would inevitably involve the Soviet Union. Mao's strategy was designed to frustrate Khrushchev's attempts to reach a détente with Washington, for as he said to his doctor, 'the islands are two batons that keep Eisenhower and Khrushchev dancing … Don't you see how wonderful they are?'

Following a successful visit to the US, Khrushchev was back in Beijing in October 1959 for the tenth anniversary of the Chinese revolution. His talks with

Chinese officials went badly, partly because of the admiration he expressed for the US. Once more he left early. Mao, in his confrontation with the Soviet leader, 'saw himself as the bullfighter and Khrushchev as the bull'.[20] Soviet engineers and economic advisers – some 1,390 in all[21] – were withdrawn from the PRC, but Mao was well rid of these 'Soviet spies'.[22]

The course was set for complete rupture between the PRC and the Soviet Union: diplomatic relations, although still maintained, reached their lowest point in 1961, when Zhou Enlai staged a walk-out by the Chinese delegation at the Moscow Congress of the Communist Party of the Soviet Union.

If, during the years (1956–64) that Khrushchev led the Soviet Union, confrontation with the US was the key factor in determining not only Soviet foreign policy but also that of the PRC, neither Mao nor Khrushchev was completely consistent in deciding between working for or against détente. Mao, however, was consistent in making clear that in confronting the US he was not going to be an instrument of Khrushchev's foreign policy: he was determined to be master in his own house.

This explains his fury at Khrushchev's attempts to establish facilities for the Soviet Navy along the Chinese coastline. Here the historical problem is why Khrushchev regarded these as so important. The answer must be that he envisaged operations in the East, and even more the South China Sea, where his ships would be separated by thousands of kilometres from Soviet naval bases north of China. With the powerful US Seventh Fleet controlling all the seas off the Chinese coast this was as much a strategic as a logistical problem. If Khrushchev had got his way with Mao, the way the facilities granted to the Soviet Navy might then have used could well have involved Mao in a confrontation with the US on terms not of his own choice. This, after all, was exactly what had happened in Korea in 1950, in a scenario orchestrated by Stalin.

CHINA AND VIETNAM BEFORE 1975

Support for Ho Chi Minh's plan to take over the whole of Vietnam, following his 1954 victory over the French at Dien Bien Phu, provided a good reason for the Soviet Navy to be active in the South China Sea. This raises the whole question of the respective Vietnam policies of Mao and Khrushchev. Given the rift between the two, Vietnam – over the long term – could not be beholden to both of them. After the end of the 1950s it was not open to Ho to ride two horses at once. It then became clear that he was casting his lot with the Soviet Union.

If the common frontier between Vietnam and China always meant that Ho had a safe supply line for his forces, what then explains his choice? One reason is that Mao never allowed Chinese forces to be committed to battle, although a number helped maintain supply lines. Although considerable war material was supplied through China – particularly in the early 1950s when the Vietminh General Giap was fighting a winning battle against the French with arms left behind, in the late 1940s, by Guomindang forces in south China – once the French had been defeated at Dien Bien Phu, the Viet Minh could also be supplied by sea through the North-Vietnamese harbour of Haiphong, which was in their hands. If, then, as proved to be the case, the Soviet Union was to be the main source of supply, there was good reason for a strong Soviet naval presence in the South China Sea. In the event this was not necessary: the US Seventh Fleet took great care not to attack Soviet merchant ships either at sea or in any Vietnamese harbour open to them. On any cost-effective analysis the sea-route to Vietnam was also much to be preferred to the tenuous rail links across China. Even so China's material support continued until the end of the war in 1975.

At all events, after Dien Bien Phu (1954), the Viet Minh's continuing successes suited Mao's book, without his being at all over-committed. Particularly after the break with the Soviet Union in 1961, there was everything to be gained by not being militarily involved in Vietnam, a policy ultimately rewarded by US recognition of the PRC following President Nixon's visit to Mao in 1972. In the early 1960s Mao wrongly interpreted the US involvement in Vietnam as a prelude to hostilities that would involve the PRC. By the late 1960s, however, the 'Brezhnev doctrine', proclaimed, in 1968,[23] by Khrushchev's successor in Moscow to justify military intervention in any recalcitrant satellite state, finally convinced Mao that the Soviet Union was a much greater threat. This view was confirmed in 1969, first by a number of skirmishes along the Soviet-Chinese border – which Mao feared might lead to outright war – and then by a conference of communist states convened in Moscow at which the PRC was expelled from the international communist movement.[24]

THE CULTURAL REVOLUTION

While all this was going on, Mao was committed to pushing through the Cultural Revolution, which he had proclaimed in 1966, and which continued until his death ten years later. In part the revolution was the result of a faction fight within the CCP, with three members of the radical Shanghai party, together with Mao's wife, Jiang Qing, constituting the 'Gang of Four', which Mao chose to support rather than the moderate Beijing party, led by Peng Zhen. In the vanguard was a vast supporters' club of young people, organized as 'Red Guards', whose task was to launch a massive attack on 'the capitalist roaders inside the party'.[25]

To direct the Cultural Revolution Mao chose Lin Biao – not a member of the Gang of Four, but equally committed to the cult of Mao: he was responsible for publishing *Quotations from Chairman Mao* – a.k.a. the 'little red book' – in 1964. In his preface he enjoined readers – who by the end of the 1960s numbered hundreds of millions – to 'study Chairman Mao's writing, follow his teaching and act according to his instructions'.[26] Jiang Qing – a merciless woman with any number of personal vendettas to pursue – together with Lin, and with the help of the Red Guards, kept the Cultural Revolution on course while the great leader chose to remain in the background. Their strategy required the elimination of all possible rivals, some of whom, such as Deng Xiaoping, had been close to Mao for thirty years.

In the end, Zhou Enlai – prime minister of the PRC and almost the only man whom the Gang of Four dared not touch – helped unearth a plot, orchestrated by Lin Biao, to usurp Mao. The evidence, although very thin, was sufficient to convince Mao and seal Lin's fate. On 12 September 1971, a plane hastily organized to take him to exile in the Soviet Union crashed in Outer Mongolia – an event characterized by Mao as 'the most ideal ending'.[27] Although not a member of the Gang of Four, with his death it lost much of its power.

NIXON IN CHINA AND THE DEATH OF MAO

Within a year Zhou became the man behind the most successful foreign policy achievement in the history of the PRC: this was US President Nixon's official visit to China in February 1972. Preparatory to the visit Henry Kissinger visited China, to observe that 'the Chinese were cold-blooded practitioners of power politics, a far cry from the romantic humanitarians envisaged by western intellectuals'.[28] In 1972 Zhou's concern for the Soviet threat to China justified a radically new approach to Washington. The meetings between Mao and Nixon were a success, and left Nixon convinced that his visit 'had changed the world'.[29] The main credit must go to Zhou, who to Nixon was 'one of the most extraordinarily gifted people I have ever known, with an incandescent grasp of the realities of power'.[30]

Zhou's ascendancy over the time of the Nixon visit enabled him to ensure the rehabilitation of Deng Xiaoping as vice-premier. Together they were in a position to hold the Gang of Four at bay, particularly since Mao no longer trusted his wife, Jiang Qing. She attempted a comeback in the early months of 1976, after Zhou had died on 8 January, and Deng prudently left Beijing. Mao himself was dying, but he did nothing to help the Gang of Four take over after his death – which occurred on 9 September 1976 – and in the event they were powerless to do so. Instead they were all arrested before the end of the year, and in November 1980 put on trial together with six close associates of Lin Biao. By this time there had been a significant transfer of power, which became apparent during the meeting of the Central Committee in the third plenum of the eleventh[31]

Chinese Communist Party Congress in December 1978, when the party leaders decided to undertake a programme of gradual but fundamental reform of the economic system – a milestone in the history of the PRC. Deng, although only a vice-premier, effectively gained control of government in the PRC, with Hua Guofeng, Mao's named successor as party chairman, almost completely sidelined. In the ensuing months a great number of party members – both military and civilian – whose political credentials were largely achieved as a result of the Cultural Revolution were purged.

CHINA, VIETNAM AND CAMBODIA AFTER 1975

Nixon's visit to Beijing was linked to his policy of reducing US involvement in Vietnam, and derivatively, Cambodia. At the same time the official Cambodian government under Lon Nol strongly supported South Vietnam, while the revolutionary Khmer Rouge, led by Pol Pot, was fighting to take over and apply the principles of Mao's Cultural Revolution to Cambodia. Given the strong – and somewhat contradictory – Soviet support for the Viet Cong on one side, and Lon Nol on the other, Beijing inclined to support the Khmer Rouge. This turn of events foreshadowed a situation in which the PRC would align with Cambodia under Pol Pot and the Soviet Union with Vietnam under Ho Chi Minh's successor,[32] Ton Duc Thang, as actually happened after the US forces abandoned both countries in April 1975.

On 3 November 1978 Vietnam and the Soviet Union signed a Treaty of Friendship and Cooperation, in which the sixth clause provided that the two states would 'immediately consult each other' if either were 'attacked or threatened with attack ... with a view to eliminating that threat'. At the end of December 1978 Vietnam invaded Cambodia, and within weeks occupied the capital, Phnom Penh, and toppled the government of Pol Pot: this was a clear threat to Chinese interests.

Beijing normalized its relations with the US on 1 January 1979, thereby completing the process which started with Nixon's visit in 1972, so that, in the words of one commentator,[33] 'two strategic alliances had been created in the closing months of 1978, a Soviet-Vietnamese alliance and a Sino-American alliance, and they would prevail for about a decade'. Then, on 15 February 1979, the very day on which the Sino-Soviet Treaty of 1950 entered its final year (as provided for in its sixth clause), China announced its intention to invade Vietnam. The actual invasion, when it began three days later, started a war fought by both sides with ground troops without any air-support. Although some ground, including three provincial capitals, was lost to the Chinese forces, Vietnam put up a very strong resistance – so much so that within a month, after heavy casualties on both sides, the Chinese abandoned all the territory they had occupied and hostilities ceased.

From one perspective China had lost the war, without achieving a single one of its obvious objectives: the Vietnamese did not withdraw from Cambodia, border clashes continued, and the US refused to be drawn into an anti-Soviet coalition. Seen in this light, China was a 'paper tiger'; the Soviet Union, however, by failing to provide Vietnam with the support to which it was committed by a treaty agreed only three months earlier, was represented by Beijing as a 'paper polar bear'. On 3 April 1979 this perception lay behind China's announcing its intention to terminate the 1950 Treaty. Although, on Moscow's initiative, negotiations to extend it did open in October 1979, the Soviet invasion of Afghanistan on 21 December provided Beijing with a pretext for ending them – which had always been its intention. The treaty therefore expired in February 1980, leaving nothing to replace it. Instead Moscow was offered three pre-conditions for improving relations with Beijing: first, Soviet troops should be withdrawn from the Chinese border areas; second, they should be withdrawn from Afghanistan, and third, Soviet support for Vietnam's invasion of Cambodia should cease. There was no possibility of the Soviet Union, under Brezhnev, accepting any of the pre-conditions. All this, as Beijing well realized, was grist to the mill for the US, while sensitive issues, such as Taiwan, were put on the back-burner.

THE COUNTER-REVOLUTION OF DENG XIAOPING

The changes in foreign policy went hand in hand with the transformation of the Chinese economy under the leadership of Deng Xiaoping. In 1982, after a two-year period of readjustment during which the standard of living improved spectacularly, with strong growth rates in almost all sections of the economy, the reform programme came into its own, so that a market economy was created for both agriculture and industry, allowing managers a remarkable free hand in both investment and the employment of labour – a complete reversal of everything the Cultural Revolution had stood for in the 1960s. This was the beginning of an era of unprecedented economic growth, accompanied by opening up the country to foreign trade and investment – a process that over the last quarter of a century has transformed China's role in the world economy. The guiding hand was that of Deng, whose voice, if muted, was still being heard when he died, aged 92, in 1997. The process has yet to complete its course, and there are still poorly performing state-owned enterprises listed for transfer to the private sector.

It is arguable that already, in the early 1980s, Deng foresaw the fall of the Soviet Union. However that may be, the Soviet position in Southeast Asia changed radically following Gorbachev's becoming General Secretary of the Communist

Party on 11 March 1985. Support for Vietnam more or less ceased after 1986, and by early 1989 Gorbachev had withdrawn all Soviet forces from Afghanistan. Since, at the same time, the number of troops along the borders with China were substantially reduced, all the three pre-conditions laid down by Beijing in 1980 were met before the end of the 1980s. Finally, just before Gorbachev resigned on Christmas Day, 1991, Soviet relations with China were normalized. This then was the culmination of a process by which a major threat to the security of the PRC, that from Soviet Russia, was reduced to insignificance – as was well realized in Beijing.

In 1985, when Gorbachev came to power, the Soviet Union, much more than the PRC, had carried the economic burden of the Cold War for forty years – Brezhnev's costly and futile venture into Afghanistan was the last straw.[34] This contrasts with the PRC, which, with no empire of satellite states, hardly any navy or airforce, and only a small nuclear capability, was in a much stronger position. In 1985 Deng Xiaoping abandoned the Maoist view of inevitable global and nuclear war.[35] This left him free to open up China even more to the outside world, with vast increases in trade, foreign direct investment (FDI) and holdings of US external debt and other foreign bonds. In particular, with his eye on the prospective return of Hong Kong to China in 1997, he developed the 'one country, two systems' principle that would then come into effect.[36] In all this Deng was supported, first by Hu Yaobang, who, after becoming General Secretary of the CCP in 1982, was forced to resign in 1987, as a result of the soft line he had taken in response to students' demonstrations for more democracy. Deng's second key supporter was Zhao Ziyang, who having been first prime minister (1980–87) then succeeded Hu as General Secretary – during which time he also emerged as a leading reformer, if one more cautious than Hu. Then, in the early summer of 1989, Deng and Zhao, and all they stood for, were overtaken by events in Tiananmen Square at the heart of Beijing.

TIANANMEN AND ITS AFTERMATH

The starting point was the death of Hu Yaobang on 15 April. Of the thousands who then came to Beijing for the memorial service on 22 April many remained in Tiananmen Square as a protest against the way that Hu's reforms had been blocked. On 13 May students began a hunger strike, which was taken up by the world media when, on 15 May, Gorbachev arrived in Beijing for critical discussions with Deng. On 19 May, Zhao, the man most trusted by the students, made a tearful appeal for the demonstrations to cease. It was ignored. On 20 May martial law was declared, but the demonstrators still refused to depart. Finally, on 3 June the army, complete with tanks, moved in to clear Tiananmen in a scene broadcast world-wide on TV. At a critical moment a single man stood his ground in front of a column of advancing tanks, which, for half an hour, stopped quite literally in their tracks – a sublime and very public moral victory that caused immense embarrassment to the Chinese leaders. By the end of the day on 4 June the masses of humanity that for weeks had occupied Tiananmen were gone.

The suppression of the Tiananmen demonstrations reflected a significant shift in the balance of power in China: after 4 June those who took a hard line were plainly on top. Inevitably those responsible for allowing events to get out of hand would have to pay a price: first among them was Zhao Ziyang, who having called political reform 'the biggest test facing socialism',[37] had no choice but to allow Jiang Zemin to take over as General Secretary of the CCP. His failure, on 19 May, to persuade the students to stop demonstrating, was unforgivable, and for the rest of his life, until his death on 17 January 2005, he was subject first to four months' house arrest and then to severe restrictions on his movements and on the visitors to his home. Deng Xiaoping's own position became much weaker, and he was soon eclipsed by Jiang, who went on to become president of the PRC in 1993.

There were also immediate repercussions outside China. In August 1989 the UN Sub-Commission on Human Rights passed a resolution of the 'Situation in China' by 15 votes to 9. Although no mention was made of Tiananmen, this was the first time ever that a permanent member state was censured by the Security Council for its human rights record.[38] The resolution was mildly worded, but human rights in China remained on the agenda.

Predictably the strongest reaction to Tiananmen came from the US. There would be no more arms sales, nor exchanges between the US and Chinese military. The US Congress also wanted trade sanctions to be imposed by depriving the PRC of its 'most favoured nation'[39] status, but when, at the end of every year, this came up for renewal, Congress was held at bay, first by President George H.W. Bush and then, after 1993, by President Clinton.

Beijing's sensitivity to its standing in the US was shown, in the summer of 1992, by its muted reaction to the approval by President Bush – who wanted to keep open the production line in Texas in an election year – of the sale of F-16 fighters to Taiwan. In general European reactions echoed those of the US, although there was never any threat to withdraw 'most favoured nation' status. Deng was also less critical of Europe, although there was a drastic reduction in imports from France after Mirage 2000–5 fighters were sold to Taiwan. The Western world readily granted visas to both dissidents and students from China. Japan's main adverse reaction was to suspend 'yen' loans, but in principle trade with China was too valuable to be jeopardized by a strong human rights stand. In 1992, although there were state visits both by Emperor Akihito to Beijing, and by Jiang Zemin to Tokyo, both press and public in Japan were hostile to China.

In the field of human rights, however, China was only too ready to remind Japan of its own record up to 1945, for which it had made few amends. Any interest shown in Taiwan, which had been occupied by Japan for fifty years, was particularly mistrusted. As for the rest of Asia, China worked hard to maintain good relations with its neighbours, for 'Asia is [above all] the centre of Chinese power and influence, the nucleus of ever-expanding circles radiating outwards in all directions'.[40]

In 1990 Beijing was able to take advantage of Saddam Hussein's invasion of Kuwait on 2 August, for China's vote was essential for the resolution – passed by the UN Security Council on 6 August – condemning Iraq. This opened the way for the US-led Operation Desert Storm, which began on 16 January 1991, followed by the ground attack on 24 February. Although Beijing knew well that the restoration of independence to Kuwait was as important for China – which was soon to become a net importer of oil – as it was for the rest of the world, its cooperation with the UN heralded better relations with US. The matter became even more important with the collapse of the Soviet Union in 1991, if only because of the way it increased the PRC's influence over events in Southeast Asia. Beijing's new-found strength became apparent on 23 October 1991 when it became a party to the Paris agreement that finally resolved the conflict in Cambodia, leaving the way open for it to become a member of the UN. This was particularly important for the US, given the power politics played by the Soviet Union in Cambodia's neighbour, Vietnam. Effectively, by the end of 1991, the US and the PRC were the only two major powers that counted in Southeast Asia, a part of the world of considerable importance to both sides. Here the PRC's involvement was unusually close, if only because of the substantial Chinese expatriate communities throughout the region, which together with Taiwan, Hong Kong and Macao defined a 'Greater China' economic area.[41] By the mid-1990s Beijing was convinced that the PRC was the only power capable of challenging the Pax Americana. In terms of military potential this was far from being true. In spite of high expenditure on men and material the PRC remained a medium-sized military power, with mainly outdated weapons: at sea, in spite of developing a small blue water navy in the 1980s, it was no challenge at all to the US.[42] The China seas are still the domain of the USN Seventh Fleet.

TAIWAN

This is at the heart of Beijing's problems with Taiwan, which with the Taiwan Straits crisis in 1995 nearly led to a major showdown with the US. The crisis goes back to 1988, when the Guomindang regime in Taiwan – which dated back to Jiang Jieshi's arrival from the mainland in 1949 – finally yielded to a new popular government led by Li Denghui, a native Taiwanese. In one way this development was advantageous to Beijing, because Li abandoned the pretensions, maintained by the Jiang dynasty, to reconquer mainland China. On the other hand, as Li's government proved to be much more successful than that of the Guomindang – both politically and economically – it was perceived as a growing threat to the PRC, the more so seeing that Li showed few signs of working towards an accommodation agreeable to Beijing. On the contrary Li was assiduous in cultivating relations with members of the Japanese Diet and the US Congress, while at the same time defying the Beijing-imposed arms embargo by acquiring ships and aircraft from France and the US. Even so, in spite of Li's obvious success, not a single country – not even the US – was prepared to recognize his Taiwanese 'Republic of China' as an independent state.

The Taiwan Straits crisis arose out of an invitation to Li Denghui to revisit Cornell University – where he had been awarded a PhD in agricultural economics in 1968 – in May 1995; Li, who had accepted the invitation, was refused a visa by the US Secretary of State, Warren Christopher. He set off nonetheless, but could travel no further than Hawaii after President Clinton, mindful of the impact that the visit would have on relations between Washington and Beijing, barred him from entering the US. By a resolution of the US Congress, carried with a large majority, this decision was reversed, so that Li could proceed to Cornell for a 'private' visit. The considerable political capital that Li made out of this success helped re-elect him as President of Taiwan in March 1996.

The Chinese, on the other side of the line, were furious. After 1992, when Jiang Zemin became head of the Taiwan Affairs Leading Small Group of the CCP, Beijing had proceeded on the basis that Deng Xiaoping's policy of peaceful engagement of Taiwan as the prelude to 'reunification' had failed. Taiwan, far from falling like overripe fruit into Beijing's basket, clung tenaciously to its autonomy, while popular support for a formal declaration of independence gathered momentum. In 1994, Jiang's supporters, who by this time completely overshadowed Deng, saw Li as increasingly committed to a separate Taiwanese state in the face of the growing popularity of the opposition Democratic Progressive Party, which had made Taiwanese independence the main platform in its appeal to electors. In the event Li won the election in March 1996, but even so Beijing's misgivings were not allayed. Although Li wisely announced the end to his 'vacation diplomacy', he still insisted that 'Taiwan's destiny isn't China's to decide'.[43]

The Taiwan Straits crisis ran its course in the period between Li's US visit in May 1995 and his re-election to the Taiwan presidency in March 1996. The PLA was ordered to plan for action against Taiwan, with additional troops deployed in Fujian, the mainland province on the other side of the straits. This accorded with a widely publicized new strategy of 'local war under high-technology conditions' agreed in November 1994. The high technology became apparent in July 1995 with a new nuclear weapons test and the firing of six ballistic missiles, followed by air and sea exercises in the straits; although there was no direct action against Taiwan, in December Washington reacted by sending the aircraft-carrier USS *Nimitz*, with its support group, through the straits. This was just the beginning. In the first three months of 1996, fourteen US warships, including a second carrier, were deployed in the straits – the largest show of US force since 1950s. This was enough to convince Beijing that there was no military short-cut to the reunion of Taiwan with mainland China. After the stand-off in early 1996, Beijing, reluctantly convinced that its show of force had been counter-productive, brought it to an end. This was definitely a setback to Beijing's attempts to enhance its 'Pacific profile', after the collapse of the Soviet Union in 1991 had greatly increased the security of the PRC on the mainland. On 24 March 2000 Beijing's worst fears were realized in Taiwan when Chen Shuibian, leader of the Democratic Progressive Party, won the presidential elections on a pro-independence platform. The people of Taiwan were plainly not put off by Beijing's threats of firm action; the years since 2000 have witnessed little substantial change in the relations between Taiwan and the PRC, although the opportunities for travel between them have increased considerably, as has also the volume of Taiwan's trade with and investment in the PRC – the two go together.

HONG KONG

In the long term the best that the PRC can offer Taiwan is the 'one country, two systems' principle, worked out by Deng Xiaoping for the incorporation of Hong Kong in 1997, after it had been ceded by Britain.[44] Hong Kong, however, was always a different case. Hong Kong Island was ceded to the UK in 1842 at the end of the first opium war, to become, in principle, a British colony in perpetuity; it was then extended to include the Kowloon peninsula, opposite it on the mainland, in 1860. Then in 1898, China granted a 99-year lease of the so-called 'New Territories', much larger in area and comprising both mainland and countless islands – on one of which, Chep Lak Kok, the new international airport was opened in 1998. The city of Hong Kong was the seat of government of both the colony and the new territories.

Hong Kong fell to the Japanese in the first month of the Pacific War, but after the defeat of Japan in 1945 the British colonial administration was restored with surprisingly little difficulty – but in a high-handed way which, although it humiliated Jiang Jieshi, did ensure that his Guomindang government had no part to play in the future of the colony.[45] Until 1 March 1946 the British forces that had entered Hong Kong in August 1945 to accept the Japanese surrender maintained a military government, but Hong Kong then returned to civil government, with

Sir Mark Young – governor at the time of the Japanese invasion in 1941 – restored to his office. Nonetheless, in the 'euphoria of victory'[46] the local people preferred to identify themselves with China. Oddly enough, the establishment of the PRC in October 1949 hardly threatened Hong Kong: Mao had already decided that the economic value of both Hong Kong and the Portuguese Macao, as European colonies, was not to be jeopardized.[47] While the British accepted that the return of Hong Kong to China was, for Mao, no more than a long-term objective, his victory over the Guomindang in 1949 brought about a very considerable increase in the British garrison. Behind this policy lay the Amethyst incident of the early summer of 1949, which occurred when the PLA, advancing southwards, confronted the forces of the Guomindang across the Yangze River. The frigate, HMS Amethyst, on a routine mission, was caught between the two Chinese armies, with its way back to the sea cut off by the PLA. Although it made a dramatic escape on 31 July, the Royal Navy's failure to rescue the ship was seen in Hong Kong as a great humiliation. London, already confronted with the Soviet blockade of Berlin – which was not lifted until May 1949[48] – felt equally committed to holding on to Hong Kong. At the end of 1949 it was decided that a sufficiently strong garrison could hold 'Hong Kong against full-scale attack by Chinese Communists unless the latter were receiving appreciable military help from Russia'.[49] On the other hand the British cabinet had already recognized, in August, that the lease of the New Territories was unlikely to be renewed when it expired in 1997, and that without them Hong Kong would be untenable. It was also anticipated that the PRC would survive until then – as it did. Events at the end of the century already cast their shadow before it was half over. Even so, until the 1970s, little was done to reform a colonial administration in which the governor, supported by two government-appointed councils, ruled Hong Kong without any form of popular representation.

In the first year of the PRC Hong Kong benefited greatly from being an entrepôt between China and the outside world. After all the China trade had always been its *raison d'être*. Then, at the end of 1950, the whole situation changed radically as a result of the PRC committing troops to the Korean War, to fight against the UN forces in which the British contingent was second only to that of the US. An immediate result of the war was that the US Seventh Fleet 'neutralized' the Taiwan Straits, so making it next to impossible for the PRC to take over Taiwan. Hong Kong, however, was much harder hit by the trade embargo against the PRC imposed by the US. As a result it confronted two problems: the first was to find a new basis for its economy, while the second was to establish a position of strict legality and impartiality in Chinese political issues, in other words striking the right balance between the PRC and the Guomindang – a considerable challenge given that both sides wished to exploit Hong Kong to their own advantage. The history of Hong Kong, in the years between the Korean War in 1953 and the reversion of the colony to China in 1997, is a story of its success in solving both these problems.

In the course of the 1950s, investment in the Hong Kong economy following the US trade embargo switched from commerce to industry. Here Chinese industrialists who had fled Shanghai as China fell to Mao at the end of the 1940s played a major role, particularly in developing textile production. The colony, with a cheap adaptable labour force, a first-class harbour, and a rapidly growing home market, proved to be well-suited to light industry – which also provided employment for hundreds of thousands of refugees from the PRC, who were unlikely to return home. All this was done with local capital: foreign investment, mainly American or Japanese, only began in the 1960s. While business, mainly Chinese, was left with a free hand, the essential role of the colonial administration was to maintain political and social stability, investing at the same time in the infrastructure, industrial estates and public housing, with greatly increased budgets for health and education. With so many different commitments, the government was always the largest employer and the biggest property developer and landlord.[50] At the same time, the loss of the inland China trade was more than made good by developing Hong Kong as an entrepôt for the rest of East Asia, a process in which British banks, such as the HSBC, played a major role. Every year Hong Kong became more prosperous.

By the 1970s, however, it was clear that if the boom was to continue, the economy had to develop beyond commerce and industry: the answer was to be found in developing Hong Kong as a major financial centre and regional hub for business services, a process made easier by the government relaxing bureaucratic restrictions. 'The Stock Exchange of Hong Kong',[51] together with the Hang Seng index,[52] count for much in international finance.

Hong Kong also became much more committed to mainland China as a result of Deng Xiaoping's economic reforms in the 1980s.[53] So large was the scale of the transfer of industrial production that by 1997 some five million Chinese, mainly in Guangdong province, were employed by Hong Kong companies. Even so, the local climate was hardly business-friendly when judged by Hong Kong standards.

Although, until the end of the 1960s, democracy had never been the name of the game in Hong Kong, this was acceptable to a population consisting largely of immigrant Chinese only too anxious not to be involved in the politics of the mainland. They were more than content with the steadily increasing prosperity enjoyed under the UK's benevolent despotism in the years after the Pacific War. Even so, long before the 1997 deadline it was clear that radical reform was in order, not only because of what the future held in store but also because of the transformation, social, demographic and economic, from the 1960s onwards, of Hong Kong.

This was in part the result of Hong Kong's unique position, as an outpost of capitalism in the heart of the PRC, although here it only came into its own after Deng Xiaoping had reopened his country to foreign trade and investment in 1978 and the US had lifted the embargo imposed during the Korean War. Politically, in the thirty-odd years of Mao's China, his ideas had made little headway in Hong Kong – so much so that after the end of the Korean War in 1953, the British military presence, greatly increased as a result of the Amethyst incident in 1949, was gradually reduced to a level sufficient only for internal security. Mao's supporters in Hong Kong, such as they were, wisely maintained a low profile among a population which preferred to support the Guomindang. On 10 October 1956, however, they were the target of nationalist riots on the occasion of a popular celebration of the anniversary of the fall of the Qing dynasty in 1911. The police had then to call on a British armoured regiment, the 7th Hussars, to help restore order.

In the summer of 1967 young Maoists – inspired by the role of Mao's Red Guards in the Cultural Revolution – themselves took the initiative in causing labour unrest, going on to besiege Government House at a time when Chinese Communist propaganda referred to Europeans as 'white-skinned pigs' and the Chinese police in Hong Kong as 'yellow running dogs'. There were also a number of border clashes between Red Guards and the Hong Kong police, but at the end of the day the situation was contained by the colonial government, and peace restored. The lesson to Mao was clear: inside Hong Kong he could count on little effective support for his regime, or for any policy of taking over the colony by force. Time, nonetheless, was on the side of the PRC.

Almost everything began to change in the 1970s. The end of the war in Vietnam in 1975 soon brought a flood of refugees to Hong Kong, so that whatever policy was adopted to deal with them was bound to involve the government in controversy, both within the colony and outside it. This was at a time of great instability within the PRC following the death of Mao in September 1976. By the end of the 1970s, Hong Kong was the main source of FDI in the fastest growing parts of China's economy: Hong Kong industrialists, facing high local labour costs, began setting up plants on the other side of the border, so that in the end the number of their employees there was greater than that of the entire Hong Kong labour force. The PRC itself responded by setting up special economic zones close to Hong Kong. Inevitably Hong Kong became the key to good relations, always somewhat problematic, between the UK and the PRC. It also provided the bridge between the PRC and Taiwan.[54]

The future of Hong Kong, once the lease of the New Territories ended in 1997, was finally decided on 19 December 1984, when Margaret Thatcher, for the UK, and Zhao Ziyang, for the PRC, signed the Sino-British Joint Declaration providing for both Hong Kong and the New Territories to revert to Chinese sovereignty on 1 July 1997.[55] The Hong Kong Special Administrative Region (SAR) would then be governed according to the 'one country, two systems' principle, to be enshrined in the Basic Law which would in effect be the new region's constitution. After 1997 Hong Kong was promised a 'high degree of autonomy' for at least fifty years, during which time it would be largely exempt from the PRC's version of socialism. All this represented a British climbdown, for it was only in November 1983 that the British conceded that 'they intended no link of authority between Britain and Hong Kong after 1997'.[56]

Once the joint declaration came into operation (on 27 May 1985) the first task was to agree the contents of the Basic Law. The process took five years and ended only when the final text was adopted on 4 April 1990 by the Seventh National People's Congress of the People's Republic of China. Its significance to the PRC is made clear by the preamble:

> Hong Kong has been part of the territory of China since ancient times; it was occupied by Britain after the Opium War in 1840. On 19 December 1984, the Chinese and British Governments signed the Joint Declaration on the Question of Hong Kong, affirming that the Government of the People's Republic of China will resume the exercise of sovereignty over Hong Kong with effect from 1 July 1997, thus fulfilling the long-cherished common aspiration of the Chinese people for the recovery of Hong Kong.
>
> Upholding national unity and territorial integrity, maintaining the prosperity and stability of Hong Kong, and taking account of its history and realities, the People's Republic of China has decided that upon China's resumption of the exercise of sovereignty over Hong Kong, a Hong Kong Special Administrative Region will be established in accordance with the provisions of Article 31 of the Constitution of the People's Republic of China, and that under the principle of 'one country, two systems', the socialist system and policies will not be practised in Hong Kong. The basic policies of the People's Republic of China regarding Hong Kong have been elaborated by the Chinese Government in the Sino-British Joint Declaration.
>
> In accordance with the Constitution of the People's Republic of China, the National People's Congress hereby enacts the Basic Law of the Hong Kong Special Administrative Region of the People's Republic of China, prescribing the systems to be practised in the Hong Kong Special Administrative Region, in order to ensure the implementation of the basic policies of the People's Republic of China regarding Hong Kong.

The question then was how much of the 'systems' evolved in Hong Kong before 1997 would thereafter be acceptable to the PRC as compatible with the implementation of its 'basic policies'. One problem confronting the British in their determination to ensure a democratic future for Hong Kong after 1997 was that the legislative council, although first established in 1843, had no popularly elected members until 1985, the year the Joint Declaration came into effect. This was a very late stage in history for Britain to see the light. Even so, it was only in 1995 that all sixty members were elected, and of these only twenty came from geographical constituencies. Of the remaining forty, thirty came from functional constituencies, which the last governor, Chris Patten (1992–97) described as an 'abomination'.[57] While some of these constituencies represented large professional groups, such as lawyers and teachers, others were the home of narrow special interest groups, effectively dancing to the music of China. Nor, surprisingly, was this an arrangement welcome to the PRC, and one which they would take advantage of after 1997. Until then Beijing, somewhat reluctantly, allowed British rule to continue, in order to preserve 'Hong Kong's stability, good order … and prosperity'.[58]

In the event the twenty constituency members made the running in Hong Kong politics in the five years leading up to 1992. Internationally the best-known was Martin Lee, a brilliant lawyer, who made a point of attending, even in 1997, the silent vigil held every year to commemorate the victims of Tiananmen Square. He was not alone in seeing Hong Kong as let down by the British, particularly when its citizens were denied the right to British passports as they faced the inevitable alternative of becoming citizens of the PRC. In the event some 40,000 heads of families, with particularly uncertain prospects after 1997, were granted such passports, and of these about 10,000, with their families, emigrated – with Vancouver so favoured as a destination that it became known locally as 'Hong-couver'.[59] Needless to say they were hardly a cross-section of the Hong Kong population.

During the years leading up to 1997 much time was spent by both sides on reaching 'convergence' between what the PRC and Britain expected from the Basic Law. Given their 'climbdown' in 1983 the British held a weak hand: even so the Chinese were persuaded to accept 'the through train arrangement', according to which the legislative council, to be formed in accordance with the Basic Law in 1995, would continue to function after the handover in 1997.[60] In the event the 1995 council remained in office until 1999, but true to character the Chinese did their best to ensure that only legislators they approved of could stay on the train after the handover. Already, in 1993, the PRC had set up a Preliminary Working Committee – effectively a sort of shadow cabinet – recruited from members of the legislature likely to be sympathetic to their cause, and from this base a select committee hand-picked C.H. Tung as the man to be president of the SAR after 1997, to take over from Patten when he retired as governor. The result, according to Patten, was that 'on 1 July 1997 Hong Kong became the only example of decolonization deliberately accompanied by less democracy and a weaker protection of civil liberties'.[61] Even so he did accept that 'on the whole … the case for pluralism, the rule of law and open markets continued to thrive after the hand-over of power'.[62]

Tung, who was getting his new act together some time before 1 July, was always guided by the invisible hand of the PRC: otherwise he would never have been appointed Chief Executive of the SAR. Although three out of the eleven members of his new Executive Council were probably members of the Chinese Communist Party, another two were carried over from Patten's old executive council. At the same time, Chung Sze-yuen, the man chosen as Convenor of the Council, had been a senior member of the Executive Council during the 1980s, when the terms of the Joint Declaration were being negotiated.[63] In this whole process British views played little part.

To the PRC the handover of Hong Kong was seen as the culmination of Deng Xiaoping's[64] pragmatic approach to building 'socialism with Chinese characteristics'. Centuries of humiliation by Western imperialism had finally come to an end, which was widely celebrated by a gigantic street party in Beijing. Hong Kong witnessed the greatest public celebration since the founding of the PRC in 1949, with Jiang Zemin representing China, and the Prince of Wales, Britain – each with a considerable and distinguished supporting cast. There was no one to represent the people of Hong Kong, who were no more than spectators and providers of entertainment, nor was there any role for Patten, who would shortly see much of his legacy, particularly as it related to the structure of government, dismantled by Tung. The PRC, having incorporated Hong Kong, then screened it from the rest of China by a cordon sanitaire, so that, for instance, foreign travellers across the border require a Chinese visa. In the Chinese bureaucratic hierarchy, in which rank is always significant, that granted to the Chief Executive of the SAR was higher than that of a government minister, reflecting Jiang's policy, as stated at the founding ceremony, that 'no central department or locality may or will be allowed to interfere in the affairs' of the SAR.[65]

The 'one country, two systems' arrangement has now lasted for some ten years, while Tung resigned, two years before the end of his second five-year term, on March 2005 – a significant event for China-watchers, as well as for the people of Hong Kong. Always rightly seen as a puppet of the PRC, his local popularity declined drastically when he tried to introduce a draconian anti-subversion bill in accordance with Article 23 of the Basic Law. He also condemned the candle-lit vigils on the anniversary of Tiananmen Square. Then, on 1 July 2003 as many as 750,000 people demonstrated on to the streets, leading the new president of the PRC, Hu Jintao – who had succeeded Jiang Zemin on 15 March – to receive Tung in Beijing on 20 July in what was perceived as a face-saving gesture, and emphasize that Hong Kong needed to pass the Article 23 legislation. Tung, nonetheless, bowed to popular pressure and on 5 September announced the withdrawal of the subversion bill. Then, twice in the year 2004, up to 500,000 people demonstrated in favour of direct popular representation in the legislative council. Beijing, anxious to present a favourable image in Taiwan at the time of the critical 2004 presidential election, hardly reacted, but did note Tung's failure to maintain public order.

It had also become clear that he was failing as an administrator: he had dealt ineffectively with avian flu and the Hong Kong SARS epidemic, having earlier failed to have the new international airport open on time. In the end Beijing saw him as more of a liability than an asset, and on 20 December, Hu Jintao, in a speech in Macau made to commemorate the former Portuguese colony's successful first five years as an SAR, admonished the Hong Kong administration on its recent performance. Tung got the message, and on 24 June 2005 he was succeeded as chief executive by Donald Tsang, a successful civil servant during the British administration who, having become Chief Financial Secretary in 1995, was retained by Tung in 1997, to end up, from 1 May 2001, as Chief Secretary – altogether a man much better suited to govern Hong Kong.

FACING THE FUTURE: DISSENT AND HUMAN RIGHTS

China, at the beginning of the twenty-first century, faces two specific and intractable issues in foreign policy, Taiwan and North Korea, and a single major problem, that is to work out how to adapt its communist form of government to the need to maintain an expanding free market economy. As recounted above, in the final quarter of the twentieth century major problems, concerning the PRC's relationship with both the United States and Russia, its involvement in Southeast Asia and the transfer of power in Hong Kong and Macao, were solved – mainly on its own terms.

As for the problems still unsolved, the PRC, when it comes to Taiwan and North Korea, must, by force of circumstance, be reactive rather than proactive. Although the status quo in Taiwan, however anomalous, is best left undisturbed, this does suit the PRC in the long run. As the Taiwan Straits crisis showed, diplomacy is the only answer but Beijing is far from finding a formula for taking over Taiwan acceptable to its inhabitants. In the event adapting to the status quo has suited them very well: the island is on any count much more prosperous than the mainland. The same, however, was true of Hong Kong, where the lesson so far is that incorporation into China as an SAR has not demanded an unacceptably high price from the local population. For both historical and geographical reasons, however, there was no real alternative to the transition of power in 1997. One reason for the exceptional degree of autonomy allowed the government of Hong Kong by the PRC is the need to reassure the people of Taiwan that they, too, could live as an SAR. So far, however, they are not convinced, and as long as foreign trade and investment support their economy, they are unlikely to be won over by Beijing – in spite of their present diplomatic isolation. In the short term Taiwan – despite its anomalous political status – is economically extremely useful to the PRC, which explains why Beijing sanctions the steady improvement of the island's communications with the mainland, including travel in both directions. For both Beijing and Taipei, therefore, the best policy is to accept a situation in which the left hand does not know what the right hand is doing. The present stand-off could last for a long time.

As to North Korea, the problem is that as a result of the dire economic consequences of its self-imposed isolation, combined with a near complete lack of allies willing to help, the state's only instrument for dealing with the outside world is its nuclear weapons potential – as described in Chapter 5. A population on the threshold of starvation is crying out for help – or at least would do so if the state allowed it. Over the years food relief has been provided by the outside world, but Kim Jong Il's government does not welcome foreign aid officials who are bound to observe and report on the sorry state of the country and the miserable condition of most of its inhabitants. In recent years representatives of North and South Korea, China, Russia, Japan and the United States have met to negotiate a non-nuclear regime acceptable to North Korea but Kim Jong Il remains intransigent, blowing hot and cold, while hiding the extent, both actual and potential, of his nuclear arsenal. Here the position of the PRC, which supported North Korea in the Korean War, is critical. With thousands of North Korean refugees in China, Beijing has no illusions about life under Kim, and has little to gain by supporting his regime. But then, what for China are the alternatives? And if there was a good alternative, what sort of action would bring about the necessary regime change in a country prepared to launch nuclear missiles? If, in North Korea, Kim were to orchestrate reforms similar to those which have transformed, say, communist Vietnam since 1975, that could be the answer. He shows no such inclination. In the worst-case scenario he would prefer to exercise the nuclear option, a step certain to provoke a reaction that would destroy him, and his country. For China, South Korea and Japan – to say nothing of the world outside East Asia – the collateral damage is simply too appalling to contemplate.

Turning back to the Chinese heartland in the post-Maoist era, the success of the PRC in introducing a market economy open to the outside world, has transformed not only the life of hundreds of millions of its citizens, but also the structure of international finance and trade and industry world-wide. The process, however, has not been cost-free. The gap between the mainly urban rich and mainly rural poor has steadily widened, a process inevitably accompanied by large-scale migration from the countryside to the cities. The result, particularly in the cities, has been the emergence of a global consumer culture supported by every modern means of communication. Mobile phones, websites and email are as much part of everyday life as Coca-Cola and KFC. In Shanghai and Guangdong there is little echo of the traditional isolation of the middle kingdom. In 1989 the student protest on Tiananmen Square was a world-wide media event. In spite of the reforms of Deng Xiaoping and his successors, this is not life according to the book, but Beijing now knows only too well that a price must be paid for the suppression of dissent – as C.H. Tung discovered in Hong Kong.

The essential question relates to human rights in the PRC, and the extent to which the outside world should be concerned about them. This is opening a real can of worms (which I am inclined to close as soon as possible). In the late 1990s there were a series of attempts to place the Chinese human rights record on the agenda of the UN Human Rights Commission, but even the US representatives, who were usually in the vanguard, lost heart. The EU was only too eager to discern 'encouraging results of the EU-China human right dialogues', such as the release from prison in 1997 of the high-profile dissident writer Wei Jingsheng, noted by the UK Foreign Secretary Robin Cook – a view, incidentally, rejected by Wei himself,[66] and condemned by Human Rights Watch. Needless to say the pusillanimous Western politicians were concerned about the loss of trade and investment opportunities, but it is doubtful whether condemning the Chinese human rights record makes much difference to prospects. After all Beijing also needs the business, and knows that tolerating dissent – within limits – is good for public relations outside China, and perhaps even for maintaining law and order at home. Henry Kissinger's description of the Chinese as 'cold-blooded practitioners of power politics' remains true.[67]

3

The restoration of Japan

GENERAL MACARTHUR'S SHOGUNATE

The reconstruction of Japan (see map on page x) after the end of World War II was largely the work of a single man, the American General Douglas MacArthur, who had been appointed *Supreme Commander of the Allied Powers* (SCAP).[1] On 2 September 1945 MacArthur had accepted the formal surrender of the Japanese government on the deck of the American battleship *Missouri*. On the allied side the act of surrender was also signed by representatives of Australia, Britain, Canada, China, France, the Netherlands, New Zealand and the Soviet Union. Although these countries were also represented in SCAP, there was never any doubt that MacArthur ran a one-man show from his office in the Dai Ichi building in Tokyo. He was Japan's new *Shōgun*[2] and his remit was to enforce the terms of the Potsdam agreement made between the allied powers in July 1945, which in addition to establishing SCAP as the government of the country, confined Japan within its historic boundaries – as they were before its imperialist expansion in the half century before World War II – providing also for complete and permanent disarmament and the punishment of war criminals.

With this remit MacArthur had little alterative but to work with entrenched Japanese officials, who despite their country's catastrophic defeat were anxious to preserve its traditional institutions – almost as if, in the broad sweep of history, the Pacific War was something that could be glossed over. At the same time the Diet – the Japanese parliament – continued to function. It is not surprising then that since 1945 there has been continuous debate, both in and outside Japan, about the degree of continuity in government from before to after the war.[3]

Two immediate practical tasks faced post-war Japan. First, a country devastated by allied bombing (which culminated in the destruction of Hiroshima and Nagasaki by atomic bombs) had to be rebuilt. Second, there was the need to repatriate not only hundreds of thousands of servicemen left in the territory still occupied by Japan at the end of the Pacific War, but also large numbers of civilians in Korea, Manchuria and Taiwan, which together constituted the pre-war empire forfeited by Japan under the terms of the Potsdam agreement.

Slowly but surely Japan was rebuilt and public services restored so that the way was open for a new civil society. Nothing could bring back the millions, both servicemen and civilians, who had lost their lives in the war, but then post-war Japan – following Potsdam once more – would not be burdened with the need to maintain armed forces, nor an armament industry to support them. At a mundane level the problems were logistic, involving the allocation of resources and the deployment of labour. At another level, however, there was the whole question of the culture of government, obsessed – at least since the time of the Meiji restoration in 1868 – with the unique status of the Japanese people, particularly in relation to their emperor. This was an immediate concern of SCAP.

A major question to be resolved was that of the responsibility of the Shōwa Emperor – then known, particularly outside Japan, as Hirohito[4] – not so much for the war, as for the atrocities perpetrated by Japanese soldiers, who fought in his name. For many the horror evoked by the Rape of Nanking, the Bataan Death March or forced labour on the Burma Railway, is on the same scale as Auschwitz. How could a man, who became emperor long before the war, and was still only 44 years old at its end, not be responsible? Why did his name not head the list of those to be tried for war crimes?

Although with Hiroshima and Nagasaki the end of the war came much earlier than expected, there had already been months of discussion, in and around Washington, about the future of the Shōwa Emperor.[5] The military government of a defeated Japan was regarded as extremely problematic, and the problems were likely to be compounded if the emperor was treated in a way abhorrent to the Japanese people. At the beginning of the twenty-first century we only need Iraq to show how badly a military occupation can fail in government. Moreover, there was never any certainty that the Shōwa Emperor would be convicted in a fair trial. Although there was no doubt that he was the focus of almost mystic reverence, so that in the front line every action was not only taken in his name, but popularly believed to reflect his own supernatural will, the reality of his actual command of events was extremely uncertain. Even in 1941, when events moved inexorably towards the Pacific War, the media outside Japan seldom mentioned the name of the emperor. The men that counted in that fateful year were Matsuoka, Konoye, Tōjō and Yamamoto – almost forgotten names of men who, if not already dead, were no longer in power in 1945. So it was in the years before 1941. In the kaleidoscope of Japanese politics, those who changed the course of events were themselves continually changing, whether they were generals in China or politicians in Tokyo. A line can be traced, historically, through a succession of key figures, whose actions, largely uncoordinated, led to the disaster of the Pacific War, but the Shōwa Emperor is not among them. It is doubtful whether he even had the power to restrain them: the balance of evidence is that he did his best.[6] What he had, quite uniquely, was a position as head of state, defined as the result of a very long and complicated history, that was his as a result of the laws of succession to Japan's Chrysanthemum Throne. Continuity in office distinguished him from everyone else in the Japanese power structure. It is no proof that he was ever in command of events: to quote an American scholar '... in the last analysis, the Shōwa Emperor was the unwilling symbol, not the maker of chaos and catastrophe'.[7] The Shōwa Emperor did, however, change the course of history at least once, when, in August 1945, his voice, as the Japanese cabinet met in the aftermath of Hiroshima and Nagasaki, carried the day, and the decision was taken to surrender.

MacArthur, in any case, had always accepted that the position of the emperor should be preserved. If MacArthur had doubts, they were assuaged when the Shōwa Emperor, on 27 September 1945, on a quite spontaneous visit to the Dai Ichi building, stated that he was ready to accept full responsibility for 'every political and military decision made and action taken by my people in the conduct of the war'.[8] In these words MacArthur recognized 'the First Gentleman of Japan', and after this meeting there was no longer any question that only political expediency governed their relationship.

There was little doubt about the popularity of the Shōwa Emperor: opinion polls at the end of 1945 showed 95 per cent in favour of retaining the Chrysanthemum Throne.[9] The emperor himself took a further significant step when, on New Year's Day, 1946, he made a public statement disclaiming the status of *arahitogami*, which means 'divine present emperor', and then went on to deny that 'the Japanese people are superior to other races, and fated to rule the world'.

When it came to the question of his status, the problem lay not so much with the emperor himself, but with members of the old guard who still held office. As a purely practical matter these men were indispensable to SCAP, few of whose members had any detailed knowledge of Japan or any useful command of its language. At a very early stage the Japanese mandarins bucked the trend of MacArthur's government. The matter at issue was the Rescript on Education, an official statement, dating from 1890, and declaring, in convoluted language, the mystical status of the imperial line, and derivatively, their subjects, the Japanese people – 'infallible for all ages and true in all places'. Although this document did not originate in the imperial court, but was rather the product of a committee of the Ministry of Education, it was accepted as the basis for moral instruction in all Japanese schools. On ceremonial occasions an entire school, lead by the principal, would recite it in unison. It rapidly became the centre of a new cult of the emperor, based largely on traditional Confucian ethics. Although, on the face of it, the rescript[10] was innocuous, it represented everything about the emperor's place in Japanese society that SCAP was intent on suppressing. Here SCAP's will was law, and in October 1946 the Japanese Diet passed a resolution terminating the use of the rescript. Even so successive ministers of education continued to see its suppression as a disaster for the people's morals.[11]

THE TOKYO WAR CRIMES TRIBUNAL

One of the first of the allied tasks to be taken up in Japan was the trial of those responsible for the war, and the crimes committed as part of it. A special International Military Tribunal for the Far East (IMTFE) was set up, and during a period of two and a half years, from May 1946 until November 1948, a heterogeneous collection of twenty-eight wartime leaders, civilian and military, were tried before it. At a lower level a further 6,000 were tried, of whom nearly 1,000 were sentenced to death. In contrast to Germany, the Japanese government took no initiative in trying its own citizens for war crimes. The law which guided the IMTFE was the Tokyo Charter, the product of a SCAP executive degree modelled on the Nuremberg Charter under which German war criminals went on trial. There were eleven judges, one from each of the nine countries represented at the act of surrender on 2 September 1945, plus India and the Philippines. In the event the concept of law implicit in the Tokyo Charter was that common to the English-speaking world, and it was not for nothing that the president of the tribunal was an Australian, Sir William Webb, and the chief prosecuting counsel an American, Joseph B. Keenan. The indictment contained 55 specific counts, but their common basis was conspiracy 'to secure the domination and exploitation ... of the rest of the world and to this end to commit crimes against peace, war crimes and crimes against humanity ...'

Conspiracy – in jurisprudence an essentially Anglo-Saxon concept – is the political crime *par excellence*. It is particularly useful for prosecutors whenever the underlying events, whatever their criminal character, can be linked to contacts between different accused. The essential rationale of conspiracy is guilt by association. In Tokyo its use by the prosecution was all the more open to question given that the drafting of the charter, the framing of the indictment, the appointment of judges and prosecutors, and the choice of the accused were all part and parcel of one political operation carried out by SCAP, which the Japanese were powerless to resist. No wonder that General Tōjō, at the end of the trial, referred to it as 'victors' justice'.

By the final judgment of the court seven were sentenced to death, and several more of the accused were convicted and sentenced to imprisonment. Of these, only General Tōjō, prime minister at the time of Pearl Harbor, was well-known outside Japan. The whole scenario was quite different to that of Nuremberg, as was its historical background. Unlike in Germany under Hitler there was never in Japan any mastermind directing policies, such as the 'final solution to the Jewish problem', which inevitably involved crimes against humanity. There was no Japanese Auschwitz. The horrors of the Rape of Nanking or the Burma Railway were incidental rather than essential to Tokyo's war policy, and after the war, justice – so far as possible – was done at the trials held at a lower level, where, after all, nearly a thousand Japanese, mainly soldiers, were sentenced to death.

No one got much satisfaction from the Tokyo Tribunal. Without the Shōwa Emperor among the accused, Australia, Britain, China, New Zealand and the Soviet Union, all regarded the final verdict as incomplete. The Japanese people accepted it with resignation, but with little sense of being answerable for the events on which it was based – most of which had taken place far from the shores of their country, a critically important psychological point. Hiroshima and Nagasaki were the complete expiation of whatever wrongs had been committed by Japan. If the Tokyo Tribunal was acceptable to the Japanese, it was because it passed judgment on men whose policies had led large parts of their country to be reduced to dust and ashes, a view echoed in the words of the Indian judge, Radhabinod Pal: 'If any indiscriminate destruction of civilian life and property is still illegitimate in warfare, then, in the Pacific War, this decision to use the atomic bomb is the only near approach to the directives of … the Nazi leaders during the Second World War'. Twelve years later the Dutch judge, Bernard Röling, representing a country whose losses in the Pacific War were never made good, noted that '… from the Second World War above all two things are remembered: the German gas chambers and the American atomic bombings'.[12]

The real charge at Tokyo, in 1946, even if seldom made explicit, was that the Japanese had destroyed a political, economic, social and cultural system, which took for granted the domination of the Western world. The destruction of this system, as a quite explicit aim of Japanese policy-makers, went back to the end of World War I. According to an article published at the end of 1918 by the young Prince Konoye, as he looked forward to the coming peace conference at Versailles (where he would be a junior member of the Japanese delegation), 'the present position of Japan in the world … demands the destruction of the status quo … [with] the minimum *sine qua non* the eradication of economic imperialism and discriminatory treatment of Asian peoples by Caucasians … Should their policy prevail, Japan, which is small, resource poor, and unable to consume all its industrial products, would have no resort but to destroy the status quo for the sake of self-preservation'.[13]

Konoye went on to become one of Japan's leading politicians. In the four years (1937–41) preceding the Pacific War he was three times prime minister, so his share of responsibility for the war can hardly be denied.[14] On 6 December 1945 SCAP ordered him to be arrested to stand trial before the IMTFE, but he took the law into his own hands. Ten days later he committed suicide by taking poison, so pre-empting the sentence that the tribunal undoubtedly would have passed upon him. History has since proved Konoye's words written in 1918 to be prophetic: every objective he stated has been realized. Somewhat ironically, Morihiro Hosakawa, prime minister from 1992 to 1993, was his grandson.

For MacArthur the Tokyo trial cleared the way to rehabilitating Japan. The first step, completed before the end of the trial, was the new constitution imposed by SCAP in 1947. Presented by the emperor to the Diet on 20 June 1946, and passed on 7 October 1946, it came into effect on 3 May 1947 – a public event celebrated by large crowds. Although in form an amendment to the existing constitution of 1889, it radically reconstructed the form of government. This was immediately clear from Article 1: 'The Emperor shall be the symbol of the state and of the unity of the people, deriving his position from the will of the people with whom resides sovereign power'. This established in law the emperor's declaration of 1 January 1946. Certain residual duties are reserved to the emperor by Article 7 but these are all ceremonial.

THE 1947 CONSTITUTION

Significantly, even before the new constitution became law, the Imperial House Law of 3 January 1947 had already abolished the Japanese peerage (and with it the Peers' House in the Japanese parliament) and drastically reduced the number of recognized members of the imperial house. Later in the year the imperial house became completely reliant, financially, on appropriations – in actual practice extremely generous – made by the Diet, while the actual household was degraded to become subject to an agency (Kunaichô) attached to the prime minister's office. These reforms established the Diet, unequivocally, as the highest organ of the state in the form of a responsible elected government on the Westminster model.[15]

The new constitution further defined the place of religion in Japan: Article 20 guaranteed 'religious freedom, forbidding (a) the exercise of political authority by religious organizations, and (b) the use of compulsion to bring about participation in 'any religious act, celebration, rite or practice' while Article 89 prohibited public funds from being 'expended or appropriated for the use of any religious institution or association'. These two articles were important for ensuring that the state support of Shintō, Japan's ancient religion, introduced for political reasons in the late nineteenth century and abolished by SCAP in 1945, could never be revived. The background is involved, but many outsiders attributed the rise of Japanese nationalism – culminating in the Pacific War – to the way that Shintō had been appropriated by the state, with priests appointed as public officials employed by the Shrine Bureau of the Home Ministry. Traditional Shintō, whose origins are to be found in a sacred eighth-century text, the Kōjiki, defined the mystical status of the emperor in a line starting with the Jimmu, a direct descendant of the Sun Goddess, Ameterasu Omikami, who became the first emperor on 13 February 660 BC – a day celebrated as *kigensetsu*.[16] State Shintō was inaugurated as the means of incorporating all this into the fabric of a modern state – a sort of Japanese answer to the Church of England. The fact that traditional Shintō has continued to thrive after 1945 is proof enough that the state version was never essential to it.

The 1947 constitution did not, however, quite settle the matter. Neither the cult of the Yasukuni Shrine in Tokyo, where Japanese war dead have been commemorated since 1869, nor the use of the ancient Shintō ceremony of Daijôsai for the inauguration of the emperor – both described later in this chapter – are in the spirit of the 1947 constitution.

In the second half of the twentieth century events were to prove that Article 9 of the constitution, renouncing 'war as a sovereign right of the nation' and forbidding the maintenance of 'land, sea and air forces and other war potential', would be the most far-reaching in its effects. This decisively ended Japanese militarism. To this day, Japan maintains little more than a modest Self-Defence Force, which means that its defence budget is extremely small compared to that of any comparable nation. Article 9 was regarded by SCAP as fundamental in 1947, but since then the US military has often enough had reason to regret that no Japanese forces can be deployed in support of its operations. The American military presence in Japan is still essential to its defence. Slowly ways are being found to bypass the drastic restrictions imposed by Article 9, as witness the small contingent sent by Japan to Iraq in 2003. Even so, many Japanese are content with Article 9, and it remains a political hot potato.

The new constitution brought in its train a number of major reforms: universal franchise extended the vote to women, freedom to organize trade unions greatly strengthened the position of labour, the freedom of the press was guaranteed and millions of tenant farmers were freed of their ties to rural landlords. Social engineering even extended to abolishing the formal legal status of the *ie*, the traditional rural household, regarded by SCAP as a conservative force which had buttressed the old order of Japanese society. Over time the importance of these reforms declined as Japan completed the transformation, already well under way before the Pacific War, from an agrarian to an industrial society.

The reforms imposed by SCAP went furthest in education, which, in the pre-war years, had been unashamedly used, as a matter of government policy, for indoctrinating pupils and students in nationalistic values: the Imperial Rescript on Education was but one extreme instrument of educational policy. SCAP's policy, enshrined in the Fundamental Law of Education of 1947, was essentially to impose a typical American school and college system, based on decentralization, co-education and equal opportunity. The established authority of the Ministry of

Education (Mombushō) in Tokyo was drastically curtailed. One immediate result was to strengthen the union movement among teachers, so that in 1947, 95 per cent of primary school teachers had become members of the nationwide union *Nikkyōso*.[17] Given his increasing concern for the communist threat, this went too far for General MacArthur, who introduced drastic new measures to reduce the power of public-sector unions. *Nikkyōso* was deprived of the right to represent its members in collective bargaining, teachers denied the right to strike, and even their rights to run and campaign for political office were restricted. SCAP even supported an unsuccessful *Mombushō* proposal to control left-wing university faculties. These extreme measures were largely counter-productive: *Nikkyōso* did not lose its support among teachers, many of whom, in later years, proved to be the most articulate critics of government policy.

As, in the two years following the end of the Pacific War, SCAP was busy imposing one legal reform after another, Japan still had its own government, complete with prime minister and cabinet. Their immediate task, subject to SCAP's guidelines, was simply to rebuild their devastated country and create a new economy. The leading figure in this process was Shigeru Yoshida, who, except for a break in the years 1947–48, was prime minister of Japan from May 1946 to December 1954. The Liberal Party – or *Jimintō* – which he led, has been in power almost continuously since he first took up office.

Yoshida, essentially an unreformed conservative, was at odds with SCAP in its early reforming days, but then, in 1948, its course changed. As SCAP's priority shifted from democratization to 'rebuilding Japan as an ally of the United States in its escalating Cold War confrontation with communism in Europe and Asia',[18] Yoshida's government willingly cooperated, supporting, among other moves, SCAP's 'red purge' of communists in government. Its position was greatly strengthened first, in 1949, by Mao's victory in China, and second, in 1950, by Kim Il Sung's invasion of South Korea. The latter led Yoshida, with full SCAP support, to create a new 75,000 strong National Police Reserve, whose true character can be seen in the fact that in 1954 it provided the hard core of the Self-Defence Forces – or *Jieitai*. The remit of the *Jieitai* was unmistakably the defence of Japan against outside aggression rather than the maintenance of civil order at home. At the same time Yoshida was allowed to rehabilitate many top Japanese with an unacceptable wartime record, including a number who had been given prison sentences by the Tokyo Tribunal. In the course of the 1950s some of these even returned to high government office.

THE 1951 PEACE TREATY

By this time the main concern of Japan was that the US should accept indefinite responsibility of its defence, and the much increased numbers of American troops sent to Japan were welcomed by the Yoshida government. The key matter to be resolved was that of a peace treaty for Japan, restoring its autonomy as a sovereign state. As early as 1948 MacArthur was beginning to doubt the wisdom of continuing the allied occupation.[19] The problem lay not so much in Japan, but in winning outside support, both internationally and in the United States. Among the Western allies there was not only resistance from all who had suffered at Japanese hands during the Pacific War, but also concern about future Japanese competition in the world economy. By the end of the 1940s there was no question of Soviet Russia or the People's Republic of China agreeing to a treaty put forward by Washington. In the end the Peace Treaty was signed in San Francisco in September 1951 by all the Western allies, together with the Latin American countries that had entered the war against Japan. From Southeast Asia, not even the Philippines were ready to sign.

Even within Japan Yoshida did not get much credit for the treaty. Many saw the continuing American military presence – coupled with extra-territorial rights for US citizens – as little more than SCAP continuing in a new guise. Outside Japan, critics in Australia, Britain and the Philippines saw the treaty as giving too much away in exchange for what would be, essentially, a US monopoly of power. This was particularly unwelcome in France and the Netherlands whose colonial empires in Southeast Asia never recovered from the devastation of the Pacific War. What is more, when it came to ratification of the treaty, Yoshida had to write a letter, intended for the US Senate, promising not to seek any ties with Beijing, at the same recognizing the continuing legitimacy of Jiang Jieshi's nationalist government in Taiwan. With these assurances the Senate ratified the treaty in April 1952, and Japan became once more an independent state.

The omens for the future of Japan were more favourable than anyone could have foreseen when the Pacific War ended on 15 August 1945. Six years of allied military government had left the country with a popular and stable regime, led by Shigeru Yoshida, who had come to power under the new democratic constitution of 1946. By 1952 the rebuilding of the cities destroyed by war, and the repair of the communications infrastructure, were well under way, while at the same time Japan, by virtue of Article 9 of the new constitution, was free of the burden of maintaining its own armed forces and the industry needed to support them. What is more, it had no overseas empire to govern, so that the focus of politics – and of society as a whole – was on developing a wholly peacetime national economy.

The radical transformation of Japan in the six post-war years meant that millions, both at home and among Japan's former enemies, who had been traumatized by the war, had little choice but to accept that the slate had been wiped clean. Japan's new standing in the world was open for all to see on 10 November 1952: countless foreign dignitaries then witnessed the emperor preside over the traditional ceremonies held for the coming of age of Crown Prince Akihito, who had the advantage of having been only 11 years old when the war ended in 1945. In 1953, the standing of the imperial court was further enhanced when the crown prince accepted an invitation to represent Japan at the coronation of Queen Elizabeth II in London. As things worked out – during a reign that lasted until 1989 – the Shōwa Emperor's state visits abroad, and to Europe in particular, led to demonstrations that made clear that not all the traumas of the Pacific War had healed; in his own country, however, he was completely rehabilitated – if, indeed, he had ever fallen from grace. Successive Japanese governments, in their international relations, also suffered little from the fact that their head of state was the same man as first sat on the Chrysanthemum Throne in 1926. Enough has been said: if the identity of Japan's head of state was ever a significant political factor in the years after 1952, it was mainly on occasions, such as the aborted *coup d'état* and ritual suicide of the ultra-patriotic novelist, Yukio Mishima, on 26 November 1970 – an event related later in this chapter – which were beyond the control of either the court or the government of the day.

THE ECONOMIC MIRACLE

The question then is, what sort of governments ruled Japan, under the new constitution of 1947, in the years after 1952? And even more important, what did they achieve? Historically the first point to make is that – at least until the 1970s – the economic climate under which Japan operated internationally was largely determined by the strategic imperatives confronting the United States in East and Southeast Asia. These meant that Japan, together with South Korea – whose history in many ways ran parallel – were in the front line in the US confrontation with communism. There were two results: first, both countries agreed to admit, support and supply a massive local US military presence – extending across all three arms, on land, sea and air. US bases were established in many parts of Japan, with US occupation of Okinawa continuing until 1972 – with many critical implications related later in this chapter.

Second, next to US strategy in the Far East, prosperity born out of unfettered economic expansion was seen as a key factor in ensuring that communism had little popular appeal in Japan. On this view the Japanese economic miracle was almost an American political expedient.[20] This was already apparent in the 1950s, when both Japanese industry and finance were organized for massive production for both foreign and domestic markets, with few restrictions on the import of key capital goods and a currency managed at highly competitive rates – particularly in relation to the US dollar. With these advantages Japan was soon building ships more cheaply than any other country, while the big names in cars and consumer electronics, such as Toyota and Sony, were beginning to count internationally. In 1964 Japan's buoyant economy had made it possible to run the *shinkansen*, the world's first high-speed train, between Tokyo and Osaka – the first link in a network now extending across the whole country – while in the same year Tokyo was host to the Olympic Games.

On the Japanese side, the most important contribution was political stability, and for almost the entire period since 1952, this has been ensured by a single party, the *Jimintō* – which, while known in English as the 'Liberal Democratic Party', little resembles the eponymous party in the UK.[21] At least until the 1990s, the *Jimintō* hardly ever failed to deliver, and was rewarded accordingly. The party, however, was far from monolithic: on the contrary it was always divided into factions, each with leaders competing for support among members of parliament, whose shifting allegiances were largely opportunistic. This was a system in which even strong leaders, such as, notably, Kakuei Tanaka, prime minister from June 1972 to December 1974, overplayed their hand, to fall from power amid accusations of favouritism and corruption – which, in the case of Tanaka, included accepting a $1,800,000 kick-back from the US Lockheed Aircraft Company. Even so the Tanaka faction – from which two subsequent prime ministers were recruited – remained for many years a power to be reckoned in Japanese politics. Significantly, in the years since 1952, only Satô, Tanaka's predecessor and prime minister from 1964 to 1972 – and Nobel prize-winner (1974) – served longer than Yoshida, the *Jimintō*'s founder in 1955.

In Japan the way members are elected to parliament, and their influence once elected, depends upon an informal principle by which the same people move back and forth between the top levels of industry and the civil service. This is known to the Japanese as *amakudari* – literally, if somewhat ironically, 'descent from heaven'. At the same time family and local ties count very highly, with the expectation, also, that party support should not go unrewarded. The state of the roads in a country constituency can indicate whether the local member belongs to the *Jimintō*, and if so, just how high he stands within it.[22] One result is that political opponents are zealous in tracking down corruption, and remarkably often succeed in finding it. If, however, they are too successful, and so succeed to office – local or national – they soon find that this is a game that two can play.

If all this is background, it is still critical for the state of modern Japan, particularly since the rules of the game have hardly changed in the years since 1952. The principal actors, however, changed constantly, often in response to events whose significance was only apparent to expert Japan-watchers.

Shinzo Abe, who succeeded Junichiro Koizumi (2001–06) in September 2006, is the twenty-fourth prime minister – and also, aged 52, the youngest – since independence was granted in 1952, without there being a single case of a former prime minister returning to office. (In the same period the UK had ten prime ministers, and the US, ten presidents.) The question inevitably arises as to how far the government of the day, given the inherently insecure position of its leader, can shape events, rather than simply react *post hoc*. Here Koizumi, with a somewhat maverick profile, achieved more than most of his predecessors. Abe may not do as well, for if there is one lesson constantly learnt by Japanese prime ministers, and their cabinets, it is that 'pride comes before a fall'.

OKINAWA AND THE US

Typically for Japan, change only came in its Pacific politics when the opportunity was ripe. The case of Okinawa, which bedevilled US-Japanese relations for nearly twenty years, is exemplary. The American invasion of the island, leading to its ultimate capture on 21 June 1945, was the last major battle of the Pacific War. On 7 September 1948 the strategic importance of the Ryukyu Islands, of which Okinawa was the most important, led President Truman to approve a National Security Council order separating them from Japan. With a US civil administration already established on 15 December 1950, the Peace Treaty of 1951 confirmed the United States' 'exclusive strategic control of the Ryukyu Islands': Japan was left with no more than 'residual sovereignty', which was sufficient, nonetheless, for Okinawans to be designated as Japanese citizens in the US.[23]

On 7 January 1954 President Eisenhower, in his State of the Union address, stated, 'We shall maintain indefinitely our bases in Okinawa', making clear the US' long-term strategy to establish the island as its main base in the Far East. These words foreshadowed the relocation of US forces from Japan itself, to start in 1955 and coupled with the compulsory acquisition of land for new bases in Okinawa. In 1956 the transfer of land was met by popular demonstrations throughout Japan, while at the same time Tokyo was busy negotiating a peace treaty with Moscow. The Soviet draft then provided for the complete transfer of sovereignty of the bleak Kuril Islands north of Japan – as far away as possible from the semi-tropical Ryukyus. This was too much for Washington, and on 27 August, John Foster Dulles, the US Secretary of State, warned that if the transfer went ahead, the US, relying on a clause in the 1951 Peace Treaty with Japan, would claim sovereignty over the Ryukyus. It would be tit for tat. Moscow then accepted a limited agreement, terminating the state of war between Japan and the Soviet Union, exchanging ambassadors, returning Japanese prisoners of war – there were still hundreds of thousands in the Siberian *gulags* – and supporting Japan's admission into the United Nations, which took place on 21 December.

Four days later, Kamejiro Senaga, leader of Okinawa's communist People's Party, was elected mayor of Naha, the capital city, by a minority vote. The Americans, much displeased, reacted immediately. The CIA began funding opposition parties opposed to communism, orchestrating at the same time a vote of no confidence in Senaga by the Naha city council. The first attempt failed after the People's Party, by increasing its vote in new municipal elections, was able to deny the opposition the two-thirds quorum required for such a vote. The newly appointed US High Commissioner, exercising powers specially conferred by President Eisenhower, then changed the local ordinances so that a simple majority would suffice. On 25 November 1957 the city council duly voted Senaga out of office, leaving the way for a new socialist major to be elected on 12 January 1958.

By this time the US Ambassador in Tokyo was advising Washington that the whole American position in Okinawa, which was proving to be a diplomatic disaster, should be renegotiated. Although Eisenhower first reacted favourably, in the end he listened to the US Chiefs of Staff and affirmed the status quo. The result was that the provisions of a new security treaty with Japan, signed in Washington on 19 January 1960, did not extend to the Ryukyus. The Japanese prime minister Nobusuke Kishi then had to use all his parliamentary skills to secure ratification by the Diet in Tokyo. Daily demonstrations, riots and strikes, which continued until final ratification on 22 June, meant that Kishi cancelled an official state visit by Eisenhower planned for 16 June. On 19 June, however, the president did visit Okinawa, to be greeted by a quarter of the population. On 22 June, the US Senate, with none of the problems facing the Japanese Diet, ratified the treaty by 90 votes to 2.

After 1960 Japan did better with a new president in the White House. On 19 March 1963 President John Kennedy stated, 'I recognize the Ryukyus to be a part of the Japanese homeland, and look forward to the day when the security interests of the free world will permit their restoration to full Japanese sovereignty.' Given the deteriorating situation in Vietnam that day had not come, but Kennedy did strengthen the civil administration of the Ryukyus. Then, in 1964, a new Japanese prime minister, Eisaku Satô, assumed office, having previously released a campaign pamphlet, 'The Fight for Tomorrow', calling for the reversion of Okinawa to Japan within the context of the 1960 security alliance. By this time Lyndon Johnson was US president, but his administration did not react to Satô's claim to the Ryukyus. Instead, on 29 July 1965, US B-52s stationed in Okinawa bombed North Vietnam. Local protests and rallies did, however, lead to further missions being cancelled. Near the end of his term of office Johnson did make one concession: on 1 February 1968 he signed Executive Order 11395 allowing Okinawans to directly elect their own Chief Executive.

The real breakthrough came with President Richard Nixon in the White House. On 28 May 1969, after only four months in office, he signed National Security Decision Memorandum 13 authorizing negotiations with Japan for the reversion of the Ryukyu Islands. Then, on 18 July, *The Wall Street Journal* reported that chemical and biological weapons were stored on Okinawa. With this background and after a three-day meeting (19–21 November) at the White House between Nixon and Satô, a communiqué announced the return of Okinawa and the Ryukyus. With this behind him Satô called a general election for 27 December which the *Jimintō* won with its largest ever majority. The momentum of the 1969 communiqué finally led to a treaty which came into effect on 15 May 1972, after much deliberation in both Washington and Tokyo. While all this was going on there were rallies and riots right across Japan, culminating in Tokyo on 19 November 1971 in a battle in which a crowd of 78,000 fought the police with firebombs. By this time, however, all the chemical and biological weapons had been removed from Okinawa.

THE NIXON SHOCKS

The events relating to Okinawa were only part of the so-called 'Nixon Shocks'. In July 1971, the President, without consulting Satô, announced that he would visit Beijing in February 1972, so heralding a fundamental change in US-China policy. All this fitted in with the decision to allow the Ryukyus to revert to Japan. It was up to Satô's successor as prime minister, Kakuei Tanaka, to take the full measure of these changes: free, as he saw it, from the commitment imposed by the US in 1951 to maintain diplomatic relations with Nationalist China in Taiwan, in September 1972 his government recognized Mao Zedong's People's Republic. (While the US did not follow until 1979, this did not prevent US President Ford making the first ever official US state visit to Japan in November 1974.) In 1974 the reward, in the form of a Nobel Peace Price, went not to Tanaka, but to Satô, whose initiatives in the cause of peace during his eight years (1964–72) of office – starting from a friendship pact agreed with South Korea in 1965, then extending to restoring Japan's relations with the countries it had fought in the Pacific War (which included, in 1966, an attempt to mediate in Vietnam), to end, in 1970, with signing the international Nuclear Non-Proliferation Agreement – had contributed greatly to Japan's standing in the world. Even so, within Japan, his success in the Ryukyus, achieved in the face of constant unrest, probably counted most.

This was not all. On 15 August 1971 Nixon ended the historic tie of the US dollar to gold, at the same time imposing a ten per cent surcharge on imports. This move, which had long been foreseen, made good sense economically, at least for Americans. For one thing it made Japanese imports much less competitive, which was fair enough given Japan's success as an exporter, built up over the 1960s.[24] The initial reaction of many Japanese was to interpret Nixon's decision, together with his new China policy, as signs that Japan had become strategically less important to the US, while at the same time being regarded as an economic adversary. In a very real sense, therefore, the 1970s were the time that post-war Japan came of age: if, following the end of the Vietnam War in 1975, its strategic importance diminished, it was still sufficient to play a part in US-Japanese relations. More important in the long run was the fact that by the 1970s the giant Japanese corporations were already playing the FDI game, otherwise known as *foreign direct investment.*

JAPAN'S OVERSEAS ECONOMY

One of the winners was Toyota, whose first foreign manufacturing operation started in Brazil in 1959, to be followed in the next twenty-odd years by countries in almost every other part of the world, Australia, Europe, Africa and Southeast Asia. Finally, in May 1988, a new assembly plant in Georgetown, Kentucky, produced the first Toyota cars in the US, thirty-one years after Toyota vehicles made in Japan were first imported. Although both Honda and Nissan were earlier in the race, Toyota was soon the leader by a wide margin. The success of the Georgetown operation has been phenomenal, with more than six million cars so far produced. Toyota's Camry was the best-seller of all cars, nationwide, in seven of the eight years up to 2005. Today Toyota in the US is second only to General Motors, and in 2005 it started to manufacture hybrids. Whatever the economics of manufacture and distribution, the political dimension is critical. Not only in Kentucky, but also in Alabama, West Virginia and Missouri – all states in which Toyota subsidiaries manufacture components – the company's contribution to local employment, to say nothing of taxes, means that it has good friends not only at state and county level, but also in Washington, as the established American manufacturers know only too well. It may also count that Toyota – as also other Japanese car-plants in the US – has located in states that incline to vote Republican, where its long-established US competitors are concentrated in Democratic states – notably Michigan.[25] Whether this is accident or design is a moot question. The car-makers' strategy was adopted, with comparable success, by the giants, such as Sony, in consumer electronics and other hi-tech industries. What is more, where Japan led, others, such as Korea and, in increasing measure, China, followed.

The switch to FDI inevitably hurt the export of cars made in Japan. The best year for exports was 1986, with some four and a half million cars sent abroad. In

1993, for the first time, more Japanese cars were manufactured in the US than were exported to the US from Japan, and the margin has increased every year since then. The same is true of other countries where Japanese assembly plants are located. The downward trend continued, and in 1995 and 1996 less than three million were exported world-wide; the trend then slowly reversed and in 2002 there was a break to more than four million. Following a serious earthquake in Kobe on 17 January, 1995 was a bad year for the Japanese economy, the more so after the US Treasury, in April, forced Japan to open up its own domestic market to American car imports.

The number of cars actually produced in Japan peaked in 1990 at just under ten million, to dip below eight million in 1994, 1995 and 1996; there was then something of a revival to a level which, in the present century, seems to have stabilized between eight and nine million. These figures show, quite consistently, an export level of just under half the cars made in Japan, whereas in the mid-1980s it was well above this level. On the other hand the number of Japanese cars manufactured abroad as a result of FDI was much greater than the lost exports.

Although the question is been put often enough, it is still worth asking what was the secret of Japanese economic success in the second half of the twentieth century. One answer is to be found in Japan's monolithic corporate structure, in which very large units in banking, industry and government are linked together, with the same people at the top constantly shifting from one position to another. The face presented to the world outside Japan is that of MITI, the *Ministry of International Trade and Industry*, whose pro-business stance is the envy of Wall Street and the City of London. It helps, of course, that top civil servants know that *amakudari* means that being friendly to business can bring a good job after retirement – although there are some legal limits to what is now acceptable.[26] The industrial giants supported so effectively by MITI are, by Western standards, surprisingly lean and mean, operating with minimal inventories and outsourcing the manufacture of every possible component to countless small and often marginal local businesses which can count on cheap, but nonetheless skilled labour. This is essentially the *kanban* system pioneered by Toyota. The logistical problems, although considerable, are not beyond the capacity of Japan's remarkable communications infrastructure. On the other side of the line, in the main industrial plants – where all the outsourced components end up – Japan leads the world in labour productivity and above all in technology, much of which is simply not available outside the country: industrial secrets are very well kept.[27] Here lifetime employment and pay based on seniority are fundamental principles, which is one good reason for the exceptionally high level of outsourcing. Furthermore, as a result of Japan's interlocking corporate structure, shareholder pressure for higher dividends counts for far less than in

Europe and North America – another factor giving Japanese manufacturers a competitive advantage.

JAPAN'S DOMESTIC ECONOMY AND RESURGENT NATIONALISM

The social consequences of the devolved and highly fragmented micro-economy are quite drastic: for millions of Japanese the benefits of a welfare state, taken for granted in the modern industrial world, are on a much smaller scale. On the other hand – almost as an alternative to welfare payments – millions of small-holders, often women, cultivating rice in the margins of the agricultural economy are kept in business by substantial government subsidies. Next to them equal numbers of small 'mom-and-pop' stores somehow manage to survive, while rates of taxation and social security contributions are kept low. The resulting deprivation is exacerbated by the poor state of consumer financial services, so that it is standard practice, for instance, to pay utility bills in cash. One result is an exceptionally high rate of household saving – with housewives buying stock over the counter[28] – while another is that money-lending institutions are on the fringes of the informal economy, with loan enforcement only too often entrusted to the *Yakuza* – Japan's high-profile version of the Mafia – whose attentions are best avoided. In these matters there has been some improvement since the late 1980s, following tighter official control of interest rates and increasing involvement by the large city banks in consumer finance, but by Western standards Japan still has a long way to go.[29] What is more, legislation and bureaucratic regulation discourage foreign corporations from setting up retail operations in Japan, whether in sales or services – including consumer finance. Concessions only come in response to extreme foreign pressure, such as resulted in allowing American cars into Japan in April 1995 – at a time when the American market had been open to Japanese cars for forty years.

Japan's monolithic closed-door economy, or rather its impact at grass-roots level, have long defined the background to considerable popular discontent: this in turn supports ultra-patriotic right-wing movements – known generically as *uyoku* – whose influence on government policy is much greater than their relatively small number of members justifies. As with many such movements a high-profile figure occasionally emerges to attempt a *coup d'état*. In Japan this happened on 25 November 1970, when a well-known novelist, Yukio Mishima, wearing a military uniform of his own design and supported by four members of his own patriotic movement, *tate no kai*, or 'shield society', overpowered the local Tokyo commander of the self-defence force – the closest approach to an army allowed by Article 9 the 1946 constitution – and addressing some thousand off-duty soldiers on the parade ground, urged them to follow his lead and demand the repeal of Article 9.[30] This piece of theatre left the soldiers unmoved, and after ten minutes' railing at them, Mishima withdrew into the garrison commander's office to commit ritual suicide.[31] Although Mishima's suicide certainly promoted his book on the *samurai* ethic,[32] it was otherwise completely counter-productive. The soldiers had laughed at him; the *Jimintō* disowned him, while one of its leaders, Yasuhiro Nakasone – later prime minister from 1982 to 1987 – called his gesture 'madness'.

Even worse was to come in 1995, when, on 10 March, five members of *Aum Shinrikyo*, a fanatical religious cult with a charismatic leader, Shoko Asahara, released deadly *sarin* gas on Tokyo metro trains during the morning rush-hour. In an earlier incident in Matsumoto in 1994 seven had died, but this had nothing like the same impact. Asahara was finally apprehended and put on trial in 1996, to be convicted and sentenced to death only in 2004.

The extremist acts of Mishima and Asahara – who in fact had little in common with each other – never discredited mainstream *uyoku*. *Jimintō* leaders consistently made concessions to popular patriotic sentiments, even at the cost of increased cultural isolation. The *nengô* calendar, according to which years are numbered from the date of accession of the ruling emperor, was restored in 1979 – a matter that can confuse Japanese almost as much as it does foreigners.[33] Much more questionable, internationally, was the increasing official support given to the cult of the Yasukuni shrine in Tokyo. This shrine, close to the imperial precinct, was founded in 1869 by the Emperor Meiji 'for the worship of the divine spirits of those who gave their lives in defence of the Empire of Japan' – to quote a hand-out given to foreign visitors. After the Pacific War the cult extended to the spirits of those convicted as war criminals, some of whose achievements are commemorated in the Yûshûkan, a small museum in the shrine precinct, where the exhibits almost suggest that Japan won the war.

The official rehabilitation of Yasukuni can be dated back to 1975, when, on 15 August – thirty years to the day after the Japanese surrender – the prime minister, Takeo Miki made a private visit. His two successors as prime minister followed in his steps, but then, on 15 August 1985, Nakasone came with most of his cabinet and some two hundred *Jimintō* members of the Diet. This caused considerable outrage abroad, particularly in China, and in his two last years as prime minister Nakasone, under diplomatic pressure, stayed at home on 15 August. The *Jimintō*, however, still turned up in strength at Yasukuni. Nakasone's discretion did not, however, establish a precedent for his successors. Koizumi paid several visits to Yasukuni as prime minister, and his successor, Shinzo Abe, may well do the same. From time to time also, the negative impact abroad resulting from such visits has been heightened by the official approval given to school history-books which ignore Japanese atrocities during the Pacific War. In April 2005 this led to violent anti-Japanese demonstrations ending in Beijing – after tens of thousands in Shanghai had taken to the streets, chanting 'Japanese pigs, get out'. The Japanese reaction in such cases is to equivocate, explaining that approval of the controversial text-books does not mean that they are required set-books for public examinations. In practice the teaching profession, which is strongly unionized, can for the most part be relied upon not to adopt them.

THE LONG SHADOW OF THE PACIFIC WAR

However uncertain public support may be for Yasukuni, on one point it is certainly on the side of official policy. This is the consistent refusal of Japanese governments even to contemplate paying compensation to those – mainly British, Dutch and American – interned during the Pacific War. For almost all Japanese, of whatever generation, the slate was wiped clean by Hiroshima and Nagasaki. Both the present emperor, Akihito, and leading politicians have expressed regret, if somewhat guardedly, but this cannot be interpreted as any sort of promise of compensation. Particularly in Britain and the Netherlands the ex-internees constitute a powerful lobby with considerable popular support. Their voice is heard in Japan, but that is all; only time will, in the end, heal this trauma.

In 1997 some 180 Chinese, whose health – as the Japanese government conceded – had been impaired by Japan's notorious *Unit 731* germ warfare programme, based in the Chinese of Harbin, tried another approach: each individual claimed some ¥10,000,000 (about £45,000) in damages. Finally – and predictably – in July 2005, they all lost their cases, and that on two grounds. First, international law gives individual foreign citizens no right to such an action. Second, it was barred by the post-war peace treaties. Following the anti-Japanese demonstrations in April, this could only damage a cause close to the heart of Japanese politics, which is to gain a permanent seat on the UN Security Council.

ECONOMIC CONSERVATISM AND ITS COSTS

One perspective on Japanese history since 1952 (when the peace treaty became effective) is that nothing essential ever changes – which would explain the gradual reversion to low-keyed nationalism described above. This theme, starkly presented by Karel van Wolferen in 1989 in *The Enigma of Japanese Power*,[34] resonated among Japan-watchers at a time when the economic miracle was almost played out. The dominant institutional force was a sort of mindless conservatism that successive *Jimintō* governments, mainly through lack of will, failed to counteract. The problem, which became acute in the 1990s, was that Japan, whatever the mind-cast of its people and their leaders, was not alone in the world. The economic problems of the 1990s seem to have forced reform upon reluctant and long-established holders of power: MITI – with, since 2001, a new name, METI, for Ministry of Economy Trade and Industry – has seen its dirigiste influence on business much reduced, largely by changing its own policy so as to favour deregulation and privatization. This, under Prime Minister Koizumi, extended, in 2005, to the Japanese Post Office, a vast conglomerate whose involvement in consumer finance – alongside communications – made it, with assets worth more than three trillion dollars, the world's largest financial institution.[35] Many in the *Jimintō*, who had long valued it as a vehicle for government patronage, were reluctant to see it go.

One critical dimension, economically, was the foreign exchange standing of the Japanese yen. The long-term boom in export markets owed much to the consistent under-valuation of the yen – in part a legacy from the days of the fixed exchange rate imposed by the US in 1951, and only abandoned, with floating of the dollar, in 1971. At the beginning of the 1980s this could be seen as a consequence of the world-wide inflation that followed in the wake of the oil crises of the 1970s. The world market in oil trades in US dollars, so that, internationally, a shortage of oil goes hand in hand with a shortage of dollars: with scarcity prices go up so that by the mid-1980s the dollar exchange rates were exceptionally high – a boon to countries like Japan with the capacity of increase manufactured exports to the US. (If the exchange effect of the high oil prices in the mid-2000s was less drastic, this was probably because of a long-term reduction of the share of oil in world trade.)

In 1984 the Yen-Dollar Accord between Japan and the US committed Japan, for the first time, to reforming its domestic banking system while at the same time recognizing yen transactions in the international foreign exchange markets. Only after these reforms were confirmed in September 1985 by the so-called Plaza Accord,[36] in which Japan and the US were joined by the UK, France and West Germany, did they really began to impact on the Japanese economy. In the years from 1985 to 1995 dollar exchange rates decreased spectacularly, to stabilize, in the case of the yen, at a level at about half of that prevailing before the Plaza Accord. Inevitably the economic consequences for Japan's export economy were drastic – particularly in the steel industry, when more and more Japanese cars, as a result of FDI, were being manufactured abroad, while, at the same time, Japanese shipyards faced increasing competition from Korea and, later, China. This is one aspect of the economic crisis of the 1990s, which, in 1993, opened the door for Morihiro Hosokawa to become the first post-war Japanese prime minister not to be a member of the *Jimintō*. Inevitably he had made his political career in the party; it was only in 1992 that his disgust at continuing high-level corruption led him to form the New Japan Party to contest the election due in 1993. When the *Jimintō* failed to gain a majority of seats, Hosokawa was chosen to form a new government out of a coalition of eight opposition parties, including his own. In a typically Japanese scenario his time in office lasted only eight months: ironically he was felled by corruption charges relating to the 1980s, when he was still a loyal member of the *Jimintō*. After two successive prime ministers, in the years 1994–96, failed to hold the coalition together, the *Jimintō* returned to power in January 1996, but only by forming a coalition with the Buddhist *New Komeitō*.[37] This was still the line-up in 2005.

JAPAN IN EAST AND SOUTHEAST ASIA

From the 1990s onwards Japan, by force of circumstance, has had to pay much more attention to its relations with Korea, China and the countries of Southeast Asia – all of which have gained significantly in their relative importance on the world economic scene. On one side Japan has gained new export markets and promising new locations for FDI; on the other, it faces greatly increased competition – in which South Korea has led the way. In spite of bilateral trade running at $70 billion a year, relations with South Korea are still bedevilled, not only because of the legacy of the Pacific War, but also because of disputed ownership of a number of small islands in the Japan Sea: both fish, which are abundant, and uncertain prospects of minerals and natural gas lie behind the dispute.

Korea is also important for Japan's close involvement in the fate of North Korea, which has meant that it is, together with Russia, China and the US, one of the states concerned to persuade Kim Jong Il's government to change its course in nuclear politics – North Korean rockets, capable of carrying nuclear warheads, have already over-flown Japan. Here Japan also seeks redress for the deliberate abduction, by North Korean special forces, of a number of its citizens from coastal areas opposite the Korean peninsula, during the 1980s: North Korea, after admitting these operations for the first time in 2002, then allowed those abducted to return to Japan. Even so, Japan is still concerned by the fact that at least eight were not accounted for.

With the remarkable take-off of the Chinese economy in recent years, Japan's relationship with China became much more important – a trend that is almost certain to continue. According to the official Statistical Handbook of Japan for 2004,[38] the percentage of Japan's total exports going to China increased from 5.6 to 12.2, and that of imports from China from 13.8 to 19.7 – with the balance of trade being consistently in favour of Japan. With the volume of trade steadily increasing this is a critical factor in the political relations between the two, at a time when China's oil imports and its trade surplus with the US are greater than Japan's.[39] (This is not the whole story, because factories built as a result of Japanese FDI employ about a million Chinese.) Although, significantly, China, in 2001, became a more important Japanese export market than Taiwan, Tokyo's concern for a peaceful solution for the future of the island – particularly when expressed in a joint statement with Washington, as in February 2005 – is calculated to provoke a strong reaction from Beijing.[40]

Japan's part in the Southeast Asian economic crisis of late 1990s was also critical in a part of the world where newly industrialized economies – notably Thailand and Malaysia – were doing their best to follow in its footsteps. In both these countries mounting consumer demand and a high level of capital investment – which the state encouraged rather than restrained – led to considerable balance of payments deficits, at a time when their currencies were pegged to the dollar. Throughout 1996, in the foreign exchange markets the dollar appreciated considerably against the yen and the D-mark: the result, in Southeast Asia, was that local industry could compete neither with cheap imports from Japan nor with local products from factories set up by Japanese FDI – in effect, a double whammy. The absence of any effective government counteraction left the field open to speculators, who attacked first the Thai baht, and then the Indonesian rupiah, forcing the central banks to abandon the dollar-peg. The result was not only a spectacular fall in the value of Southeast Asian currencies, but also an economic crisis throughout the area; as for Japan, both exports and the return on FDI inevitably suffered.

THE SECRETS OF SUCCESS

However uncertain the future of Japan, the reconstruction of the country in the years since 1952 is still remarkable. What then are the secrets of its success, and what, on the other side, are the blemishes on its record? Given the conflicts in East and Southeast Asia in the first quarter century of restoration, Japanese capitalism – whatever its distinctive and restrictive attributes – was marked out for economic success. It mattered little that it was critically short of raw materials – these could always be imported. What counted was cultural solidarity, free from significant ethnic challenge and supported by a skilled, well-educated and disciplined work-force with a remarkable team spirit. The extreme density of population, in a country in which no one lived far from the sea, meant that investment in the communications infrastructure almost always paid off. At the same time, however, the Japanese mind-cast, at its most profound level, was not tuned to the outside world. Japan is for the Japanese: it is not for nothing that foreigners are *gaijin*, 'outside men', best kept at a distance. The other side of the coin, however, is a remarkable insensitivity to what *gaijin* see as their legitimate claims on Japan – of which many examples are given in this chapter. It is not sufficient to buy goodwill by being the UN's second largest contributor to development aid, while at the same time ignoring restrictions imposed by the International Whaling Commission – however much catching and consuming whales was part of Japan's traditional way of life. It is also worth questioning Japan's supporting the US and its allies in Afghanistan and Iraq – here, as also in the case of Taiwan, Japan might have been wiser to have kept its distance. In coming to terms with its own past Japan must become less inward looking, and accept that, for much of the outside world, the slate was not wiped clean by Hiroshima and the 1951 Peace Treaty. Americans may be able to accept this, but others, particularly around the Pacific – Chinese, Koreans, Indonesians and Australians – are not.

The death of the Shōwa Emperor in 1989 gave Japan the chance to improve its image abroad. It certainly opened the way for Queen Beatrix of the Netherlands to pay a state visit to the new Emperor Akihito. The Shōwa legacy, however, is still significant, particularly in the way Japan finds its leaders. In the years since 1952 Japanese names that resonate internationally are not those of prime ministers – unless they become notorious for corruption, like Kakuei Tanaka, after the million-dollar kick-back from Lockheed – but of business tycoons, such as Akio Morita, the founder of Sony, film-directors, such as Akira Kurosawa, or writers, such as Nobel prize-winners, Tanizaki, Kawabata and Oe. At the beginning of the twenty-first century Japan's greatest need – as it has been through much of its long history – is to learn how to find and support leaders who are trusted both at home and abroad. This, however, is not a formula that ever fitted in with the essential structure of Japanese politics.

4

Korea: a country divided by war (1945–53)

THE PARTITION OF 1945

Geography has always been the key to understanding Korea,[1] a country defined by a peninsula projecting south from north China, into the Japan Sea, over a length of some 800 kilometres. In the north its main land frontier is the Yalu River – separating it from China – but in the far north-east there is also a short, but extremely important frontier with Russia; in the south the Japanese island of Kyushu is some 200 kilometres away across the Tsushima Straits. The width of the peninsula varies between 150 and 300 kilometres, and there are also a number of islands off its shores. Located between latitudes 34ºN and 43ºN on the east side of the great Asian land-mass, Korea has a temperate continental climate, with bitterly cold winters – when much of the country is covered in snow – and hot humid summers. It is a land of hills – with altitudes up to some 2,500 metres – rather than mountains. Its original natural vegetation was deciduous forest, but the need of its inhabitants for cultivable land, combined with the depredations of its rulers – particularly the Japanese in the first half of the twentieth century – created today's sparse, somewhat barren landscape.

Until the beginning of the twentieth century, Korea had been for thousands of years a feudal society, with a settled population mainly engaged in the cultivation of rice. For hundreds of years it had been united in one kingdom, whose successive rulers, for the most part, were intent on denying their subjects all contact with foreigners. This 'hermit kingdom' was the face that Korea presented to the outside world: its few visitors found a remarkably uniform culture, with a single language little related to any other. The dominant outside influence was that of China, where the imperial court always regarded Korea as a tributary, a role that it was ready to accept. This meant that Buddhism became the dominant religion, and that Chinese characters were adapted for writing Korean (which since the fifteenth century has also had its own quite distinctive orthography).

From about the middle of the nineteenth century Korea's small ruling elite – which was closely tied to the court – began to divide into two factions, one intent on maintaining the kingdom's traditional isolation, and the other equally intent on opening it up to the outside world. In the event Japan, by a show of force off the west coast of Korea in 1876, forced the issue, so that by the Treaty of Kangwa the country accepted normal diplomatic and economic relations. The Americans soon followed and in 1883 the first minister, Lucius M. Foot, arrived in Seoul, the capital of Korea. His diplomacy led not only to Americans coming to the country to set up a light and telephone system ahead of much of the rest of the world, but also to missionaries being admitted to preach the gospel – so that within a very short time Protestant Christianity won many converts (one of whom was to become the father of Kim Il Sung – of whom more later. The Presbyterian Church is still very strong).

As related in chapter 1 Japan, with considerable moral support from Washington, annexed Korea.[2] In 1905, a young member of the Korean elite, Syngman Rhee, went to the US, to make his first protest on behalf of the Korean people – presented it to President Theodore Roosevelt – and got nowhere. This was at the beginning of a long exile, during which Rhee lost no opportunity to make his lone voice heard, but the only Americans who listened were those who supported the Christian missions in Korea. As late as 1941, the year of Pearl Harbor, Rhee published a book, *Japan Inside Out*, warning of the dangers of Japanese aggression. Even the outbreak of the Pacific War did not much help the Korean cause: finally, late in 1943, when the two allied war leaders, Roosevelt and Churchill, met in Cairo to lay the first plans for the post-war world, Jiang Jieshi – already fighting Mao's communists in China – prevailed upon them to take up the cause of Korean independence as essential to blocking Soviet plans to take over the country. The final communiqué then contained a declaration that Korea '... in due course should become free and independent' – offering some small comfort to Rhee and his supporters.

Given the oppressive regime imposed by Japan on Korea, which brought many young girls to work as prostitutes, and young men as unskilled labourers, in Japan itself – where they counted as a despised ethnic minority without any rights to citizenship – it is not surprising that in the period between the two world wars many Koreans were attracted to communism. Protest actions, however peaceful, within Korea were suppressed with such brutality that the only way forward was to organize the revolution from outside its boundaries. Soviet Russia, with its short frontier with Korea, was always one possible base, but an alternative was provided by the revolutionary cadres of Mao Zedong in China. This was one reason why Chiang insisted on the Cairo declaration of 1943. Behind Stalin's agreement, at the Teheran Conference in February 1945, to bring Soviet Russia into the war against Japan three months after the defeat of Nazi Germany, lay the prospect of regaining everything that had been lost to Japan at the beginning of the century. Both Manchuria (where in the early 1930s the communist guerrillas resisting the Japanese takeover were mainly Koreans) and Korea itself (where until 1905 Russia had a strong position) had a significant part in Soviet planning.

As the end of the Pacific War approached, both Washington and London had come to accept that some arrangement had to be made for the occupation of Korea, seeing that the Soviet Union was almost certain to send troops to both Manchuria and Korea as soon as it entered the war. Once in either country, it would be difficult to dislodge them. At the last minute, two US army colonels were given the task of finding a line to divide Korea, first to limit the impending Soviet occupation, and second to define the part of the country to be occupied by US forces. At this time few in the West found the question important. The solution found was to divide Korea along latitude 38°N, an east–west line that crossed the country just to the north of Seoul and divided it, geographically, into two roughly equal halves. Unknown to two colonels, at the beginning of the century the same line, in negotiations between Japan and Russia, had been suggested as a possible frontier between their respective spheres of influence in Korea, which may explain why Stalin so readily accepted it on 15 August 1945, the day of the Japanese surrender.[3] Soviet and American forces lost little time in taking up positions along the agreed frontier, an exercise for which the Soviets were clearly better prepared: after all, their common land frontier with Korea was immediately open for the movement of troops and equipment along already existing lines of communication.

The Soviet military government immediately set about organizing North Korea politically. A Korean leader, with unquestionable loyalty born out of combat experience, was essential to their plans. The Soviet man of the hour was Kim Il Sung, who during most of the 1930s had proved himself an effective guerrilla commander in the resistance to the Japanese in Manchuria. His greatest victory came late in 1940, when his guerrillas defeated Japanese police forces near Kapsun. A strong Japanese counter-offensive then forced him to seek refuge in the Soviet Pacific Primorski province. There he joined the Special Independent Sniper Brigade, whose task was to gather military intelligence relating to the Japanese occupation of Korea and Manchuria. At the end of the Pacific War this brought him back to his own country, probably for the first time in fifteen years. In February 1946, Kim Il Sung, as the senior Korean officer present in Pyongyang – the largest city occupied by the Soviets and the seat of their military government – was chosen, almost as a matter of temporary expediency, to head the North Korean Provisional People's Committee.[4]

In principle Kim Il Sung's task was to cooperate with the Americans in South Korea in arranging national elections, but this was blocked by the Soviets. President Truman then referred the matter to the United Nations General Assembly, with the result that the elections were held, but only in South Korea. Following elections in May 1948, Syngman Rhee, who had at last returned to his native country – after more than forty years in exile – was inaugurated as president of the new Republic of Korea (ROK) on 15 August, exactly three years after the Japanese surrender. On 9 September Kim Il Sung reacted by proclaiming the Korean People's Democratic Republic (KPDR), with himself as head of state, totally dependent on 'Our Beloved Comrade' – none other than Joseph Stalin. From then on there were two states in Korea separated by the 38th parallel. Before the end of 1948 the Soviet troops were withdrawn from Korea, and within a few months devoted by Kim to outmanoeuvring his rivals, he consolidated his position as leader. Almost from the beginning of 1949 he was in sole command of substantial armed forces, trained by the Soviet occupation forces and equipped with war material left behind by the Japanese, supplemented by modern Soviet armaments – including military aircraft with Russian pilots.[5] In the same year his position became much stronger and more significant as a result of Mao's successful revolution in China. His loyalty to Stalin was the secret of his success, as he made clear by declaring that 'all the most precious and best things in life of the Korean people are related to the name of Stalin'. With fateful consequences for its future, he was equally dedicated to the unification of Korea. On the other side of the line Syngman Rhee was equally committed to the same end, but militarily he had been left very weak by the Americans. His own army – small, poorly trained and ill equipped – was never conceived of by the Americans as an effective fighting force. He was also weak politically: when elections were held for the ROK assembly his party failed to win a majority, although his own position as president was secure. At the same time communist guerrillas were active, leading major rebellions on the island of Cheju-do and the port of Yosu, which were suppressed by loyal ROK troops with appalling brutality.[6] Even so Kim Il Sung still believed that he had considerable popular support south of the 38th parallel – a matter on which he was able to convince Stalin.[7]

After the main US forces had been withdrawn in June 1949 all that remained of the military occupation was a small Korean Military Advisers' Group with some five hundred members.[8] There was no doubt at all that the balance of power in the Korean peninsula strongly favoured Kim Il Sung's People's Republic. That even the CIA recognized this is clear from an assessment made in July 1949, according to which the relevant factors were so adverse to the ROK that they could not 'prevent ultimate Communist Control of the whole of Korea'; furthermore, in the event of a Soviet invasion, 'the life expectancy of South Korea would be, at best, only a few days'.[9] Even so Syngman Rhee's request for sufficient arms and munitions to give his army 'a fighting chance' was turned down by President Truman, who feared that with such encouragement Rhee might decide to 'drive north'.

By the end of 1949, a number of small-scale military actions had indicated that both sides were spoiling for a fight. Kim Il Sung had spent much of the year trying to sell his plans for an invasion of South Korea to his Russian and Chinese allies. At Kim's insistence Mao, in January 1950, did arrange for 14,000 Korean nationals serving in his People's Liberation Army to return home to join Kim's Korean People's Army, but made it clear that he would go no further. In April 1950 Kim, on a visit to Moscow, gained Stalin's reluctant consent to the planned invasion, but with the clear understanding that if things went wrong, and the US intervened, the Soviet Union would not join the battle. In May Kim went to Beijing, and by misrepresenting Stalin as an enthusiastic supporter of the proposed invasion, also gained Mao's hesitant consent. In particular both Stalin and Mao allowed themselves to be persuaded by Kim that the Americans would not intervene to save Syngman Rhee – a reasonable conclusion given the cursory way they had been dealing with him. Rhee himself knew only too well that any ROK invasion of the north was doomed to failure. On every count, both in men and equipment, the north outnumbered the south by a wide margin, so that the operational plans of the Korean People's Army, which envisaged total conquest and occupation of the south within 22–27 days,[10] were well-founded. That is almost the way things happened.

KOREA AT WAR (1950–53)

A full-scale North Korean invasion of the south began on 25 June 1950. Seoul, the ROK capital, was captured within three days, with Syngman Rhee and his government retreating ahead of the invading forces. Although the invasion caught Washington by surprise, President Truman and his cabinet reacted very quickly, and with full congressional support, organized local US forces, based mainly in Japan, to support the ROK. There was concern that the invasion was the opening phase of a general Far East war, orchestrated by Moscow. On the morning of 29 June – by which time the ROK forces had been driven back to the Han River, in the far southeast corner of the peninsula – General MacArthur, who was still in Tokyo as head of the allied military government, flew to the frontline to witness the disintegration of the ROK army. Back in Tokyo on 30 June he asked for the commitment of US ground forces, to which President Truman immediately agreed: the USAF had already successfully engaged the Korean People's Air Force (KPAF).

By the end of the first week of July a whole US division had been landed at Pusan, and several more followed in the course of the month. On 7 July the United Kingdom sponsored a resolution in the UN Security Council, committing UN member states to the defence of the ROK, with the US designating the commander of the forces to fight under the UN flag; the Soviet Union, which had withdrawn from the Security Council in January 1950 as a protest against the continued membership of Jiang's nationalist China, was not therefore present to exercise its right of veto. With some misgivings – which later proved to be well-founded – on the part of the US State Department, General MacArthur became the commander in chief of the joint UN forces. The first UN troops, apart from the Americans, were British: two infantry battalions disembarked on 19 August, and on 5 September were in action for the first time. They were sorely needed. By 20 August the US and ROK forces had been driven back to a small perimeter around Pusan; the loss of the enclosed territory to the Korean People's Army (KPA) would have meant final defeat in the land war, and the new British troops played an important part in its successful defence. In the end fourteen countries: Australia, Belgium, Canada, Colombia, Ethiopia, France, Greece, Luxembourg, the Netherlands, the Philippines, Thailand, Turkey, South Africa and the United Kingdom, joined the US in providing military support for the war in Korea, while Denmark, India, Italy, Norway and Sweden sent medical units.[11]

Kim Il Sung was not only mistaken in his conviction that the US would not intervene to save the ROK, but also failed to take into account the American potential to deploy vast forces from its secure base in Japan. Once the Pusan perimeter held – and it was, to quote the Duke of Wellington, 'a damned close-run thing' – it was only a matter of time before the tables would be turned on the KPA. It did not take MacArthur long to do so. On 23 August 1950 he announced his plans for a counter-attack based on landing a strong force at Inchon, the harbour for Seoul, which at that time was some hundreds of kilometres from the Pusan perimeter. This would be a very bold move. The approaches to Inchon were hazardous, and the risks of landing were increased by a tidal range that could exceed ten metres. Nonetheless, Washington approved MacArthur's plans on 28 August, allowing the operation to begin on 13 September with US and British naval and air strikes to soften up the KPA defences in and around Inchon. On 15 September, at 5am, US Marines landed on Wolmi-do, a heavily fortified island just offshore that guarded the sea approaches to Inchon. This fell to the marines after three hours of heavy fighting during which no American, but countless KPA, lives were lost – not a good augury for the superstitious Kim Il Sung. With the next high tide American forces landed on the Korean mainland, and the KPA, overwhelmed by the supporting fire-power, abandoned Inchon, and retreated to secure the defences of Seoul. By this time also the UN forces were strong enough to break out of the Pusan perimeter, and advance north to join the troops landed at Inchon.

The breakthrough at Pusan began on 19 September and within four days the KPA had abandoned their positions along the whole perimeter, leaving the way open for the UN forces to move north to link up with the troops landed at Inchon. General MacArthur, somewhat prematurely, claimed the capture of Seoul on 25 September – three months to the day after the KPA invasion – and on 26 September he joined Syngman Rhee in a liberation ceremony in the ruined capital city. By the end of the month the UN forces had linked up, and the ROK was soon to be cleared of all KPA troops.

If MacArthur's first objective had been achieved, it was by no means certain how he should proceed further. The KPA, although driven north of the 38th parallel, was still a fighting force. Beginning on 1 October, MacArthur issued a series of ultimatums demanding the surrender of all North Korean forces.[12] They were all rejected by Kim Il Sung, so the war was still on. Already, on 29 September, Washington had signalled MacArthur that he was 'to feel unhampered strategically and tactically to proceed north of the 38th parallel'. Furthermore he was authorized to take on any Chinese forces found in North Korea if such action offered a 'reasonable chance of success'. All this was grist to the mill for Syngman Rhee. Addressing a vast cheering crowd at Pusan four days after the successful Inchon landings, he proclaimed, 'We have to advance as far as the Manchurian border until not a single enemy soldier is left in our country'.[13] There was never much doubt that a united Korea was as much part of his agenda as it was of Kim Il Sung's.[14] The only question, for either of them, was which side it would belong to, that of the US and its allies, or that of Mao's China and the Soviet Union.

On 2 October, China's foreign minister warned K.V. Pannikar, the Indian Ambassador in Beijing, that China would enter the war, in support of the KPDR, if the UN forces crossed the 38th parallel. In the same week the Soviet delegate to the UN proposed a ceasefire and the withdrawal of all foreign troops. The US was not to be held back, although it did declare, in a message intended for Beijing, that it had 'no desire for war nor even the establishment of a US military regime in North Korea'. The advance continued in North Korea: Pyongyang fell to UN forces on 19 October, and within the week Syngman Rhee, pursuing his own agenda, arrived to address another mass rally. By the end of October forward units had reached the Yalu River, to face Chinese soldiers on the other side of the frontier. Stalin was furious at the failure of the KPA to hold the line after the Inchon landings, and his ambassador to the KPDR reported that Kim Il Sung and his lieutenants were 'confused, lost, hopeless and desperate'.[15] Kim, in turn, pleaded for Soviet and Chinese aid to save his regime. Stalin, at first, wished to end the conflict, and on 13 October actually ordered the abandonment of all North Korea, and the evacuation of Kim and what was left of the KPA to northeast China and the Soviet Far East. A day later this order was countermanded: China, unknown to the UN, had notified Stalin that it was ready to enter the war.

By the end of November the UN line of advance had stabilized some 100 to 150 kilometres short of the Yalu River frontier with China, where Kim Il Sung, together with his government, had taken refuge in the city of Sinuiju. By this time the KPA counted for nothing and the Chinese called the shots, as the UN forces were soon to discover. From the middle of October onwards, Chinese troops took over in the front line facing the UN forces, but the UN commanders only realized this on 23 November, even though Chinese prisoners had already been taken in battle before the end of October. The moment of truth came with the four-day battle of Chongchon, fought at the end of November in sub-arctic weather. Although some UN units held the line, others retreated and abandoned their equipment. MacArthur saw the position correctly, declaring 'we face an entirely new war' and announcing plans 'to pass to the defensive'. And so it came about, in spite of the fact that MacArthur, in a press interview, had argued for the right to pursue Chinese forces into Manchuria.[16] To this Truman reacted, on 6 December, with a Presidential Directive instructing US officers not to comment publicly on sensitive issues. By Christmas, when the UN forces – or their more gung-ho American generals – expected to be looking at China across the Yalu River, they were in full retreat before what one of the generals had once called a 'bunch of Chinese laundrymen'.[17]

The UN forces, for the most part, retreated in good order, inflicting considerable casualties on the Chinese in rearguard actions. Even so Seoul was abandoned in January 1951, but shortly thereafter the new UN C-in-C, General Matthew Ridgeway, finally succeeded in establishing a line that could be held. The turning point came when a Chinese attack at Chipyong-ni, in overwhelming numbers, was defeated by French and US troops, who inflicted heavy casualties. Seoul was recaptured on 14 March, and when the harsh Korean winter ended the battle lines were much as they had been in the first days of the war in June 1950. President Truman then made a guarded statement suggesting that with South Korea almost cleared of communists the UN should be willing to agree to a ceasefire. This was not part of MacArthur's agenda. On 15 March, in another press interview, he insisted that the UN forces should not halt short of their true objective, 'the unification of Korea'. At the same time, in the US Congress, Joseph Martin, an old friend of MacArthur, was arguing for the deployment of Chinese Nationalist forces in Korea, a move that was almost certain to be seen by China as a *casus belli* vis-à-vis the United States. On 5 April he was able to read, on the floor of the House of Representatives, a supporting letter from MacArthur ending with the words 'There is no substitute for victory'. This was too much for Truman, who, relying on his directive of 6 December 1950, dismissed MacArthur.

The general, returning home as a hero, was invited to give a valedictory address to a joint session of the US Congress. In the early summer of 1951 two Senate committees, behind closed doors, debated the UN strategy in Korea, with their Republican members only too ready to show Truman as 'soft on communism'. In the end the Congress realized that the American public, for all its admiration of MacArthur, did not want to risk a third world war. Even a wider conflict was too high a price to pay for victory in Korea. If the war was ending in a draw, in the spring of 1951 the Chinese were not ready to admit it: UN positions faced a succession of offensives, and against one of these the British Gloucester Regiment fought an epic and heroic defence, which earned an American Presidential Unit Citation for 'the most outstanding example of united bravery in modern warfare'. The Glorious Glosters were credited with the preventing the fall of Seoul for the third time.

By the end of May, after five offensives, with heavy Chinese casualties, had failed to achieve a breakthrough, Mao Zedong decided to accept the wisdom of President Truman, and give up hope of total victory in Korea. At the beginning of June 1951 Kim Il Sung was summoned to Beijing to be told of Mao's change of heart: with great misgivings he accepted the new Chinese strategy. Already, on 16 May, a declaration of the US National Security Council, subsequently approved by President Truman, had stated that the 'United States would seek to conclude the fighting in Korea with a suitable armistice'.[18] In the result negotiating teams from both sides met at Kaesong, an ancient capital of Korea, on 8 July, moving to a more secure site at Panmunjom, about five miles to the west, in October. Although the fighting was largely over it would be nearly two years before peace-terms were finally agreed, with a new dividing line separating North and South Korea.

THE PEACE SETTLEMENT OF PANMUNJOM

In the half-century since the final armistice was agreed in 1953, historians have argued about why, after stalemate had been reached in the summer of 1951, it had taken so long to get there. Reason, particularly for China and the KPDR, was all on the side of an immediate armistice. Their casualties, at close to a million, were three times those of the ROK and the UN combined. Even so, on 13 June, Mao, in a secret cable to Stalin, stated: 'In July we will be stronger than in June and in August we will be even stronger'.[19] General Ridgeway, on the UN side, contemplated an autumn offensive to establish a better defensive line, further north up the Korean peninsula,[20] and refused to accept the 38th parallel as the demarcation line, which, at this early stage in the peace process, was acceptable – according to recent intelligence[21] – to China and North Korea. On the other side the problem was that Stalin wished to temporize, and it is significant that peace was only agreed after his death in March 1953. On this matter he had on his side not only his devoted follower, Kim Il Sung, whose reputation, in the summer of 1951, had reached its lowest point, but also – somewhat ironically – his sworn enemy, Syngman Rhee, who still saw himself as the President of a United Korea.[22]

Of the many issues arising during the peace negotiations at Panmunjom – a name that could count on headlines in the world press for nearly two years – two were particularly important. The first was the establishment of a military demarcation line and a demilitarized zone (DMZ), and the second, the repatriation of prisoners of war (POWs). Continued activity, and in particular air-strikes, by the UN forces, led the communists – who were suffering heavy losses – to accept the current battle line as the basis for the DMZ separating North and South Korea. There was then considerable wrangling about the composition of a neutral supervisory organization to monitor the armistice, with Czechoslovakia, Poland, Sweden and Switzerland being finally agreed as its members. Even so the war continued – it seems simply because Stalin wanted it to: his rationale was that 'the war tied America's hands ... provoked tension with America's allies and cemented the Sino-Soviet alliance'.[23]

The POW question was also crucial. The Geneva Convention of 1949 provided that 'Prisoners of war shall be released and repatriated without delay after the cessation of hostilities', a principle honoured more in the breach than in the observance by the victorious allies after the end of World War II. (The Russians delayed as long as ten years in releasing German and Japanese POWs.)[24] The basic understanding was that POWs invariably wished to return home: this, however, was not the case with tens of thousands of Soviet POWs held by the Germans who feared, on largely ethnic grounds, that repatriation would lead to persecution, if not worse. Forced repatriation, in which the Western allies cooperated with the Soviets, proved these fears to be well-founded.[25]

When the peace talks began in 1951 UN camps in South Korea held some 132,000 POWs, together with 37,000 civilian internees.[26] Of the POWs, some were North Koreans in the KPA; others, from South Korea, had been forcibly recruited during the three-month occupation following the invasion in June 1950, while the remainder were Chinese, captured after China entered the war at the end of 1950. Repeated screening in the camps revealed that at most 83,000 prisoners were willing to accept repatriation. Among those unwilling to do so many were 15,000 Chinese, who, if not repatriated, were likely to join up with Jiang Jieshi's nationalists in Taiwan.[27] Such, at least, was the not unreasonable fear of the Chinese negotiators at Panmunjom. For the US this was crucial, since it still recognized the Guomindang in Taiwan as the legitimate government of China. This did not please the Foreign Office in London, which minuted that Britain had 'no interest at all in UK and Communist POWs having to stay captive in order to build up the Guomindang forces'. In the end the decision not to yield was that of President Truman. There was, however, as London had foreseen, a price to be paid in human lives and the destruction of property. As the negotiations dragged on until 1953, tens of thousands, both soldiers and civilians, died on both sides, while many of those who survived saw their means of livelihood destroyed.

Although, as the negotiations continued in Panmunjom, there were only intermittent local skirmishes on the ground, the USAF put pressure on the Chinese and North Koreans with intensive strategic bombing: North Korea, which had begun the war with East Asia's highest hydro-electric generating capacity – the Suiho plant was the world's fourth largest – saw this reduced by more than 90 per cent. Power could no longer be exported to Manchuria and Russia, with considerable loss to their manufacturing economies. China and the KPDR had no means of retaliating. There is little evidence of a change of heart, whether in China or the KPDR, following this massive destruction.

Then, on 5 March 1953, Stalin died, by which time Eisenhower had succeeded Truman as US President. On 19 March the Soviet Council of Ministers approved a letter to Kim Il Sung and Mao concluding that 'We must achieve the exit of Korea and China from the war according to the basic interests of other peace-loving peoples'.[28] Armistice talks were revived on 26 April; agreement on voluntary POW repatriation was reached on 8 June and a week later the demarcation line was agreed. On the same day the Chinese and KPDR high command ordered all offensive operations to cease. To the exasperation of Eisenhower, Rhee did his best to disrupt the peace process by securing the premature release of 25,000 non-communist POWs held by the ROK, but Mao rightly concluded that US pressure would force him to accept the armistice. At the same time he had not failed to note that the US Joint Chiefs of Staff favoured air and sea operations against China, together with the use of nuclear weapons. (They were restrained by Eisenhower.) Armistice terms were finally agreed at Panmunjom on 27 July 1953, in a ceremony orchestrated by the communists to humiliate, as far as possible, the UN delegates – so that later Kim Il Sung's official biographer could later report that 'On July 27, 1953 the US imperialists were taken to Panmunjom, where they bent their knees to the national flag of the Democratic People's Republic of Korea and signed the armistice agreement'.[29] Mao was content to claim that 'US imperialism is not terrifying, nothing to make a fuss about'. At the end of day Korea remained divided along much the same line as it had been at the beginning of the war, three years earlier, and no POW was repatriated against his will.

Looking back on the Korean War, one discovers a world with many different facets. What they mean is largely a question of perspective. The war had important consequences for the US, the UN (and in particular the member states that took part), the Soviet Union, China, Taiwan, Japan, Australia, Britain, Europe – on both sides of the Iron Curtain – and above all for Korea itself, both North and South. To the US the war made clear what Mao's victory in China in 1949 involved for the balance of power in the Far East: Japan, South Korea, Taiwan, to say nothing of the various states of Southeast Asia, could not just be left to look after themselves. It was in America's interest to support them, politically and economically, and to deploy its armed forces to defend them. These were new frontline states in the battle against communism, so that where, before 1950, South Korea made do with 500 US military advisers, after 1953 it was defended by a hundred times as many US combat troops. At the same time the US accepted that Japan was also essential to its strategic interests, a role it could only fulfil if it regained the independence it had lost after being defeated in the Pacific War – a process completed before the end of the war in Korea, much sooner than would otherwise have been the case. On a narrow view, such as that of Winston Churchill, this was all that mattered. In his words, spoken after the Panmunjom armistice, 'Korea does not really matter now. I'd never heard of the bloody place until I was seventy-four. Its importance lies in the fact that it has led to the re-arming of America'.[30]

There was, however, more to it than that. The United Nations, almost by accident, discovered that it could be effective in the cause of peace by mobilizing its members to resist aggression: in the half-century after the Panmunjom armistice the United Nations, for all its many peacekeeping operations, was never more effective. Its role in Korea was exemplary. The Soviet Union and China gained little from the war, save the knowledge that the US and its allies were resolved to stand fast in the Far East, just as they were in Europe. China, in particular, lost, for some twenty years, any chance it might have had of being accepted as a member of the world community: its intervention in Korea made certain that the US would continue its support for Jiang Jieshi, recognizing his Guomindang regime in Taiwan as China's legitimate government. Mao's new China, true to the tradition of the old imperial China, had good reason for wanting to retain Korea as a tributary – the more so after what China had gone through in eight years of war against Japan. After the division of the country, in 1945, along the line of the 38th parallel, Mao could only reluctantly accept that 'half a loaf was better than no bread'. From a Chinese perspective, destiny was on the side of Kim Il Sung when he invaded South Korea in 1950, and that was certainly how he saw the future. In forty years after Panmunjom, until his death in 1994, he never learnt the lesson that he was mistaken, and his country, now led by his son, Kim Jong Il, still pays the price – a history related in Chapter 5.

On the other side of the DMZ, the challenge to the ROK to rebuild the devastated country, together with the massive support received from the US, led to the creation of a new state of unprecedented prosperity. If the world needs a demonstration of the inherent superiority of Western democracy and the capitalist society, there is no better place to find it than South Korea. This is the other half of the history related in Chapter 5.

Finally, the Korean War was exemplary in the moderation displayed, if often reluctantly, by the leading protagonists. It was always contained within the historic frontiers of Korea, and both sides resisted the temptation to let the war escalate. Truman, at the critical moment, did not hesitate to relieve General MacArthur of his command, when he, and his political supporters, wished to follow this path. Truman's successor, Eisenhower, restrained his generals when they contemplated the use of nuclear weapons. Kim Il Sung, a man incapable of moderation, was the biggest loser in the war, taking his desperate country, which lost more than a million soldiers in the war,[31] with him. South Korean casualties, although fewer, were still considerable. For both North and South, equally committed to reunification, the war settled nothing. On the other side a new pattern of confrontation, between East and West, did emerge from the Korean War, as can be seen by looking at the much more devastating war that followed it in Vietnam.

5

Korea: North and South (1953–2006)

THE POLITICS OF SEPARATION

From an international perspective, defined by membership of the UN, Korea has only been two separate nations – with on one side, the Republic of Korea (ROK), and on the other, the Korean People's Democratic Republic (KPDR) – since 1991. Nonetheless, the actual division of the Korean peninsula into two separate countries goes back to 1945, as related in Chapter 4. The present frontier between them is defined by the *demilitarized zone* (DMZ) as shown by the map on p. xi, agreed at Panmunjom in 1953. Since then the presence of a rival state of Korea on the other side of the DMZ has been a dominant factor in the politics of both the ROK and the KPDR. The result is that any modern history must have three components: the first two relate to the two states considered apart from each other, while the third relates to the interaction between them – consistently unproductive, mainly because when it comes to progress in any field the ROK has always out-distanced the KPDR. Why this is so and how it all came about are the main themes of this chapter.

THE REPUBLIC OF KOREA

Starting then with the ROK, Panmunjom, in 1953, left it with an old, blinkered leader, Syngman Rhee, who had the very considerable advantage of having the US as an ally committed, if largely in its own interests, to investing heavily in his country. The US, however, having fought the war to a standstill in 1953, had lost almost all interest in the cause dearest to Syngman Rhee's heart, the reunification of Korea – if possible under his leadership. It did not help matters that the Soviet Union and China had made much the same problem with Kim Il Sung in the KPDR.

Syngman Rhee, having first been elected President of the ROK in 1947, had, as his major achievement after Panmunjom, the reconstruction of his devastated country. Politically the war left the ROK, in 1953, with an unprecedented level playing-field, which made it possible for Syngman Rhee, a year later, to put through a major programme of land reform: the great mass of peasant farmers, in what was still an essentially rural economy, acquired their own land, at the expense of their former landlords. Then, following a special amendment of the constitution to make this possible, the re-election of the 85-year-old Syngman Rhee as president in 1960 led almost immediately to nation-wide rioting, in which students – long a volatile force in Korean politics – played a major part. Syngman Rhee, having failed to control events, lost the support of his cabinet, and fled to exile in Hawaii, where he died, aged 90, in 1965 – a sad end to the life of a man who had given everything he had to his country.

In spite of having banished Syngman Rhee, the ROK government was still unable to bring the country to order. In 1960, after Syngman Rhee, the ROK had three successive acting presidents until Yun Po Sun became the official president at the end of the year. He was not, however, the strong leader the country needed. The man who assumed this role had an inauspicious beginning. In 1940, a young school-teacher, Park Chung Hee, volunteered to serve in the Japanese Army, where he did so well that – quite exceptionally for a Korean – he was given a commission. After the war he was admitted to the new Korean Military Academy, to graduate as an officer in 1946. There he became the leader of a communist cell, which, in 1948, organized the Yosu rebellion and proclaimed a short-lived people's republic. For this he was sentenced to death by a military court, but Syngman Rhee, following the advice of his American military adviser – who knew Park as a 'damned good soldier'[1] – commuted the sentence. Park, having turned over a list of communists in the armed forces, was reinstated as an intelligence officer at army headquarters, and by 1960 he had become a major-general.

Using his position in the ROK military Park staged a coup in 1961, and effectively took over the government of President Yun – making sure that no one mentioned his communist past. Under pressure from Washington, Park, who in his own words had taken over a 'bankrupt firm', returned the ROK to civilian rule. Even so, obsessed by the need to keep national security in his own hands and independent of the US, Park lost no time in setting up his own Korean Central Intelligence Agency (KCIA), which by 1964 had some 370,000 employees. With the KCIA behind his new Democratic Republican Party (DRP), Park was elected president in 1963, to become the virtual dictator of the ROK. If, in domestic politics, he was where he wanted to be, he had still to contend with Kim Il Sung in the KPDR, at the same time retaining the level of support he required from Washington – where his high-handed methods won few friends.

Park's place in history, according to his own plans, was to be found in his economic policy. Almost immediately after seizing power he introduced a policy of 'guided capitalism', based on the principles that had enabled the Japanese economy to take off at the end of the 1950s. Part of Park's programme was to normalize relations with Japan, a goal achieved in 1965. This led to a Japanese aid package worth $800 million, with millions more coming into Korea as a result of foreign direct investment.

Central to Park's economic policy in the 1960s was the Heavy and Chemical Industries Promotion Plan, judged to be over-ambitious by both Washington and the World Bank. This led to problems in financing the first major project, an integrated steel mill at Pohang, but then Japanese loans saved Park. Events justified the project: Pohang became the centre of the world's largest steel production complex, which became the foundation of the ROK's heavy industry. The instrument for carrying out Park's was found in *chaebols*, vast business conglomerates, each one an empire in itself, controlled by a single family. This is true even of such world-ranking businesses as those of Hyundai or Samsung.[2] The problem with the *chaebols* was over-capacity; within almost every one of them there was simply too much diversification. Their unprecedented growth, and indeed their very survival, depended on almost unlimited access to credit, guaranteed, at least for those he favoured, by Park's control, through the Central Bank, of the whole banking system. If this resulted in debt-equity ratios that horrified foreign economic observers, it mattered little to Park, because the whole operation was in-house – and what is more, it was successful.[3] For some 25 years real GDP increased at an average annual rate of 8 per cent, a process that only ended with the Asian financial crisis of 1997.[4]

Needless to say, a political price had to be paid. In 1964 the concentration of ownership inherent in the corporate structure meant that the nine largest chaebols between them accounted for 38 per cent of all bank credit: the ruling family in each of them enjoyed powerful positions in the DRP or the state bureaucracy, always with the understanding that this would be paid for with substantial political donations proportionate to the credit granted – the accepted level in the 1960s was between 10 and 20 per cent.[5] If not Park himself, those close to him became millionaires, with Kim Hyung Wook – head of the KCIA from 1963 to 1969 – probably accumulating the largest fortune.

The sanctions for not playing the game were harsh: when finally Kim was called to account by a congressional investigation in Washington, he provided a long list of businesses[6] that had been ruined after Park had come to doubt their corporate loyalty. Charges were fabricated and directors imprisoned. The system outlasted Park's own time: in 1985, his successor, Chun Doo Hwan, orchestrated the bankruptcy of the Kukje group – the seventh largest chaebol – after the owners of its equity, the Yang family, failed to come up with the contributions demanded by Chun. This was a quite straightforward operation: outstanding loans were called in, and government credit was discontinued.

Park's success owed much to his exploitation of relations with the US on one side, and the KPDR on the other. As for the US he faced a number of problems.

First, Washington was anxious to reduce the number of US troops supporting the ROK in its confrontation with the KPDR on the other side of the DMZ. Second, there was widespread criticism of the financial regime supporting the expansion of the ROK economy, and that not only because of the high level of corruption involved. Third, Park's record on human rights was lamentable.

US troop reduction was unwelcome to Park not only on the point of security (where in the view of Washington his own forces could take over) but also because of the considerable economic benefits flowing from a large US military presence. The facilities provided by the Daewoo chaebol for repairing US aircraft carriers helped considerably in making its shipyard the largest in the world. Towards the end of the 1960s Park, by sending two ROK divisions to support the US forces in Vietnam, ensured that a corresponding number of US troops would not be withdrawn from Korea. As for the finances of the ROK, Park was always able to deflect criticism so long as the economy grew at a rate sufficient for profits to cover the service of its chronic indebtedness. Since in each decade after he seized power in 1961 the economy grew by some 30 per cent, he was almost always ahead of the game. If, during the presidency of Syngman Rhee the economies of the ROK and KPDR had been level pegging, from 1960 that of KPDR began to lag ever further behind, as that of the ROK raced ahead.

The endemic corruption in the ROK was accepted as the price to be paid for the country's success, during the 1960s, in transforming its basic economy from import substitution to export-oriented industry. Finally an attack on Park's human rights record was for him an attack on ROK sovereignty at a time when it was under continuous threat from the KPDR. On this point his outside critics got little satisfaction, even in cases as notorious as the kidnapping of the opposition leader, Kim Dae Jung, in a Tokyo hotel in 1973 – related later in this chapter. Washington, although continually mistrusting Park – even to the point of having the CIA bug his office – accepted in the end that this was an 'internal' matter. As for confrontation with the KPDR, this was consistently useful to Park as a pretext for any high-handed policy. The long shadow of the Korean War (1950–53) was sufficient to remind his critics of the costs of disregarding the threat from the north. What is more, there was always some low-keyed action across the DMZ, sometimes hostile but more often consisting of fruitless negotiations to resolve disputes arising as a result of perceived hostile action.

If, during the 1960s, Park's economic successes made him acceptable as president, in the 1970s he overplayed his hand. Having forced through a constitutional amendment, during his second term as president (1967–71), to allow him to stand again in 1971, he did so and won a third term on the promise that he would never again ask the people of the ROK to vote for him. Park's most effective challenger in 1971 was Kim Dae Jung, who, from exile in Japan, warned of the consequences of Park's third victory.

The warning proved to be well-founded, when, a year later, Park, by staging an auto-coup, made sure that the question of re-election would never arise. On 16 October 1972, he declared martial law, disbanded the National Assembly, and imposed a new regime for the indirect election of the president – supplanting the existing constitution, in a scenario remarkably similar to that in the Philippines, where Ferdinand Marcos had staged a coup three weeks earlier. Senior political leaders were arrested as Park's new *yushin* system took over, justified by the need to maintain, internationally, the independence of the ROK, and to strengthen its hand in confronting the KPDR. Washington, preoccupied with the need to resolve the war in Vietnam, with a presidential election due within three weeks, turned a blind eye. Kim Dae Jung, still in Japan, repeated his dire warnings.

At this stage, the ROK and the KPDR were actually engaged in low-level dialogue, offering people in the ROK some hope of opening up the KPDR for possible family reunions, and giving Kim Il Sung the chance to improve its international standing. This was the beginning of a process by which the KPDR increased, over a period of four years, the number of countries linked by diplomatic relations from 35 to 93, gaining also the right to observer status at the UN in New York and Geneva. In practice the diplomatic links added up to very little: Sweden was the only Western country ever to open an embassy in Pyongyang.[7] Even so the turn of events was seen as favourable by both Seoul and Pyongyang, and was used by the leaders on both sides to improve their political standing. In the ROK Park used it to justify his *auto-coup* in October 1972, while in the KPDR, Kim Il Sung proclaimed a new principle of *juche*, defined as 'a creative application of Marxist-Leninism' and had himself upgraded from prime minister to president.

On 8 August 1973 Park showed his true colours, by orchestrating the kidnapping of Kim Dae Jung in Tokyo. This provoked a furious reaction from Seoul, where US Ambassador Philip Habib was almost immediately able to expose the KCIA as responsible. It was made clear to Park that Kim, who was already on his way to Korea, must be released – a move that probably saved his life. Five days later he was free, for 36 hours, to speak of his ordeal, but then he was placed under permanent house arrest. Pyongyang then had a pretext for breaking off the dialogue with Seoul, welcome because there was no sign that it was leading to the hoped-for reduction in US troops.

Park at first reacted by trying to salvage the talks, dismissing the KCIA director, Lee Hu Rak, who had not only represented the ROK in Pyongyang but was also the man behind the kidnapping of Kim Dae Jung. Making no progress, Park changed tack. Having noted India's successful test of a nuclear weapon in 1974, he announced plans to raise the ROK's military profile by setting up his own nuclear arms programme, in conflict with Washington's long-standing policy on proliferation, even among its allies. To add insult to injury he invited the French to supply the necessary technology for his own programme: this was too much for Washington, and he was forced to climb down. A contract with the French was also ruled out when Park switched to a nuclear energy programme to be carried out by the Korean Nuclear Fuels Development Corporation. The nuclear programme, however, remained on the back-burner, to be decisively abandoned, under US pressure, in 1980.

In the ROK 15 August is a national holiday celebrating the country's liberation from the Japanese in 1945. On this day, in 1974, President Park was reading a long speech to an invited audience in Seoul's National Theatre, when a young man, firing a gun wildly, rushed towards the stage. The president, who ducked behind the bullet-proof lectern, was safe, but his wife was not so lucky. Hit by a single bullet, she collapsed in a pool of blood, and died later in the day. The proceedings followed their course, and the president finished his speech. He was shaken, nonetheless, and had plenty to worry about. Not only had his long-standing fear of assassination proved to be justified, but there was no mistaking the resentment for his regime, particularly among students, counted in hundreds of thousands, and Christians, counted in millions. This did not go unnoticed abroad, as Park was to discover when Jimmy Carter became US president in 1977. By this time also, Kim Il Sung, noting, from the other side of the DMZ, the defeat of the US in Vietnam, was sounding out Beijing and Moscow for support for a new invasion of the ROK. He had no success, but the period of dialogue, which had lowered tension across the DMZ in the early 1970s, was definitely over.

This became only too apparent on 18 August 1976, when a small detachment of US troops started to trim the branches of a poplar tree in the Joint Security Area (JSA) at Panmunjom. This small enclave was the only location in the DMZ open for contacts between the local forces of the ROK and the KPDR. The object in trimming the tree was to improve the line of sight between two adjacent ROK guard posts, but this was too much for a lieutenant of the Korean People's Army, who after giving a warning, ignored by the American soldiers, ordered troops to attack them. This led to the deaths of two US officers, the first such event since the armistice of 1953.

The immediate reaction in Washington was to consider plans for extensive mobilization of its forces in the area around Korea. President Ford, however, regarded this as massive overkill, with the risk of dangerous escalation. In the end it was made clear to the KPA that the US detachment in the JSA would complete the trimming of the poplar tree, but with heavily armed support. The KPA got the message, and the operation was completed without any further incident. There was never any sign of an apology from the government of the KPDR.

While all this was happening Richard Sneider, US Ambassador in Seoul, was urging Washington to increase military and economic support for the ROK. In particular he wanted to reassure Park that US forces would remain indefinitely in Korea. Otherwise Park would have the ROK develop its own sophisticated weapons, a follow-up to the aborted nuclear programme most unwelcome to Washington. Park had in any case increased military expenditure to the point that in absolute, though not relative terms, the ROK was spending more than the KPDR. He also increased public investment in his heavy chemical programme.

In October 1976 the *Washington Post* revealed how agents of the ROK had bribed some 90 members of the US Congress. In November Jimmy Carter, having defeated Ford in the US presidential election, was resolved to take action on Korea. Quite apart from the bribery scandal, like many others in the US and elsewhere, Carter disliked what he saw. He threatened Park with the withdrawal of US forces and a reduction in aid, and unless Park took action to release political prisoners, Washington would no longer turn a blind eye to human rights abuses in the ROK.

If Carter had had his way, the majority of the 40,000 US servicemen in the ROK would have been withdrawn, but times were against him. Although, in the end, only 3,000 were pulled out, the number of nuclear warheads was reduced from 700 to 250, while at the same time ROK troops took over all the frontline positions along the DMZ. By this time the ROK economy was in deep trouble as a result of world-wide inflation in the wake of the 1973 oil crisis. Dissidents, released from prison as a result of pressure from Carter, emboldened opposition politicians. When their leader, Kim Young Sam, used an interview published in the *New York Times* to appeal to the American public to end its support of Park's 'minority dictatorial regime'[8] this all went too far. Park had Kim expelled from the National Assembly. This led to mass resignations by opposition deputies, and the country was in a deep political crisis. Starting from Pusan (Kim's home turf) anti-government demonstrations, led by students, spread throughout the country. The US Embassy was concerned about where Park's harsh policies would lead to.

The end came soon and very suddenly. On 26 October 1979, at a dinner in a KCIA safe house in the presidential precinct, Kim Jaw Kyu, the director of the KCIA, after being abused by Park for failing to pacify the country, left the room for his own office. There he pocketed his .38 Smith & Wesson, and returning to the dinner, shot first the presidential security chief, Cha Chi Chol, and then Park, leaving both severely wounded. His pistol then jammed, so he borrowed another from a KCIA guard, and finished off the job.

The US, thought by many to have been involved in the assassination, reacted by moving to a higher state of alert. In the KPDR, on the other side, Kim Il Sung, after taking the opportunity to point out that 'our country is truly a socialist paradise', simply temporized. In the ROK – which was far from being any sort of paradise – Park was succeeded by his prime minister, Choi Kyu Ha, who declared martial law and announced a presidential election for 6 December 1979, which he went on to win – but without any significant military support.

By this time it was clear that the position of the top military in the ROK was being threatened by lower-ranking generals, who claimed that the Chief of Staff had played a part in Park's assassination. On the night of 12 December, their leader, Major-General Chun Doo Hwan, supported by troops withdrawn from the frontline along the DMZ, staged a coup which left them in control of the country. The US Ambassador, William Gleysteen, was powerless to take any action to counteract this most unwelcome turn of events. His answer to criticism was simply, 'I cannot act as a colonial governor'. He got nowhere with Chun, and nothing was to be gained by dealing with Choi, who had been reduced to little more than a figurehead. In fact no one was any match for Chun, whom successive US ambassadors described as 'almost the definition of unreliability ... unscrupulous ... ruthless ... a liar' and 'one of the shrewdest, most calculating politically smart people I've known'.[9]

In April 1980 Chun, to consolidate his control of the ROK, had Choi appoint him head of the KCIA. From this commanding position he proceeded, on the night of 17–18 May, to arrest a number of student leaders, together with the three leading opposition politicians, Kim Dae Jung, Kim Young Sam and Kim Jong Pil. At the same time he declared full martial law, clamped down on the press and closed the National Assembly at bayonet point.

A warning from the US Embassy that the arrest of Kim Dae Jung would be 'incendiary' proved to be correct, when, the following day, 19 May, a popular uprising occurred in Kwangju, where local support for him was very strong. It took Chun more than a week to suppress the uprising, for which he held the US Embassy largely responsible. Protests from the ambassador achieved next to nothing, for as one top security official in Washington advised, 'the only way to get leverage on this guy is to start a dialogue with the north'[10] – a course of action which no one could contemplate. In the long run, however, Chun lost out at Kwangju: in the uprising the seeds were sown of what, by the end of the century, would become a powerful labour movement.[11] It is an irony of history that Kim Dae Jung, as president of the ROK, would then have to rein it in to save the country's economy.

On 7 August 1980 Chun became a four-star general. On 17 August, after being elected by a special National Conference for Unification, convened for just this purpose after he had dispensed cash handouts to his supporters on a scale unprecedented even for Korea, Chun displaced Choi as president. In the meantime Kim Dae Jung, after a show-trial, was sentenced to death. US protests at every stage were of no avail: Chun realized that Carter, confronted with an election in November, had his hands full with the need to secure the release of more than a hundred staff members of the US Embassy taken hostage in Iran.

After Carter's defeat by Ronald Reagan Chun realized that nothing was to be gained from negotiating with a 'lame duck'. On the other hand Richard Allen, nominated as the new National Security Adviser, held out hope of an early official visit to the Reagan White House. This was formally announced on 21 January 1981, the day following Reagan's inauguration. On 24 January Chun commuted Kim Dae Jung's death sentence to life imprisonment and lifted martial law.

On 2 February Chun was received at the White House, his arrival preceded by advice from Gleysteen not to regard the visit as a 'crude trade-off' for the life of Kim Dae Jung. Chun need not have worried. In dealing with Chun Reagan was as effusive as Carter had been distant. For the new Secretary of State, Alexander Haig, the visit symbolized 'the normalization of US-ROK relations after a period of prolonged strain'. Chun was assured that there were no plans for US troop reduction; on the contrary, Reagan eventually increased the number serving in Korea to 43,000. He also promised, informally, to sell F-16 warplanes to the ROK, leaving much of the opposition, driven underground by Chun, to conclude that Washington was behind the military coup of 12 December 1980.

Although the ROK economic miracle continued, the 1980s, under Chun, were more than a prolongation of Park Chung Hee's harsh regime. In 1983 one event, in particular, highlighted the vulnerability of the ROK. On 1 September, a Korean Airlines flight, KAL 007, from Anchorage in Alaska, failed to reach its destination, Seoul. The airliner was shot down by a Soviet fighter-plane after it had veered wildly off course over territory belonging to the Soviet Far East. While President Reagan denounced the incident as a 'massacre', an 'atrocity' and a 'crime against humanity', the Soviet authorities, after first denying responsibility, then admitted shooting down the plane, justifying their action on the grounds that it was engaged in espionage on behalf of the US and the ROK. Finally, in January 1993, after the collapse of the Soviet Union, it became clear that a local Soviet air defence officer had ordered an attack by a ground-to-air missile: the airliner had in fact strayed some 600 kilometres off course as a result of navigational errors. It was never involved in espionage, but the incident seriously hindered the promising development of a rapprochement between the Soviet Union and the ROK.

KOREAN PEOPLE'S DEMOCRATIC REPUBLIC

The 1980s witnessed the opening of a new era in international relations for both the ROK and the KPDR. This was not so much the result of radical new policies adopted by either side as of changes in the relations between the US and its allies on one side, and the Soviet Union and China, on the other. From 1973, when the US first established diplomatic relations with China, and even more from

1975, when it withdrew from Cambodia and Vietnam, both sides had become increasingly reluctant to let Korea, North or South, stand between them. The result, inside the Korean peninsula, was to weaken the international standing of Kim Il Sung at a time when he could see his own country, the KPDR, lagging far behind the ROK in economic development. Inside the KPDR his tight hold on the country stifled all opposition, while a million troops were deployed along the DMZ to confront the ROK.

Then, on 9 October 1983, a remarkable incident in Burma lost Kim Il Sung the goodwill of one of the few countries in the world sympathetic to his regime. The occasion was the visit of ROK President Chun to Rangoon, the Burmese capital. The first event was a ceremony at the Martyr's Mausoleum at the National Cemetery, which only minutes after the scheduled opening time was shattered by a vast explosion. Nearly twenty people lost their lives: among them were four ROK cabinet members, the Ambassador to Burma and two presidential advisers. President Chun, however, had not yet arrived – the result of a change in his flight plan from Seoul made for security reasons.

The Burmese police, realizing that only the KPDR could be behind the explosion, lost little time in arresting the North Korean officers responsible for it. One of these, Captain Kang Min Chul, in a full confession exposed the advance planning in Pyongyang, led by the 'Great Leader's' son (and future successor), Kim Jong Il, who was responsible for the KPDR's foreign clandestine operations. Burma broke off diplomatic relations, and expelled all the KPDR diplomats. In China, Deng Xiaoping refused all contact with delegates from the KPDR.

Whoever was responsible in Pyongyang, the Rangoon incident remains a puzzle, because at that time Kim Il Sung was working hard at improving his isolated country's relations with the outside world. The incident can only be explained as an attempt to destabilize the ROK by assassinating its head of government, so that new revolutionary forces, suppressed after the popular uprising in Kwangju in May 1980, would emerge to establish a regime more acceptable to the KPDR. In the event, the US reacted by delaying the scheduled departure of the aircraft carrier USS *Carl Vinson* and its support group from Korean waters, while at the same time persuading Chun not to retaliate with force of arms.

It may be that the Rangoon incident was a last desperate attempt, by Kim Il Sung, to create a situation in which he could finally realize his dream of a united Korea under his leadership. According to later reports[12] he had commando units ready to land in the ROK to support the expected uprising. With the failure to eliminate Chun it all came to nothing, and later in 1983 the US Defense Secretary Caspar Weinberger, learnt from Deng Xiaoping in Beijing that the KPDR had 'neither the intention nor the capability' to attack the ROK, but that if the ROK attacked the KPDR, 'China will not be able to stay out'. Given the frequent contacts between Washington and Beijing – following the resumption of diplomatic relations in 1979 – Beijing provided the obvious route for indirect negotiations between Pyongyang and Washington. Once, however, Pyongyang began to take the idea seriously, Washington became cool, and President Reagan – after an apparent change of heart – proposed that negotiations should begin with bilateral talks between Pyongyang and Seoul, which, in the event, is the way things happened. After a few family reunions between North and South, the first high-level talks took place on 26 December 1984. From then on, beginning in May 1985 and continuing until November 1991, there were 42 meetings between named representatives of the ROK and the KPDR: if, as at first contemplated, there should be at some stage a direct meeting between Chun Doo Hwan and Kim Il Sung, lack of will on both sides ensured that this never took place. The final blow, for the KPDR, was the resumption, in 1986, of the joint US-ROK Team Spirit military exercises, denounced by Pyongyang as a 'nuclear war manoeuvre intended against North Korea'.[13]

Throughout the 1980s the main diplomatic challenge to Kim Il Sung was to ensure the continued support of both China and the Soviet Union for his regime. This was essential not only politically, but economically, in a world which the KPDR had little to offer by way of trade. While during the 1960s the split between China and the Soviet Union confronted Pyongyang with the need to decide where its allegiance lay – a problem exacerbated by Kim Il Sung's unrelenting commitment to Stalinism and distaste for Khrushchev's reforms, which in 1963 had led to the Soviet Union cutting off military and economic aid – by the 1980s he had learnt how to play off the two sides against each other.[14] Neither Moscow (where Khrushchev's fall in 1964 had restored Kim to grace) nor Beijing could afford to abandon the KPDR: Moscow, seeing 'North Korea, for all the peculiarities of Kim Il Sung, [as] the most important bastion in the Far East in our struggle against American and Japanese imperialism and Chinese revisionism', increased its military and economic aid. Early in 1984, Kim Il Sung, having learnt of a visit to Beijing by President Reagan planned for April, arranged to visit Moscow in May – his first visit since 1961. There, after telling the Soviet leader, Konstantin Chernenko, that his greatest fear was that 'socialism [was] not being maintained in China', he was rewarded with a whole package of modern weapons,[15] in exchange for over-flying rights for Soviet military aircraft – much to the concern of the American military south of the DMZ. There was also a valuable economic package, so that KPDR imports from the Soviet Union increased fourfold in the period 1984–88, with Moscow financing a growing trade deficit, while at the same time supplying coal and oil at well below world-market prices. The end-result, that two-thirds of all imports came from the Soviet Union, was in the 1990s to prove disastrous for the economy of the KPDR.

Even as early as his 1984 Moscow visit, Kim Il Sung should have been able to read the writing on the wall. Shortly afterwards a top Soviet adviser had noted, 'It is obvious that South Korea is a successful and respected country which is genuinely interested in being our friend. To respond positively to Seoul's overtures correlates with the U.S.S.R. national interest'.[16] Then, in 1985, Gorbachev succeeded Chernenko. If, to begin with, Gorbachev continued his predecessor's military and economic support for the KPDR, it was not long before he came to see Kim Il Sung as 'a burden he had from the past'.[17] This, apparently, was also the view of Deng Xiaoping, who, in July 1987, announced that China would no longer support KPDR military action – at the same time opening secret diplomatic links with the ROK.

THE OLYMPIC SHOWDOWN OF 1988

The Olympic Games of 1988 were a critical turning point in the history of Korea, North and South. Both Chun's own opponents in the ROK and the United States – followed by the numerous other countries likely to compete – knew that it was critically important for him to prevent any disturbance in the run-up to the games. This was doubly important given the history of the games held in Moscow in 1980 and Los Angeles in 1984. The Moscow games were a disaster for the Soviet Union after the US, followed by thirty-one other countries, including Japan and West Germany, dropped out in protest against the Soviet invasion of Afghanistan. As a result the Soviet Union, together with twelve other countries, declined to send teams to Los Angeles four years later. China, however, did send a team in 1984, which won fifteen gold medals. In 1988, not only the US, but also China and the Soviet Union, were determined to make a success of the games.

The US leverage, in the light of the forthcoming games, was used to the advantage of political reform in the ROK. Chun, when elected in 1980, had promised to serve only one term, and Washington – and his own wife – meant to hold him to his promise. On 2 June 1987 Chun's proclaiming Roh Tae Woo, the second man in his administration, as his chosen successor, led to uprisings throughout the ROK. In Washington, President Reagan reacted with a letter stating that the peaceful transfer of power was crucial, demanding, also, the release of political prisoners and guarantees of press freedom. On the day the letter was received, demonstrations throughout the ROK decided Chun to call in the military the following day, but this decision was almost immediately reversed under pressure from the US Embassy. Roh Tae Woo agreed to direct elections for the next president, accepting also a complete amnesty for Kim Dae Jung. This proved to be the advantage of all concerned. There were three principal candidates for the elections held in December 1987: Roh Tae Woo, Kim Young

Sam and Kim Dae Jung. The two Kims split the opposition vote, allowing Roh to be elected with only 36 per cent of the votes cast. This allowed Roh to claim the moral high ground as the true founder of democracy in the ROK, conveniently overlooking the fact that he originally expected to be manoeuvred into office by Chun bypassing democratic procedures. Both the Kims went on to be elected president in the 1990s, so the 1987 election had a happy outcome for everyone. It also opened the way for China, the Soviet Union and its East European satellites to send representatives to the ROK, as a prelude to their teams competing in the Olympic Games.

The 1988 Olympics were a disaster for the KPDR. After first ignoring the award of the games to Seoul, Pyongyang, following a suggestion made by Fidel Castro, proposed that it should join Seoul as co-host. The International Olympic Committee (IOC), with the agreement of the ROK, accepted the transfer of some events, beginning with table-tennis and fencing, but for Pyongyang nothing less than a third was acceptable. This was never on the cards, particularly after the Soviet Union and the East European states made clear that they would send teams to Seoul, however much Pyongyang might protest. In August 1987 Pyongyang rejected the IOC's final compromise offer, leading a friendly ambassador, Hans Maretzki, of East Germany, to make the following judgement: 'North Korea is once again putting itself in self-imposed isolation. Through its stubborn behaviour, North Korea is granting advantages to South Korea, which will enjoy an improved image'. This is precisely what happened.

On 19 November 1987 Pyongyang saw to it that things went from bad to worse. Flight KAL 858 was lost in flight from Abu Dhabi to Seoul as a result of sabotage carried out by KPDR agents – a man of 70 and a woman of 25 posing as father and daughter, who had left a bomb on the airplane after taking the flight from Baghdad to Abu Dhabi. Their escape plans were foiled in Bahrain, where the man committed suicide. The woman, however, failed in her attempt, and was sent for trial in the ROK, where, after eight days of interrogation she told the whole story of how she had been selected and trained in the KPDR for this operation. The US placed the KPDR on the list of countries practising state terrorism, new economic and political sanctions were imposed, and new sophisticated security devices were installed for the Olympic Games – which were free of any terrorism.

Roh made good diplomatic use of the success of the games. Shortly before the opening ceremony moves were made, with the help of the US Embassies in Moscow and Beijing, to improve relations with Pyongyang, while the US also promised 'positive steps' if the KPDR did not attempt any disruption of the games. Once they were over, Roh made clear that the ROK would no longer object to direct dealing between Washington and Pyongyang, and following a visit to Washington and the UN in New York in November 1988 he was able to reveal a new four-point plan for facilitating contacts with the KPDR. On 5 December 1988, in Beijing, this led to the first meeting ever between diplomats representing the US and the KPDR: this was followed by thirty-three more in the period ending in September 1993.

THE SOVIETS BETRAY THE KPDR

The Olympic Games, where Soviet athletes won the largest number of gold medals, foreshadowed a change of heart in Moscow. A meeting of the Politburo on 10 November 1988 formally recognized that in Korea, the ROK had far more to offer economically than the KPDR, which was consistently defaulting on debts owed to the Soviet Union. By this time the Gross National Product of the ROK, which had been equal to that of the KPDR in 1960, had become seven times as great. Already, on the day before the opening ceremony, Gorbachev had spoken of 'the opportunities ... for forging economic ties with South Korea', proposing at the same time a reduction of military forces and operations 'in the areas where the coasts of the USSR, PRC, Japan, DPRK and South Korea merge close'.[18] A month later this was taken up by Roh suggesting at the UN in New York the setting up of a 'consultative conference for peace' involving both the ROK and the KPDR, together with China, Japan and the Soviet Union – with the US to join later. The Soviet Union had even more reason to be grateful to the ROK when both the official Economic Development Cooperation Fund and leading chaebols showed interest in investing in Siberia. A request from Moscow for a $300 million commercial loan would also be favourably considered. Pyongyang, needless to say, watched such developments with dismay, which was only partly allayed by an assurance given by Edward Shevardnadze, the Soviet foreign minister, that there no 'intention [to] establish diplomatic relations with South Korea'.[19] He would soon have to eat his words.

The fortunes of the KPDR had always been tied to those of the Soviet Union, whose collapse during the period 1989–91 inevitably foreshadowed unprecedented disaster. The events of these three critical years are too well-known to be deployed at any length. The final phase began at the end of 1989, when the Berlin Wall was opened up and Gorbachev abandoned the 'Brezhnev doctrine' assuring military support for the communist governments in Eastern Europe. Already, in May 1989, Gorbachev, after successfully resolving the long-standing Sino-Soviet dispute in Beijing, had refused to go on to Pyongyang. The KPDR's trust in Chinese support was also shaken by a $3 billion trade deal between Beijing and Seoul. A year later, in September 1990, Kim Il Sung, meeting Deng Xiaoping in Shenyang in northeast China, asked him pointedly, 'How long will the red flag fly?' He was reassured that China, Vietnam and Cuba were still solid, but by this time neither China nor Russia attached much worth to their relations with the KPDR.[20]

Kim Il Sung was powerless to turn the course of history. In January 1990 Gorbachev, by welcoming ROK opposition leaders in Moscow, was able to broker an alliance between Roh and Kim Young Sam, opening the way for the latter to become the next president of the ROK. On 22 May Anatol Dobrynin, representing Gorbachev in Seoul, offered a meeting between Roh and Gorbachev in San Francisco two weeks later, following directly on a meeting between Gorbachev and President Bush in Washington. Roh made it clear that further support would be contingent on full diplomatic relations being established between Seoul and Moscow, and this was then agreed at San Francisco. In September Shevardnadze – going back on his own word – had to break the bad news to Pyongyang in the course of what he described as 'the most difficult, most unpleasant talk of my life'. In the face of the hostility he encountered (made clear by Kim Il Sung's refusal to meet him) Shevardnadze advanced the date for opening diplomatic relations with Seoul by three months, to 30 September 1990, provoking veiled threats from Pyongyang to 'go nuclear'. Worse still for Kim, China, a month later, disregarding his express wishes, opened a trade office in Seoul while the ROK did the same in Beijing.

At the end of 1990, in December, Roh paid an official state visit to Moscow. By this time the days of the Soviet Union, under Gorbachev, were numbered. Moscow's refusal to extend the 1961 Treaty of Friendship and Cooperation[21] made clear that support, of any kind, for the KPDR was out of the question. Moscow itself was desperate for finance,[22] from any source, and in the early months of 1991 a $3 billion aid package was negotiated by Yuri Maslyukov, Gorbachev's special representative in Seoul, on the condition that Soviet arms shipments to the KPDR must be suspended. This would have happened in any case after Gorbachev's government of the Soviet Union collapsed in the late summer (by which time about half the aid package had been taken up). Boris Yeltsin's new Russian successor state, with next to no funds to repay the ROK, worked off its debt to the ROK by supplying tanks, helicopters, missiles and spare parts – a final irony for the KPDR, which in the years following 1945 owed to Moscow its emergence as an independent state.

THE CHINA CONNECTION

The KPDR did better with China, where the survival of the People's Republic was hardly threatened by events in Russia. Until the twentieth century, Korea had long been a tributary of China, which it knew as *dae guk*, that is, the 'big state'. For the KPDR the relationship with China was also important, not only because of the common frontier at the Yalu River, but also because of the years before 1945 which Kim Il Sung spent fighting against the Japanese in Manchuria. With a near perfect knowledge of both its language and culture, Kim saw friendship with China as 'an invincible force that no one can ever break ...'[23] At the same time his government was based upon the Confucian principle that 'the political system is a reflection of a universal moral order', with the corollary that 'loyal and legitimate opposition cannot ... exist'.[24] In the KPDR the heavenly mandate, upon which the Chinese emperor's authority was based, was assumed by Kim Il Sung.

Although, by the early 1990s, China had long abandoned any such extreme interpretation of Confucianism, good relations with the KPDR were seen as essential for preventing it becoming too close to Moscow, but even after the collapse of Soviet Russia, KPDR was valued for its support of Beijing's claims to Taiwan, particularly after the ROK had granted it diplomatic recognition. On the other hand Pyongyang was let down by Beijing's decision not to block the ROK's becoming a member state of the UN. Although this opened the way for Pyongyang also to become a member, it put an end to the dream of a united Korea subject to the Great Leader, Kim Il Sung. Finally, after the ROK had agreed to break off diplomatic relations with Taiwan – a move welcome to Pyongyang – it entered into full diplomatic relations with China on 24 August 1992. All this fitted in with the China's Korean policy, based on the principle of 'neither unification nor war'.[25]

THE KPDR: ECONOMIC DISASTER AND NUCLEAR CONFRONTATION

By 1991 the KPDR, seen by one American observer as 'a strange land left deserted by some invisible plague',[26] was in dire straits. The need to pay cash for essential imports from China and Russia led to a severe fuel crisis – disastrous for KPDR industry[27] – and the cost of maintaining more than a million men under arms was an additional heavy burden for the economy. In early December, 1993, the Workers Party Central Committee in Pyongyang admitted the failure of the seven-year economic plan then coming to an end: in four years of continuous decline the economy had reached a point where GNP was one-sixteenth that of the ROK, with the gap still widening. The focus of a new three-year transition plan was mere survival, based on agriculture and light industry and exports to an uninterested world. The full horror of the KPDR as a failed state became clear when, following devastating floods in July 1995, an appeal was made for nearly $500 million in flood relief. The UN aid agencies insisted on opening an office in Pyongyang, with its director free to visit the devastated countryside. He then found 'people scavenging in the fields looking for roots and wild plants to prepare soup for their families ... [with] not a cabbage to be seen'.[28] As many as two million lives were lost to famine, leading one commentator to describe what happened as 'perhaps the greatest humanitarian disaster of the 1990s'.[29] In the year 2000 the KPDR had a nominal gross national income of $17 billion, a mere fraction of the $455 billion of the ROK.

Circumstances such as these lie behind the KPDR's nuclear weapons programme: this, the most recent chapter in Pacific nuclear history, is still being written. As far back as 1965 the Soviet Union supplied a research reactor for the Yongbyon nuclear centre that had been set up some 85 kilometres north of Pyongyang. Until 1974 the Soviet Union also supplied the fuel elements needed for the reactor, but in that year North Korean specialists took over, increasing the reactor's capacity and switching to fuel containing 80 per cent enriched plutonium. Activities increased significantly during the 1980s, and in 1988 US satellite photographs suggested that North Korea had embarked on a nuclear weapons programme.

The outside world, whether it is China, Japan, Russia, the US or the ROK on the other side of the DMZ, became resigned to accept the status quo north of the DMZ, however appalling the record of the government responsible for it. Given Pyongyang's potential for a nuclear reckoning, it is no more than prudent to let this sleeping dog lie – if it will. The problem lies in 'the cornered rat syndrome' – to adopt words used by the US military commander in Korea in 1994 – but then more than ten years have passed since these words were uttered. Looked at objectively, the record of the years since 1990 suggests another metaphor: Kim Jong Il has effectively imposed on the ROK an unremitting game of snakes and ladders. The historic meeting in Pyongyang, in June 2000, between the 'dear leader' and Kim Dae Jung, brought the latter to the top of a ladder, but the KPDR's withdrawal from the non-proliferation treaty in January 2004 brought his successor, Roh Moo Hyun to the end of a snake. Given its present position, this is the best game in town for the KPDR. It could continue indefinitely, particularly since China has repeatedly stated that it will not tolerate a forceful reunification of Korea.[30]

The 1990s, however, began favourably. In 1990 itself, a White House spokesman made clear that 'the United States is not a threat to North Korean security, and we seek to improve relations with that country'.[31] At the end of 1991 Roh announced that the last US nuclear weapons had been removed from the ROK, making it quite inconceivable that the ROK, on its own initiative, would open hostilities with the KPDR: the war that would follow would be devastating for its people and their flourishing economy. This was in accordance with the Joint Declaration of the Denuclearization of the Korean Peninsula, signed in October, to be followed in February 1992 by an Agreement on Reconciliation, Non-Aggression and Exchange and Cooperation. Then in May 1992 North Korea, in a declaration required by the International Atomic Energy Authority (IAEA), admitted to the operation of seven nuclear sites and the possession of 90 grams of enriched plutonium, claimed to come from the reprocessing of 89 defective fuel rods in 1989. Inconsistencies in the evidence supplied by North Korea convinced the IAEA that there had not been full disclosure. On 9 February 1993 the IAEA claimed the right to inspect two undeclared sites relevant, in its view, to North Korea's nuclear programme. Access was denied on the grounds that these were military installations unconnected to the programme – contrary to the allegations made by the IAEA. On 12 March North Korea's announcement of its intention to withdraw from the Non-Proliferation Treaty of 12 June 1985 provoked a major diplomatic confrontation with the US. The situation deteriorated even further after the Rodong-1 missile was test-fired over the Japan Sea in May 1993.

Talks between North Korea and the IAEA were resumed at the beginning of 1994, and on 15 February it was agreed that the inspections asked for could be resumed, with the exception of two nuclear waste sites that had been declared. The IAEA inspectors resumed work immediately, but while at some locations they encountered no obstacles, at others they were denied admission, even to plants specifically mentioned in the agreement. When on 15 March the inspectors were barred from taking samples at key locations in the plutonium reprocessing plant, noting at the same time that their own seals had been broken, the IAEA called a halt. This was the start of a cat and mouse game played out between North Korea and the IAEA.

In the summer of 1994, after learning of American plans for attacking Yongbyon with guided missiles, North Korea – following an initiative of former US President Jimmy Carter – had second thoughts, and agreed both to accept inspection at locations previously barred and to consult directly with the US – a change of policy probably connected with the death of President Kim Il Sung on 8 July, and the succession of his son, Kim Jong Il as the 'dear leader'. This left the weapons programme as a card to be played by a man no less enigmatic and un-predictable than the late lamented 'great leader'. Kim Jong Il never took over this title, although in 1998 he did declare his father to be 'President for Eternity'.[32]

After preliminary talks confirming the immediate extension of the areas open to inspection, representatives of the US and North Korea, meeting in Geneva on 21 October 1994, signed a Framework Agreement to resolve the nuclear issue once and for all. This required North Korea to freeze and eventually dismantle all the nuclear facilities suspected of being part of a secret weapons programme. In return, Pyongyang would be provided with two 1,000 megawatt light-water nuclear reactors – which would be safer and would produce much less plutonium – to increase the supply of electricity in North Korea. Moreover, 500,000 metric tons of heavy fuel oil for North Korea's existing conventional generating stations would be supplied in every year until the new reactors were completed.

In 1995 South Korea, Japan and the US established the well-funded Korean Peninsular Energy Development Organization (KEDO) to implement the key provisions of the Geneva Framework Agreement. This was always intended to be an international organization, and Canada, Australia and New Zealand joined it in 1995, Indonesia, Chile and Argentina in 1996 and the EU in 1997.

All key operations would be carried out under the supervision of IAEA inspectors, and spent fuel would not be dealt with in any way that involved reprocessing in North Korea. Until the end of 1999 American experts remained on site to look after the canning of spent fuel, and until the end of 2002 North Korea maintained a freeze on its nuclear operations consistent with Geneva. In the meantime, however, North Korea had carried out a test launching of a long-range missile, the Taepodong-1 – much more powerful than the Rodong-1 of 1993 – across the northern part of Japan in August 1998. The fact that almost every city in Japan was within its range caused considerable alarm in Tokyo.

Then, at the end of 2002, everything became unstuck. To begin with, some 20 tons of TBT,[33] a chemical used in extracting plutonium from spent nuclear-reactor fuel, was shipped to North Korea by a company in Dalian, a north Chinese harbour. Then the freeze was lifted, and at Yongbyon the IAEA's surveillance cameras were removed from a power plant suspected of producing weapons-grade plutonium, while many of the security seals were broken. A request by Mohamed El Baradei, the head of IAEA, for talks, was refused. On 10 January 2003 North Korea announced its withdrawal from the UN Non-Proliferation Treaty. There was no doubt that the North Koreans' nuclear weapons programme had been resumed, and in January 2004 an unofficial American delegation was actually shown a sample of weapons-grade plutonium: by this time, also, a cooling pond where some 8,000 spent fuel-rods had been stored, was empty. In the meantime every effort was made to resolve the issue by diplomacy. Three-party talks in April 2003, between the US, China and North Korea, were followed by four rounds of six-party talks – with Japan, South Korea and Russia as additional participants – in August 2003, and February, June and September 2004. To begin with KEDO went ahead with the light-water plants, but then, on 21 November 2003 it announced that construction would be suspended for one year, to begin on 1 December – North Korea had failed to keep its side of the bargain.

In 2002 any doubt about North Korea's nuclear weapons programme was dispelled when Dr. A.Q. Khan, the head of Pakistan's programme – which in 1997 had led to a series of successful tests – admitted to providing North Korea with all the technology it needed for a weapon based on uranium. Even so, North Korea, in July 2004, denied its uranium enrichment programme, which it had earlier admitted. At the end of 2004 a new diplomatic approach was made on the basis that this programme would be ended, while North Korea could continue retrieving plutonium from spent fuel-rods. It was to no avail: in February 2005

North Korea announced not only that it had nuclear weapons, but also that it was withdrawing indefinitely from the six-party talks. Kim Jong Il gave several reasons for this decision, among them a speech by Condoleeza Rice (who had just been appointed US Secretary of State for George W. Bush's second term of office) in which she included North Korea in the category 'outposts of tyranny'.

In the summer of 2006, Kim Jong Il orchestrated a series of rocket launches,[34] to demonstrate the power of North Korean nuclear warheads to reach targets as far away as the west coast of the US. Finally, in September, it was announced that the KPDR was planning an actual test of its nuclear weapons – without any details as to time and place being specified. The world did not have long to wait. On 9 October the KPDR claimed to have carried out a successful underground nuclear test in a remote northeast region of the republic. This was later confirmed by seismic evidence, although the device was very low-powered – suggesting, perhaps, a failure in KPDR nuclear technology. The test was universally condemned, particularly by Japan and the United States, but the UN Security Council was unable to agree what sanctions, if any, should be imposed as a result.

All this was too much for China, which had already cut off oil supplies to the KPDR after the test was announced in September. Then, some three weeks after test, Chinese diplomatic pressure brought about a meeting in Beijing between Chinese, North Korean and American officials – a first step towards resuming the six-party talks. The cards may have been shuffled once more, but the new hands look much the same as the old. Given the character of KPDR foreign and defence policy as dictated by Kim Jong Il it could hardly be otherwise.

While there is no certain answer to the question why North Korea changed course at the end of 2002 it is significant that President Bush's plans to invade Iraq were then an open secret. Their justification was Iraq's alleged concealment of research into and production of weapons of mass destruction. Then, even though UN inspectors found no supporting evidence, the invasion still went ahead in March 2003, with devastating consequences for the regime of Saddam Hussein. President Bush had already designated North Korea as part of an 'axis of evil' – also including Libya and Iran. In the perception of Kim Jong Il, North Korea could well be next in line for an US-backed invasion: what better deterrent then than the capacity for nuclear retaliation? It is more than likely that this point has already been reached – as claimed by Kim Jong Il – even if no one outside North Korea knows exactly how many nuclear warheads are ready for use, nor what targets are within range of the missiles that would carry them. The most terrifying scenario is a pre-emptive nuclear strike, undertaken by Kim Jong Il as a desperate measure to defend the integrity of a state that he, and his father, have tyrannized for sixty years. A confrontation now seems less probable after a new six-nations agreement made with North Korea in February 2007, under which its nuclear facility at Yongbyon must within 60 days be 'shut down and seal[ed] for the purpose of eventual abandonment'. In return, aid equivalent to 50,000 tonnes of fuel oil was to be sent within the same periods. With Kim Jong Il it is impossible to know what this will add up to in the long run.

The hope that this will never happen depends on the certain knowledge that Kim Jong Il must have that his regime's survival, after whatever counteraction the US and its allies might take, would be counted in days, if not hours. This assumes, however, a capacity for rational and pragmatic thinking hardly justified by recent history. Those concerned for the peace of the world in the twenty-first century should keep their eyes on Korea.

THE ROK TURNS TO DEMOCRACY

Apart from the continuous confrontation with the KPDR, across the DMZ, there are three facets to the history of the ROK in the same period. First, the election, on 16 December 1987, of Roh Tae Woo as president was the beginning of effective democratic government, following the oppressive and dictatorial regimes of Syngham Rhee, Park Chung Hee and Chun Doo Hwan, which together spanned a period of more than forty years dominated by the ideology known as *bukuk gangbyong*, or 'rich state, strong army'.[35] Second, at the end of 1995, large-scale corruption, which had been endemic for thirty years or more, was exposed as never before, so much so that two former presidents, Chun and Roh, were tried and sentenced to prison, as a result of a succession of dealings that also involved their successors, Kim Young Sam (1993–98) and Kim Dae Jung (1998–2003). Third, the economy could no longer maintain the remarkable growth achieved under Park and Chun (1961–88), so that in 1997 the ROK suffered, as much as any other country, from the Asia economic crisis.

As for new style democracy in the ROK, there have now been four presidents, Roh Tae Woo (1988–93), Kim Young Sam (1993–98), Kim Dae Jung (1998–2003) and Roh Moo Hyun (2003–) elected since 1987. Roh Tae Woo was the last president from the military, but by force of circumstance he was denied the chance of adopting the authoritarian style of his predecessors. Neither he nor his successors to date made any serious attempt to bypass or subvert the reform the constitution adopted in 1988. None of them had an easy ride, but then they were all, in varying degrees, authors of their own misfortunes, which proved to be a grave handicap in dealing with the other factors mentioned in the previous paragraph.

The new democratic regimes were confronted by two opposing forces, the chaebol, long entrenched in power, on one side, and organized labour, which only came into its own at the end of the 1980s, on the other. The brutal suppression of the Kwangju uprising, in 1980, was a major set-back to labour, and it was only in 1987, as the Chun regime neared its end, that unions could operate effectively on a large scale, free of government-supported harassment.[36] In the mid-1990s the admission of the ROK to both the World Trade Organization (WTO) and the Organization for Economic Cooperation and Development (OECD) led to multilateral pressures for economic liberalization.[37] This meant that although the conflict of interests between the chaebol and organized labour only became acute at the end of the 1990s, following the economic crisis of 1997, attempts to reform both sides were essential to the policies both of Kim Young Sam and Kim Dae Jung. Kim Young Sam's earliest reforms, in 1993, were designed to reduce the scope of government intervention in the financial sector, encouraging, at the same time, greater foreign participation.[38] If, in principle, this should have reduced the chaebols' involvement in politics (which had involved widespread corruption), in practice it gave them access to new foreign funds at a time when they were already drastically over-committed to new investment.

On the labour side this meant that wage rates raced far ahead of gains in productivity,[39] at a time when new legislation, introduced to meet trade union demands, made effective sanctions almost impossible. Attempts by Kim Young Sam to allow lay-offs to the chaebols led to nation-wide strikes with some 500,000 workers on the streets. The legislation sponsored by the president was withdrawn, but by this time the eighth largest chaebol, the Kia Group, had collapsed, preceded by other high-profile business failures. This was the last straw for the ROK economy.[40] In December 1997 there was a run on the Korean *won* by foreign investors, and the ROK faced the prospect of defaulting on its foreign debts. In just over a year per capital income, measured in US dollars, fell by nearly 40 per cent.[41] Daewoo, the second largest of the chaebols – which in the 1960s had built the world's largest shipyard – was only saved from complete bankruptcy by a radical restructuring which left nothing to shareholders.[42] For the country as a whole rescue by the IMF was the only way out, and the $58.35 billion loan finally agreed was the largest in its history. In exchange the ROK had to agree an austerity programme – including the lay-off of tens of thousands of workers – to stabilize its currency: this was to be the first challenge confronting Kim Dae Jung after he defeated the candidate adopted by Kim Young Sam's party in the presidential election of December 1997.

Given the history of Kim Young Sam's administration, particularly in its final days, it was to be expected that Kim Dae Jung, who in 1992 had formed his own National Congress for New Politics (NCNP) to oppose Kim Young Sam's Democratic Liberal Party (DLP) – a familiar strategy in the politics of the ROK – would win the presidential election of 1997. Given his past history, as related in this chapter, he had all the qualifications for carrying out a policy of radical reform. In the election, however, Kim Dae Jung's NCNP had only won 78 out of 299 seats in the National Assembly, while his opponent's party – a successor to the

DLP – had a majority. After state prosecutors and tax inspectors had done their work on opposition members, several were ousted, while a sufficient number of others changed sides to enable Kim Dae Jung to form a coalition government enjoying a small majority – a poor reward for a man who had given so much to the cause of democracy. If this was a typically Korean way of dealing with a problem known as *yeoso yadae*, or 'small government, large opposition,'[43] it was no formula for the strong government the country needed. Although, during his critical first year, 1998, Kim Dae Jung largely failed to reform the chaebol or reduce their power, the trade unions did hold back from organizing large-scale strikes. In his second year, with his hand strengthened as the economic crisis began to bite, he did much better, and did more to remove the barriers to economic liberalization characteristic of 'Confucian capitalism' than any of his predecessors.[44] Per capita income was restored to its level before the 1997 Asian economic crisis.[45]

Internationally Kim Dae Jung did better still: his 'sunshine policy' led to a summit meeting with Kim Jong Il in February 2000, with the award of the Nobel Peace Prize 'for his work for democracy and human rights in South Korea and in East Asia in general, and for peace and reconciliation with North Korea in particular' later in the year. Already, in October 1998, a state visit to Tokyo had ended with an official apology from the Japanese prime minister Keizo Obuchi, for atrocities committed during the colonial era. In the final two years of his administration Kim Dae Jung's greatest success was hosting the 2002 World Cup, leaving his successor, Roh Moo Hyun, to preside over the remarkable recent recovery of the ROK economy, which is now the twelfth largest in the world.[46] As for the KPDR, Roh has promised to continue his predecessor's sunshine policy: his somewhat unexpected election at the end of 2002 could well have been a reaction, on the part of voters, to President Bush declaring the KPDR to be part of the 'axis of evil'.

6

Thailand: a history of success

THE ACCIDENTAL HISTORY OF THAI INDEPENDENCE

In the history of Southeast Asia, after the end of the Pacific War, the kingdom of Thailand was a special case. In spite of the fact that the country was occupied by Japanese forces throughout almost the entire war, there was a continuity in government from the capital, Bangkok, which had no parallel elsewhere.

Thailand retained its independence throughout the nineteenth century largely because of the diplomatic skill of two remarkable kings, Monkut (1855–68) and Chulalongkorn (1868–1910). Siam, as the kingdom was then known, still paid a high price in terms of rights granted to foreign powers, similar to those that China had been forced to accept for the treaty ports. Although the court lost its monopoly rights, this was compensated for by stronger control over opium, alcohol and gambling. At the same time commodity trade with the West, based mainly on rice, but supplemented by teak and tin, expanded beyond all bounds. Roads were built, new canals dug, shipyards opened, a state printing office was set up, silver money was coined for the first time and the learning of foreign languages encouraged.

For all this it was essential to recruit foreign specialists who would westernize Siam. The appointments made, particularly in the field of public finance – where traditional institutions were archaic and corrupt – reflected the dominant position of Britain in Southeast Asia. This also meant that intellectually promising princes were sent to be educated in England's top schools.

At the other end of the scale Chinese labour was brought in for irrigation and other infrastructural programmes. These included the railways, which over a thirty-year period extended to cover the whole area from the upper Chao Phraya River, down to and across the frontier with Malaya, to reach Johore, opposite Singapore, in 1918, with a new causeway completing the link in 1923. This meant that Siam had to give up its claims to the sultanates of Kedah, Kelantan and Trenganu, although cession only became complete with the Anglo-Siamese treaty of 1909. (Already, in 1824, the sultanates of Perak and Selangor, by agreeing a treaty with Britain, had ensured that they would not be incorporated in Siam.)

Considerable territory in both Laos and Cambodia acquired by Siam in the eighteenth century was also ceded to France in a series of treaties agreed during the period 1867–1907.

In return for its loss of territory Siam benefited, in 1896, from a joint declaration, by both Paris and London, guaranteeing the independence of the Chao Phraya valley, the heartland of the kingdom. A year later, a secret agreement between London and Bangkok provided that no third power should be allowed in Siam without prior agreement by the British. Bangkok also agreed not to accept any French or Russian proposal to build a canal across the Kra isthmus, where at some points less than 50 kilometres separates the Indian Ocean from the Gulf of Thailand. This ensured the dominant role, in world commerce, of Singapore, Britain's major investment in Southeast Asia. The Entente Cordiale of 1904, between London and Paris, made certain, however, that Siam, in spite of all that it had ceded as a result of treaties made with the great powers, would always retain its independence.

On the economic side, the rights acquired by Europe and America following the series of treaties agreed in the period 1855–68, made it extremely difficult for Siam to protect any infant industry, even one producing exclusively for the domestic market. Instead the kingdom had to be content to be a market for Western manufactured goods, to be paid for by the export of primary products – in twentieth-century terms, a typical dependency situation. On the other hand, the half-century preceding the death of Chulalongkorn in 1910 witnessed a vast expansion of rice cultivation, and a tenfold increase in Siamese exports. There was no longer any military threat from Siam's historic enemies, Burma and Vietnam – whose rulers, if not overthrown, had been rendered harmless by British and French imperialism.

In 1910, therefore, with the present frontiers of the country all laid down by treaty, the stage was set for the indefinite future. In the developing world Siam, in keeping its independence, had proved to be luckier than almost any other state, and as the rest of this chapter will show, its good fortune has continued to this day in its successor state of Thailand.

The most critical shortcoming, in 1910, was that the greater part of the population, consisting of peasant cultivators of rice, hardly shared in Siam's prosperity, although – in contrast to the Dutch East Indies and the Philippines – they had abundant land. The king, supported by an extensive royal and noble elite, controlled the greater part of the land, labour and capital resources. What is more, the treaties with Britain and France encouraged the elite to devote their country's increasing economic surplus to conspicuous consumption rather than to capital investment. It was mainly the Chinese merchant community that exploited the window of opportunity provided by export surpluses. To judge from population growth this was considerable: in the first half of the twentieth century, the number of Chinese increased from 300,000 to 3,000,000, representing an increase from 5 to 15 per cent of the total population.[1]

After 1910 Siam stagnated under two weak kings, Vajiravudh (1910–25) and Prajadhipok (1925–35). On 24 June 1932, during the reign of the second of these a secret cabal of 141, calling itself the People's Party, seized power in less than three hours. The leaders of this *coup de théâtre* were minor bureaucrats and junior officers – many with radical ideas acquired while studying in France – who had long been dissatisfied with the backwardness of the monarchy and its disregard of their potential contribution to government service. The king, who already had his own reform programme, but had been persuaded to postpone it, accepted the coup's reforms, and so brought to an end Siam's absolute monarchy. By the end of the year a new constitution gave Siam a new National Assembly with half its members elected by popular vote and the others appointed.

At this point politics began to polarize between a young radical reformer, Pridi Phanomyong (Pridi), and a military faction led by Luang Phibunsongkhram (Phibun), who had played an important part in suppressing a revolt of provincial garrisons in October 1933. Although both Pridi and Phibun had taken part in the 1932 coup, the former's main support came from the elected members of the National Assembly, and the latter's from the appointed members. This was no simple balance of power, since at least three other factions were represented in the National Assembly. The political line-up became too much for King Prajadhipok, particularly since the 1933 revolt had led the military, who were strong among the appointed members, to distrust him. Concerned at the lack of key military support, he abdicated on 2 March 1935. The National Assembly then offered the throne to his son, Prince Mahidol, a ten-year-old boy at school in Switzerland: there he remained – with his powers being entrusted to a Regency – until after the end of World War II. This increased the power of Phibun, who became minister of defence, and diminished that of Pridi, who became foreign secretary until a cabinet reshuffle lost him his office and banished him, effectively, to study in Europe. Finally, following national elections in November 1938 – the first ever with universal suffrage – Phibun became prime minister for the first time on 26 December, recalling Pridi to become his minister of finance.

Phibun soon established himself as a major, and at the same time ruthless figure in the history of his country. Within a month of becoming prime minister he discovered a plot against his government, and after arresting some forty of his opponents, had eighteen executed after a show trial – the first political executions in more than a century. He also amended the constitution to extend from ten to twenty years the period during which half the members of the National Assembly would be appointed.

At popular level Phibun's most significant move was to change the name of the country from Siam to Thailand. The policy of 'Thailand for the Thai' was designed to encourage the allegiance of all ethnic Thais, including the millions outside the country, at the expense of the ethnic Chinese inside it. Here the war between China and Japan, which had begun in 1937, was a key factor. The Chinese community not only remitted vast sums of money to China, but organized anti-Japanese boycotts at a time when Japan was becoming a major trading partner. One leading supporter of Phibun even compared the Chinese in Thailand with the Jews in Germany, with obvious implications for government policy. New laws, discriminating against the Chinese, were enacted. They were barred from certain professions, while Chinese language schools and newspapers, together with new immigration, were severely restricted. Xenophobic policy was not, however, confined to the Chinese. Because a good Thai was Buddhist, both Muslims (an important minority in many parts of Thailand, particularly the southern provinces bordering on Malaya) and Christians were denied fundamental economic rights, particularly in employment. Even so, there was little outright persecution.

THE JAPANESE OCCUPATION AND ITS AFTERMATH

Thailand's position during the Pacific War was equivocal, with Phibun on record as having allied his country with Japan, while Pridi had maintained a low profile. Fundamentally, Bangkok, true to form, reacted at every stage to the way the wind was blowing. Following Pearl Harbor, Thailand soon became an ally of Japan – for which it was rewarded by recovering provinces whose cession to the British in Malaya and the French in Indochina was agreed in the 1909 treaty. This was not pure opportunism by the Thais: in the immediate aftermath of Pearl Harbor the alternative to the Japanese alliance was a Japanese military occupation, with all that meant for the treatment of local populations.

Long before Hiroshima, however, a very successful Thai resistance movement opened the way for the country to be counted as an ally by Britain and the United States. With the unexpected Japanese surrender on 15 August 1945 Bangkok reacted immediately to the new situation; Pridi, taking advantage of the fact that Seni Pramoj, Bangkok's Ambassador in Washington at the time of Pearl Harbor, had conveniently failed to deliver the note declaring war, pronounced the alliance with Japan not only illegal but null and void. Seni Pramoj's reward, in 1945, was to be invited by the National Assembly to return to Thailand and become prime minister.

Washington was ready to accept the newly reconstituted Thai government at face value. Thai troops had never actually engaged in war against the allies, and the alliance with Japan had certainly spared Thailand much of the devastation suffered in the rest of Southeast Asia. London took a different view. Japan had invaded both Malaya and Burma from bases in Thailand, but Japan, in any case, would have overrun Thailand in a matter of days. Thailand would then have suffered not only considerable losses in men and equipment but also a much harsher regime under Japanese occupation. In the end few British demands – which included the right to station troops indefinitely in Thailand – were met, but the Thais readily agreed to withdraw to the frontiers with Burma and Malaya agreed in the 1909 treaty. They also accepted the obligation to sell a substantial annual quota of rice, at concessionary prices, to other countries in Southeast Asia which had suffered much more under Japanese occupation. This form of reparation proved to be a considerable break on economic development until it was cancelled in 1949.[2]

France had more difficulty in recovering the parts of Laos and Cambodia lost to Thailand in 1941. Given the war record of the Vichy government, US support could not be counted on, and Thailand only yielded when, in 1947, France threatened to veto its application to join the UN. This surrender was very poorly received within Thailand.

Thailand, with strong US support, lost little time in restoring representative government. In December 1945, the young King Ananda Mahidol returned home to occupy the throne for the first time in his own right. Then in January 1946 elections were held and in March Pridi became prime minister. By May he had brought in a new constitution, providing for a bicameral legislature on the American model with a fully elected lower house.

If, in 1946, the outlook for the future could hardly have been more promising, events soon led to a period of chaotic government. First, in April, the Thai Supreme Court halted the prosecution of Phibun, and his wartime associates, for their collaboration with the Japanese. This was a popular decision, since most Thais accepted that what Phibun had done, when confronted by the Japanese in 1941, was in their best interests. At this stage, in 1946, Phibun and his supporters among the military prudently decided to keep a low profile, but the court's decision meant that sooner or later they would be a force to be reckoned with.

A much more sinister event occurred on 9 June 1946. The young king was found dead in bed, shot through the head with a pistol. The government first declared the death to be an accident, but after American and British doctors had concluded that this was a case of murder, the three most likely perpetrators were summarily tried and executed. The Thai people, remembering Pridi's pre-war anti-royalist stance, held him indirectly responsible, and in August he resigned and left Thailand to travel abroad. He was also condemned for having agreed to France recovering the provinces surrendered by Cambodia to Thailand in 1941. Prince Bhumibol, who succeeded to the throne – and is still king – was himself no more than a boy at school in Switzerland, and so the country was destined to work for some five years with a regency. Only in 1951 did Bhumibol return to occupy his throne.

SARIT'S KLEPTOCRACY

On 8 November 1947 Phibun, supported by a number of senior officers, including a new figure in Thai politics, Colonel Sarit Thanarat, staged a *coup d'état* which established him as the real power in the Thai government. The front man was Khuang Aphaiwong, who had already been an interim prime minister following the end of the war. After elections, called for early 1948, gave Khuang's party a majority, the coup leaders, whose party had won little support at the polls, forced his resignation in favour of Phibun. By this stage in history Phibun was able to play the anti-communist card with some effect, and Pridi, with help from the British and US Embassies, took the chance to leave the country on a Shell Oil tanker. As in the Philippines, at much the same time, American interests led to support for a man with a poor record in the Pacific War, while one with a good record was consigned to the political wilderness. Under Phibun the Chinese community also suffered, as it had in 1938, but this time for its being associated with Mao Zedong's new China. In the early 1950s Thailand's military government actively supported the United Nations in the Korean War and France in Indochina – making clear its stance in the international politics of Southeast Asia. Washington showed its appreciation when, on 8 September 1954, the Treaty of Manila designated Bangkok as the headquarters of the new Southeast Asia Treaty Organization (SEATO). This was essentially an American initiative in response to the communist threat in Vietnam, following the defeat of the French army at Dien Bien Phu.

Phibun, once in office, became the focus of attempted coups, and critically, Sarit, who commanded the first army, located in Bangkok, turned against him in 1956. Phibun tried to save his position with a rigged election in early 1957, but this only gave Sarit the pretext he needed to take over the government. This he succeeded in doing by means of a bloodless coup – enjoying considerable popular support – on 17 September 1957. Sarit, after making a pretence of respecting democratic process, both so as to reassure Washington and to tide over a period of ill health requiring treatment abroad, finally assumed direct power in October 1958, arresting many of his critics and severely restricting press freedom. Parliament was sent home, the 1946 constitution was annulled, and 'communist sympathizers' were arrested. Such was the beginning of a 15-year period of autocratic government, first under Sarit, and then, after his death in December 1963, under Thanom Kittachorn, who had been his deputy.

Sarit, as a charismatic leader, took such diverse characters as JFK and the

Egyptian Gamal Nasser as his role models. Political instability in Thailand was blamed on alien institutions – particularly those associated with radical politics – so that Sarit readily identified his opponents as communists. King Bhumibol accepted the role of a semi-sacred monarch, to be the focus of ancient ceremonies revived by Sarit. Visits abroad, much encouraged by Sarit, also showed the king to be an excellent ambassador for Thailand. Although the government was paternalistic, Sarit still claimed to be a revolutionary, intent on restructuring the social and political order of Thailand.

Sarit assumed power just at the time that the US was beginning to become deeply involved in Vietnam, and Washington was not slow to recognize how important a part Thailand must play in the conflict in Southeast Asia. Since the mid-nineteenth century, Thailand's foreign policy had always been anchored on support from one major power, chosen according to sound principles of *realpolitik*. Until the beginning of the Pacific War in 1941, this had been the United Kingdom; then, as related above, Japan took over until its defeat in 1945. After the war it was soon clear that only the US could guarantee a prosperous future for Thailand.

Sarit's unequivocal opposition to communist forces earned Thailand massive American aid, both economic and military, combined with a promise that the US would defend Thailand against any outside aggression. Sarit was already concerned that civil war in Laos would end with the Pathet Lao, supported by North Vietnam, gaining power, so bringing communism to the borders of Thailand. (In 1961 the Rusk–Thanat agreement of 1961 – signed as a result of the continuing crisis in Laos – also committed the US to defend Thailand against internal subversion.) In Cambodia also, King Norodom Sihanouk's close ties with communist forces also threatened Thailand – at least in the perception of senior Thai officers intent on increasing their power. On the other hand, although Thailand had been a member of SEATO since 1954, Sarit could not persuade the other members to promise to support him in any conflict with Laos and Cambodia.

Washington's support was therefore critical, and enabled Sarit to invest massively in the economic development of his country. Particularly in poor and densely populated areas there were vast improvements in roads, irrigation, agricultural support services and electricity supply, while education expanded at every level, from primary schools to universities. The Friendship Highway, linking Bangkok to the banks of the Mekong River, opposite Laos, in the impoverished northeast of Thailand, was a major achievement, only made possible by US aid.[3]

At the same time a new National Economic Development Board became responsible for centralized planning, encouraging both local private investment and foreign direct investment – with such success that the average growth rate of the economy in the ten years from 1959 to 1969 was 8.6 per cent.[4]

Sarit, already in poor health when he assumed power in 1958, died on 8 December 1963. As with almost any other successful dictator in the region – just think of Marcos and Suharto – his five years of power gave him ample opportunity to feather his own nest. He died worth some $150,000,000, leaving two wives and more than 50 mistresses. His rule, as he always intended, had proved to be revolutionary, in that he had sowed the seeds for a transformation of Thailand's economy. In the end Sarit's policies would be killed by their own success, since the new middle classes, educated and prosperous as never before, would insist on adopting Western values incompatible with Sarit's traditional ordering of society.

THE WASHINGTON CONNECTION

Sarit was succeeded by Thanom Kittikachorn, who, once in office, pursued his own agenda in foreign policy, based on good relations with the non-communist governments of Laos and Cambodia. When it came to actual intervention in Laos, the low profile maintained by both Thailand and the US encouraged both North Vietnam and China to support insurgency within Thailand.

Thanom reacted with even greater willingness to grant the US every possible facility for intervention in the conflict in Vietnam. In 1964 the USAF established an air-base at Nakhom Sawan, 255 km north of Bangkok, and other military installations soon followed. By 1968 there were some 45,000 US troops – mainly air-force – in Thailand, actively engaged in both air and ground operations in Laos and Vietnam. By 1969 Thanom had also committed 11,000 Thai servicemen to supporting the US in South Vietnam. One result was the development of a road network which, while meeting the needs of the military, also brought great economic advantages to rural areas.

The growing prosperity resulting from Thai involvement in the war in Southeast Asia brought unprecedented opportunities for corruption, particularly in connection with construction projects undertaken by the local Chinese commercial elite. Many of these provided the basis for what would later become an extremely lucrative tourist industry.

By the beginning of the 1970s the tide was beginning to turn against Thanom. US President Nixon, committed to disengagement in Vietnam, adopted a policy of 'Vietnamization', which meant 'letting Asians fight their own battles'.[5] For Thailand this meant rural revolt, not only in the poor northeast of the country, close to Laos and North Vietnam, where the rebels enjoyed Chinese support, but also in the extreme south, where ethnic Malays – with their own language, Yawi – were taking up the banner of Islam. Thanom, intent on his own survival, appealed in vain to the new middle classes, pointing out how they had benefited from the economic, social and educational transformation of Thailand under his regime. While students rebelled, demonstrating particularly against the influence of the growing Japanese trading community, the middle classes, questioning the traditions so dear to the heart of Sarit, preferred to adopt a Western way of life.

As with Suharto in Indonesia, the authoritarian regimes of Sarit and Thanom in Thailand subverted the country's harmony and stability. Where in 1960 the Thai economy was based on agriculture, forestry and mining, by 1970 it had been transformed by massive diversification, urbanization and a steady increase in population. With a predominantly young population, Thailand was becoming crowded and overpopulated, although, significantly, the Chinese population, partly as a result of assimilation, had declined. A policy of import substitution had stimulated manufacture for the home market, with considerable increase in industrialization – so much so that by 1975 industry's contribution to the Thai economy, in terms of value added, was greater than that of agriculture.[6] Here rice lost its lead, and in the late 1970s tapioca became the main agricultural export. At the same time the phenomenal growth of tourism continued.

By the end of the 1960s Washington, concerned for the local impact of its policies for Southeast Asia, was no longer comfortable with Thanom's authoritarian military regime. In 1968 this dissatisfaction, combined with that of Thailand's new middle classes, led Thanom to introduce a new constitution, with a bicameral parliament similar to that introduced by the 1932 constitution. In February 1969 elections under the new constitution, by giving Thanom's party a majority in the lower house, enabled him to continue as prime minister.

THE DEMOCRATIC COMEBACK

In spite of his success in 1969, by the end of 1971 Thanom perceived the need to strengthen his position, and so in November he staged an *auto-coup*,[7] dissolved parliament and set up, once again, a military government under an interim constitution.

This was a last-ditch stand when the old order was collapsing under historic forces, but an old style military coup worked no more. Finally students, who constituted a major political force – with as many as 500,000 demonstrating at one time – demanded a new democratic constitution and the release from prison of critics of the government. In this crisis the army, supported by King Bhumibol, refused to act against civilians. On 14 October 1973, Thanom and Praphas resigned and went into exile.

There followed a new civilian government, led by Sanya Dharmasakti, who, with a new constitution providing for a fully elected unicameral parliament, called elections for January 1975. The left, with unprecedented freedom of action, went to town with many different parties competing in the election. With no single party gaining a clear majority the result was a succession of weak coalition governments, based on the minority Democratic Party. Of these two were led by the veteran prime minister, Seni Pramoj – who was no more successful than he had been in 1945. At the same time the political situation changed radically when, in March 1975, the US, confronted by a popular outcry, began to withdraw its troops from Thailand – just a month before it abandoned Vietnam and Cambodia. Finally, in July Thailand established diplomatic relations with China.

In a chaotic political situation, characterized by strikes, demonstrations, and agitation for land reform – all quite out of character with traditional Thai doctrine of *mai pen rai*, or 'live and let live' – new elections were held in April 1976. Although the coalition leaders' Democratic Party just survived, the poor performance of the left-wing parties led to both student extremism and right-wing backlash – in which Buddhist monks were particularly active. Several left-wing leaders, harassed by the police, fell to political assassins.

Then, in October, Thanom, under the pretext of entering a monastery to acquire merit on behalf of his dying father, returned from exile. Students, enraged by the welcome he received, protested violently. The reaction of right-wing forces, with police and military connivance, led to many brutal killings, particularly at Bangkok's Thammasat University. Although Thanom did not regain power, after 6 October 1976 a new authoritarian and repressive government drove many into exile or insurgency in the hills. Once again Thailand acquired a new constitution, with elections to be held in 1979. By this time the Vietnamese invasion of Cambodia had led to thousands of refugees finding sanctuary in the east of Thailand, where they lived side by side with guerrilla groups operating across the border. Thailand, confronted at close range by the military power of Vietnam (which far exceeded the combined power of ASEAN) appealed, successfully, to both China and the US for support. This was not enough to save the government. With only 24 per cent of those qualified voting, the planned elections, held on 22 April 1979, drastically failed to confirm its claim to popular support.

This was the last straw. The result of the events of the late 1970s, both in Thailand and in the world at large, was economic downturn and the collapse of the military government. In March 1980 the commander-in-chief of the army, General Prem Tinsulanonda, although not a member of parliament, was asked to form a government by the major parties. Assured of majority support in parliament under the new constitution, Prem chose a mainly civilian cabinet, appointing experts to key positions in the economy. This was critically important since by the end of the 1970s the new middle classes had been hard hit by a high rate of inflation caused by vastly increased petrol prices and a world slump in primary commodities. At the same time, Prem's good record, both as an effective leader of counter-insurgency operations in northeast Thailand, and as being free from corruption, won the support of King Bhumibol.

In the 1980s Prem succeeded in neutralizing the Vietnamese threat in border areas. Thailand could call not only on US military support, but also on help from ASEAN in getting Vietnam to withdraw its troops from Cambodia – so making possible a broader government there. China also played a significant part by helping the Khmer liberation movement led by King Norodom Sihanouk, described in chapter 8.

After governing for longer than any other prime minister in Thai history, Prem retired in July 1988. By and large Thailand, during his years in office, was strong and resilient, largely as a result of his skilled diplomacy. In 1983 national parliamentary elections rightly confirmed Prem's version of military government. He was greatly helped by King Bhumibol, who was popularly regarded as being disinterested and accessible, looking after the interests of all Thais. The long-term legacy in the 1980s was a new sense of national community, with middle class commitment to a hierarchy structured by 'nation, religion and monarchy', while the power of the military steadily declined. It also helped that the economy enjoyed an annual growth rate of 13 per cent.

Although after Prem's retirement Thailand enjoyed the first all-civilian, all-elected government in its history, good times could not last. By the end of the 1980s, government corruption, at the highest level, was again rampant – this time encouraged by a new factor, the traffic in drugs produced within the so-called Golden Triangle, described in Chapter 15. On 23 February 1991, the head of the National Council for Public Order (NCPO), General Suchinda, staged a *coup d'état*, which led – in a way only too familiar to the Thai population – to a new constitution, under which elections were held in March 1992. This would have been all very well, had not Samakkhitham (meaning 'solidarity') been the party winning the greatest number of seats. Its leader, however, was implicated in the drug traffic, and so was not acceptable to Washington.

The NCPO intervened to impose Suchinda as prime minister. Another leading political party, Phalang Dharma (meaning 'force of Dharma') reacted with increasingly violent mass demonstrations in Bangkok. On 17 May Suchinda declared martial law, leading to three days of rioting. Government offices were set on fire and the police fired on the crowds of demonstrators, leaving some fifty dead and hundreds of wounded. This was all too much for Suchinda, who resigned on 24 May.

The way was open for a coalition government formed by the four parties which had done best in the March elections. Each of these had its own regional base, although only one, Prachathipat ('democracy'), was strong in Bangkok and the economically dominant south of Thailand. Its leader, Chuan Leekpai, was the obvious choice for prime minister, but when, in the spring of 1995, he was implicated in a financial scam in the international resort of Phuket, he dissolved parliament and called a new election for 2 July. This led to two short-term governments, each formed by one of the other parties in the 1991 coalition, with yet another election – judged to be 'the dirtiest in Thai history' – on 17 November 1996. Particularly in the face of the Southeast Asian financial crisis which was already brewing, neither was any improvement on that led by Chuan Leekpai.

By 1994, although money still flowed in from abroad, the boom was clearly past: property firms could no longer pay their debts, and foreign creditors began to withdraw their funds. Exports declined drastically and the balance of payments deficit – already too high for a sound economy – increased. Not surprisingly the many companies with substantial foreign debt resisted any devaluation of the Thai *baht*, which had long been pegged to the US dollar. The government tried to support failing businesses through its Financial Institutions Development Fund (FIDF), but it could only do so by using its international reserves to speculate on the foreign currency market. In all this Thailand suffered from the economic malaise afflicting almost every country in East and Southeast Asia, from South Korea to Indonesia – and including, most notably, Japan. What is more, in all these countries there was bound to be considerable political fall-out.

The day of reckoning came in Thailand on 2 July 1997, when the baht was floated. The Thai government appealed to the IMF for rescue – a familiar strategy for developing countries in crisis – but Washington first insisted on a full disclosure of the FIDF's true balance sheet. This revealed a financial position so disastrous that currency speculators lost no time in hammering the baht, while the net outflow of private capital added up to nearly 20 per cent of Thailand's GDP. Within a year the baht, followed by the Thai stock-market, lost more than half its value while at the same time businesses closed down – with staff inevitably laid off – consumption decreased, and banks refused new credit. In 1998 Thai banking losses added up to $8.4 billion while the economy contracted by 9.4 per cent.[8]

With the floating of the baht at a time of a conspicuously failed government new elections were inevitable. With his party, Prachathipat, gaining the largest number of votes, Chuan Leekpai became prime minister for the second time. Given the dismal record of the two governments that followed his retirement in 1995, his return to power was greeted with wide rejoicing, particularly from the hard-hit business community. In the event the Thai economy, from his second year in office, did begin to recover, but this was not enough to save him, when elections were next held, in 2001.

THE CHARISMA OF THAKSIN SHINAWATRA

Thaksin Shinawatra, whose *Thai Rak Thai* ('Thais love Thais') party, with some 70 per cent of the votes cast, defeated Chuan's Prachathipat in 2001, is a man with a clear sense of destiny. Born in 1949, Thaksin as a young man set out to make his career in the Thai Police. After graduating from the Police Academy in 1973, Thaksin went on to an American master's degree and doctorate in criminal justice. In all he served nine years in the police, but plainly he had set his sights higher than his final police rank of lieutenant-colonel.

After two early business failures, Thaksin in the late 1980s set up a new venture to sell computers to the police. This time he struck pay dirt, while vehemently repudiating any suggestion of crony capitalism. One thing led to another and by the end of the century his Shin Corporation was the largest media and telecommunications business in Thailand, and he was the richest man in the country. Money counted as always in Thailand, and in 1998 Thaksin used his money to found Thai Rak Thai, with key positions in the party going to members of his family and Shin Corporation associates.

Thai Rak Thai fought the 2001 election from a populist platform, with Thaksin claiming that the prevailing austerity resulted from Chuan's unquestioned acceptance of the regime imposed by the IMF in 1997. In any case, Thaksin was intent on being proactive in government, following in the footsteps of Mahathir in Malaysia and Lee Kuan Yew in Singapore – the two most successful strong men in Southeast Asia.[9]

Whatever the IMF may have thought, Thaksin had the wind behind him. His policies have greatly increased the prosperity of the countryside at grass-roots level, while foreign corporations have returned to invest in Thailand. (General Motors' new Thai plant now exports Opel Zafiras to Germany.)

Thaksin, ever the policeman, fought a brutally effective campaign against drug-dealers, with hundreds being gunned down in shoot-outs – many occurring in turf-wars in which the police were involved. He was equally brutal in dealing with Islamic militancy orchestrated by members of the Yawi ethnic minority in Thailand's three southern provinces.[10] With some 1,700 deaths, both Yawi and Thai, to account for, Thaksin's methods of enforcing law and order were clearly failing.

With Thaksin, as with any charismatic leader, much had to be taken on trust. Not everything went right with his economic policies. Foreign direct investment was much lower in 2002 (Thaksin's first full year in office) than in 2001. State-owned banks became heavily committed to Thaksin's rural development programme – with which he effectively bought the votes of the countryside – when there was little certainty about the economic returns. Although in 2004 his favoured candidate in the election for mayor of Bangkok was defeated,

Thai Rak Thai still won the 2005 parliamentary elections.

In spite of this success, Thaksin soon ran into trouble, which was largely of his own making. In January 2006 the sale of his family's controlling stake in Shin Corp. to Singapore's state-owned Temasek Holdings for a tax-free $1.9 billion was seen as a monstrous sell-out to a foreign power. There was also growing dissatisfaction at Thaksin's abysmal human rights record, characteristic of his failure to deal effectively and fairly with Islamic separatist violence in the three southern provinces adjacent to Malaya. Faced with protest rallies orchestrated by the Bangkok middle classes – who had paid much for and benefited little from his economic policies – Thaksin called new elections in April 2006. After being boycotted by the opposition parties, these were annulled by the supreme court, so leaving Thailand without an effective legislature. New elections, on terms acceptable to the opposition parties, called for on 15 October were never held. In mid-September the army Commander-in-Chief General Sondhi Boonyaratkalin staged a bloodless coup – nominating himself as acting prime minister – while Thaksin was in New York for the UN General Assembly. Significantly Sondhi was a Muslim, who had particularly resented the repressive and ineffective policies that the army had been required to carry out in the south of the country.

There was little popular reaction to the coup; rather it was accepted that Thaksin had forced the military to act. In the words of former Prime Minister Chuan Leekpai, 'as politicians, we do not support any kind of coup but during the past five years, the government of Thaksin created several conditions that forced the military to stage the coup. Thaksin has caused the crisis in the country'. At the end of September, Sondhi appointed a retired general, Surayud Chulanont, with an impeccably clean political record, to take over as acting prime minister, imposing, at the same time, a new constitution under which elections will be held in October 2007. Thaksin, having left New York for London, renounced the leadership of Thai Rak Thai. If, as seems likely with the new government, the courts rule that the party must disband following its abuse of election laws, it is unlikely ever to revive. By the end of September, 2006 two-hundred of its members of parliament had resigned. Thaksin's chances of being the 'come-back kid' are not good.

For all the political upheavals over the years since 1945 – including that of September 2006 – almost all Thai governments have been reactive, rather than proactive, when faced with the logic and pressure of economic conditions.[11] Thailand is essentially a 'soft state', in which the private sector of the economy has benefited from a climate of market-friendly dirigisme – in contrast to Malaysia or Japan. Thaksin's intent on changing course to a 'hard state' was one reason for his downfall.

All in all, Thailand has been for two centuries and more the most fortunate country in Southeast Asia. It is not for nothing that Robert Muscat's 1994 study of Thai economic development was entitled 'The Fifth Tiger'. There is, however, one considerable problem. Too much of everything – government (including the military), commerce, industry, finance or education – is concentrated in Bangkok. King Bhumibol has done his best to redress the balance by spending time in the provinces far from Bangkok, showing particular concern for irrigation – a field in which he is an expert.

As to culture and society, the country is held together by two important institutions, Buddhism and the monarchy. If Thai Buddhism has not always been free from scandal, the monarchy has been able stand above it, earning, at the same time, the loyalty of ethnic and religious minorities. In the last half-century this has been the achievement of King Bhumibol, who, while loved by almost all his subjects, has rarely intervened in politics. Finally, much is due to the Thai people themselves. As a French scholar[12] once wrote of medieval Thailand,

> Thais have always been remarkable assimilators: they never hesitated to appropriate from the civilisations of their neighbours and masters, what was necessary to get the better of them.

As to late-twentieth-century Thai politics, two views are possible about a country described as a 'semi-successful, semi-democracy':

> '... on the one hand, politics in Thailand is ... successful, pragmatic, balanced among principal forces, stable and capable of coping with the needs of the people. On the other hand Thai politics is ... self-serving, corrupt, cumbersome, inappropriate for the kingdom, and ultimately unable to solve the fundamental problems of poverty, too rapid urbanization, and inequitable economic development. Both positions can easily be substantiated by a selective use of the evidence'.[13]

In spite of Thaksin, with all his pretensions, this is still a fair description of the fundamental contradictions in modern Thailand.

7

The battle for Indochina

DIEN BIEN PHU AND THE END OF FRENCH COLONIALISM
(1945–54)

Although the image of Indochina, as presented by the French in the years leading up to the Pacific War, was of a country at peace, Vietnam, (see map, page xii) at least, was seldom free of local unrest. Before 1900 resistance to French colonialism was essentially xenophobic and inspired by traditional Confucianism.[1] In the twentieth century, and particularly after the end of the World War I, it became nationalistic, and found inspiration in radical movements outside the colony. In the mid-1930s large-scale rural uprisings led to a breakdown of colonial authority in north central Vietnam, for which the French were only too ready to blame Bolshevik agitators. At the same time, in the less accessible areas of forest and mountain, isolated populations maintained traditional cultures little disturbed by what happened in the outside world.

The roots of the Vietnam War go back to the 1930s, when, in the underground politics of French colonial Indochina, a new actor – who took good care to avoid the limelight – entered the stage. His name, Nguyen That Thanh, was authentic Vietnamese – as was to be expected for a man born in Tonkin. In the year of his birth, 1892, France's Indochina Union was only five years old. Although born to a poor rural family, he took advantage of such education as the French offered to children of his background. This was sufficient for him to leave home in 1912, when he was only just twenty: his travels took him first to London and New York, but from 1918 he spent most of his time in Paris, where in 1922 he was one of the founders of the French Communist Party. By 1924, after visiting Moscow, he was a leading figure in the international movement. In 1930, he returned home with a new name, Ho Chi Minh, and founded the Indochinese Communist Party.

The 1930s were a time of considerable popular unrest, supported by the Moscow-based Comintern. The French reaction was ruthless. Popular rural uprisings were suppressed, their leaders jailed, and sometimes executed – particularly if they were communists. Ho, however, kept out of harm's way: as often as not he was not even in the country. On the other hand the initial success of the uprisings convinced him that there would be a very considerable grass-roots support for communism, when the time was right. That time would not be long in coming. The collapse of French authority in 1941, following the concessions made to Japan (related in Chapter 1) provided Ho with the ideal scenario for taking the first step to restore the Communist Party as an effective political force. Back in Vietnam he organized a new movement, known as Viet Minh. Although local resistance to the Japanese occupying forces defined its first field of operations, Viet Minh never lost sight of its long-term objective, the end of colonial rule.

Ho's first attack on a French garrison was at the end of 1943, and such attacks, supported by partisans from China, continued sporadically throughout 1944. The Japanese, in an attempt to win support, appointed Bao Dai, who since 1932 had been head of the Nguyen dynasty – with their court at Hue the traditional rulers of Vietnam – as emperor of Vietnam, and allowed him to proclaim the country's independence on 11 March. From this time onwards Ho directed the only effective local resistance to the occupying forces. On 22 August Bao Dai, following the defeat of Japan a week earlier, renounced his rights to the imperial throne, to become, as a private citizen, Vinh Tuy, supreme counsellor to the government in Hanoi. His abdication left the way open to the full independence of Vietnam. On 2 September 1945 – the day of the formal Japanese surrender – Ho, who had taken advantage of the disintegration of the Japanese armed forces to return to Hanoi, proclaimed the independence of the Democratic Republic of Vietnam (DRV). His political credentials, based on successful resistance to both the Japanese and the French, could hardly have been better. The realization of his programme – which would not be complete until after his death in 1969 – would involve the longest and most bitterly fought struggle of the second half of the twentieth century.

On 24 August 1945, Colonel Cédille, appointed official representative of the French High Commission, was parachuted into south Vietnam. Within three days he contacted Viet Minh leaders, with the object of persuading them to negotiate their country's future on the basis of promises – long on rhetoric if short on specifics – made by de Gaulle in Paris earlier in the year. Cédille had hoped that the prospective arrival of British troops – to take over from the defeated Japanese in mid-September – would encourage the Viet Minh to come quickly to an agreement.

The position of the French in Saigon remained precarious, at least until 12 September when a company of French colonial infantry disembarked as part of a mainly British force. The British soldiers re-armed some 1,400 French prisoners held by the Japanese, and French sailors gained control of the Saigon arsenal. On 23 September 1945 the Viet Minh, forced to abandon Saigon, broke off negotiations with Cédille, and took revenge on the city of Héraud where they killed a large number of French civilians, mainly women and children. On 30 September the formal Japanese surrender was sealed by General Terauchi handing over his sword to Admiral Mountbatten, commander of all allied forces in Southeast Asia, who had come to Saigon for this occasion. In the last three months of the year the rhythm of colonial life began to be re-established in Saigon, to extend gradually to the rest of south Vietnam. Not only new British troops, but also, in much greater numbers, French troops, arrived, to restore and maintain order.

The situation in north Vietnam was somewhat different because the forces sent to take over from the Japanese came from Jiang Jieshi's China. While their commander succeeded in maintaining order in Hanoi, he did nothing to help some 5,000 French prisoners, locked up since March by the Japanese – who still guarded them. It was only on 9 October 1945, nearly a month later than in the south, that the first French troops reached north Vietnam. At the same time a new high commissioner, Jean Sainteny, who had joined up with de Gaulle in 1940, took over. In Tonkin, the northern part of Vietnam, he was immediately confronted by General Giap, in command of the Viet Minh armed forces, whose position was much stronger than in the south.

By the end of 1945, with new French troops constantly arriving, both the British and the Chinese began to withdraw their forces. While the last British soldiers left on 28 January 1946, the departure of the Chinese had to await the signing of an agreement with Jiang Jieshi at Chongjing on 28 February. This provided not only for the withdrawal of the Chinese forces from Vietnam – a process only completed on 15 September – but also for the renunciation, by the allied powers, of their extraterritorial rights in Chinese sea-ports, which, 46 years earlier, had been the *casus belli* of the Boxer Rebellion.

The French position in Tonkin was not at all easy. Although a new administration was set up in Hanoi, including, in key positions, a number of officers finally released from Japanese imprisonment, it still had to come to terms with the Viet Minh. On 6 March 1946 Sainteny and Ho signed an agreement stating the terms on which French forces would be allowed to re-occupy Tonkin, and providing that the future of Cochin China as an independent state would be decided by a plebiscite.[2] On the same day the Viet Minh engaged in combat new French troops, who had just disembarked at Haiphong. The military stand-off was then dealt with by an agreement between the French General Salan and General Giap on 3 April.

In the summer of 1946 Ho made another official visit to Paris, which led the way to negotiations at Fontainebleau broken off after two months without any result. Even so, on 14 September Ho returned to Paris to sign a *modus vivendi*, but this made no provision for the plebiscite agreed in March. Ho pleaded to Sainteny, 'Don't leave me this way; arm me against those who seek to surpass me

... You will not regret it ... If we must fight, we will fight. You will kill ten of our men, but we will kill one of yours. And in the end it is you that will tire.'[3] The die was cast.

On 25 October Ho was back in Vietnam, and on 30 October he formed his third government, in which only Marxist parties were represented. This was followed by local uprisings by Viet Minh supporters, and Ho himself, having organized one to take place in Hanoi on 21 December, withdrew to the countryside to be out of reach of French forces.

In the course of 1947 the French worked hard to establish a legitimate government, acceptable to the people of Vietnam, to counter the appeal of the Viet Minh. The process started on 14 January when Sainteny sounded out Bao Dai, who was in self-imposed exile in Hong Kong. On 5 July 1947 he offered to return as emperor of Vietnam, and following a demonstration in his favour at Hue on 13 August, the French, on 27 August, agreed to negotiate his possible return. In the meantime the French army had had some success in clearing rural areas in Tonkin of Viet Minh, and on 19 June Ho announced that he was ready to cooperate with the new French Union proposed by de Gaulle. (This did not, however, prevent the Viet Minh from organizing a general strike in Tonkin on 30 June, nor General Giap from issuing a declaration of independence on 15 September.) Finally, on 23 December, Cambodia and Laos – where, at this stage, the Viet Minh was hardly active – joined the French Union.

Six months later, on 5 June 1948, Bao Dai signed an agreement by which Vietnam would become an associate member of the union proposed by the French, but only on the understanding that its independence was recognized by Paris. This was the basis of the Elysée Accords, signed in Paris on 8 March 1949, and formally accepted on 5 June, with the result that on 30 June, Bao Dai – once again emperor of Vietnam – was able to form a new government.

By this time events in China had greatly strengthened the position of the Viet Minh in Vietnam. Long before the end of 1948 Mao Zedong's soldiers were clearly defeating the Chinese Nationalist Army. On 21 September 1949, in Beijing, Mao became the first president of the People's Republic of China. On 29 November Jiang, with the last of his soldiers, evacuated the nationalist capital, Chongqing, and on 8 December they took refuge in Taiwan. On 6 January 1950 the British government recognized Mao as Chinese head of state, and on 19 January Mao recognized Ho Chi Minh as the sole head of state in Vietnam. On 7 February the British and Americans countered by recognizing the states associated in the French Indochinese Union, and on 6 March an American mission arrived in Saigon to assess Vietnam's foreign-aid requirements. On 11 June the first shipment of arms and war material arrived at Saigon, to be followed by an American military mission on 15 July.

The name of the game was escalation, both internationally and within

Vietnam. A successful Soviet test of a nuclear bomb on 29 August 1949 raised the stakes in the Cold War. In April 1950 a top secret report of the National Security Council concluded that 'the global equilibrium was at stake in Indochina'[4] and advised that the United States must assume the unilateral defence of the entire non-communist world.

This commitment became critical on 15 June 1950 with the beginning of the Korean War, which added greatly to the strategic importance of Vietnam, particularly in the eyes of America. Also, on 27 October the Chinese Army invaded Tibet, although it was only on 9 September 1951 that the capital, Lhasa, was captured. (Two days earlier, on 7 September, the United States signed a peace treaty with Japan.) Within Vietnam there were popular demonstrations in Saigon, and the Viet Minh was actively, and often successfully, engaging French forces in rural areas. The French also began to operate in conjunction with Vietnamese troops, who, in principle, were defending their own country.

During the year 1951 the French prospects in Vietnam seemed remarkably promising. In December 1950, General de Lattre de Tassigny, a well-known war hero, was appointed high commissioner and commander of the French. Although he made little progress in resolving the conflict with the Viet Minh, on balance he held them at bay – so much so that his troops' morale was greatly improved. He made one extremely significant contact on 3 September 1951, when, on a visit to Paris, he met General Eisenhower and the influential American Senator Henry Cabot Lodge – who later was to become the US Ambassador in Vietnam. Eisenhower was already favoured as the Republican candidate for president in the election due in November 1952, so this contact had important implications for future American policy. Two weeks after the meeting in Paris, de Lattre, accompanied by Robert Schuman, the French foreign minister, arrived in Washington, where they successfully negotiated an increase in US military aid to $600 million. To reassure the Americans, de Lattre, at a press conference on 20 September, stated that the war in Vietnam was 'no longer a colonial war since Vietnam was no longer a colony … everything has been handed over to the governments of three independent states'. This went down so well that he was awarded the Congressional Medal of Honor, and by the end of the year the US was meeting a third of the French expenditure in Vietnam.[5] Then de Lattre, already diagnosed with terminal cancer, died in France on 11 January 1952. For the French in Vietnam, times would never be so good again.

The predicted election of General Eisenhower as US president, in November 1952, was particularly significant for Vietnam because of his appointing, as Secretary of State, John Foster Dulles, who had long been the man behind the foreign policy of the Republican Party. World-wide containment of communist expansion was an obsession, already explicit, during the election campaign, in the Republican platform. In the very first days of Eisenhower's administration Dulles made clear his view that the Soviet Union was intent on taking over not only Korea (where the war begun in 1950 was still being fought), but also Indonesia, Thailand, Malaya and Burma, with the control of Japan and India as more distant goals. The main threat, however, was to Indochina, which was 'in some ways more important than Korea, because the consequences of loss there could not be localized, but would spread throughout Asia and Europe'.[6] This doom-laden perspective was shared by Eisenhower, who, at a news conference in April 1954, characterized it as the 'falling domino'.[7] If Indochina was lost to the West, a whole row of dominoes, going even as far as Australia and New Zealand, would then topple. This accorded with the American mission to defend people *against* colonialism – as the Dutch had already learnt to their cost in Indonesia.[8] Just where the French would stand if the American mission succeeded in Indochina was, at this stage, an unanswered question – de Lattre's Washington statement of 20 September 1951 could hardly be taken at face value.

The war in Indochina acquired a new dimension on 13 April 1953 when the Viet Minh invaded Laos. Although – as shown by the map on page xii – Vietnam and Laos had a common frontier some thousand kilometres long, each country presented a quite different face to the outside world. They were also traditional enemies. In Vietnam itself almost all that was important, politically or economically, related to its long coast along the South China Sea. The strip of land close to the sea defined the main line of internal communications, with busy road and rail links – running mainly north–south – built by the French in the colonial era. In Tonkin in the north the delta of the Red and Black Rivers, with the major sea-port of Haiphong and the capital city of Hanoi, was the home to the greater part of the population, with a commensurate share of the economy. In the south the delta of the Mekong River defined an area of similar character with the city of Saigon, capital of Cochin-China, just to the north. Between the north and south the old kingdom of Annam occupied a relatively narrow strip of land between the sea and the frontier with Laos. Tonkin, on the other hand, contained a considerable area of densely forested hills behind the delta, so that there the frontier with Laos was much further from the sea. Topographically, however, there was little difference in the Laos frontier regions of Tonkin and Annam – both consisted of endless mountain and forest, home to hill tribes with their own culture, language and agricultural subsistence economies: opium poppies were the most likely export crop, if there was one. The terrain ruled out any modern form of communication.

Laos must be counted as one of the world's least accessible countries. A US National Intelligence Estimate of July 1955 described it as 'a primitive sparsely populated kingdom'.[9] Like Vietnam Laos' main orientation is north–south, which is also the direction of its main river, the Mekong, that for several hundred miles is its western frontier, with Thailand on the other side. Although both

Luang Prabang, the old royal capital, and Vientiane, the administrative capital established by the French, are on the Mekong, the former, surrounded by hills and forest, is extremely isolated, while the latter has the plains of Thailand on the other side of the river – which is undoubtedly why its location appealed to the French. Outside access to Laos – historically never of any great economic or political significance – was either across the Mekong from Thailand (with its own substantial Laotian minority population), or up the Mekong – not always a navigable river – from the delta in Vietnam, passing through Cambodia on the way.

All these factors made the country extremely attractive to the Viet Minh. For an army of locally recruited foot-soldiers, with relatively few heavy weapons, the cross-country trails allowed for movement and communication free from hostile interference. For modern mechanized forces, such as the French in Vietnam, the terrain was an almost insuperable obstacle. The local communist forces in Laos, known as 'Pathet Lao', could also offer powerful support to the Viet Minh – at least if the long-standing enmity between the two countries could be overcome. The part of Laos just across the frontier with Vietnam, if held by the Viet Minh and its local allies, would greatly increase its power to operate against the French forces in south and central Vietnam. When, therefore, the Viet Minh invaded Laos in 1953, and within a week were close to Luang Prabang, the situation for the French was very serious.

On 8 May 1953 the French forces in Indochina acquired a new commander-in-chief, General Henri Navarre, a man whose poor knowledge of the country was considered an advantage by the government that appointed him. The hope that he would have a fresh approach to dealing with the Viet Minh was soon justified. Within two months Navarre presented a new plan for a large-scale airborne operation to be carried out at the end of the year.

The target area of Operation Castor, launched by Navarre at dawn on 20 November 1953, was a long valley in the remote northwest corner of Tonkin, close to the Laotian frontier to the west, and not all that far from China to the north. The name of the valley was Dien Bien Phu. Although surrounded by densely forested hills characteristic of the whole region, the actual area of the valley was – according to intelligence sources – suitable for modern warfare on French terms. If occupied in sufficient force, it would prove to be a stronghold for attacking Viet Minh supply routes through Laos. Given that Dien Bien Phu was separated from the main French bases in the delta area of Tonkin by territory held by the Viet Minh, a successful airborne assault was essential to the capture and occupation of the valley.

Operation Castor, at least in its early phases, was carried out according to plan so that by the New Year, 1954, Dien Bien Phu had become a French stronghold, which with newly constructed airstrips could be supplied and reinforced, to the point that the Viet Minh in Laos would be fighting a losing battle. This, at least, was Navarre's rationale for the whole operation. On the other side, the Viet Minh commander, General Giap, well realizing what he was facing, was determined to recapture Dien Bien Phu, and formulated his own plans for achieving this end.

Giap had the advantage that his forces surrounded Dien Bien Phu, commanding, on all sides, the high ground overlooking the valley. The terrain occupied by his forces may have been difficult, but for troops hardened in battle who had never used mechanized transport, it was far from being impossible. Navarre had planned Operation Castor on the basis that infantry was the only arm available to the Viet Minh, and Dien Bien Phu could be defended against any infantry assault. Giap, however, did have artillery – supplied by China in the aftermath of the Korean War[10] – and by dismantling his guns and using human transport to carry their various parts to suitable emplacements on the high ground above the valley, acquired the capability to bombard the French positions in Dien Bien Phu. It was a slow laborious process but in the space of three months Giap's gunners were ready for action, as were also engineers who would mine French positions.

The first Viet Minh assault, on 13 March 1954, was followed by a second assault on 30 March. In April, as the French became ever more hard-pressed, they asked for an American carrier to be positioned in the Gulf of Tonkin, to provide additional air-support. It was already too late to make any difference. After weeks of hard fighting, with heavy casualties on both sides, Giap's forces broke through Dien Bien Phu's defensive perimeter on 1 May 1954, and on 7 May they completed the occupation of the whole valley, having captured the local French commander, General de Castries. In an operation designed to inflict a decisive defeat on the Viet Minh, the French had themselves been decisively defeated. They had under-estimated both the strength of their enemy and the tactical skills of General Giap.

THE PARTITION OF VIETNAM (1954–1964)

As a result of the defeat at Dien Bien Phu, North Vietnam was clearly lost to the French. On 26 April 1954, only a week before the French defeat, an international conference opened at Geneva to settle the future of Korea and Vietnam. Already, on 13 April, Washington had made clear that the US would intervene in Indochina. Then, in the period 13 to 20 June, the last week of the Geneva conference, the French prime minister, Mendès-France, together with the foreign ministers of China, the Soviet Union, the UK and the US and a representative of the Viet Minh, met together and agreed a treaty, signed on 20 June, for ending hostilities in Indochina.

In the first week of August ceasefires came into effect in central Vietnam, Laos and Cambodia, and on 10 August an international commission arrived at Hanoi to supervise the carrying out of the terms of the armistice. On 14 August an agreement for the exchange of prisoners was signed by the French and the Viet Minh. During October 1954 the French Army began to evacuate North Vietnam (a process only completed on 13 May 1955 when the control of Haiphong was ceded to the Viet Minh), and on 16 December Jean Sainteny, appointed to represent French interests, was received by Ho. On 8 December China agreed to send aid to the Viet Minh to help reconstruct North Vietnam, and two days later, on 10 December, Washington agreed to help South Vietnam, Laos and Cambodia in the same way.

Effectively the year 1954 saw the end of the French presence in Indochina. The French had nothing to gain by remaining. Whatever the character of French policies for the future of Indochina, they always had an underlying colonial rationale. This was acceptable neither to the people of Indochina, nor to the United States, whose support, both political and economic, was essential to the survival of South Vietnam, Laos and Cambodia outside the communist bloc. In the context of international politics, France's historical commitment to the defence of these countries was taken over by the United States. This was not entirely what Washington had intended, but then to quote Henry Kissinger, 'Why France should risk lives in a war designed to end its presence in Southeast Asia was not explained'.[11]

Every post-war president of the United States made clear that his country had 'no selfish interests' – to quote from Truman's inaugural address in January 1949 – in intervening, where necessary with force, in any part of the world threatened by the advance of communism. The first test came in Korea in 1950, while Truman was still president, but the result of the armistice in 1953 was clear-cut: North and South Korea would continue as separate states, separated by a *demilitarized zone* (DMZ), roughly following the line of the 39th parallel, the frontier in the pre-war period (1945–50).

The Geneva accord of June 1954, although only provisional, adopted the same principle in dividing up Vietnam. A DMZ, separating North and South Vietnam, was established roughly along the line of the 17th parallel, which ran across the old kingdom of Annam, just north of Hue. On the east the zone was bounded by the sea, on the west, by Laos.

The American strategy for Vietnam, until well into the 1960s, was based on the principle that the government of South Vietnam, with Saigon as its capital, could defend the country against any threat from the Viet Minh north of the DMZ, simply by holding the line on its northern boundary. This line was only 70 kilometres long, and the terrain was suitable for defensive positions. If things had been that simple, the army of South Vietnam, equipped and trained by

Americans, could well have defended the country effectively into the indefinite future.

In the event two key factors ensured that a strategy that had succeeded in Korea would fail in Vietnam. The first was that the DMZ, for obvious political reasons, could not extend, at its western end, into Laos. The second factor was that from the very beginning Viet Minh enjoyed grass-roots support from locally recruited guerrillas – the so-called 'Viet Cong' – throughout South Vietnam. The Viet Cong, if supplied with sufficient arms, could be an effective military force, acting behind the lines.

Although the Americans, from the very beginning of their intervention in Vietnam, were aware of both these factors, they proceeded on the basis that the threat they represented could be contained, at least so long as there was a strong government in Saigon. The key, then, to American policy was to find, and maintain in office, a strong leader, with the greatest possible popular support. The approach was essentially different from that of the French, who, so long as they were in Vietnam, intended to maintain a colonial regime, however many political concessions were made to the Vietnamese people.

The French, if things had gone their way, were in Vietnam to stay; the Americans, from the beginning, were there to get out as soon as possible. When, following the defeat of the French in Dien Bien Phu, they began to call the shots on location in Vietnam, no one could foresee that their intervention would last more than twenty years, or that, in the end, their policy of containment would fail.

The American search for an effective leader for South Vietnam lighted upon Ngo Dinh Diem, who having served the Emperor Bao Dai in the early 1930s, resigned in 1933 in protest at the restrictions imposed by the French – but nevertheless accepted by Bao Dai. After 1933, Diem, a Catholic and a nationalist, had lived as a recluse, spending much of the time in the United States. In the years before 1954 Diem had built up something of a reputation for integrity, by consistently refusing office in the Japanese, Viet Minh and the French supported Vietnamese administrations.

Diem, with no record as a popular democratic leader, was still seen by Dulles as 'the only horse available', and so, in October 1954, became prime minister under Bao Dai. Eisenhower then sent a letter promising aid to South Vietnam contingent on Diem's 'performance ... in undertaking needed reforms ... [with] a strong government responsive to the nationalist aspirations of its people'.[12] When Diem proved to be no more acceptable to Bao Dai than he had been in Hue in 1933, the latter, on 18 October 1955, issued a decree depriving him of all his functions. Diem retaliated by staging, on 23 October, a referendum on the question 'Do the people wish to depose Bao Dai and recognize Ngo Dinh Diem as the Chief of State of Vietnam with the mission to install a democratic regime'. Diem won with 98 per cent of the votes cast, and the Democratic Republic of

South Vietnam was proclaimed on 26 October. The American Embassy would at last be able to deal with a legally constituted government.

Diem's regime was corrupt, authoritarian, cruel and, most critically, unpopular. Although Diem had nothing like the charisma of Ho Chi Minh, this did not matter to Dulles. It was sufficient that Diem was anti-communist. In the spring of 1956 he had no hesitation in detaining 15,000 to 20,000 peasants, identified as 'Viet Minh sympathizers' in 're-education camps'. Later on in the year, the American Ambassador, G. Frederick Reinhardt, after accepting that Diem was not 'running a Jeffersonian democracy', added, 'I must say that Mr Dulles makes my life a lot easier by taking a philosophical view of the question … saying that a truly representative government was certainly our objective in the long run, but one shouldn't be unrealistic in thinking it was something to be achieved in a matter of weeks or days'.[13] The American Embassy, by allowing Diem to see the Viet Minh behind all opposition, gave tacit approval to every act of oppression. There was also a price tag: by the end of Eisenhower's presidency his administration had given more than a billion dollars in aid to South Vietnam.[14] Ho's outside supporters' club was not half as generous.

By the time Eisenhower left office in 1961, the vast amounts of American taxpayers' money poured into Vietnam had created so convincing an illusion of prosperity that there was even talk of a Vietnamese economic miracle. The middle-class suburbs of Saigon, with shops full of luxury items, may have suggested this, but the development of industry and agriculture was almost completely neglected. Peasants coming into town could look into the shop windows but they could not afford to buy. Most of the money went to the military, which is what Washington really wanted. The Republic of Vietnam, under Diem, never came near to being an 'Asian tiger'. In January 1956 Eisenhower allowed himself to be persuaded that Saigon's army was 'now prepared to do a first class fighting job', dismissing the absence of any social programme, such as land reform, as a matter to be dealt with after pacification. He was also advised that 'the Communists will eventually stew in their own juices … although this might take twenty-five years'.[15]

Eisenhower's perception of reality was deeply flawed. Whatever the Americans did to equip and train the Vietnam local forces, the South Vietnam military command was based on corruption, financed by either extortion in the provinces or embezzlement of funds furnished by the Americans. The local militias never left their own outposts at night, and daytime operations were planned to go to places where, according to intelligence reports, the Viet Cong would not be present.[16] Because engaging the enemy was not part of the agenda, the Viet Cong effectively called the shots. In twenty years this pattern was not to change – not even when, in the final years, the American forces had withdrawn from the country.

In his second term of office (1957–61) Eisenhower scarcely modified his Vietnam policies. Although during this time there was something of a lull in communist pressure,[17] local guerrillas were continuously active, often with weapons and other supplies captured from local government forces. Government officials were often their targets, and by 1960 some 2,500 were being assassinated every year. Expedients, such as fortified villages, quite failed to curtail these operations of the Viet Cong. The character both of the land, and even more of the agricultural economy and society it supported, lends itself to guerrilla tactics. The vast core area of South Vietnam defined by the delta of the Mekong River is mainly devoted to the intensive cultivation of rice, the staple food of Southeast Asia. This creates a landscape of paddy fields, flooded for much of the year, separated by a network of ditches and dikes. Those who cultivate this land live in insubstantial houses built mainly of reeds, clustered in countless small villages – some with a modest Buddhist temple – connected to each other by paths, rather than roads, along the dikes. As to communications local knowledge counts for everything, and the best way to get around is on foot or by bicycle. Although this means that the distances travelled are short, this is all the local economy needs. At the same time many of the waterways are open for small craft. All in all this is a variant of so-called 'hydraulic civilization', subject, in Marxist terminology, to the 'Asiatic mode of production', in which 'villages are relatively self-sufficient, but surpluses are drawn off by a despotic state'.[18] (This summarizes how Ho Chi Minh and his followers presented it to the outside world.) The land under cultivation is not a terrain suitable for the mechanized transport of modern warfare.

In 1959 Hanoi, by establishing a continuous and reliable supply line to the Viet Cong, achieved a decisive change of gear in the war in South Vietnam. The route chosen was through Laos where the Pathet Lao was already well-established in the northeastern provinces of Laos along the frontier with North Vietnam. The Pathet Lao were allied with Prince Souvanna Phouma, the head of the ruling house, who in August 1960 seized power from the local American-backed government. As a result a large part of Laos became open to the forces opposed to Diem in South Vietnam. This was the origin of the Ho Chi Minh trail, which wound its way under a forest canopy for some 650 miles in the strip of land, some ten miles wide, just inside the frontier with Vietnam.

So much had Laos, by 1960 – Eisenhower's last year in office – become the main concern of his Vietnam policy, that he had declared himself ready to fight for the country 'with our allies or without them'.[19] When he left office in January 1961, he urged his successor, John F. Kennedy, to follow the same line. By this time, however, the Soviet leader, Nikita Khrushchev, in a speech made on 6 January, described 'wars of national liberation' as 'sacred'. This, in turn, was described by Kennedy, during his inaugural address on 31 January, as proof of the Soviet Union's and China's 'ambitions for world domination'. (It is now accepted that Khrushchev's speech was directed at Beijing, where he was being criticized both for his policy in the then current Berlin crisis and for his reservations about nuclear war.) Kennedy was also worried about credibility, as is clear from his comment that 'Now we have a problem in trying to make our power credible, and Vietnam looks like the place'.

Eisenhower's advice to fight the war in Laos was that of a soldier rather than a politician, and Kennedy, only three months in office, decided against it in April 1961. The Bay of Pigs fiasco in Cuba had already taught him about the risks involved in new foreign intervention. Kennedy, and his advisers, decided therefore that the line of defence against communist aggression must be drawn in South Vietnam, and not in a foreign country almost completely unknown to the American public – and for that matter the world at large. American diplomacy was to be the key to ensuring the neutrality of Laos – some hope when Ho Chi Minh was the adversary on the other side.

The Ho Chi Minh trail was a diplomatic as well as a logistical triumph, particularly after it had been extended into Cambodia, as described in Chapter 8. With the essential lines of communication in both Laos and Cambodia running along a north–south axis, the frontier areas to the east of the trail were of little economic importance, and they were also sparsely populated. Effectively these areas could be taken over with very little impact on either Laos or Cambodia. There was some out-migration of local populations, but these were far from the mainstream of national culture. Any local attack on the communist forces operating along the Ho Chi Minh trail would have meant fighting a losing battle against them on their own terms. Any attack on its hinterland in either Laos or Cambodia would be an egregious assault on a neutral country, responsible for little more than passive collaboration with the Viet Cong. In any case the support system maintained by the Ho Chi Minh trail would have remained intact. Withdrawal of all foreign forces from Laos and Cambodia was a pre-requisite to the restoration of the South Vietnamese Army's control of South Vietnam, and although Ho Chi Minh had agreed to this in principle, he left his own forces in place.

Kennedy's administration was always deeply involved in the internal politics of South Vietnam. This was largely the result of the situation inherited from Eisenhower combined with Kennedy's decision to ignore the advice given to him relating to Laos. Although, in South Vietnam itself, there was little threat to the survival of Diem, continuous guerrilla activity both prevented him from consolidating his position and provided him with a pretext for delaying the reforms he had promised. Any lull in guerrilla activity during 1961 was no more than the result of the Viet Cong consolidating their supply lines along the Ho Chi Minh trail. The first step in combating the Viet Cong, according to the advice of one senior State Department official, was to reduce it to 'hungry, marauding bands of outlaws devoting all their energies to staying alive'.[20] In practice, however, the Viet Cong, if ever in trouble, could always rely on support along the supply lines from North Vietnam. By the end of the year, however, the guerrilla threat, as reported by the American Embassy, was so serious that a military mission was sent to Saigon in December to assess the situation and advise on policy. In early 1962 the Viet Cong reacted by creating the National Liberation Front (NLF) in South Vietnam as its force to combat the government and its American supporters.[21]

The American position, at best, was one of stalemate, but the price to be paid for this was constant escalation in the number of US troops in Vietnam, which, during the Kennedy administration, increased from fewer than 1,000 to more than 16,000. If, in principle, South Vietnam was bound to accelerate the pace of reform as the price for increased military support, this never happened in practice. The increased number of American soldiers simply meant more money and supplies coming into the hands of corrupt officers and officials – a scenario familiar, if on a larger scale, in Indonesia and the Philippines. All the time Diem and his ineffective government were held responsible for the troubles afflicting their country. In due course Americans thought the same – although Diem was their man – so that Senate majority leader, Mike Mansfield, at the end of 1962, stated, on the basis of his own observations, that the Diem government 'appears more removed from, rather than closer to, the achievement of popular responsible and responsive government'.[22] This, needless to say, greatly increased the strength of the NLF.

Buddhist sects, long powerful in Vietnam, were prominent opponents of the government led by Diem, a Christian. This led to a show-down on 8 May 1963, when, in Hue – a traditional Buddhist stronghold – South Vietnamese troops opened fire on Buddhists demonstrating against a government order forbidding the flying of flags by religious groups. The deaths of several of the Buddhist demonstrators led to a wave of international media protest, but Diem was unmoved.

The most disliked of the men close to Diem was his brother, Ngo Dinh Nhu, who was head of the security forces responsible for the events of 8 May. Diem refused to yield to Washington's demand to replace his brother, who on 21 August had his forces raid a number of pagodas and arrest some 1,400 monks. Three days later the new US Ambassador, Henry Cabot Lodge – who as a senator had accompanied General Eisenhower to Paris in 1951 to meet de Lattre de Tassigny – made clear not only to Diem, but to Saigon's leading generals, that Nhu must go if US aid was to continue.

The generals, assured by the ambassador of 'direct support in any interim period of breakdown of central government mechanism', finally overcame their mutual mistrust and on 1 November 1963 orchestrated the murder of both Diem and Nhu. So much for the authority of the government of South Vietnam: the generals were in no way able to take over from Diem. The result was political chaos, leaving it to the Americans, led by Ambassador Lodge, to call the shots.[23]

Hanoi lost no time in taking advantage of the new situation in South Vietnam as a result of the coup of November 1963. Not only were support for the guerrillas and the level of infiltration across the frontiers with Laos and Cambodia increased, but soldiers from the regular army of North Vietnam were sent to support the Viet Cong. Then, on 22 November 1963, the assassination of President Kennedy led to Lyndon Johnson succeeding to the White House. The new president was faced, almost immediately, with a stark choice in relation to the war in Vietnam. Quite simply, either the US must substantially increase its own armed forces in Vietnam, or the collapse of South Vietnam must be accepted. The advisers Johnson took over from Kennedy all urged escalation, in spite of a number of signs that Kennedy himself was thinking about détente.

ESCALATION AND THE GULF OF TONKIN (1964–69)

Two major incidents in the war in Vietnam occurred under the Johnson administration. The first, in August 1964, was an alleged attack on the USS Maddox, an American destroyer, in the Gulf of Tonkin, off the shores of North Vietnam. The second was the Tet offensive, launched by North Vietnam on 30 January 1968. The first of these incidents occurred during Johnson's short first term in office, the second, as his second full term was in its last year. Between the two incidents the character of the war and the climate of public opinion – both in the United States and outside – changed radically.

The reality behind the Gulf of Tonkin incident, which was deliberately concealed by the Johnson administration – to be revealed only in 1971 when Daniel Ellsberg orchestrated the publication of the top secret Pentagon Papers – was that at the end of July 1964 covert raids, code-named '34A ops', were being carried out both along the coast of North Vietnam and on offshore islands. This was known both to the Pentagon, and to the commanders of USN destroyers patrolling the same stretch of coast. The official story, as then released to the public, was that the raids were carried out by South Vietnamese ships, with the object of hindering infiltration from the north. They were quite unrelated to the destroyer patrols, which belonged to a quite different operation, code-named 'DESOTO'.

On the night of 30 July 1964 South Vietnamese junks raided two offshore islands: this may have been a normal 34A op (as related, thirty years later, by US Defense Secretary Robert McNamara,[24] but it could also have been a separate joint venture controlled jointly by the CIA and the Military Assistance Command Vietnam (MACV), as recorded by Daniel Ellsberg[25]). The distinction is critical for an accurate assessment of the reaction from North Vietnam.

In broad daylight, on the afternoon of 2 August, high-speed boats attacked the USS Maddox, a destroyer on DESOTO patrol, some twenty-eight miles off the coast of North Vietnam. Torpedoes were launched and there was also automatic weapons fire. There was no damage, although McNamara relates[26] receiving a shell fragment from the deck of the Maddox, while for Ellsberg[27] this becomes a 14.5 mm bullet lodged in one of its funnels – much more likely, given the nature of the attack.

This, the first attack on a USN vessel since World War II, was reported immediately to President Johnson, who, in deciding how to react, accepted the advice given to him that the decision to attack could have been taken by a local North Vietnamese commander acting on his own initiative. On this basis Johnson was content with a note sent to Hanoi, warning that 'any further unprovoked offensive military action against United States forces [would] inevitably [result in] grave consequences', even though General Maxwell Taylor, his ambassador in Saigon, had advised that failure to retaliate would be seen as an 'indication that the US flinches from direct contact with the North Vietnamese'. Johnson did, however, order a second destroyer, the USS C. Turner Joy, to join the Maddox. In any further attack the North Vietnamese boats were to be repulsed and destroyed.

Then, on the night of 4 August 1964, the USS *Maddox* reported a torpedo attack, on both ships, by North Vietnamese patrol boats. None of the torpedoes, if they even existed, hit their targets, so the two American ships suffered no damage. The torpedoes were detected by radar, which at first also received signals possibly originating in the ships that launched them. Although the early signals from the Maddox reported 'continuous torpedo attack', so that in the end 26 torpedoes had been launched, with at least one of the attacking boats being sunk. By this time planes from American carriers were firing rockets at targets revealed by the C. Turner Joy's radar. Then, after two hours of frantic messages from the Maddox, there was suddenly an hour's silence. This was broken by a new signal from the Maddox: 'Review of action makes many reported contacts and torpedoes fired appear doubtful. Freak weather effects on radar and overeager sonarmen may have accounted for many reports. No actual visual sightings by Maddox. Suggest complete evaluation before any further action taken'. In other words, the torpedoes and the ships that launched them had about as much reality as Saddam Hussein's weapons of mass destruction nearly forty years later.

Quite simply, the instrumentation, at the level of 1964 technology, could have detected phantom signals. Even so, at a press conference on the evening of 4 August, US Secretary of Defense McNamara announced that US warships, on 'routine patrol in international waters', had suffered 'deliberate, unequivocal and unprovoked' attacks, forming part of a pattern of 'naked aggression'.[28]

The fury of the American people and of their Congress in Washington had been aroused. The president's immediate response was to order bomb attacks on North Vietnam by planes launched from the two offshore carriers, the *Ticonderoga* and the *Constellation*. Dean Rusk, Secretary of State, told Congress that 'the present attacks are no isolated event. They are part and parcel of a continuing Communist drive to conquer South Vietnam ... and eventually dominate and conquer other free nations of South Asia'.[29]

This was followed on 7 August by the Senate's Gulf of Tonkin resolution, affirming that Congress 'approves and supports the determination of the President, as Commander in Chief, to take all necessary measures to repel any armed attack against the forces of the United States and to prevent further aggression'. The president took this as the legal basis for unlimited escalation of the war in Vietnam. The American people stood by their president; Johnson won the November presidential election with a substantial majority over his Republican opponent, Senator Barry Goldwater (whose militancy, in relation to Vietnam, extended to contemplating the use of nuclear weapons).

There was no immediate change in strategy. For one thing Johnson had reason to fear that escalation in Vietnam would jeopardize the chances of success for his 'great society' programme, which had played a decisive part in winning the election. But then, at the beginning of January 1965, shortly before the inauguration, the Viet Cong twice defeated elite South Vietnamese units in battle, while at the same time North Vietnamese regular soldiers had begun entering South Vietnam. On 27 January, just a week after the inauguration, this led two of Johnson's closest advisers to present a memorandum too long to quote in full, but one passage neatly sums up the sense of stalemate in Saigon:

> The basic directive says that we will not go further until there is a stable government [in South Vietnam], and no one has much hope that there is going to be a stable government while we sit still. The result is that we are pinned to a policy of first aid for squabbling politicos and passive events we do not try to control.[30]

The choice presented was essentially between negotiation from a position of weakness and escalation of the war. This so-called 'fork-in-the-road' memorandum had almost immediate results. In the six-month period from 28 January 1965 the US troop strength increased from 23,000 to 175,000, while at the same time US National Security Adviser McGeorge Bundy, sent to Saigon by the president on the day he received the memorandum, advised that 'the current situation among non-communist forces gives all the appearances of a civil war within a civil war'.[31] The generals, when they were not fighting Buddhists, fought each other, while the politicians did nothing.

Then, on 30 January, the NLF mounted a heavy attack on a South Vietnamese Army HQ and an USAF air-base 240 miles north of Saigon, close to the DMZ. With eight American dead, and more than a hundred wounded, the way was signposted to escalation. This was the view of a meeting of the National Security Council convened by Johnson on 8 February. The only dissenting voice was that of Senator Mike Mansfield, who pointed out that 'the local populace in Vietnam is not behind us or else the Viet Cong could not have carried out their surprise attack'. If escalation went ahead, America would no longer be in 'a penny ante game'.[32] These wise words were ignored. On 19 February Johnson ordered regular air-strikes against North Vietnam to begin, and on 2 March a hundred aircraft launched from both carriers offshore and air-bases in South Vietnam bombed an ammunition depot in North Vietnam. This was the first strike in Operation Rolling Thunder, which in something over three years would lead to more bombs being dropped than had been on the whole of Europe in World War II.

During this period there was little prospect for any peace negotiations involving Washington and Hanoi, since President Johnson had made it clear that the NLF would not be allowed to participate, while Ho Chi Minh declared that it was the 'sole genuine representative of the people of Vietnam'.[33] The status of the NLF in the communist world was clear from the fact that it had its own offices in both Beijing and Moscow.[34]

In 1965 South Vietnam did, however, acquire a new head of state, Nguyen Van Thieu – a man with an unusual capacity for leadership. Thieu was to remain president until the war ended in 1975, when the American withdrawal from his country would leave him in the lurch. In the judgement of Henry Kissinger, he 'was unquestionably the most formidable of the military leaders of South Vietnam, probably the ablest of all political personalities ... He inherited a civil administration torn apart by the reckless coup against Diem, a guerrilla army threatening to overwhelm his country through systematic terror, and an invasion along a trackless border of 600 miles. He was saddled with an ally who first flooded the country with hundreds of thousands of troops and trained his army for a war not relevant to Southeast Asia; and then, while withdrawing at an accelerating rate, urged on him escalating concessions to an implacable enemy'.[35] In writing these words, for a book only published in 2003, Kissinger was no doubt being wise after the event. But in considering all that happened in the critical period, 1965–75, the fact that Thieu remained president of South Vietnam must not be forgotten.

As, in the course of 1965, the war escalated in Vietnam, two events, outside the country, changed its significance for the balance of power in Southeast Asia. The first was a declaration by Mao Zedong that China was no longer concerned to intervene in wars outside its own frontiers. Although it was no doubt a relief to Ho Chi Minh to have this assurance from his northern neighbour, he also had to accept that North Vietnam must rely on the Soviet Union rather than China for outside support. China's declared non-intervention policy was also a signal to Washington that it must never be the target of any US military operations. This was something that President Johnson was ready to accept.

The second key event in 1965 was the fall of Sukarno's government in Indonesia in August. General Suharto, who then assumed power, broke decisively with China and the rest of the communist world. Although George Kennan, the leading US authority on containing communism, told the Senate on 9 February 1966 that the Chinese had 'suffered an enormous reverse in Indonesia ... one of great significance, and one that does rather confine any realistic hopes they may have for the expansion of their authority', US government policy for Vietnam remained unchanged. Escalation was out of hand, until at the end of Johnson's term of office in 1969, some 543,000 US troops were in Vietnam.

By this time the Tet offensive of February 1968 had transformed the war. For the first time NLF troops launched coordinated attacks on units of both of the US and the South Vietnamese Army. They had the advantage of surprise, because in previous years Tet, the Vietnamese new year, had always been the occasion for a temporary ceasefire.[36] The result was that NLF forces were able to occupy, if only for a short time, both the American Embassy and the Presidential Palace in Saigon. Key military installations were also captured.

In military terms the battle, for the NLF, was at best a stalemate. Losses were heavy, and the strong points occupied could not be held against US and South Vietnamese counter-attacks. On the other hand, Tet showed that the US and South Vietnamese forces were nowhere safe; there was no part of the country where they had complete control. In March 1968, after the offensive had run its course, Secretary of State Dean Rusk stated that 'the element of hope has been taken away by the Tet offensive. People don't think there is likely to be an end'.[37] A warning note had already been sounded when Robert McNamara resigned as Secretary for Defense in the autumn of 1967, realizing that the 'continuation of our present course of action in Southeast Asia would be dangerous, costly in lives and unsatisfactory to the American people'.

On 31 March 1968 Johnson, in a speech announcing a radical change of course, said, 'We are prepared to move immediately toward peace through negotiations. So tonight in the hope that this action will lead to early talks, I am taking the first step to de-escalate the conflict. We are reducing – absolutely reducing – the present level of hostilities'. In the same speech he announced that he would not be a candidate in the presidential election due in November. The president, in effect, was conceding defeat by what he had once described as a 'ragged ass little fourth rate country'.

In his last months in office, President Johnson did not find it easy to make his words come true. North Vietnam, realizing its strength, would not play his game.

Finally, in the autumn of 1968, he agreed to talks in which both the government of South Vietnam and the NLF would take part, and on 1 November he called a halt to American bombing – except along the Ho Chi Minh trail in Laos.[38] Effectively this required the South Vietnamese 'government to recognize the legal status of the enemy determined to overthrow it',[39] and this President Thieu refused to do. Nonetheless, on 1 November 1968, Johnson announced a complete end to bombing of North Vietnam, in part because this might help Hubert Humphrey, the Democratic candidate in the presidential election. At all events, the Republican Richard Nixon was elected. All this time, American casualties were extremely high – and as the North Vietnamese General Giap pointed out, 'Once American boys being sent home in body bags steadily increase … their mothers will want to know why. The war will not long survive their questions'.[40]

THE US DÉTENTE AND THE FALL OF SOUTH VIETNAM (1969–75)

This then was the Vietnam legacy left by President Johnson, to his successor, Richard Nixon. Not far short of a million South Vietnamese soldiers were supported by more than half a million Americans. Even so the NLF infrastructure extended to 80 per cent of the hamlets, which in turn paid the price in levies on their rice and other agricultural produce. This led the US Commander, General Creighton Abrams to concentrate on protecting the population, rather than undertake large-scale offences against the NLF (which had suffered serious losses in the Tet offensive) and the increasingly numerous North Vietnamese units. The main concern was to deploy troops for the defence in depth of the major cities in the southern part of the country.

It was clear to Nixon, from the very beginning, as it had been to Johnson in his last days in office, that the number of American troops serving in Vietnam must be drastically reduced. On 20 December 1968, a month before his inauguration, Nixon had declared his readiness for negotiations with Hanoi, but the response, given on 20 December, was a demand for the unilateral withdrawal of all US troops, and a replacement of Thieu's government in Saigon. Nonetheless, the Soviet Union tried to rescue the situation with a round table conference to be held a week before the inauguration, but nothing came of what was essentially an attempt to compromise Nixon's administration before it even entered office.

The essence of Nixon's policy was to de-Americanize the war (and so make possible the promised withdrawal of US troops), and at the same time to Vietnamize it, as if all that the US had ever done was to help South Vietnam defend its right to exist as an independent state. This was part of the Nixon doctrine, requiring the reduction of the United States' role as the 'world's policeman'. In Nixon's own words, 'America cannot – and will not – conceive all the plans, design all the programs, execute all the decisions, and undertake the defense of nations of the world. We will help where it makes a difference in our national interest and is considered in our interest.'

On 6 February 1969 Thieu accepted that a sizable number of American troops could depart in the course of the year, and on 6 June Nixon convened a meeting in Honolulu, attended by a galaxy of top men, both civilian and military, from his administration, to take the final decision on the withdrawal strategy. The military, in particular, realized that the process would be irreversible – as it proved to be – and that however much the quality of the South Vietnamese armed forces might be improved, they would never win in combat with North Vietnam.

Nixon, with his supporting cast, then flew several hundred miles westward to Midway Island, where a meeting had been arranged with Thieu, who was to learn that, effectively, his death warrant, or at least that of the country he led, had just been signed in Honolulu. On 8 June, in the first critical meeting on Midway, at which only Nixon, supported by Kissinger, and Thieu, with a personal assistant, were present, Thieu himself proposed the first troop reduction.

Nixon saw the Midway conference as a political triumph, but he had in practice asked Thieu 'simultaneously to win a war, adjust his own defense structure to the withdrawal of a large American military establishment, and build democratic institutions in a country that had not known peace in a generation or democracy in its history'.[41] This was an impossible assignment.

In the US Nixon's critics had won the day. They had already achieved a halt in the bombing of North Vietnam, and now they could see the end of American military intervention in Vietnam – a result longed for by the families of US soldiers fighting there. At the same time North Vietnam could see the balance of forces on the ground changing decisively in its favour. But the war was not yet over, and US forces would still be another three terrible years in Vietnam.

Nixon's first year in office was fateful not only for the future of Vietnam, but also for that of Cambodia. On 22 February 1969 North Vietnam launched a major offensive across the DMZ: for four months casualties would be at the rate of 400 a week, so that 60 per cent of all American losses during Nixon's administration occurred in its first year.

On 30 June 1969 Nixon, visiting Saigon, issued a new 'mission statement' promising maximum help to South Vietnam, but also making clear to Thieu that continued withdrawal of US troops was essential if public support in the US was not to be forfeited. On the same day the B-52 operations were cut back, in principle as part of the commitment to de-escalation; there were almost certainly budgetary reasons as well, for the raids were proving to be extremely costly. Hanoi was in any case unmoved. On 11 August, after an eight-week lull, North Vietnamese forces attacked a hundred separate targets in South Vietnam.

Nixon's reaction was to defer consideration of the next withdrawal of US troops, but so great was the outrage, in both Congress and the media, that Nixon never took such a step again. Indeed, on 16 September he announced a second troop reduction of 40,500 men at a time of vast demonstrations in the US. Once again there was no reaction from Hanoi, nor any reduced activity by the protest movements in South Vietnam. The decision to Vietnamize the war was plainly being carried out, and with every step in the process the risk of failure increased. For Nixon, however, there was no going back, simply because of the steadily increasing domestic opposition to the war in every part of the country. This meant that he could only ever negotiate with Hanoi from a position of weakness, as Hanoi knew only too well.

In the course of 1969 it became clear that there were two sides to Nixon's Vietnam policy. First, the army of South Vietnam would be provided with all the logistical support necessary for continuing the war on the ground as American troops were withdrawn. This was the essence of Vietnamization. There was also the possibility of active air-support from the USAF, but this was problematic, given the moratorium decreed by Johnson on 1 November 1968. Second, a political solution to the problem of Vietnam's future would be the main goal of US diplomacy in Moscow and Beijing.[42]

1970 was the year the tide changed, with the first substantial reductions in US forces in Vietnam. Hanoi did not make it easy for Nixon to make this change of direction. Throughout April North Vietnam, driven by the pace of events in Cambodia described in Chapter 8, used its bases along the Cambodian frontier with Vietnam for a series of attacks on the South. Many of these were launched from the 'Parrot's Beak', a small enclave, surrounded on three sides by South Vietnamese territory, and only some 50–100 kilometres from Saigon. At the end of April South Vietnamese forces, without any American support, responded with a counter-attack, crossing the border into the Parrot's Beak, where they won a significant battle against the Viet Cong. This victory probably owed much to the radically changed political situation confronting North Vietnam in Cambodia as a result of Lon Nol's *coup d'état* of 18 March, described in Chapter 8.

From April, 1970, to the end of the year, the most significant events in the conflict with North Vietnam occurred not so much in Southeast Asia but in the United States, where following the Kent State University incident in May the tide of protest against the war became impossible to ignore. Because they related more to Cambodia than to South Vietnam, the political consequences are described in Chapter 8. The US Congress' repeal of the Gulf on Tonkin resolution at the very end of the year showed how radically the political climate had changed since 1964.

Washington confronted a new problem in April 1971, when South Vietnamese ground troops invaded Laos. This time the plan originated with the American

General Abrams, who wished to make good use of the remaining US forces before they were finally withdrawn at the end of the year. The main use of the Ho Chi Minh trail as a supply route was in the dry season from October to May. Abrams' plan was for South Vietnamese forces to capture the small town of Tchepone, a key hub of the trail located some 40 kilometres inside Laos, just south of the line of the DMZ. From just inside Vietnam, American troops would provide all possible logistical support, but subject to the restriction that they would not cross the frontier into Laos.

The operation was launched with two South Vietnamese divisions on 8 February 1971. Not only was this but half the number considered necessary by Abrams, but President Thieu in Saigon had ordered his commanders to be extremely cautious, and to abandon the operation entirely after 3,000 casualties. Not surprisingly the South Vietnamese commanders found any number of pretexts for slowing down their advance, and if they ever actually occupied Tchepone, they were still three weeks too late and withdrew from Laos as fast as they could – claiming that their mission had been accomplished. The supply route along the Ho Chi Minh trail had not been disrupted. This did not bode well for 1972 when the last US troops would be gone. Vietnamization of the armed forces would have to do better than this for South Vietnam to defend itself indefinitely against the North.

With no US troops in support, the military capability of South Vietnamese ground forces was again put to the test on 3 April 1972, when North Vietnamese forces, in a major new offensive, advanced 15 miles across the DMZ. Nixon's first reaction was to send Kissinger to Hanoi for a meeting with the North Vietnamese leaders on either 24 or 27 April, but after they refused this overture, he ordered the USAF to bomb military targets in the Hanoi-Haiphong area, thus ending Johnson's moratorium of 1 November 1968. Then, on 8 May, Nixon extended the order to include the mining of harbours and the bombing of railways and military targets throughout North Vietnam, pointing out that its army had relied on arms supplied by the Soviet Union for the attack on 3 April.

As for a diplomatic solution involving both Moscow and Beijing, three obstacles had to be overcome. One was simply that Moscow and Beijing had fallen out with each other, so that it was next to impossible to win the support of both for any American initiative. The second obstacle was that both Moscow and Beijing saw Vietnam as something of a side-show. Third, North Vietnam, sooner or later, would have to be involved, for, as they say, 'it takes two to tango'.

As to the first obstacle, the US had to be content with Beijing's stated policy (reported on page 148), going back to 1965, that China was no longer concerned to intervene in wars outside its own frontiers. This, in principle, was also Moscow's policy, but not to the extent that it was inhibited from sending arms to North Vietnam. As to the second obstacle, Kissinger had already heard from

Zhou Enlai, at a meeting in July 1971, that China was much more concerned about Taiwan than mainland Southeast Asia.

The supply of arms to North Vietnam was a point on which Brezhnev, the Soviet leader, would listen to Nixon, so turning the second obstacle, in a somewhat back-handed way, to America's advantage. There would be no leverage applied to North Vietnam, say by threatening to cut off the arms supply, but this would not block negotiations with Washington on other matters, which, to Moscow, were much more important. Nixon had to accept that there was simply too much at stake in the impending negotiations between Washington and Moscow, on matters having nothing to do with Vietnam, to allow this question to block a satisfactory outcome.

Preparations went ahead for a Moscow summit in May 1972, but as a result of the heavy bombing of North Vietnam ordered by Nixon at the end of April it hung on a knife-edge, particularly since there had been some damage to Soviet ships off-loading military supplies in Haiphong. Finally, after Kissinger had promised that 'the most drastic measures would be taken to avoid any accidents to Soviet vessels in North Vietnamese ports or on the open sea',[43] and further, that the bombing of North Vietnam would be reduced during the meeting (and of Hanoi completely suspended), Brezhnev accepted that to abandon the summit would effectively give a power of veto to Hanoi. The summit, therefore, went ahead as planned.

As to the third obstacle, although talks were actually held in Paris in May 1972, Le Duc Tho – after the death of Ho Chi Minh, the strong man chosen by the almost unknown Prime Minister, Pham Van Dong, to present North Vietnam to the outside world – told Henry Kissinger, representing the US, that Nixon should stop discussing Vietnam with Moscow. In Kissinger's own words, 'The man was as defiant as if he had won the war after all'.[44] Given that Hanoi had refused to receive him in April, Kissinger could hardly have been surprised, even though Le Duc Tho's recalcitrance would mean that there would be no cessation to the bombing. In the long term, North Vietnam *had* won the war, as Kissinger himself had heard from many of his own advisers.

The position taken by Le Duc Tho in Paris was undoubtedly influenced by what had been agreed between Nixon and Zhou Enlai during Nixon's visit to Beijing in February. Although Nixon's visit was rightly regarded as a breakthrough in Chinese-American relations – with important consequences also for the relationship between Moscow and Washington[45] – Nixon had not received much satisfaction on the question of Vietnam. Although he had told the Chinese that Hanoi could not win the war there, he accepted its capacity to prolong it indefinitely. With this in mind Nixon, on returning to Washington, let it be known that if North Vietnam showed some flexibility and understanding of the American position, it would within two or three years realize all its aims, including significant changes in South Vietnamese politics. If Nixon had but known, he was giving away far more than he had bargained for. This Le Duc Tho knew only too well, and he also judged, correctly, that Vietnam would not be a major issue between Nixon and Brezhnev at the Moscow conference to be held at the end of May. In the event Brezhnev did not even raise the matter about American bomb damage to ships from the Soviet Union. Supplies from the Soviet Union continued to be delivered at Haiphong.

After the Beijing summit in February 1972, and the Moscow summit in May, Washington spent the remaining months of the year trying to broker a peace treaty between North and South Vietnam. This involved Henry Kissinger in months of shuttle diplomacy starting in Paris negotiating with Le Duc Tho, who then returned home, so that negotiations then alternated between Hanoi and Saigon, where Thieu held the fort for South Vietnam.

The breakthrough came on 8 October when Hanoi, for the first time ever, abandoned its demand for the overthrow of the Saigon government. This was the beginning of a whole series of concessions; South Vietnam would be allowed to keep its army, to receive American military and economic aid, North Vietnam would withdraw its troops from Laos and Cambodia, there would be a ceasefire in both Vietnam and Laos and there would be no more infiltration. Ideally Kissinger would like to have gone further and have free elections decide the future of the whole of Vietnam, but this was plainly asking too much of Hanoi. To some extent his hands were tied by the new restraints imposed by the US Congress on aid to Vietnam, but even so the terms acceptable to Hanoi held out the prospect of Saigon being able to continue to govern South Vietnam, with the threat of US naval- and air-power in the background to discourage major violations of the ceasefire on the part of North Vietnam. What is more, given the favourable outcome of the two summits held in the early months of 1972, Moscow and Beijing could be expected to do their best to restrain Hanoi from breaking the ceasefire.

Kissinger was back in Washington, from the first round in Vietnam, on 12 October. Nixon was so taken by Kissinger's apparent success that he ordered a steak and wine dinner to be served in his hideaway in the Executive Office Building. Everything appeared to be in order for the final agreement to be signed on 31 October. On 16 October Kissinger left Washington for Saigon, where he would try to sell the North Vietnamese terms to Thieu, with a stop in Paris on the way, to tie up a number of loose ends with Le Duc Tho's appointed deputy, Xuan Thuy.

Once in Saigon Kissinger learnt from the US Embassy of the problems that the North Vietnamese terms would pose for Thieu. It was asking much of him to accept that Saigon should cut its umbilical cord with the US,[46] and his reception of Kissinger, at their first meeting on 19 October, was frigid. Kissinger presented a formal note from Nixon, which ended with the following handwritten words: 'Dr Kissinger … and I have discussed this proposal at great length. I am personally convinced it is the best we will be able to get and that it meets my absolute condition – that the GVN[47] must survive as a free country…'

The meeting was then adjourned to another room, where Kissinger, with a large supporting cast, both military and diplomatic, had to confront Thieu's National Security Council, joined by his ambassadors to Washington and Paris. Kissinger explained what lay behind the American diplomacy, pointing out that the terms now agreed by Hanoi were based on American proposals made with the concurrence of Saigon. To sweeten the pill Kissinger promised, on a massive scale, new matériel for the South Vietnamese Army to equip it for the period, starting on 1 January 1973, after the final departure of American combat troops.

While all this was going on, Hanoi played a clever double game. On the one side military activity was stepped up, while on the other important new concessions were made on a number of points – such as the release of civilian prisoners and the replacement of military equipment – that remained unsettled. The result, as intended, was to make Thieu more nervous than ever about confronting North Vietnam, while the US had every incentive to lose no time in having the agreement accepted. Quite apart from the presidential election due in November, by 1972 US domestic politics made it impossible for the US team in Saigon to make any commitment that would stop, or even slow down, the process of US de-escalation combined with the Vietnamization of the ground forces in South Vietnam. When, however, Thieu asked Kissinger[48] what the US would do in the event of massive North Vietnamese violations, he was assured that the US would act to enforce the agreement. Within three years both his misgivings about North Vietnam and his mistrust of American assurances proved to be only too well-founded.

Once again Hanoi forced the pace in Saigon by making concessions to the US; in particular all American prisoners, both in Laos and in North and South Vietnam, would be released. At the same time Hanoi was about to go public, but even so Thieu would not yield, and on 23 October 1972 Kissinger returned to Washington without an agreement. Once Congress learnt of the terms proposed there was no way that it would vote to continue the war.

Although Kissinger had been wrong-footed all along the line, he still had to persevere in his attempt to reach a ceasefire agreement. One problem in October 1972 was that Thieu believed that Nixon's policies were part of his campaign for re-election in November. This Nixon denied in a letter sent to Thieu on 26 October.[49] Hanoi at the same time declared its willingness to resume talks after the election, which it had rightly assumed that Nixon would win. The result was that Kissinger went to Paris on 19 November to steer negotiations between the representatives of both North and South Vietnam towards agreement. In practice this meant almost continual discussion with Le Duc Tho, while the South Vietnamese delegation simply stonewalled. Nothing was achieved: Kissinger's view was simply that Le Duc Tho, aware of the rift between Washington and Saigon, had decided to go back to psychological warfare. For this Hanoi paid a high price. Nixon ordered American B-52s to resume heavy bombing of North Vietnam. This started on 18 December and lasted for 11 days in which some 20,000 tons of bombs were dropped, to add to the 150,000 tons already dropped between April and October.

The Christmas bombing led to universal outrage. Both parties in Congress condemned it, with words such as 'barbaric', 'contemptible', 'disastrous' setting the tone of the reaction. A cut-off of aid was an almost certain outcome. Foreign criticism was even more strident, and in Sweden Nixon's administration was compared with the Nazis. Moscow and Beijing were much more restrained, no doubt because they knew better what was involved.

Whatever the extent and character of the damage caused by the bombing, Hanoi did offer to resume negotiations on terms acceptable to Washington, and on 30 December the bombing was stopped. Le Duc Tho returned to Paris on 6 January 1973, committed to making a 'final' effort for a rapid 'settlement'. On 9 January he announced that Hanoi accepted the terms which he had rejected at the end of 1972. All US bombing of North Vietnam was stopped. On 13 January Kissinger was able to return to Washington with the draft agreement. The only problem was Thieu in Saigon, but on 21 January he relented, after being reassured by a unilateral statement that Washington 'recognized Saigon as the legal government of South Vietnam and that Hanoi had no right to maintain troops there'.[50] The agreement was finally signed on 27 January by representatives of Hanoi and the Viet Cong on one page, and Saigon and the United States on another. For the US this meant that all troops must be withdrawn within sixty days, by which time also all US POWs held in North Vietnam would be released. In both cases the deadline was met. After that the sole means left to the US to enforce the agreement was the threat to use its own air-power.

Given not so much the terms of the Paris Peace Agreement, but its historical and political background, South Vietnam, in the words of Henry Kissinger, 'was being asked to defend its freedom under more daunting conditions than any of America's other allies ... That [American forces] were withdrawn from South Vietnam sixty days after concluding the agreement was the principal weakness of the Vietnam agreement, far more significant than the continued presence of North Vietnamese forces ... [The US] was driven in the direction of unilateral withdrawal by domestic pressures ...'[51] These, by January 1973, included the first tremors of the Watergate scandal, which was soon to lead the US Congress to enact a law making it impossible to enforce the peace agreement. On 10 May the House of Representatives voted to cut off all funding for US combat operations in Indochina, including any new bombing. Nixon used his power of veto to buy time, but even so he had to accept a resolution of both houses of Congress to end all bombing on 15 August.

In the early months of 1973 Washington, confronted by any number of North Vietnamese violations of the Paris Peace Agreement, was continually challenged to enforce it. The only means to do so was to use air-power to attack targets appropriate to each successive violation. This only happened once. As the day for the agreed ceasefire in Laos approached, the country's ruler, Prince Souvanna Phouma, reported a 'general offensive'[52] by the communist Pathet Lao. An immediate strike by US B-52 bombers was ordered, and within 48 hours this led to the agreed ceasefire.

On the other hand, Washington, confronted by continuous military traffic on the Ho Chi Minh Trail, did nothing, although similar strikes were contemplated. Nixon simply temporized until the summer rains closed down the trail, by which time some 35,000 North Vietnamese troops had entered South Vietnam and the adjacent border areas of Laos. Nixon, threatened by Watergate, dared not retaliate, and by August it would be illegal for him to do so. At the same time Congress was drastically reducing military assistance to South Vietnam, a blow compounded by the drastic increase in oil prices caused by crisis in the Middle East. 'Not surprisingly' – as Kissinger noted – 'the tragedy ended with the entire North Vietnamese army invading South Vietnam while the United States stood by paralyzed and cultivating its own divisions'.[53]

By the time Watergate had spent its force, and Gerald Ford had succeeded Nixon as US President on 9 August 1974, the increasing number of combat deaths in South Vietnam directly reflected the drastic shortfall in US aid. By this time the US Congressional majority was convinced that South Vietnam must learn to stand on its own, with perhaps one final lump sum grant. In justification it was pointed out that Soviet and Chinese aid to North Vietnam had always been on a much lower scale – although Soviet military aid was substantially increased in the final months of the war. As it was Hanoi did not fail to notice the South Vietnamese troops' decline in firepower and loss of mobility. The fault lay mainly with the Americans. To quote Kissinger once again, 'Idealism had propelled America into Indochina, and exhaustion caused it to leave.'[54] All this was clear to Hanoi at the beginning of 1975: attacks on South Vietnam were stepped up, to culminate, on 10 March, in a major offensive in the central highlands. On 12 and 13 March the US congress voted overwhelmingly against any further aid to South Vietnam.

There was no question of turning the tide back. The central highlands fell without a struggle, and tens of thousands of refugees, both soldiers and civilians, clogged the roads south. One disaster followed another, and on 8 April Kissinger asked for a list of those who would have to be evacuated as the whole country fell into the hands of the North Vietnamese. It would include not only some 6,000 Americans still in Vietnam, but also several times as many Vietnamese whose lives would be threatened because of their collaboration with the US. The American media chose Thieu as a scape-goat, but it was too late to replace him – as if that would have helped. On 10 April President Ford pleaded in vain with Congress for renewed support for South Vietnam. The only question left to decide was how rapidly the planned evacuation should be carried out. On 21 April Thieu finally resigned, with his fierce criticisms of the United States described there as the rantings of a 'discredited and embittered Vietnamese politician'.[55] On the same day giant US military transports began a round-the-clock airlift from Saigon's airport, which, over a period of ten days, helped nearly 50,000 Vietnamese leave their country. On 29 April, in the face of a rocket attack, chaos took hold of the airport, putting an end to the airlift. On the same day President Ford ordered the final evacuation, which was carried out by helicopters landing on the roof of the US Embassy in Saigon. The US Ambassador left at dawn on 30 April in almost the last helicopter.

VIETNAM UNITED UNDER HANOI (1975–2006)

Once Hanoi had taken over in South Vietnam, it was plain that this country would not be allowed to retain any sort of autonomy, even under a communist government. The NLF, presented by Ho Chi Minh during the 1960s as the 'sole genuine representative of the people of Vietnam', simply disappeared. There would be simply one Socialist Republic of Vietnam (SRV), a unitary state with its capital at Hanoi, and Saigon renamed as Ho Chi Minh City, as formally proclaimed in July 1976.[56] Although Ho Chi Minh, the founder of the state, had died in September 1969, he remained the 'living embodiment of his people', and his successors in office followed his policies, extending to the whole country the regime what he had established in North Vietnam after defeating the French at Dien Bien Phu in 1954. They were immediately confronted by the need to reconstruct a country devastated by thirty years of war, a task made doubly difficult in the years up to 1980 by wars with Cambodia to the west and China in the north. Behind these two wars, related respectively in chapters 8 and 2, lay the fact that in fighting the US and its allies, the Vietminh of North Vietnam was allied with the Soviet Union rather than with China. This alliance was confirmed in December 1975, when the Vietnamese leader, Le Duan, secured Moscow's agreement to immediate economic aid and support for the new five-year plan. In June 1978 the SRV joined COMECON,[57] the Moscow dominated trading block, leading Beijing, a month later, to withdraw all its aid. The SRV responded, in December, by signing a 25-year friendship treaty with Moscow.[58] With the collapse of the

Soviet Union in 1991 this meant that Vietnam, effectively, was on its own. The remainder of this chapter is devoted to its history from 1980 onwards, with 1991 as a critical watershed. In this period, uniting a divided people and rebuilding a shattered economy were the leitmotiv behind every new development.

In performing the former task the SRV government soon found that it was far from welcome among some hundreds of thousands of South Vietnamese who were so deeply committed to the old regime that fell in April 1975 that they could not be won over by the populist rhetoric of Ho Chi Minh: the life they contemplated was one of persecution for having been – largely by force of circumstance – on the losing side in the war. Nearly a million, indeed, had fled North Vietnam when it was taken over by Ho Chi Minh and the Viet Minh in 1954.[59]

There was, however, more to it: countless South Vietnamese rightly foresaw the new regime destroying their traditional values, inherited from their Buddhist, or, surprisingly often, their Christian, past;[60] others, particularly among the numerous Chinese expatriates, saw their traditional livelihood being destroyed by the planned elimination of the private sector of the economy.[61] The classes, needless to say, overlapped, and between them they accounted for nearly a million people who throughout the 1980s and beyond attempted to escape – mainly by sea – communist Vietnam. Of these some 840,000 'boat people' arrived safely in 'ports of first asylum', with Hong Kong (where they became a considerable social problem) at the top of the list. In the end little more than 100,000 returned, generally under extreme pressure, to Vietnam, leaving more than 750,000 to resettle permanently overseas.

Of all the dramas that unfolded in twentieth-century Asia-Pacific that of the Indochinese – but mainly Vietnamese – boat people had the widest impact world-wide, if only because so many different countries around the Pacific Rim finally and often reluctantly offered them a permanent home. Until the late 1980s most, according to international criteria, qualified as refugees – they faced political, religious or other forms of persecution if they returned to Vietnam. Particularly in the early days those who escaped, if they survived the hazardous sea-voyage, ended up in other states of East and Southeast Asia, notably, Hong Kong, Thailand, Malaysia, Indonesia and the Philippines, where governments were ill prepared to deal with them.

Few intended to remain in Asia. Although their preferred destinations were the US, Canada, Australia, and, beyond the Pacific, Britain and France, they landed up almost everywhere – even in such places as Bermuda and Iceland. In particular, the countries actually involved in the Vietnam War, led by the US, felt obliged to the countless hapless people left behind when it ended in 1975. In many cases, just one member of a family sought to escape, hoping to acquire refugee status entitling the other members to follow – that is, if they could leave Vietnam. From 1977 to 1981 President Jimmy Carter embodied this sense of obligation, as shown by his decision to allow up to 14,000 refugees from Southeast Asia to resettle in the United States every month. TV pictures showing boats carrying refugees being pushed back into the sea from Malaysia, Thailand and Indonesia, to face the depredations of pirates, heightened their emotional appeal.

The flow of refugees continued into the 1980s, but it gradually became clear, particularly in Hong Kong, that many were 'economic' refugees, who were not so much fleeing persecution as looking for a new and more prosperous life. The UN High Commissioner for Refugees, under pressure from the international community, reacted by producing a Comprehensive Plan of Action. This provided for all those arriving in a 'port of first asylum' to be screened, so as to separate out the purely economic refugees, who would then be returned to Vietnam.

The situation was at its most critical in Hong Kong, where tens of thousands were held behind barbed-wire awaiting screening and eventual deportation under the colony's 'Orderly Repatriation Programme' – a colossal oxymoron. All this was grist to the mill both to the media world-wide and to Hong Kong's human rights lawyers – who won very few cases – but at the end of the day the repatriation programme was successfully completed, and the internment camps are now empty.[62]

Returning to the mainstream of SRV politics, Hanoi, throughout the 1980s, was effectively forced to choose between hardline communist orthodoxy and an open, decentralized market economy. With the planned economy of the second five-year plan (1976–81) failing all along the line,[63] the writing on the wall was clear. A programme known as Doi Moi, or 'renovation', was launched in 1986 as the basis of the fourth five-year plan, in 1988 the remarkably liberal new Law on Foreign Investment opened almost all sectors of the economy to foreign investment[64] and in 1989 central planning gave way to a market economy, with a proper legal framework for property rights and commercial transactions.[65] The results were palpable: rampant inflation was cured while food production increased spectacularly. At the same time the economy of the Soviet Union was stagnating, to the point that Moscow finally withdrew from Afghanistan in 1989, at the same time making clear that it could no longer afford any useful support for the SRV. In the same year the SRV withdrew the last of its forces from Cambodia; the Soviet naval base at Cam Rahn Bay was, however, maintained by Russia until October 2003. The reaction in the SRV ran parallel to Deng Xiaoping's programme in China, as described in Chapter 2. Although Nguyen Van Linh, who headed the SRV from 1986 to 1991, was an economic reformer with a reputation for modest political liberalization, his speech on the SRV National Day in September 1989 strongly opposed multi-party democracy: significantly the drama of Tiananmen Square in Beijing had unfolded only three months earlier.

With the collapse of the Soviet Union the SRV's position, internationally, was greatly strengthened, if only because it could no longer be reasonably perceived as a threat to the stability of Southeast Asia: this was particularly important for its relations with the US, which, from the 1990s onwards, had every interest in investing in the economic development of Vietnam. Given all that Vietnam had been through in the previous half-century, there was a great deal of lost ground to be recovered. Economic growth, therefore, is the leitmotiv of its history since 1990. Although, in principle, this was always the central plank in the policy of the SRV, the government, in practice, was restricted by its commitment to communist orthodoxy. The country, after all, had not fought and won a bitter thirty-year war for nothing. Even so, after 1991, it was one of only five states, world-wide, to be bound in this way: of these, China, which was much the most important, could hardly be counted on for support, given the historical background related in Chapters 2 and 8. The other three, Cambodia, Laos and Burma (of which the first two bordered on Vietnam), were, if anything, more of a hindrance than a help. Inevitably, therefore, Vietnam's economic progress in the 1990s depended on its coming to terms with its former enemies, notably the US, but also Australia – to say nothing of other states, such as those belonging to the EU. In this process, with considerable goodwill on both sides, the SRV was remarkably successful. At the same time Vietnam became something of a historical back-water, if only because its achievements echoed those of China – which, inevitably, counted for much more on the world scene.[66] Nonetheless, with more than 80 million inhabitants it has the largest population in Southeast Asia, and the twelfth largest in the world, and that with a relatively high growth rate.[67]

There were a number of significant steps along the path of economic progress in the 1990s. In 1991 foreign banks were allowed to operate while the Law on Companies and Private Enterprises recognized the rights of the private sector, allowing it to grow much more rapidly than the public sector. In 1992 Washington lifted the ban on US citizens travelling to the SRV. In 1993 the SRV was recognized by the World Bank as qualifying for support – which in the following twelve years added up to more than $5 billion. Then in 1995 the SRV was admitted to ASEAN, in 1998 to APEC and in 2005 to the WTO, in the process becoming a member of the club first, in Southeast Asia, then in the Pacific region and finally in the world at large.

The economy of the SRV, as a developing country, is based on the exploitation of natural resources and agriculture. Oil, first drilled in 1986, became, within ten years, the largest earner of foreign currency. The wells are mainly offshore, where natural gas is also exploited. Even so the SRV only ranks about thirtieth in world production of petroleum products. The problem, in increasing measure, is the apportionment of the sea-bed of the South China Sea, with the SRV's claim to be the Spratly Islands disputed by China, Taiwan, the Philippines and Malaysia.[68] Forestry and ocean fishing also exploit natural resources, often – as in so much of Southeast Asia – beyond a sustainable level. Harvesting shrimp from inland waterways is a remarkably specialized economic sector providing for the livelihood of some two million Vietnamese, whose country is the world's leading producer. In 2005 the shrimp-farmers became likely to be killed by their own success, when the US Congress moved to impose harsh anti-dumping duties to protect local producers in the world's largest national market. In agriculture Vietnam regained its position as the world's third largest producer of rice, while remarkably, in the 1990s, moving up to being the world's second largest producer of coffee. The price for this success story was paid not only by the long-standing producing nations, such as Mexico, Guatemala, Costa Rica and Colombia[69] on the other side of the Pacific, but also by Vietnam itself, which in 2003 discovered that the world coffee glut had pushed prices below its own production costs. Drastic counter-measures retrieved the situation, allowing Vietnamese industry, with its modern infrastructure developed to serve the plantations,[70] to return to profits and remain ahead of its competitors.

Although talk of long-term trends is premature, Vietnam's economy, following most of the rest of Southeast Asia, seems to have made a good start in the new millennium. This is certainly the perception of outsiders,[71] who note the country's vast human resources and its successful transition to a market economy. Land, however, is in increasing short supply, development is unbalanced between the regions – with the south prospering more than the centre and north – and dissidents still have a hard time.

8

Cambodia: a kingdom upside down

THE FINAL DAYS OF FRENCH COLONIALISM

After 1887, the year in which the ancient kingdom of Cambodia became part of French Indochina, it was allowed to survive to play a subordinate part in the colonial government, subject always to the French controlling the succession to the throne on the death of a king – an event that, in Cambodian history, had often led to crisis. In 1941 King Sisowath Monivong died. For the French the time was inopportune. Following the defeat of France by Germany in 1940, the colonial administration, as that of Vietnam, had to answer to Germany's axis partner, Japan, which had already orchestrated the return to Thailand of three provinces incorporated into Cambodia, with French support, in 1861.

Prudently, as they then saw things, the French in 1941 arranged for an unknown eighteen-year-old prince, Norodom Sihanouk, a grandson of the late king, to succeed him. They were little concerned that passing over the late king's oldest son, Prince Sisowath Monireth, might cause antipathy to Norodom Sihanouk within the extended royal family. Nonetheless, for four years, 1941–45, the young king's rule, as seen by the French, was exemplary. He even accepted two reforms central to their policy of modernization. The first was that Khmer[1] should be written in the Latin alphabet in official correspondence, the second, that the Gregorian should replace the traditional Buddhist calendar.[2] This, as the young king well knew, weakened his position with the *sangha*, or order of Buddhist monks – the traditional guardian of Khmer culture.

Then, on 9 March 1945, the Japanese, in a *coup de force*, abruptly ended the French administration in Cambodia, as part of a coordinated action relating to the whole of Indochina. Three days later Sihanouk proclaimed the end to the French protectorate. He changed the name of the country to Kampuchea, and declared his support for the Japanese. In return he was given a free hand in forming a new administration, and even before this process was complete, he restored the Khmer alphabet and the Buddhist calendar, noting that 'we are a people known for honouring old laws, and customs from ancient times. The French laws would deprive us of customs and of history'.[3] None of this was any problem for the Japanese. Cambodia never became a theatre of war, and when forced to accept the defeat of their empire in August 1945, the Japanese at least had the consolation that their policy in Indochina, in the final months of the war, would make it difficult for the French ever to re-establish their authority.

In fact the French faced a crisis as soon as they began to take over from the defeated Japanese. Its origins went back to 1942 when Song Ngoc Thanh, a wealthy French-educated Cambodian, orchestrated a *coup d'état* directed against the local French administration. Without Japanese support, which he had counted on, the coup failed, and Thanh fled to Battambang, one of the three Cambodian provinces ceded to Thailand in 1941. From there he made his way to Tokyo, where the Japanese somewhat hesitantly welcomed him, realizing that he could play a useful part in their plans for the future of Cambodia. When King Sihanouk proclaimed the country's independence in March 1945, Thanh came home, to be appointed foreign minister in May. On 9 August Thanh, supported by Prince Sisowath Monireth – the uncle of the king whom the French had barred from the succession in 1941 – succeeded in disarming a group from the local Cambodian militia (originally organized by the Japanese) that had stormed the royal palace in Phnom Penh, with the intent of deposing Norodom Sihanouk. The king, however, warned by his mother, had hidden in a nearby temple. When it was safe to return to the palace, he dismissed his entire cabinet, and asked Thanh to be the first prime minister of independent Cambodia. The following day the Japanese emperor began negotiations for surrendering to the Allies.

Thanh, concerned about what would happen to his government when the French returned in force, lost no time in making key international contacts in China, Thailand and Vietnam. He himself visited South Vietnam, where he made himself unwelcome by claiming for Cambodia much of Cochin-China. In North Vietnam he extended diplomatic recognition to the communist Viet Minh, who, with remarkable prescience, advised him to prepare his country for a protracted armed struggle.

By this time – September 1945 – the French had taken the first steps to restore their authority in Cambodia, and on 15 October their military commander, General Leclerc, flew to Phnom Penh accompanied by a bodyguard. Thanh willingly responded to a summons from the general, believing that he would be confirmed in office. Instead, he was arrested by the bodyguard and immediately flown to Saigon – the first stage in a journey which was to end in exile under 'administrative surveillance' in France.

Leclerc, having dealt with Thanh, wisely accepted Prince Monireth as prime minister, and on 23 October King Sihanouk formally welcomed the new French high commissioner. The French then proposed a *modus vivendi*, which recognized the king's autonomy in the internal administration of Cambodia. On 8 January 1946 this was agreed as the basis for negotiating a new constitution. In the same year France recovered the provinces ceded to Thailand in 1941.[4] The constitution would take longer.

The first step, the election of a constituent assembly, was scheduled for 1 September 1946. Of the two main parties which emerged to fight the election, one, the Liberal Party, was 'moderate' – at least in the eyes of the French – while the other, the Democratic Party, was radical. While the former, which emphasized 'Franco-Cambodian understanding and friendship', was secretly funded by the French, the latter, organized by a number of young Cambodians who had returned home from studying in France during the war years, campaigned on a programme promising complete independence. Once the election was held the Democratic Party won 50 out of 69 seats, and its leader, the young Prince Youtevong, became prime minister. In the election, at the end of 1947, for the first national assembly under the new constitution, the party won 54 out of 74 seats – a victory demonstrating the grass-roots appeal of a record of confronting the French, and combatting corruption and patronage.

By this time Prince Youtevong had died at the young age of 34, to be succeeded by a long line of ineffective prime ministers, who by the mid-1950s had brought the Democratic Party to the point where it could only survive with communist support. The 1947 election marked also the first appearance, in a very minor role, of a nineteen-year-old student, Saloth Sar, in Cambodian politics. Thirty years later, with the adopted name of Pol Pot, he led his country into the killing fields of the Khmer Rouge, but two years after his political debut in 1947, he left for Paris with a scholarship from the French government. He therefore missed the introduction of the new constitution at the end of 1949, to return home only in 1953, in which year Cambodia was granted full independence.

The 1949 constitution was contained in a treaty signed in Paris by the French president, Vincent Auriol and Sihanouk. While the king said later that it granted Cambodia '50 percent independence',[5] in Auriol's view the remaining limits to Cambodia's independence were 'those brought to it by its membership of the French union'. However that may be, the terms of the treaty represented a half-way stage, which, if acceptable to Sihanouk, at least for the time being, would not in the long run meet the aspirations of the Cambodian people.

The Democratic Party, having failed to gain full independence, lost many votes in the election held in 1951 according to the terms of the Paris agreement. Although the party still won a majority of the seats, its complete lack of direction gave Sihanouk the idea of bringing Thanh back from exile in France to take a leading role in government. Although his return to Phnom Penh on 29 October 1951 was greeted by vast crowds, within six months he had disappeared into the forests of Battambang. Although ostensibly a kidnapping, this was clearly a put-up job, enabling Thanh to join the Khmer Issarak, a guerrilla movement directed from Bangkok, and closely associated with the Viet Minh.

Coincidentally, on the same day in October 1951 as Thanh returned home, the French High Commissioner was murdered by his Vietnamese houseboy, who had been planted in the household by the Viet Minh to satisfy the commissioner's bizarre sexual tastes. The houseboy escaped to Vietnam to become a national hero for the Viet Minh.[6]

Although Thanh's plans to organize resistance against the French failed, the events of the winter of 1951–52 completely discredited the Democratic Party. The French became convinced of the need to move rapidly, for – in the words of one of their political counsellors – 'all Cambodians want true independence'. Given the way the war against the Viet Minh was going in Vietnam, the last thing the French wanted was trouble in Cambodia, particularly if it should mean Khmer guerrilla groups linking up with the Viet Minh. The essential first step, agreed to by both the French and Sihanouk, was to end any power still retained by the Democratic Party.

No sooner said than done. On 15 June 1952, after Moroccan troops had taken up positions in Phnom Penh, Sihanouk dismissed the Democratic cabinet and appointed himself as prime minister, with his cousin, Prince Sirik Matak, in charge of defence. French Union troops, brought in from Saigon, surrounded the National Assembly, and Sihanouk issued a royal decree banning political meetings and the diffusion of propaganda.[7] Nine Democratic delegates were imprisoned for terrorism, and although the party survived, it was taken over by communists at its last congress in 1955. The 1952 coup made clear that Sihanouk was no longer willing to be a constitutional monarch nor, as the French were soon to discover, an instrument of their colonial policy.

Sihanouk had once again shown a remarkable understanding of the mind-cast of the common people of Cambodia. With them he 'could draw on a fund of belief that he enjoyed access to beneficial supernatural forces and could ensure the country's physical prosperity'. Seen in this way, Sihanouk's coup of June 1952 allowed him to walk into the political arena unopposed. The coup nipped the prospect of pluralism in Cambodia in the bud and marked a major turning point in the kingdom's political history.[8]

In January 1953 the Democratic leaders in the National Assembly once more attempted to assert their power, but Sihanouk, with military support, dissolved it and suspended a number of civil rights. After a short delay Sihanouk left for a holiday in France, just as Saloth Sar and other young revolutionaries were returning home from Paris. Once in France Sihanouk devoted his holiday to a campaign for Cambodian independence, but only got as far as having lunch with President Auriol. Returning home via Washington he was warned by US Secretary of State John Foster Dulles that independence was meaningless without French protection, for otherwise Cambodia would be 'swallowed' by the communists. (President Eisenhower's failure to invite him to the White House led to lasting antipathy against the United States, for which later a high price would be paid.) Almost immediately after meeting Dulles, Sihanouk, in an interview he had requested with the *New York Times*, stated that if independence were postponed the Cambodian people might 'rise up against the present regime and join the Viet Minh'[9] – the very last thing that either the French or Dulles wanted. On the other hand this was certainly the intention of Saloth Sar and the revolutionaries back home in Cambodia.

Throughout 1953, Sihanouk, with his own distinctive ideas about diplomacy, worked hard for Cambodian independence from a new headquarters close to Angkor Wat. Although, to the French, his political style was highly original – to the point that their top general described him as 'a madman, but a madman of genius' – no one could gainsay the immense popularity of his cause. Both the High Commissioner in Phnom Penh and the US *chargé d'affaires* agreed that 'the king has excited people to such an extent that it may be difficult to keep control'.[10] Since, by this time, the main concern of both Paris and Washington was to defeat the Viet Minh, almost any price was worth paying for peace in Cambodia, particularly since the Communist Party there had scarcely a thousand members.

THE GRANT OF INDEPENDENCE

In October 1953 the French agreed to independence on Sihanouk's terms, so long as they could retain a strong military presence east of the Mekong River, to counteract the threat from the Viet Minh. Cambodia became independent on 9 November 1953, and Sihanouk, the 'father of independence', became a national hero.

Although Sihanouk has been described as the 'most gifted and popular politician to take command of Cambodia at any point between 1945 and 1979 … [with success mostly] due to his genuine patriotism, his capacity for hard work, and his rapport with the aspirations of Cambodia's rural poor',[11] he came to power without any constructive policy or understanding of democratic government. The king, according to one Western observer, considered 'immediate independence more important than long term survival', while, according to another, 'it mattered little if Cambodia is unbalanced, internally, by a demagogic policy'.[12]

This is exactly what King Sihanouk brought to his newly independent country. In Cambodia power was always seen as legitimate, and until 1970 – when events got out of control – almost everyone revered Sihanouk. Travelling everywhere by helicopter villagers saw him as coming from heaven. This was a society in which status was more important than comfort, hierarchy was unquestioned, and the superiority of Khmer culture – with its roots in an empire which had collapsed some five hundred years previously – taken for granted.[13] History had created a common people resigned to cruelty and exploitation, hospitable but at the same time duplicitous, and accepting passion and intrigue as a normal part of life. With almost all these different attributes, Sihanouk, although their unquestioned ruler, was a true representative of the Cambodian people.

In early 1955 Sihanouk decided that his authority should be confirmed by a referendum, which, with local police overseeing the way votes were cast, produced 925,667 votes in his favour, and only 1,834 against him.[14] With Cambodia recognized as his personal domain, Sihanouk arrested the editors of Khmer language newspapers that had campaigned against him and started rewriting the constitution. After his proposals had proved unwelcome in the diplomatic community, Sihanouk seemed to lose interest, noting that since the constitution had 'emanated' from him, he could amend it whenever he chose. This meant that a second referendum, to approve his proposed amendments, was never held.[15]

True to his character, Sihanouk changed direction once more, and on 4 March 1955 announced his abdication, a move later described in his memoirs as his 'atomic bomb'. His father, Prince Suramarit, took over to become a somewhat reluctant king, but Sihanouk, who had taken the title of *upayuvareach* – 'the prince who has left the throne' – left him with little choice.

The next step was to form a new national movement, *Sangkum Reastr Niyum*, or the 'People's Socialist Community'. According to its statutes, 'Our association will attain the aspirations of the Little People, the real people of the Kingdom of Kampuchea, which we love. Our community … fights against injustice, corruption, exactions, oppression and treason committed against our People and our Country'. Sihanouk's underlying intent was to dissolve the existing political parties, since belonging to Sangkum excluded membership of any other political group. Everyone was expected to join, so it is not surprising that in the election held at the end of 1955 Sangkum, with 83 per cent of the votes cast, won all the seats. The Democratic Party did not stand a chance. In elections held in 1958 and 1962 Sangkum candidates, most of extreme mediocrity, were returned unopposed – so much for the principles stated by Sihanouk in its founding charter.

Once the 1955 elections had been resolved in his favour, Sihanouk enjoyed ten years of more or less absolute power. His foreign policy, at a time when the American commitment to Vietnam was steadily increasing, was determined by the way he was received in the course of state visits – which he always enjoyed. In this way his new friends were Zhou Enlai (following a successful visit to Beijing early in 1956), Sukarno and Nehru, while he saw the first US Ambassador in Phnom Penh as dogmatic, imperious and gauche.[16]

Inevitably Sihanouk was seen as a communist sympathizer, although he always made clear that his Khmer or Buddhist version of socialism was essentially different from Marxist communism. As always he was incurably vain, and long on rhetoric while short on policy – not a man to appeal to Americans. Closer to home the result was that both Bangkok and Saigon became hostile to Sihanouk's new regime, but given his sense of Cambodian history this only confirmed his view that he was on the right track. He had an unmistakable popular touch, and in his speeches 'berated his enemies, joked about his love life, insulted foreigners, praised the people listening to him, and invoked the glories of Angkor'.[17]

The years 1955–65 were something of a golden age. Exports of rice, rubber and pepper brought in sufficient foreign exchange in a country where most of the population were peasant farmers cultivating their own land. At the same time foreign aid from France and the United States on one side, and China and the Soviet Union on the other, built hospitals, schools, harbours and highways, accompanied by massive improvement in health and education.

In April 1960, the death of King Suramarit after a long illness, led to a crisis of succession dealt with by Sihanouk in his usual high-handed way. After persuading his uncle, Prince Monireth, to preside over a regency council, Sihanouk refused to allow either his eldest son, Prince Rannaridh – still a minor – or his mother, Queen Kossamak, to succeed to the throne. In either case Prince Monireth would have become too powerful. Once again Sihanouk called a referendum to confirm his policy, so that some two million Cambodians voted to abandon a thousand-year-old monarchy. Sihanouk had twice as many votes as in 1955, the opposition, with only 266, one seventh. Sihanouk – perhaps under the influence of his mistress, Monique Izzi – moved out of the royal palace, but his mother stayed on with the court regalia, the Brahmins, the astrologers and the *corps de ballet*.

THE END OF NEUTRALITY

Although it clearly paid Cambodia to be neutral, events outside its frontiers in the end destroyed Sihanouk's dream-world, which enjoyed, in his own words, a level of 'democratization … never attained by any other country'.[18] However, as related in Chapter 7, the Viet Minh's struggle to take over the whole of Vietnam, owed much of its success to operating first from bases in Laos, and then from Cambodia. To begin with Sihanouk, true to his character, turned a blind eye. The fact that a substantial part of his country was beyond his control hardly disturbed him: the region along the Vietnam frontier had always been marginal, and the small ethnic Khmer population had mostly chosen to move elsewhere rather than confront the Viet Minh. From 1961 Sihanouk may also have been reacting to the fact that the new US President, John Kennedy, had decided not to engage the Viet Minh outside South Vietnam. This was a clear signal that neutrality was the best policy for Cambodia.

Much more important in the long term was the position of communists at the centre of Vietnam politics. As far back as 1951 a Khmer People's Revolutionary Party (KPRP) had been formed, but it was essentially little more than a supporters' club for the Viet Minh in their fight to take over Vietnam – a war with little popular appeal to Cambodians. Then, in September 1960, the Vietnamese Workers' Party (VWP), at a national congress in Hanoi, agreed a strategy committing the KPRP to an active role in the war against South Vietnam. This seriously compromised the KPRP inside Cambodia, and the party reacted by holding its own national conference at the Phnom Penh train station on 30 September. There a new central committee was agreed, with three young members who particularly resented the way policy was dictated by Hanoi, where there was little interest in Cambodia's need for its own revolution. Significantly one of the three was Saloth Sar, who in the 1950s had fought with the Viet Minh. The most that the Cambodian party could achieve at this stage, however, was to change its name to the Khmer Workers' Party (KWP).

The KWP's position changed radically in February 1963 as a result of continual demonstrations by high-school students in the province of Siem Reap, close to Angkor Wat. With the unrest spreading to Phnom Penh and Battambang the police intervened, and although several students were killed, order was only restored with the help of the army. The cabinet, accepting responsibility, resigned, while Sihanouk, then on a state visit to China, made clear that he would not. Returning to Phnom Penh, he was reluctant to blame communists directly, but instead asked his Minister of Defence, Lon Nol, for a list of subversives, which included the names of two KWP members, one of which was Saloth Sar.

Sihanouk, having invited 32 out of the 34 men listed to his residence, asked them to form a government, in which they would hold every office except that of prime minister and minister of defence. Although terrified by what would happen if they refused, the dire consequences of accepting Sihanouk's proposal still led them to do so. In the event Sihanouk took no further action, but in May 1963 the two KWP members left Phnom Penh to join the Viet Minh in the forests of eastern Cambodia, where they were to remain for the next eight years. This left the KWP with negligible influence on Cambodian politics, while at the same time Saloth Sar, protected and encouraged by his Vietnamese friends, began to organize the movement later to be known as Khmer Rouge.

The KWP was not the only threat to Sihanouk. Another political force, the *Khmer Serei*, founded in 1956 by Song Ngoc Thanh after he had returned from exile in France, was operating from bases in South Vietnam and Thailand. This, in Sihanouk's thinking, was only possible because of US support – not surprising given *Khmer Serei*'s outspoken anti-communist stance. Sihanouk's misgivings about the US were confirmed in November 1963, first by the murder of the Diem brothers in Saigon on the first day of the month,[19] and then by the arrest of two

Khmer Serei envoys who had entered Cambodia from Vietnam. In both cases Sihanouk saw, not implausibly, the hidden hand of US diplomacy, particularly since hostile Khmer Serei broadcasts continued to come from Bangkok and Saigon when the Americans could easily have suppressed them. His reaction was to order the immediate suspension of US military and economic aid, and a down-sizing of the US Embassy in Phnom Penh.[20] Of the two hapless Khmer Serei envoys – who had entered Cambodia expecting to negotiate with Sihanouk – one, who admitted that the US were aiding Thanh and supplying radio-transmitters to the Khmer Serei, was set free, while the other, who failed to do so, was tried by a military court and executed early in 1964.

The way Sihanouk dealt with the US benefited Cambodia in so far as it closed the door to US diplomatic (or more likely CIA) personnel intent on gathering intelligence along the border with Vietnam – a development that encouraged the Viet Minh to leave the rest of Cambodia at peace. On the other hand Sihanouk was left to confront communism alone, while the end to military aid meant that the equipment of his army, supplied by the Americans, rapidly became unserviceable. The KWP, at the behest of the Viet Minh, maintained a very low profile, while many potential supporters were in exile in North Vietnam. The status quo in Cambodia suited the Viet Minh, whose programme never included annexation of any part of the country. For the Viet Minh the KWP threatened to be more of a hindrance than a help, particularly since Saloth Sar was close to Beijing while the Chinese no longer supported North Vietnam.

The final months of 1966 witnessed a significant change of direction in Cambodian politics. In August, President de Gaulle made an impressive state visit to Cambodia. France had drawn the borders of modern Cambodia in the nineteenth century, and de Gaulle, whom Sihanouk had long admired, pledged to respect them, while the US, committed to both South Vietnam and Thailand, dragged its feet.

Following his success with de Gaulle, Sihanouk seemed to lose his grip, and in the election due in September 1966 failed to nominate Sangkum candidates. The result was the election of a new assembly, with members from many different parties, owing nothing to Sihanouk, who in the course of the campaign had labelled many of them as enemies of his regime. The new assembly voted a reluctant General Lon Nol into office as prime minister, but when he began to form a cabinet unacceptable to Sihanouk, the latter – as if taking a cue from the fourteenth-century popes in Avignon – formed a counter-government, and did his best to call the shots in Cambodian politics.

Times had changed for good. Lon Nol, who had always been loyal to Sihanouk, proved to have a mind of his own. In the face of a chaotic political situation in China, escalation of the war in Vietnam, local insurgency within Cambodia itself and a worsening financial crisis, Lon Nol did his best to establish some sort of order but his attempts to do so led to increasing unrest, among both students in Phnom Penh and peasants forced to sell their harvests at less than black market prices. A major uprising, which took place in Samlaut, a district close to the Thai frontier and far from Vietnam, was taken by Sihanouk to be communist-inspired, and on 7 April 1967 he threatened to 'treat the Khmer Reds as I have treated the Khmer Serei' – and arranged for the public execution of three agents of the latter group.

All this was too much for Lon Nol, who pleading ill-health, resigned as prime minister to seek medical treatment in France. Sihanouk formed a new Exceptional Government containing no assembly delegates. In spite of his hostility to the Khmer Rouge Sihanouk, behind the scenes, was seeking some sort of guarantee of Cambodia's territorial integrity not only from the communists in both North (Viet Minh) and South Vietnam (Viet Cong[21]) but also from Moscow. In this he was successful, but only at the cost of further unrest in Phnom Penh, for which local ethnic Chinese, loyal to Mao Zedong at the height of the Cultural Revolution, were largely responsible. Sihanouk's style of government inevitably alienated pro-Western members of the urban elite in Phnom Penh, long distrusted by him for their support of the Democratic Party in the early 1950s. The result, for Sihanouk, at the end of 1967, was that he was left with hardly any allies.

THE RAPPROCHEMENT WITH WASHINGTON

A new change of direction was called for, and so Sihanouk sought to restore relations with the US. This step was in the interest of both sides: Sihanouk was anxious to prevent US ground forces attacking Viet Cong bases in Cambodia, while the US wanted the frontier area opened to international inspection teams. In January 1968 Chester Bowles, the US Ambassador to India, visited Phnom Penh for four days of negotiations, which left the way open for the resumption of diplomatic relations.

Cambodia, having insisted on pledges by the US, South Vietnam and Thailand to honour its frontiers, had to wait for a year until Washington finally persuaded both Saigon and Bangkok – both with claims to Cambodian territory – to agree to this demand. This meant that the US Embassy in Phnom Penh only reopened on 22 May 1969, two weeks after the Viet Cong had raised its diplomatic representation to embassy status.

In May 1969, therefore, Cambodia completed the process of establishing its neutrality on all possible sides – in principle at least, since practice was quite another matter. In August Sihanouk once more appointed Lon Nol prime minister – describing him as 'the only person I could trust because of his faithfulness to the Throne and nation' – with his long-standing political ally, Sirik Matak, as his deputy.

By this time the American involvement in the war in Vietnam had reached maximum intensity, to include, from March 1969, bombing of Viet Cong positions inside Cambodia – according to US claims with the secret acquiescence of Sihanouk. With a new president, Richard Nixon, inaugurated in January, the commitment of US forces was almost certain to be reduced. In the meantime, Khmer Rouge guerrillas had become increasingly active inside Cambodia, so whatever the success of Sihanouk's diplomacy, he had to contend with an unprecedented level of internal unrest – caused mainly by the Khmer Rouge – whose reach by 1969 had long extended far beyond the frontier areas adjacent to Vietnam. So critical had the situation become that President Thieu of South Vietnam, meeting Nixon in Saigon on 30 July 1969, had warned him that 'if the balance in Cambodia were upset by the overthrow of Sihanouk the Communists would win in the end'.[22]

On 7 January 1970 Sihanouk, true to character, left his country once again on a lengthy trip abroad. He started with a two-month health-cure on the French Riviera, where, in late February, he stated his intention to visit 'those great, friendly countries', the Soviet Union and China, on the way home – hoping for their support in persuading North Vietnam to pull its forces out of Cambodia. At home the situation was getting out of hand. On 8 March villagers in Svay Rieng, the province geographically closest to Saigon, demonstrated against the North Vietnamese occupation, and on 11 March 20,000 young militants in Phnom Penh sacked the North Vietnamese and Viet Cong embassies. A day later the government acted, with Sirik Matak announcing the suspension of a trade agreement with the Viet Cong, combined with the recruitment of 10,000 new soldiers for the Cambodian Army. North Vietnam and the Viet Cong were told that their forces must leave Cambodia by dawn on 15 March.

LON NOL AND HIS MISSION TO SAVE CAMBODIA

Sihanouk, whose first reaction was to return directly to Phnom Penh, changed his mind and on 13 March announced that the planned Moscow visit would go ahead. On 18 March, his last day in Moscow, while on his way to the airport with Soviet Premier Kosygin, he learnt that the ninety-two members of the Cambodian National Assembly and Council of the Kingdom, led by Lon Nol and Sirik Matak, had voted to depose him. Even so he still went on to visit Beijing, to be assured there by Zhou Enlai that China still recognized him as head of state.

After only two days in Beijing, Sihanouk, attributing the 'turbulence' in Cambodia to collusion between the American CIA and Lon Nol's government, accepted the presence of North Vietnamese forces in Cambodia as necessary for 'resisting American imperialism'. A day later he proclaimed a struggle 'until victory of death' against the 'stooges of American imperialism' – notably Lon Nol and Sirik Matak.

All hell was let loose, and the fruit of months of Sihanouk's successful shuttle diplomacy went for nothing. While in Phnom Penh the National Assembly voted to charge Sihanouk with treason; Hanoi described Cambodia's new leaders as a 'pro-American ultra-rightist group' and affirmed its support for 'the struggle of the Cambodian people against them'. Far worse than the rhetoric were new attacks by North Vietnamese and Viet Cong forces, launched from their bases in Svay Rieng province, which with local support from the Khmer Rouge, penetrated deep into Cambodia, and across the frontier into South Vietnam. On 4 April, Le Duc Tho, representing North Vietnam at a meeting with Henry Kissinger in Paris, effectively declared war on Cambodia.

At the end of April the escalation of the war along the frontier between Cambodia and South Vietnam led to the Parrot's Beak incident described in Chapter 7, in which South Vietnamese forces won a battle against the Viet Cong in Svay Rieng, a province of Cambodia. If, in military terms, this was a relatively minor event in the war, it was seen by many in the US as a major breach of a long-standing commitment not to commit ground troops outside South Vietnam. Although no US troops took part, this was denounced by the *New York Times* as a 'virtual renunciation of the President's promise of disengagement from Southeast Asia'. This was the general reaction of the media, and not only in the US, and politicians, particularly in the US Congress, were bound to take notice.

Lon Nol's new government in Cambodia soon learnt that US help in its resistance to conquest by North Vietnam was regarded by the chairman of the Senate Foreign Relations Committee as 'additional [and by implication, unacceptable] extension of the war'. Nixon, in a speech made on 30 April 1970, tried to stem the tide of criticism, but the view of the *Washington Post* that he was defending 'a self-renewing war [supported] by suspect evidence, specious argument and excessive rhetoric' was widely accepted.

The result was campus unrest and violence in many different parts of the US, and on 4 May, four students at Kent State University, demonstrating against the war, were killed by rifle fire from the Ohio National Guard. Five days later up to 100,000 people demonstrated on the Ellipse in Washington, facing the White House. The government was completely demoralized, and from the summer of 1970 the Congress, with a succession of new amendments,[23] created a position in which, in the words of Henry Kissinger, 'the ultimate victims of America's domestic crisis [were] the people of Cambodia',[24] so that 'with the inevitability of a Greek tragedy ... there descended on that gentle land a horror that it did not deserve and that none of us have the right to forget'.[25]

In 1970, however, the full impact of the horror was still some six years in the future. For five years Lon Nol's government continued to defend Cambodia against Khmer Rouge onslaughts, backed up by the Viet Minh. In May 1970 Saloth Sar had returned to Cambodia via the Ho Chi Minh trail, and although he at first concentrated on helping the Viet Minh in South Vietnam, in 1972 he changed his policy to one of fighting Lon Nol on his own ground.

From 1970 to 1972 Lon Nol's forces more or less held their own, helped first by American bombing of communist positions inside the country, and second by material aid supplied by the US. On the other hand they were unable to prevent Khmer Rouge commandos disrupting the life of the countryside – after the manner of the Viet Cong in South Vietnam – and even, in January 1971, from destroying the entire Cambodian air-force – consisting of ten airplanes and four helicopters – at Phnom Penh's Pochentong Airport. This last attack shook the morale of the inhabitants of the capital city, whose number had greatly increased with refugees from the countryside.

The strain was too much for Lon Nol, who after suffering a minor stroke, was flown to Hawaii to recuperate in a US military hospital. He returned home in April 1971, and as a result of involved political manoeuvres, including his resignation as prime minister and directed mainly to reducing the power of Sirik Matak, the assembly voted him the rank of marshal. With this new status he launched a campaign designed to open the road to Kompong Thom, a town north of Phnom Penh in the heart of the area controlled by the Khmer Rouge, and a major base for supplying the Viet Cong in Vietnam.

Cambodian forces actually reached Kompong Thom in October, and Lon Nol proclaimed a major victory. This was premature. The opposing forces, which had never lost control of the forest areas on both sides of the road, counter-attacked, and on 1 December 1971 Lon Nol ordered his forces to retreat. The retreat became a rout, with some three thousand of Lon Nol's best troops killed in action, with many thousands more fleeing in all directions after abandoning their weapons and equipment.

Lon Nol, in spite of the acclaim greeting his *coup d'état* in March 1970, was completely discredited. His army was being defeated, his government was riddled by corruption, and what energy he had was devoted to maintaining his own power. In the last three years, up to 1975, hundreds of thousands came as refugees to Phnom Penh, while others, seeing the way the tide was going, joined the Khmer Rouge. Indiscriminate American bombing, about the only military operation still not blocked by Congress, killed thousands of civilians – although some of the alleged victims may actually have died as a result of Khmer Rouge atrocities. Finally, in August 1973, after half a million tons of bombs had been dropped on Cambodia – three times what had fallen on Japan in the last year of the Pacific War – the Congress called a halt, a move which led General Alexander

Haig to tell Nixon, 'We've lost Southeast Asia'.[26] Lon Nol certainly took the view that he had lost Cambodia, but even so his government held on, through one military defeat after another, until April 1975.

The three years, 1972–75, witnessed significant changes in both the membership and the objectives of the communist forces fighting in Cambodia. Where, before 1972, strategy reflected the paramount need to win the war in Vietnam, it then changed, together with the forces deployed, to take into account that there was also a war to be won inside Cambodia. At this stage, also, Saloth Sar emerged as pre-eminent among the Khmer Rouge, taking the popular name, Pol Pot, by which he became known to the world at large. Even so, his leadership of the top cadres was not uncontested, at least in the period preceding the final defeat of Lon Nol's republic in April 1975. The new orientation of the Khmer Rouge also reflected Pol Pot's enthusiasm for Mao Zedong's Cultural Revolution, whose governing principles he hoped himself to apply once in power in Phnom Penh. Beijing, although concerned about where Pol Pot's extremism might lead him, nonetheless welcomed, with some reservation, the prospect of Cambodia under the Khmer Rouge as a counterweight to a new Vietnam allied to Moscow. That the confrontation between Moscow and Beijing was also played out in Cambodia is shown by the way the former supported Lon Nol to the very end, while the latter supported Sihanouk.

The change in Khmer Rouge strategy after 1972 led to a remarkable visit to Cambodia, made in the early months of 1973, by Sihanouk, from his exile in China. After travelling down the Ho Chi Minh trail for eight days in Soviet jeeps, Sihanouk, with his customary entourage, entered Cambodia where he was joined by Pol Pot. A week later the party reached its final destination, a typical Khmer House in Phnom Koulen, a city just north of Angkor. Ceremonies were held in honour of Sihanouk, a visit was made to the Angkor Wat temple complex, and Sihanouk composed a song entitled 'Thank You, Ho Chi Minh Trail'.[27]

After returning to China in April 1973, Sihanouk once again set off on a foreign tour, to practise his own distinctive personal diplomacy, although it must have been uncertain just whom he was representing. In May he told Oriana Fallaci, a well-known journalist, in Rome, that he was '100 percent with the Khmer Rouge'.[28] He coupled this statement with a remarkable political insight: 'I am useful to them because without me they wouldn't have the peasants and you can't make a revolution in Cambodia without the peasants'. He added, however, 'The Khmer Rouge do not love me at all … I understand very well that when I shall no longer be useful to them, they'll spit me out like a cherry pit'.[29]

By the end of 1973 Khmer Rouge forces had begun closing in on Phnom Penh, and by January 1974 they were sufficiently close to attack the city with both rockets and artillery. Surprisingly Lon Nol's forces were able to hold the Khmer Rouge at bay for the whole of 1974, perhaps because the Viet Minh kept it short of weapons and ammunition. Plainly this could only be a temporary respite, and by the end of 1974 the Khmer Rouge could obtain almost unlimited supplies. A country-wide offensive was launched on 1 January 1975, and Cambodia without new American support was helpless.

The US Ambassador in Phnom Penh worked hard to negotiate a political solution involving both the Khmer Rouge and Sihanouk, and the State Department even went so far as to enlist the support of the heads of government in Singapore and Indonesia. Beijing, claiming that the dire position of Cambodia was a purely internal matter, did its best to block access to Sihanouk, but on 28 March John Holdridge, deputy chief of the US mission, did succeed in getting an invitation to discussions through to him. This was rejected the next day, and the last chance of achieving an acceptable political solution was gone.

On 1 April Lon Nol left Phnom Penh 'on vacation', but in reality for exile. On 10 April Sihanouk let it be known that he did not want the Khmer Rouge to take over completely, but it was far too late for any intervention on his part to prevent this happening. Even so Holdridge, acting on State Department instructions, offered to arrange with Beijing for Sihanouk to make a last-minute return to Phnom Penh. If anything had come of this, Sihanouk would have found no Americans left to talk to. During the morning of 12 April helicopters evacuated 82 Americans, 159 Cambodians and 35 other nationals from the US Embassy compound. Unlike in Saigon two weeks later, many prominent members of the government, having been offered the prospect of exile, preferred to stay behind. These included Sirik Matak, who in 1970 had led the coup that brought Lon Nol to power. Just before he himself left Phnom Penh, the US Ambassador received the following letter:

> Dear Excellency and Friend:
>
> I thank you very sincerely for your ... offer to transport me towards freedom. I cannot, alas, leave in such a cowardly fashion. As for you, and in particular for your great country, I never believed for a moment that you would have this sentiment of abandoning a people which had chosen liberty. You have refused us your protection, and we can do nothing about it.
>
> You leave, and my wish is that you and your country will find happiness under this sky. But, mark it well, that if I shall die here on the spot and in my country that I love, it is no matter, because we are all born and must die. I have only committed this mistake in believing in you [the Americans].
>
> Please accept, Excellency and dear friend, my faithful and friendly sentiments.
> S/Sirik Matak

Phnom Penh fell to the Khmer Rouge on 17 April 1975. Sirik Matak, shot in the stomach and denied medical help, took three days to die. All the others who had governed with him, including civil service employees, were executed by the

Khmer Rouge, together with their families. Two million Cambodians in Phnom Penh – a number including many who had sought refuge there from outside – were ordered to leave the city, to chance their luck in a countryside ravaged by war. A reign of terror, unprecedented in the history of Southeast Asia, had begun. The driving force behind it was just one man, Pol Pot.

POL POT'S KILLING FIELDS

The history of the revolutionary years in Cambodia must largely be reconstructed from the oral testimony of those who survived the Pol Pot regime. But it is above all the numbers involved which give some measure of the price exacted by Pol Pot from the country he ruled. In four years, 1975–79, a million people died, and half a million more survived only by fleeing into exile. Cities became a wasteland, lives were ruined, families broken up, treasured possessions expropriated, if not destroyed.[30] One thing which can be said is that the revolution was carried out with extraordinary speed. The devastation, summed up by 'the killing fields',[31] for which it now mainly known to history, was ruthlessly carried out from the very first days. It is as if Pol Pot worked from a blue-print with which he was already thoroughly familiar. This could well be the case for the top cadres of the Khmer Rouge had had five years odd to plan the revolution. As Pol Pot saw it, everything he did was dictated by inexorable historical laws – the classic Marxist position. One former colleague, borrowing words first applied to Lenin, described him as 'the only man who had no thoughts but thoughts about revolution, and who in his sleep first dreamt of revolution'.

Two questions arise: first, what was Pol Pot aiming at, and second, how and why did his revolution fail? As to the first question, Democratic Kampuchea – the new name bestowed on Cambodia by the Khmer Rouge after their victory on 17 April 1975 – was chosen to signify the end of two thousand years of history. Traditional Cambodia was to give way to a new state inspired by ideals of the French Revolution, Chairman Mao's Great Leap Forward of the 1950s and the Cultural Revolution that followed it in the 1960s, the Soviet collectivization of agriculture and the North Korean *juche* doctrine of self-reliance. Pol Pot saw himself as destined to overthrow the wicked king (*sdach piel*) of Cambodian prophetic literature and to lead his country in a twentieth-century war against unbelievers, or *thmil* – that is, in his perception, people who rejected his teaching.

Pol Pot professed to abjure the cult of personality, but standing alone at the pinnacle of the party and the state he drew on traditions of command that made it hard for him to distinguish between disagreement and treason. In this he resembled Sihanouk and Lon Nol, for all three men can be seen as dynastic founders whose one-reign dynasties collapsed.

In the event, power corrupted the top cadres of Pol Pot's Democratic Kampuchea, who looked after themselves while even the poor peasants it claimed to represent suffered unprecedented hardship: inevitably popular support declined. For most of the millions of Cambodians his ideas were alien and incomprehensible. It was not sufficient to emphasize Khmer uniqueness and Kampuchea's glorious past, or to capitalize on the ubiquitous hatred of Vietnam. The elimination of markets, money and master–servant relationships was bought at the price of an appalling reign of terror. Kampuchea may have had a long history of violence, but under the Khmer Rouge there was no social restraint, so 'violent death became a national phenomenon'.[32]

Pol Pot, realizing how popular Sihanouk was in the countryside, allowed him to return to Kampuchea as Chief of State in the autumn of 1975. The early months of 1976 Sihanouk spent visiting rural cooperatives – the hard core of the new agricultural programme – factories and hydraulic works, but what he saw convinced him the prospects held out to him during his 1973 visit were far from being realized. He repudiated the role assigned to him, and Pol Pot, furious with this treachery, banished five of Sihanouk's children, and fifteen grandchildren to rural cooperatives: none of them ever returned. Sihanouk himself became a virtual prisoner in the Royal Palace, where occasionally Khieu Samphân – his successor as Chief of State and a close associate of Pol Pot – would come with a black Mercedes to take him for a ride in the countryside, where he could look at smiling peasants digging canals.[33]

Pol Pot, once in power, conceived of his role as leading combatants (*yothea*) in offensives (*vay samrok*) against enemies (*khmang*) of his new Kampuchea. On 1 January 1978 Khmer Rouge officials, visiting Beijing, announced, publicly, that their country was at war with Vietnam. Pol Pot, never rational, contended that the failure of his regime was caused by Vietnamese infiltration, as described in a policy document entitled 'Black Paper: Facts and Evidences of Vietnamese Acts of Aggression and Annexation against Kampuchea'.[34] In fact the Khmer Rouge, very soon after their victory in 1975, expelled some 300,000 Vietnamese – almost the entire community – resident in Kampuchea.[35] This is not recorded in the Black Paper.

INVASION FROM VIETNAM

Vietnam was forced to react, not so much because of what happened in Beijing on 1 January 1978, but because they could see that if they failed to take over in Kampuchea, when the Khmer Rouge regime faced collapse, forces hostile to Vietnam would do so.[36] By the end of 1978 there were already considerable numbers of Cambodians in Vietnam. Some had trained with the Viet Cong and never returned home, some were refugees from Pol Pot, and some had served with Pol Pot in 1975 but had rebelled against him to organize resistance in the frontier areas of Vietnam. Hun Sen, one of the leaders of this last group, later played a key role in a reconstituted Cambodia: in 1978, he was one of the organizers of the Kampuchean National United Front for National Salvation (KNUFNS), which was in the spearhead of the Vietnamese invasion planned for the end of the year.

In the event, even before the end of 1978, invading Vietnamese forces, together with troops from KNUFNS, penetrated deep into Kampuchea, to go on to capture Phnom Penh on 7 January 1979. Once in the city the Vietnamese soon discovered Tuol Sleng, the notorious Khmer Rouge interrogation centre. The documentation left behind included not only the forced confessions of its victims, but official records of the appalling ways in which they had been put to death. The horrors of Pol Pot's 'killing fields' were becoming open to world scrutiny.

Vietnam, having won the war against Pol Pot's Democratic Kampuchea – with 224,000 soldiers committed to it and some 50,000 casualties – still had to win the peace in a devastated and mainly hostile country. To provide an alternative to that of Democratic Kampuchea, Vietnam – shortly before the fall of Phnom Penh – established the People's Revolutionary Party of Kampuchea (PRPK) as the legitimate local successor to the old Indochina Communist Party. This in turn formed a government in which most offices were filled by Cambodians returning home from some twenty-five years of exile in Vietnam.

The new government allowed the gradual return to Phnom Penh of the tens of thousands of people whom Pol Pot had forced to leave the city. Against this background a new administration was created, for the first two years (1979–81) under Khieu Samphân (who had been chief of state under Pol Pot in the period 1977–79 following the departure of Sihanouk), and then under Chan Si (1981–85) and Hun Sen (1985–89). The latter's service with the KNUFNS in the invasion of 1978–79 marked him out for an important role in any PRPK government, and after 1985, when he became prime minister, he played a key part in establishing a new kingdom of Kampuchea.

The PRPK recruited very widely to find the personnel required for its new administration. Many non-communists, particularly minor bureaucrats who had managed to survive Pol Pot's reign of terror, were willing to rebuild the state under Vietnamese guidance. The result was a new style of socialism, wide open to the world market, whether by trading along the coast or across the land frontier with Thailand, with little state intervention.

Whatever its success in restoring order to Kampuchea, Vietnam still needed to find a long-term political solution for the future of a country which only the force of circumstance led it to occupy. Hanoi's policy had never been to extend its empire beyond Vietnam's historical frontiers. On the other hand, following the Vietnamese invasion some 400,000 Khmer Rouge had found refuge in the forests along both sides of the frontier with Thailand. There they were joined, if in smaller numbers, by others who had fled the country to escape from Pol Pot in 1975 and Lon Nol in 1970.

Since the border population was normally very small – little more than a quarter of million – the presence of vast numbers of refugees, at odds with each other, did not bode well for the future of Kampuchea. The Thai government, on its side of the frontier, worked hard to keep the opposing factions apart, setting up separate camps for each of them. In this situation two new parties emerged: the first of these, the Khmer People's National Liberation Front (KPNLF), was the party for those who had worked with Lon Nol until his regime was overthrown by Pol Pot in 1975; the second, Funcinpec,[37] was established by Sihanouk in March 1981 to provide a political home for those who had supported him against Lon Nol in 1970.

To the Vietnamese in Phnom Penh the problem, throughout the 1980s, was to find an exit strategy that would not create a void that one or other of the Khmer Rouge, the KPNLF and Funcinpec was bound to fill if it had the chance. The doom scenario did not only worry the Vietnamese; it was a major concern to the United States, China, the Soviet Union and all the countries of Southeast Asia.

The United States, given the success of both its China policy following Nixon's visit to Beijing in 1972, and its condemnation of the Soviet Union as the result of Brezhnev's invasion of Afghanistan in 1979, would in principle welcome the collapse of the PRPK government in Phnom Penh, which was supported by Moscow.

But then the way would be open to the Khmer Rouge, with its appalling human rights record, to return to play a major, if not a dominant part in Kampuchean politics. Given, however, the strength of the Khmer Rouge in the border areas, it could hardly be left out of the equation – the more so, given the level of the support it enjoyed in Beijing.

As for Southeast Asia the country that counted most was Thailand, whose main wish was to clear the camps along the border with Kampuchea – making certain, at every stage, that it had US support. If, however, the camps were cleared, their occupants had no alternative to making some kind of a living in the forest areas just inside Kampuchea. The results were chaotic, with warlords emerging with their own private militias and fighting turf-wars to protect their own smuggling operations; these in turn were only possible because of clandestine support from Thai officers on the other side of the border.

This situation particularly favoured the Khmer Rouge, simply because both Beijing and Washington continued to recognize it as the legitimate government of Cambodia. Since Bangkok consistently followed Washington, the PRPK, although in control of most of the country (including its capital, Phnom Penh), was unable to prevent supplies reaching the Khmer Rouge across its porous Thai frontier. This deprived the PRPK of its chance of starving the Khmer Rouge to death.[38]

AN UNEASY PEACE

In spite of this unstable situation, time, during the 1980s, was on the side of restoring peace and order in a united Kampuchea. For one thing the numbers still adhering to the rump of the Khmer Rouge were steadily declining, which allowed the Vietnamese to withdraw the last of its own forces in September 1989.[39] Pol Pot, who only died in 1998, no longer played any significant part. Hun Sen, who had been prime minister under the Vietnamese since 1985, then proclaimed the new State of Cambodia (SOC), with a one-party government, that of the People's Democratic Party of Kampuchea (PDPK), of which he was the leader. Whereas in 1985 the chances of a peace settlement were slender – simply because Washington would then block anything acceptable to Vietnam – by 1989 Hun Sen's position was much stronger, both because of changes in Soviet policy relating to Southeast Asia, and because of Washington's perception of these changes following George H.W. Bush succeeding Ronald Reagan as President.

Nearly two years earlier, on 2 December 1987, Sihanouk and Hun Sen, the PRPK prime minister, found it safe to meet in Paris and discuss the future of Kampuchea. At this meeting Sihanouk, supported by his son Prince Ranariddh, represented the remarkable Coalition Government of Democratic Kampuchea (CGDK), whose members were Funcinpec – his own party – the KPNLF and the Khmer Rouge. The result, as described by one observer, was 'a strange creature, a shotgun marriage of three partners whose mutual hatred was only exceeded by their antipathy for the PRPK and Vietnamese'. If, at one time or another, all the factions represented in the CGDK had been rejected by the people of Kampuchea, it provided, at the end of the 1980s, the only foundation for negotiating the country's future with the PRPK and its leader, Hun Sen.

Also in 1989 two major events outside Kampuchea were favourable to its future. On 15 February, the ten-year Soviet occupation of Afghanistan came to an end. Moscow, by accepting this radical change in foreign policy, sent a clear signal to Vietnam that it would be on its own in Southeast Asia. In Beijing, in June, the brutal suppression, by Chinese soldiers, of a student demonstration in Tiananmen Square proved, internationally, to be a public-relations disaster, occurring at a time when Li Peng's government was working hard to improve its relations with both the Soviet Union and the United States. Faced with a diplomatic crisis, and with the Soviet Union no longer an important factor in Kampuchea, Beijing had much to gain, and little to lose, by disowning the Khmer Rouge. Inside Kampuchea the traditional market economy was beginning to revive, with consumer goods and property speculation once more a normal part of life. The PRPK, having lost control of the border regions, realized only too well that a decisive victory for its own low-key communism was no longer on the cards. The only way forward was for all the parties involved – the PRPK, the Khmer Rouge, Funcinpec and the KPNLF – to accommodate each other.

The process was directed to setting up an interim national government called the Supreme National Council (SNC), which would provide the foundation for a new constitution to be drawn up with the help of the UN. The SNC was established on 17 September 1990, following conferences – in Jakarta and Tokyo – attended by all the parties earlier in the year. In 1991 two further conferences – in Jakarta and Pattaya[40] – paved the way for the Paris Agreements signed in October 1991.

Not only were all five permanent member states of the UN Security Council represented in Paris, but they had also agreed, in advance, on a framework for a political settlement. Essentially all the Cambodian factions would abandon the military option and play a part in the democratic process, under the supervision of a new United Nations Transitional Authority in Cambodia (UNTAC).

THE UN PEACEKEEPERS

The military component of UNTAC would be critical to its success. It had five essential tasks: first, it would supervise the permanent withdrawal of all foreign forces, together with their weapons and equipment. Second, it would collaborate with the governments of neighbouring states – primarily Vietnam and Thailand – to restrain any local developments threatening the implementation of the Paris Agreements. Third, it would monitor the cessation of military assistance to any of the Cambodian factions. Fourth, it would locate and confiscate caches of weapons and military equipment within Cambodia. Fifth, it would organize training programmes enabling the people of Cambodia to clear land-mines.

The stated aim of the so-called P-5 framework was to 'safeguard the neutral status of Cambodia [and] prevent foreign aggression against Cambodia or interference in the affairs of that state',[41] at the same time ensuring 'the non-return to the policies and practices of the past'.[42]

As intended by the parties to the Paris Agreements the new order in Kampuchea would put an end to the polarization between the SOC, led by Hun Sen – the main political force inside the country – and the CGDK, a coalition led mainly by Sihanouk from outside. The three parties in the CGDK would then compete on equal terms with the SOC in the elections to be held under the new constitution. At the same time Sihanouk returned to Kampuchea to be chairman of the SNC until elections were held in 1993.

In the election line-up the government party of the SOC named itself the Cambodian People's Party (CPP), while the KPNLF became the Buddhist Liberal Democratic Party (BLDP). Funcinpec kept its name, and the Khmer Rouge tried to spoil the whole electoral process, first by boycotting it and then by attacking the CPP and capturing UNTAC personnel. The Khmer Rouge was not alone; in Battambang province the CPP repeatedly attacked party offices of Funcinpec and the BLDP, causing more than two hundred deaths in the early months of 1993.

More than four million people voted in the election, which was held in May 1993 – a remarkably high turn-out. Voters, in the judgement of almost all observers, were 'able to make a free and fair choice'.[43] Funcinpec and the CPP won more than 90 per cent of the 120 seats in the new parliament, but neither had a majority. The BLDP won only ten seats while the small Moulinaka party got one. There were also sixteen parties left without a single seat.

The result was that a new Royal National Government of Cambodia (RNGC) was constituted by a vote of the National Assembly on 29 October 1993. Sihanouk (after 38 years once more King of Cambodia following an earlier vote of the National Assembly in September 1993) had already appointed his oldest son, Ranariddh (leader of Funcinpec), as First Prime Minister and Hun Sen (leader of the CPP) as Second Prime Minister in the new coalition government – the order of precedence being the result of Funcinpec winning marginally more seats than the CPP. UNTAC, having completed its mission, was wound up, and Washington reluctantly accepted a coalition including the CPP.[44]

The Khmer Rouge, however, still refused all cooperation, even though in September it had praised Sihanouk – king once more – as 'the only person capable of prodding all national forces into national reconciliation'. This proved not to apply to the Khmer Rouge, in spite of Sihanouk's entreaties to the new government. Even with his son (and successor) as joint prime minister, Sihanouk was about as effective as Shakespeare's King Lear.

The new government's main problems were economic: Cambodia, heavily in debt, was one of the world's poorest nations, although some progress had been made under the SOC in the early 1990s. The Khmer Rouge, with nearly ten thousand men still under arms, was a continuing threat to law and order, but the new king's peace initiatives – which included offering ministerial posts to the Khmer Rouge – got nowhere. Prince Ranariddh blocked his father's proposals as unconstitutional. At the same time the second prime minister, Hun Sen, refused to enter into talks with Khieu Samphan, the Khmer Rouge leader. Sihanouk did not give up, and in June 1994 talks did finally take place in the Royal Palace in Phnom Penh. Nothing was achieved and in July the National Assembly voted to outlaw the Khmer Rouge, which in the same month had taken three foreign hostages. Even though Sihanouk made a direct appeal to Khieu Samphan for their release, they were still finally executed.

Outlawed by the National Assembly the Khmer Rouge revived its guerrilla war against the Cambodian National Armed Forces, at the same time not hesitating to kill civilians and UN personnel. The war was bitterly fought for more than two years, mainly in areas northwest of Phnom Penh in the direction of Thailand. Its toll on the national economy was disastrous, and its legacy included some ten million land-mines – leaving Cambodia with the world's highest proportion of disabled citizens. By denying access to land in agricultural areas, the mines were a major factor in the impoverishment of rural communities. Thousands of refugees added to the country's problems. Even so, the government was rebuilding the country, and the situation was nowhere near so appalling as it had been under Pol Pot in the late 1970s.

The fate of the Khmer Rouge during the early 1990s was greatly influenced by shifting alliances in the international community. As already noted, until 1990 Washington supported the Khmer Rouge against Hun Sen's PRPK. The scenario changed radically with the impending collapse of the Soviet Union at the end of the 1980s, so although in 1990 Washington's declared policy was still to marginalize the CPP, it was ready to enter into dialogue, making clear at the same time its 'unalterable opposition to the Khmer Rouge shooting its way back into power'[45] while showing 'growing interest in prospects for normalization of relations with Vietnam'. This was a significant change of direction.

Finally, on 4 January 1992, Washington lifted its embargo on Cambodia, and in March accepted that the 'United Nations is the best insurance against a return to power by the Khmer Rouge'. This left China out in the cold in Southeast Asia, so the Khmer Rouge was on its own. China, anxious to continue its most-favoured nation status from the US, limited its interest in the whole area to support for the local ethnic Chinese communities. Nonetheless, the Khmer Rouge continued to fight a battle it had little chance of winning, and remained a force to be reckoned with in Cambodian politics. The close ties between the state and Hun Sen's CPP, established during the 1980s, continued after the Paris Agreements, depriving the Khmer Rouge of the level playing-field which they envisaged.[46] This, at least, was its own perception, providing good reason for boycotting the democratic process. In terms of *realpolitik* there was no room for two competing communist parties. Even so, the Khmer Rouge, during the 1990s, retained considerable grass-roots support, and was able to turn many parts of the country into 'no-go areas' for government forces. This may seem astonishing given the reign of terror it maintained during its three years (1975–78) in power, but this was clearly focused on the centre, while the areas still controlled by the Khmer Rouge after its defeat in 1979 were on the periphery – and the state that emerged from the Paris Agreements was highly centralized. The Khmer Rouge cause was also helped by the close association – as perceived at grass-roots level – between the CPP and the substantial Vietnamese population of Cambodia.

COALITION GOVERNMENT

The unwieldy government that came to power following the elections of 1993 proved to be dysfunctional, if only because of the competing commitments made by both the CPP and Funcinpec to their own supporters. At every level from Phnom Penh down to the remotest villages offices were effectively created in duplicate to satisfy the demand for government patronage by supporters of both parties. With poor salaries – all that the government could afford – officials were open to corruption at every level, and the worst example was set by those at the top.

The National Assembly avoided issues likely to cause confrontation, and although Funcinpec had more seats than the CPP, the latter, having enjoyed power during the years before 1993, had far more members with experience of government service. The process of government would have been impossible without CPP personnel: officials from the Funcinpec contributed little. Hun Sen, who had first been prime minister in 1985, continually got the better of Prince Ranariddh: their ostensible collaboration was a façade and Hun Sen is on record for saying that '[although] we hug and kiss, we do not love each other. In fact, we barely speak ... because we have little to discuss'.[47]

If Ranariddh, albeit reluctantly, accepted the dominance of Hun Sen, the rank and file of Funcinpec did not. Ranariddh's occasional protests against the way his party was treated – for instance with the appointment of judges in 1995 – were ineffective, and his credibility, in both Cambodia and internationally, was seriously compromised.

In March 1996 Funcinpec forced Ranariddh's hand by convening its first party congress since the 1993 elections and using this to launch a new 'strategy of provocation' to 'gain lost political ground by creating a crisis in which [Hun Sen] would make a fatal mistake that would then benefit Prince Ranariddh'.[48] This was accompanied by a veiled threat to withdraw from the government if Funcinpec's demands were not satisfied.

Ranariddh unwisely provoked Hun Sen – who was already losing patience – in two ways. First, he tried to capitalize on Vietnam's historical role – during the 1980s – in supporting the government of which Han Sen had always been an active member (and prime minister since 1985). Second, he tried to recruit dissident members of the Khmer Rouge, which by this time was split into a number of rival factions. Here Ranariddh was pre-empted by Hun Sen, when at the end of 1996 Ieng Sary, a leading member of the Khmer Rouge, defected to the CPP, because, in his own words, 'he did not want to be on the side of the losers'.

In 1997 Ranariddh continued to play a dangerous game, arranging, surreptitiously, for a container of arms to be unloaded at the port of Sihanoukville. This event, in Hun Sen's view, only made sense as a part of Funcinpac's strategy to encourage the 'defection of more Khmer Rouge troops'. Then, in July 1997, just as Ranariddh was about to agree to Khieu Samphan – a rival to Ieng Sary and still prominent in the Khmer Rouge – joining the government, fighting broke out between the police headquarters of the CPP and Funcinpac in Phnom Penh. This may have been an *auto-coup* orchestrated by Hun Sen, but in any event it sealed the fate of Ranariddh, who, after first resigning as prime minister, went into exile. A CPP spokesman immediately claimed the moral high-ground: 'It was within the domain of the government's responsibility to prevent and put a check on illegal armed elements and to act against the clandestine outlawed elements of the Khmer Rouge'.

A successor to Ranariddh as first prime minister was appointed from his own party, Funcinpac. Ung Huot, who had been the Funcinpac foreign minister, was in Australia in July 1997, and so missed the events that led to the fall of Ranariddh. He was acceptable to both UNTAC and Hun Sen, in the latter case because he was clearly ready to allow Funcinpac to submit to the CPP. This proved to be the case, but Cambodia paid a high price. ASEAN, Japan and, later, Europe, if reluctantly accepting the increased power of the CPP, still reduced the level of their aid. The US went further and cut off all development aid, and suspended the activities of many of the agencies working in Cambodia. Given the lasting trauma of the war in Vietnam, US politics had no room for any policy favourable to a government, such as that of the Hun Sen's newly reconstructed Cambodia, which only ever existed because of Vietnamese intervention. It did not matter that this intervention went back to 1978, nor that Vietnam had withdrawn completely from Cambodia in 1989.

The future of the political line-up, following the events of July 1997, was determined by the nation-wide elections held on 26 July 1998. Although the main contest was bound to be between the CPP and Funcinpac, the position was complicated by the emergence of a new party, led by Sam Rainsy, who had been expelled from both Funcinpac and the National Assembly in 1994, after fighting tenaciously, as Minister of Finance, against government corruption. Since Ranariddh, urged on by Hun Sen, had taken the initiative, it is not surprising that neither of them welcomed Sam Rainsy's success in founding a new Khmer Nation Party, nor that they were suspected of being involved in an attack on its leader's life in 1997. The party, renamed the Sam Rainsy Party, then contested the 1998 elections, with its candidates being harassed on every side during the election campaign. Even so it won 15 seats, compared to the 43 won by Funcinpac and the 73 won by the CPP.

Any number of foreign observers, politicians, officers who had served with UNTAC, former ambassadors, together with representatives of international agencies, turned up for the elections. Predictably their judgements were polarized: the Joint International Observer Group, and many others, found the elections 'free and fair'; others, coming mainly from Australia, Canada and the US, found them 'flawed'. Voters turned up in large numbers, voting was open and peaceful, and the counting of ballots well administered.[49]

The fact that the CPP won a majority of the seats may reflect its essential control of government agencies, but even so the party failed to win the two-thirds majority necessary for new legislation. The pattern of the 1998 elections was repeated on 27 July 2003, when elections were held under the five-year rule incorporated in the 1993 constitution: the number of CPP seats increased from 64 to 73, while the Sam Rainsy Party went from 15 to 24. The losers were Funcinpec, down to 26 from 43, doubtless as a result of Ranariddh failing to work effectively with Hun Sen.

Finally, in October 2004, Norodom Sihanouk, 82 years old, abdicated in favour of his low-profile son, Norodom Sihamoni, by his favourite, sixth wife, Monique Izzi. The succession was approved by both Hun Sen and Ranariddh – the new king's half-brother – but it was undoubtedly the former who had orchestrated it. In 2005 Hun Sen had Sam Rainsy tried in absentia – the result of prudently choosing for temporary exile in Paris – for falsely accusing him of being behind the 1997 assassination attempt. Rainsy was convicted and sentenced to 18 months' imprisonment, but early in 2006 he was able to return to Kampuchea following an amnesty granted by the new king. Even so, Hun Sen continues to be the most stable element in Cambodian politics, which must mean that his – for all its shortcomings – is still the best game in town.

9

Malaysia and Singapore: invention of Asian values

THE END OF BRITISH RULE

When, at the end of 1945, the British had to pick up the pieces of their colonial empire in Southeast Asia – following nearly four years of Japanese occupation during the Pacific War – it was clear that a new order, foreshadowing independence in the not too distant future, had to be established.

In their political status, as orchestrated by the British over a period of well over a century, the pieces were remarkably heterogeneous. There were two main regions, Malaya and Borneo, which in colonial times had developed independently of each other. Malaya (which was mainly continental and had a land frontier with Thailand) was divided up between the Straits Settlements, the Federated and the Unfederated Malay States. Borneo, on the other hand, was a very large island, of which the much greater southern part belonged to the Dutch East Indies. From east to west along the north coast there were, however, three British protectorates, North Borneo, Brunei and Sarawak.

In Malaya the Straits Settlements, defined by the three main harbour cities, Penang, Melaka and Singapore, had been under direct British rule since the nineteenth century. Melaka, historically the most important, had long before the end of the century been eclipsed, first by Penang, and then by Singapore – both, significantly, offshore islands. Singapore, which at the beginning of the century had been little more than a home for pirates and sea-gypsies, became not only a commercial centre but also, as a naval- and air-base, the key to British defences in the western Pacific.

There were four Federated Malay States, the sultanates of Perak, Selangor and Negri Sembilan, on the west coast, and Pahang on the east. In each case the sultan, as a result of British diplomacy, had accepted a British resident whose rule covered all aspects of government except for religion and culture. The residents, in turn, were subordinate to the British governor in Kuala Lumpur, which became the federal capital in 1895. The main reason for British policy was economic: tin had long been mined in the west-coast states, and these, in the twentieth century, also became the site of the new rubber plantations. Because Malaya was a leading producer, world-wide, of both commodities, they were the mainstay of the federal economy. Given that indigenous Malays provided little of the capital or labour needed for their exploitation, it made sense, to the British, to establish a system of close control. Pahang, on the other hand, was incorporated largely because the sultanate had problems with law and order: it also gave Kuala Lumpur a hold on the east coast.

The unfederated states were Perlis, Kedah, Kelantan and Terengganu – the four sultanates bordering Thailand – together with Johore, at the southern end of the peninsula, to which Singapore had belonged before it became one of the Straits Settlements. In the four northern states, which had little economic potential, the British were content to allow the sultans to rule with no more than British advisers to support them. In particular, once Thailand, by agreeing the Treaty of Bangkok in 1909, abandoned its historical territorial claims, there was little perceived threat to peace in the north of Malaya. Johore was a different case altogether. Its location made it commercially important, in step with the growth of the harbour of Singapore, to which it was connected by rail in 1923. The sultan, however, was too powerful for the British in Kuala Lumpur to wish to interfere with his rule: it was clear to both sides that the interests of Johore were closely tied to both Singapore and the Federated States. The sultan was trusted not to rock the boat.

The threefold division of British Borneo was quite different to that of Malaya. In the late nineteenth century the extreme north of the island was developed as an estate of the North Borneo Company, a British enterprise established precisely for this purpose. Sarawak, a much larger region, with a long coastline on the South China Sea to the west of that of North Borneo, was ruled by the British Brooke family. The line of so-called 'white rajahs' had established, almost by accident in 1841, a hereditary dynasty which remained in power until 1946. Finally there was the sultanate of Brunei, to which the whole coastline had once been tributary. Once the most important commercial power over a wide area of land and sea, it lost out to the sultanate of Sulu in the Philippines in the eighteenth century, and in the nineteenth to the Dutch and British. In the end it only survived by grace of the British, who, following the Malayan pattern, in 1905 appointed their own resident to rule from the Sultan's court.

In 1888 Britain declared a protectorate of all three territories in Borneo, but this was mainly to establish its prior claim to exploit them in the face of other European powers – which by this time included Germany. In the twentieth century the British pre-emptive rights proved extremely valuable with the export of tropical hardwood and rubber, and, above all, oil, in considerable quantities. Even so, the development of the infrastructure, health services and education remained far below the level of Malaya.

The question is, what explains all this complexity in British Southeast Asia? On one side there is a history of demographic and political confusion, on the other, an *ad hoc* pragmatic approach to every new situation. Taking the demography first, the whole region was home to an original population of Malays, whose domain also covered much of the Dutch East Indies and odd bits of Thailand and the Philippines. Given that they were so widespread, there was considerable variation between their different local cultures: even so, all the populations spoke much the same language, enjoyed, in common, economic and social organization, culture and religion. Many were also closely tied to the sea – above all in Borneo, where the inland populations supported a variety of cultures little influenced by contact with the outside world.

A Malay's home was in a village, known as a *kampung*. If it was inland, its subsistence economy would be based on wet-rice cultivation, if on the coast, on fishing, supplemented by part-time agriculture.[1] In the village each inhabitant would know his or her own status, defined first according to sex and age and then according to the traditional ranking of families. Villages belonged to chiefdoms, and the chiefdoms were subordinate to the prince at the head of the state to which they belonged. Because the religion was Islam, the prince was a sultan, and his realm a sultanate.

Throughout the nineteenth century, the British in Malaya, and to a lesser extent in Borneo, worked hard to stabilize the realms of rival sultans – a policy which often required unashamed support for one favoured individual. In this way, the boundaries between the different states of Malaya became fixed, allowing each one of them to invest its political capital in domestic affairs rather than conflict with its neighbours.

If Malays had been the sole inhabitants to confront the British in South Asia, and if, then, their economies were truly segmentary, in the form described above, life would have been simple for all concerned. This was far from the reality. With Asia opening up to the world market for commodities requiring considerable capital investment, like tin and rubber in Malaya, the small-scale rural society, based on the *kampung*, was only part of the picture – and from any global perspective the least important. To the British in Malaya the *kampung*-based society was entirely acceptable in regions with little potential for profitable investment, such as the unfederated states along the frontier with Thailand. At the end of the Pacific War this led one commentator to note that 'when the British came the Malay was a poor man in a poor country; when they left he was a poor man in a rich country'.[2]

In the federated states, however, and even more, in the Straits Settlements, the demands of the world economy, as mediated by the British, changed the picture entirely. In the federated states the labour force of the tin-mines and rubber plantations was Chinese rather than Malay, with expatriate British managers, and the same was true of commerce and industry in the Straits Settlements, where the Chinese also maintained a flourishing service and retail sector of the micro-economy. Only in rural areas, without either mines or plantations, could Malayan peasants maintain the subsistence economies of the *kampung*. The result was that Chinese outnumbered Malays in the economically important parts of Malaya: some of the Chinese communities, particularly in the Straits Settlements, went as far back as the eighteenth century, and their members could hardly be counted as citizens of China. Although most remained poor, the Chinese were at heart entrepreneurs, and particularly in Penang and Singapore many made considerable fortunes. Elsewhere, economic development had attracted Chinese from outside, whose status, particularly after World War II, would be extremely problematic. There was also an Indian – mainly Tamil speaking – community: while most of its members worked alongside the Chinese in the plantations, it also provided many recruits to the lowest ranks of the civil service and infrastructure of a developing export economy. Not so numerous as the Chinese, and considerably less enterprising, the Indians never attained a comparable level of business success.

The depression of the 1930s was disastrous for poor Chinese working in the mines and on the plantations: the decline in the world demand for tin and rubber led to many of them becoming unemployed in a countryside where they had no roots. This led to tens of thousands appropriating unused land at the edge of the jungle for agricultural small-holdings – to enjoy a precarious existence in a country where traditional agriculture had always been the preserve of native Malayans.[3]

Singapore was a special case: it was the largest harbour in Southeast Asia, shipping not only rubber and tin from Malaya, but oil from Borneo and Indonesia. (The Pulau Bukom refinery was opened as far back as 1905.) In the years before World War II, Britain had developed Singapore into its major base in the Far East for all three of the armed services. A new international airport became a key link in the new British and Dutch services to the Far East and Australia. In the local economy a strong financial and services sector emerged, with British, American, Dutch, French and Middle-Eastern banks all maintaining branches. At the same time, the small port and commodity trade was in Chinese hands.

The Pacific War was a catalyst in Malaysian politics. The fall of the impregnable fortress of Singapore, in February 1942, was an almost unimaginable disaster for Britain and the Commonwealth. The three and a half years of Japanese occupation that then followed was catastrophic for almost everyone in British Southeast Asia. With the loss of its sea lanes, the imprisonment of almost all Europeans, the destruction of key installations by the British Army as it retreated in face of the Japanese in 1942, Malaya's economy inevitably collapsed – a process exacerbated by incompetent administration, a reign of terror by the *Kempeitai* – the notorious Japanese secret police – and, in the end, the inflation of a worthless currency.

In the early stages the Japanese tried to win Malayan support by promising self-rule, losing out at the same time by returning to Thailand the four unfederated frontier states definitively ceded to Britain in 1909. Promises were also made to the 55,000 Indian troops captured in 1942; of these some 40,000 agreed to fight alongside the Japanese in S.C. Bose's Indian National Army,[4] while thousands of local Tamils were sent north to Thailand to work on the notorious Burma Railway. The Japanese did nothing to win over the Chinese, who suffered the worst of *Kempeitai* justice, particularly in urban Singapore where they were a clear majority of the population. On the mainland Chinese small-holders, precariously settled at the edge of the jungle, organized, in tens of thousands, as guerrillas. As the tide turned in the Pacific War, their Malayan People's Anti-Japanese Army, supplied with arms dropped from the air and supported by British military personnel parachuted in by the RAF, fought very effectively against the Japanese.

Given the history of the occupation, the British Army, not surprisingly, was welcomed back after the Japanese surrendered in August 1945. Even so, the signal defeat of the British in 1942 had shattered the pre-war image of an all-powerful empire. What is more the occupation had created a perception of a population polarized between Chinese patriots and Malayan collaborators. At all events, the British recognized that self-rule was inevitable: the problem was to plan the stages by which it, in due course, would be achieved, always bearing in mind the need to restore, and preserve, the vast overseas capital invested in the country.

The proposed solution was a Malayan Union, incorporating both the Federated and Unfederated Malay States, together with Penang and Melaka. The remit of the sultans would be restricted to religion and local culture. Singapore would be a separate colony.

Easier said than done: ethnic Malayans were concerned by the prospect of becoming second-class citizens in their own country. The position of the sultans, as it had been before the Pacific War, was seen as a guarantee that Malayan interests would be paramount. Different interest-groups came together to constitute the United Malay National Organization (UMNO), which, with the support of sultans boycotting British-organized events, demonstrated against the proposed unitary state. The movement was essentially conservative: if the old times of the traditional kampung, subject to the rule of the hierarchy of chiefs and sultans, without there being any Chinese or Indians to spoil the party, were seen as the ideal, it was one totally divorced from reality. Even so, the planners plainly had to think again.

The result was an interim proposal for a new federation, with a British High Commissioner as head of the central government, with the sultans of the different component states restored to their pre-war positions. New legislative councils would be elected at both federal and state levels on a franchise that, in every separate instance, guaranteed that the majority of members would be Malays – a principle to be buttressed by stricter controls on immigration and citizenship. Singapore, once again, would be a separate case.

Inevitably the Malays' satisfaction at seeing their privileges guaranteed under the new proposals was matched by Chinese resentment. The most effective resistance came from the Malayan Communist Party (MCP), whose members, almost entirely Chinese, had long supported Mao Zedong's revolution in China. Although the MCP was powerful among the unions, the strikes and agitation it organized lacked the popular support essential for producing any useful results: their main effect – slowing down the desperately needed post-war economic recovery – was counter-productive.

THE COMMUNIST UPRISING

In 1947, at a meeting called to confront the ineffective MCP leadership, a new leader, Chin Pang, took over on undertaking to fight a 'war of national liberation' against the government. The new militant communists, calling themselves the Malayan National Liberation Army (MNLA), claimed to be fighting for a new democratic socialist Malaya. With perhaps no more than 10,000 members, the MNLA, fighting from jungle bases with arms left over from the guerrilla war against the Japanese, orchestrated a reign of terror.

Rubber plantations and tin-mines were attacked and their European personnel murdered; roads and railways were sabotaged; finally, in 1951, the UK High Commissioner, Sir Henry Gurney, was murdered. Although the government portrayed this as an emergency to be dealt with by 'police action', some 80,000 Commonwealth troops[5] had to be called in to fight the MNLA.

In the years 1952–54, a new High Commissioner, Sir Gerald Templer, became the first man to deal effectively with the emergency. Having persuaded the Malays that the MNLA was essentially Chinese and anti-Islamic, he was able to increase their contingent in the police force from 9,000 to 60,000 men. At the same time some half-million Chinese small-holders from the jungle fringes were relocated to purpose-built new villages, complete with mains services and facilities for healthcare and education. With this move they had no longer any incentive nor the ability to supply the MNLA. Many went further and supplied the Special Branch of the police with useful intelligence. This left the way open to elite units, such as the British SAS, to fight the MNLA on its own ground. This meant its end as an effective fighting force, although sporadic fighting continued until the end of the 1950s.

Although the fundamental political problem was still unsolved, Templer made it clear in 1952 that independence was still on the agenda. While Malays were united in the UMNO, the Malayan Chinese Association (MCA), founded in 1949, finally gave the non-communist Chinese – a far from homogeneous community – a unified political voice, and in 1950 it was recognized as a full political party. After 1952 the numbers brought into the political mainstream, with enhanced access to the modern economy, as a result of the relocation into Templer's new villages, made the position of the Chinese in Malaya much stronger – to the considerable resentment of the police and army, which consisted mainly of Malays. What is more, few recent immigrants wanted to return to Mao Zedong's new China.

This time round Britain made it clear that a government answerable only to Malays would be unacceptable. On this basis, the UMNO and the MCA, together with the much smaller Malayan Indian Congress (MIC), came together in 1954 as a coalition to form the new inter-ethnic Alliance Party, led by the Malayan Tunku Abdul Rahman. In the general election of 1955 this party, with 80 per cent of all votes cast, won 51 out of 52 seats in the federal legislative council.

The success of the Alliance led to a new constitution, agreed after negotiation between leading figures in the UMNO and the MCA; the Malays from the UMNO were mostly top civil servants, while the Chinese, representing the MCA, were prominent businessmen. Together they had enjoyed an English-language education in the same schools and universities, so that they were familiar with British institutions. The new constitution recognized the special position of Malays and provided for government support to improve their economic standing. The new state would be a monarchy, with the nine Malayan sultans taking it in turn, every five years, to rule as king. Islam would be the state religion, while other religions were banned from proselytizing among Malayan Muslims. Malays would also enjoy a fixed quota of posts in the civil service, and their traditional land rights guaranteed. Malay would also be the official language, sharing that status with English for the first ten years.

In exchange for accepting the entrenched rights provided for Malays the Chinese acquired much-extended rights of citizenship, a critical matter for recent immigrants, as can be seen from the fact that after the adoption of the new constitution in 1957 Malays constituted only 58 per cent of the electorate – down from 80 per cent. Although neither side was completely happy with the new constitution, it was sufficient for the UK to transfer power to the new state on 31 August 1957.

THE PRICE OF INDEPENDENCE

As all these changes were taking place in Malaya politics was taking its own course in Singapore. While self-rule was also on the agenda, Britain was concerned about two matters: the first was the strategic importance of Singapore, which had been much increased by Mao Zedong's success in China, the emergency in Malaya and the war in Korea; the second was Singapore's considerable contribution to the British economy. As to the first concern, one-fifth of the area of Singapore was taken up by British military installations. These were not only home to large contingents from all three of the armed services but also the source of employment for some 40,000 local residents – to say nothing of a local economy dependent upon supplying services to the military. As to the export economy, the British were investing heavily in restoring Singapore to its position as the leading harbour in Southeast Asia.

Politically the fact that the rapidly expanding population was mainly Chinese counted for more than anything else. In a predominantly urban economy dependent on wage labour, the way was open to unions to organize strikes, which were often successful in improving the pay and working conditions of their members. The MCP was often in the background, and with the emergency in Malaya a new Internal Security Act (ISA) was passed to allow for detention without trial in case of threats to peace and order. The result was that many MCP leaders, if they were to escape jail, had to go either abroad or underground.

In a climate increasingly hostile to radical politics a new right-wing party, the Singapore Progressive Party (SPP), became dominant. The party was, however, much too elitist to stay the course once the franchise was extended, but even so it succeeded in doubling the enrolment in English primary schools, so that by 1956 this exceeded that in Chinese language schools. By this time, however, the broad mass of the Chinese, who had many grievances, such as poor housing and public services overstretched as result of the population explosion, could not be left out of the political equation. Their cause was taken up by the Chinese Chamber of Commerce, which demanded for Chinese equal status with English in public affairs, together with a new Singapore citizenship open to all residents on the island. At the same time, as the security restrictions eased with the end of the emergency in Malaya, trade unions began to organize low-paid semi-skilled workers. Once again young people looked to Mao Zedong's China for inspiration. The grievances of the Chinese were shared by the much smaller Malay population; this consisted mostly of wage-earners at the same level as the Straits Chinese – which was about twice any Malayan equivalent. Although a minority, the Singapore Malays still counted politically.

In 1955, in a general election held under a new constitution, by which some 300,000 qualified voters could elect 25 out of the 32 members of a new legislative council, the SPP won only four seats – a clear sign of its narrow political base. Much more successful was the Labour Front, first organized in 1954, which won ten seats. With the promised support of members nominated by the government this was sufficient to form a coalition, enabling its leader, David Marshall, to become chief minister in Singapore's first elected government. In this election another new party, the People's Action Party (PAP), led by Lee Kuan Yew, also won four seats with a broad-based appeal to English-speaking professionals, union militants and Chinese-educated voters.

Marshall failed as a political leader: his attempts to control civil unrest led Lee to portray him as a British stooge, and yet he failed, in London, to make progress in gaining independence for Singapore. Once back home he yielded office to his deputy, Lim Yew Hock, who in 1957 himself went to London, accompanied by Lee, to negotiate self-rule. Lim, after satisfying London that, with the support of the ISA, he could maintain order better than his predecessor, was offered a new constitution, which granted autonomy in everything except defence and foreign affairs. To make good his stand on law and order, Lim had showed that he was not afraid to use his powers against communists in the unions and student organizations. In 1956 the situation had become desperate when fifteen people died and hundreds were wounded during two weeks of student-led rioting. The action led extremists within PAP to form a faction supporting the students, at the same time being committed to unseat Lee as leader. This was an odd twist of fortune since Lee, in the early 1950s, had made his reputation as a lawyer by defending students and union radicals in court. In the event Lee was rescued by Lim detaining the PAP extremists under the ISA. Lee then lost no time in changing the party structure so that only a small cadre, whose members would have to be approved by the Central Committee, could elect the party's leaders. Having sewn up the party in this way, Lee, in 1959, was ready to contest the first election under the 1957 constitution.

On a broadly populist platform, which included a promise to release the imprisoned former PAP leaders from detention, Lee's reformed PAP, backed by both students and unions, won 43 out of 51 contested seats. Lee, at the age of 39, then became Singapore's first prime minister.

The eight-year period 1957 to 1965 proved critical for the future of British Southeast Asia. With self-rule granted to Malaya in 1957, and to Singapore in 1959, the question was whether they had a future as a single state. This was a long-term commitment of both sides, and in 1963 they both joined a new Malaysian Federation, which also included Sarawak and Sabah (the Malayan name for North Borneo), but not Brunei – where the sultan had opted out at the last moment. In 1965 Singapore was expelled from the federation, and had no choice but to go its own way, leaving Malaysia to get on without its wealthiest and most dynamic member state. This position has now lasted for more than forty years, and there is no immediate prospect of it changing. Even so, what lies behind this somewhat remarkable chain of events?

The simple answer is an irreconcilable conflict of interests between the Malayan and Chinese populations of Malaya, Singapore and north Borneo. The reasons why the federation failed to resolve this conflict are, however, much more complex. The support of two dominant parties, Alliance in Malaya and PAP in Singapore, was essential to the success of the federation. Alliance was an umbrella party including Malayan, Chinese and Indian components. In the Malayan general election of 1959, the new Pan-Malayan Islamic Party (PMIP), which was strong in the old Unfederated Malay States, won 13 seats after campaigning for a stronger Islamic presence in government. On the other side left-wing parties, with Chinese and Indian votes, also won a number of constituencies. The result was that Alliance only won 64 out of 104; this may seem a comfortable majority, but even so the message to the dominant UMNO faction within Alliance was that more had to be done for rural Malays – its core constituency. The answer was to be found in new land grants, development finance for industry and commerce, public investment in the infrastructure, new mosques, better schools and clinics – to say nothing of new financial institutions that would reduce the need to borrow money from Chinese shopkeepers.

To pay for all this the exchange economy would be diversified beyond tin and rubber, with foreign direct investment being encouraged, to achieve an average 10 per cent growth rate over ten years in manufacturing, commerce and construction. Malays would be favoured in the civil service. This was an essentially rural programme; in the large cities, where the population was mainly Chinese, little was offered for the improvement of housing and mains services. All this was political overkill with a vengeance; inevitably there were repercussions in Singapore.

Within the PAP left-wing members saw federation as a sell-out to Malaya, leaving Lee with the power to destroy them. After two by-elections lost by members of Lee's faction, the dissident left wing, led by Lim Chin Siong, split with the PAP to form a new 'socialist front' party, *Barisan Sosialis*. This won the allegiance of 13 PAP members of parliament, and 35 out of 51 constituency associations. Lim also organized a new Singapore Association of Trade Unions, which some two-thirds of existing union members chose to join. By July 1962, the PAP government had lost its parliamentary majority; it was only able to remain in power because the opposition was divided.

Lee resolved the deadlock by calling a referendum in September. Voters, however, could not vote against federation: the choice offered was between the terms upon which Singapore would join it. PAP urged acceptance of the terms it had already negotiated in Kuala Lumpur, and every possible means of publicity was used to win a majority of the votes. The best that *Barisan Sosialis* and others opposed to federation could do was to ask for blank votes. In the event 70 per cent voted for the government terms, while 25 per cent cast blank votes.

In February 1963 success in the referendum led Lee to detain over a hundred Barisan Sosialis leaders, union officials and 'communist sympathizers' under the ISA. Having taken care of his most effective opponents Lee then called an election in which PAP won 37 out 51 seats in the assembly, as against 13 won by Barisan Sosialis.

Once again Lee had successfully sewn up Singapore, but Malaya was much more of a problem. Ideally – at least from Lee's point of view – PAP should replace the MCA in the ruling Alliance Party. This was not acceptable, so PAP was consigned to the opposition, but when, in 1964, it was first put to the test in a Malayan election it won only one seat. Lee's reaction was to organize an opposition coalition, the Malaysian Solidarity Convention (MSC), as an umbrella covering small parties in Sarawak, Perak and Penang. With the slogan 'Malaysian Malaysia' it was designed to appeal to non-Malayan voters, particularly in the towns.

UMNO, the Malay faction in the Alliance, which dominated the government coalition, was immediately concerned for all the privileges won for the Malays in the federal constitution. Between them PAP in Singapore and MSC in the rest of Malaysia had the numbers on their side, and these could add up to an electoral disaster for the Alliance. Race riots in July and September 1964, in which Malays and Chinese confronted each other in Singapore, increased Alliance's misgivings about the future. At the same time, the Indonesian leader, Sukarno, confronted Malaysia across the common land-frontier in Borneo, and his forces could only be held at bay with the help of Commonwealth soldiers.

Times were not easy for the new federation. Extremists in the UMNO faction, for whom it was essential to get rid of Lee and those close to him, wished to have the whole PAP top detained in Singapore under the ISA. Harold Wilson, the British prime minister, then made it clear that in this case he would withdraw the Commonwealth troops from Borneo. This left the federal government in Kuala Lumpur with only one option. In August 1965, Singapore was expelled from Malaysia.

MALAYSIA AND THE INDEPENDENCE OF SINGAPORE

In spite of this drastic step Malaysia was by no means out of the wood. Too many Malays had seen little progress, while the Chinese community was divided between its mainly prosperous members who supported the Alliance and the broad mass who had gained little from its policies. The wealth of the country was unevenly divided between Kuala Lumpur and the Malayan west coast on one side and northeast Malaya and Borneo on the other. The divisions within the country were exacerbated when, in 1967, the ten-year review provided for by the National Language Act established Malay as the sole official and national language. Chinese could only be taught in private schools, while the official use of English was restricted to the courts, higher education and specialized agencies.

With so much discontent, the Alliance performed badly in the general election of 1969, gaining less than 50 per cent of the votes at both state and national level. When the two non-Malay parties that had gained votes celebrated their success by marching through the streets of Kuala Lumpur, riots followed after the chief minister bussed in rural Malays for counter-demonstrations. Government, after a national emergency had been proclaimed, was entrusted to a new National Operations Council (NOC), led by Tun Abdul Razak, a rising figure in Malay politics who went on to become prime minister in 1970.

Although the NOC succeeded in restoring law and order, a serious division emerged in the dominant UMNO faction: on one side moderates, led by Razak, insisted on closer cooperation with non-Malays, while on the other, in which a young member, Mohamad Mahathir, of the party was a key figure, demands were made for strengthening the position of Malays. Razak won the day – with Mahathir being expelled from the party – but even so, the strength of the military was substantially increased, with the percentage of Malays going up from 60 to 80 in the course of the 1970s. At the same time Razak formed a new more inclusive party, Barisan Nasional, to take over from Alliance, and in 1971 he had the Sedition Act of 1949 amended so as to define any questioning of Malayan paramountcy as treason. His policies were immediately popular. In the national election of 1974 Barisan Nasional, with more than 60 per cent of the votes cast, won a two-thirds majority in parliament, losing only 10 out of 104 seats in mainland Malaya.

Under Razak government economic policy took a new turn with the so-called Second Malaysia Plan. This had two main objects: the first was to eliminate poverty, the second, to integrate the economy to a point where race would no longer be identified by economic function.[6] Given the socio-economic position of Malays this required both the modernization of rural life and the creation of a commercial and industrial community in which Malays would have a place at all levels of operation and in all categories. Given the dominance of foreign and Chinese interests in the export, retail, commercial and manufacturing sectors of the economy, this was a very tall order.

To succeed the Second Malaysia Plan required affirmative action on a massive scale. To begin with the National Corporation, set up in 1969, would provide start-up capital for new ventures in transport, insurance, finance and manufacturing within the Malay business community. At a later stage steel, shipping and car manufacture were added, and a new Urban Development Authority was set up to enable Malays to compete with the Chinese in building shops and offices. Two new government funds were set up to buy out, at fair market value, the British companies that controlled the mines and plantations.

Two questions arise: first, how would it be possible to find a sufficient number of Malays with the educational background essential for managing the new enterprises; second, where would the finance come from? As to the first question, Malays benefited enormously from a system in which education, at every level, was in their own language – so much so that by 1957 only a quarter of the places in higher education were taken up by non-Malays. Malays, moreover, were helped by the rule that required them to be employed at every level in new ventures, and by the practice of awarding government contracts to concerns that positively discriminated in their favour. There was every incentive for Malays to work their way out of their traditional rural economy.

Civil unrest, as it was stirred up by the non-Malay communities in the 1960s, was held at bay not so much by police action as by the Malaysian economy's phenomenal annual growth rate of 7 per cent in the period 1970–90. The government, although on one side it encouraged the takeover of British interests, on the other provided considerable financial incentives for foreign direct investment. The economy was also helped by the discovery, during the 1970s, of new deposits of oil and gas offshore from Sarawak and the Malayan east coast. (By 1990 this sector was 20 per cent greater than rubber.) All in all, there was plenty left over in the new economy for Indians and Chinese left out in the cold by government affirmative action. Many, indeed, effectively excluded from higher education in Malay, had studied in the US, Britain and Australia, and with their command of English were at a premium for top-level jobs in the new multinationals operating in Malaysia. The Chinese, as elsewhere in Southeast Asia, came out in the end as winners.

THE REIGN OF MAHATHIR

Razak died in 1976, but not before appointing as minister of education the renegade Mahathir, who, in 1981, with strong business support, became prime minister. This followed a national election in 1978 in which Barisan Nasional, although the outright winner, had lost ground since 1974. It was threatened by two strong opposition parties: one, on the left, was likely to cause trouble if too much was conceded to extreme Malay interests; the other, on the right, was just as likely to do so if too much was conceded to non-Malays. Mahathir was the strong man to deal with both these threats, which he did very effectively. On the economic side he strongly favoured the private sector, which meant selling off government corporations, parts of the infrastructure and licences in the media and telecommunications to favoured Malayan businessmen.

This policy was beset by a number of problems. To begin with the Malayan business community simply did not have the background or experience essential for running enterprises in the fields where the government had given it priority. Success became even more problematic when Malayan enterprises had to meet official quotas in the number of Malays employed. To operate efficiently Malayan businesses were forced to adopt a number of expedients to overcome their own limitations. Key operations were sub-contracted to foreign businesses operating locally. In so-called Ali-Baba set-ups – also common in Indonesia – management was entrusted to experienced Chinese operating behind the scenes.

This was all very well so long as the economic boom continued at a level which could tolerate the waste inherent in the whole system. When, however, a downturn came in the late 1980s, there was considerable unrest among educated Malays, who were forced to compete with each other for jobs in government and Malay enterprises. In 1987 Mahathir faced a challenge from within his own faction, the UMNO, but by this time he was ready to use detention under the ISA to deal with recalcitrant opponents, even if they were Malays. In extreme cases he resorted to prosecution under the Sedition Act. Even so, the faction in the UMNO opposed to Mahathir still managed to pursue him in courts, claiming that his victory depended on votes coming from illegal branches of the party. In the end the President of the Supreme Court scheduled the case to be heard, quite exceptionally, by all nine judges. Mahathir then orchestrated an involved series of manoeuvres which led the king to remove three judges, including the president, who had ruled against him, leaving the way open for a majority, within the court, to rule that he had won the UMNO election. It was clear that Mahathir was not to be meddled with.

While all this was going on, Mahathir, at grass-roots level, appealed successfully to a party that had two million members – whose representatives at vast annual conferences willingly showed their support for him. He also made clear that he favoured the younger generation, represented in the new Malay middle classes, above traditional elites, which, in the early days of self-rule, constituted an old guard blocking access to newcomers. The fact that the sultans and their courts lost in status hardly concerned Mahathir, who, exceptionally for a Malay, had risen to the top from a relatively humble background. Moreover, with the media subject to government regulations, and annual licences being required of newspapers, Mahathir had unashamedly stacked the cards in his own favour.

By the end of the 1980s, after nearly ten years with Mahathir as prime minister, Malaya's economy had been transformed. By 1990, after some twenty years with an average annual growth-rate just under 7 per cent, industry, based on the manufacture of hi-tech products and components, such as computer chips, accounted for 61 per cent of all exports.[7] This was almost pure gain, since oil, rubber and tin continued to be strong throughout the period. Foreign ownership had also declined from 60 to 25 per cent, while Malay ownership, with strong official support, was up from 2 to 20 per cent. Malays, however, were still mainly engaged in agriculture and fishing, with relatively few in the middle and upper classes. It was mainly the Chinese who benefited from the transfer of ownership, so that their share in the export economy doubled in the period 1970–90. Regardless of who owned what, Malaya had become a 'tiger economy'.

Despite official support the new Malayan middle classes did not adjust easily to a city life, which was open, competitive and exposed to an alien culture that emphasized individual values rather than respect for authority. To many Islam was the way to preserving a distinctive Malay identity, a direction encouraged by Islam Youth Movement of Malaya (ABIM), founded by Anwar Ibrahim in the early 1970s. There was an increase in religious observance, with the new economy providing the means for tens of thousands, with the encouragement of Mahathir, to participate in the Haj – the traditional pilgrimage to Mecca. The UMNO came to see explicit commitment to Islam as essential for continued popular support.

The process threatened to go too far: in the mainly rural state of Kelantan an extremist party, the Pan-Malayan Islamic Party (PAS), came to power on a programme including the introduction of traditional *sharia* law, a ban on alcohol, separation of the sexes and a dress code for women. All this was too much for Mahathir, who realized only too well how easily Islamic extremism could lead to civil unrest and discourage foreign investment in a country where 40 per cent of the population were not Muslims. True to character he did not hesitate to detain extremist leaders under the ISA, appealing at the same time for pragmatic, open-minded and tolerant believers. This was all very well, but in the large cities the tensions caused by the demands of the new economy led to massive drug abuse. As in Thailand and Singapore draconian penalties, including the death sentence, were enforced, but with only limited success.

By the end of the 1980s Mahathir's pretensions for Malaysia attracted world-wide attention. A man much given to slogans, his theme that 'Malaysians can do anything' – or *Malaysia Boleh* – supported projects such as the country's production of its own national car, the Proton Saga, in 1985.

In the 1990s, Malaysia, still led by Mahathir, went over the top. In 1993 construction started of the Patronas Twin Towers – the future headquarters of Malaysia's nationalized petroleum industry – at the centre of Kuala Lumpur. The site had long been home to the Selangor Turf Club, and the last race was held in 1991, the year in which the American Cesar Pelli – the architect of London's Canary Wharf – won the competition to design the building. The twin towers were completed in 1997 and occupied in 1998. They were then reckoned to be the world's tallest building, a goal decided upon as the result of a question Mahathir put to Pelli in 1994.[8]

The story of the Purgau Dam is both involved and discreditable, not only to Malaysia but also to the UK. This hydro-electric project on the Purgau River close to the Thai border, constructed in the early 1990s with the help of a grant of £234 million from the British Overseas Development Administration – making it the largest aid project ever financed by the UK – proved to be linked to a £1 billion Malaysian purchase of British arms agreed in 1988 between Mahathir and Margaret Thatcher. In 1994 the World Development Movement, which was concerned by the environmental impact of the dam, challenged the grant in the British courts, which ruled that financing it out of the aid budget was illegal. The British Treasury covered this by finding alternative funding, but even so – as the result of an article which told the whole story in the *Sunday Times* – Mahathir announced an official ban on government contracts with British firms.

This did nothing to dampen Mahathir's taste for building large dams. In 1996 an international consortium, led by the Swiss ABB, was awarded a contract to construct a 2,400-megawatt hydro-electric power generation plant and transmission system at Bakun on the Balui River in Sarawak. Its purpose is to increase the electricity supply in Malaya, which is connected to Bakun by three transmission cables, each some 700 kilometres long, under the South China Sea. Significantly no British firms were invited to participate in this massive project.

ANWAR IBRAHIM'S FALL FROM GRACE

Towards the end of the 1990s Malaysia, together with other *tiger economies*, was riding for a fall. The vast investment in public sector projects, largely financed by foreign soft loans, led to the IMF, at the end of 1997, asking for budget cutbacks, tough financial measures and the abolition of huge state-backed infrastructure projects. In response Anwar Ibrahim, who had become Mahathir's minister of finance, announced a package of austerity measures in December which slashed government spending by 18 per cent for 1998, revised growth rates, cut ministerial salaries and deferred major investment projects.

Anwar's policies hit hardest at indigenous Malay entrepreneurs, who relied on their close contacts with UMNO and the state apparatus for preferential treatment. Powerful and politically connected businessmen were warned not to expect any protection. Anwar must have known that these formed the hardcore of Mahathir's political support, and tensions erupted at the UMNO national conference held in June 1998, where the position taken by Anwar against nepotism and cronyism was seen as a thinly veiled challenge to the prime minister.

Anwar could hardly have anticipated Mahathir's brutal reaction. He was dismissed on 2 September 1998, a day after Mahathir had announced far-reaching economic regulations controlling speculation in Malaysian currency and stocks and creating the basis for easing interest rates and bank credit to stave off a string of corporate bankruptcies. Worse was to follow. On 20 September some 50,000 people had demonstrated in Kuala Lumpur, making clear the widespread discontent among workers, small farmers, traders and sections of the middle class who had been hit by a doubling of the jobless rate and rising prices. The following day Anwar was arrested under the ISA, later to be charged with both corruption and sodomy. It made no difference that it was Mahathir who had invited him to join the UMNO in 1982, nor that for seventeen years he had loyally defended government policies, including repeated abuse of basic democratic rights.

Two months later, in November 1998, at a time when top international leaders were in Kuala Lumpur for an Asia-Pacific Economic Cooperation (APEC) summit meeting, the Malaysian government, faced with protests from the foreign delegates, suspended Anwar's trial for corruption, which had only just started. Anwar, still in detention, wrote an editorial for the Asian *Wall Street Journal* repeating his criticisms of the Malaysian government. This was just two days after US Vice-President Al Gore had told APEC that 'democracy' and an end to corruption were essential to economic recovery in Asia, at the same time praising demonstrators in Malaysia protesting against Anwar's arrest and calling for *reformasi* or democratic change.

None of this helped Anwar: the trial continued and he was convicted, and sentenced to six years in prison. Then, in 2000, after being tried and convicted on the sodomy charges, a further nine years was added. In 2002 Anwar appealed unsuccessfully against his conviction of the corruption charges. Then in October 2003, Mahathir retired as prime minister, to be succeeded by Ahmad Badawi, who had been his deputy prime minister – a post held by Anwar until his arrest in 1998. This left the way open for Anwar to appeal to Malaysia's Supreme Court against all his convictions. In September 2004 the court allowed the appeal on the sodomy charges – without there being any suggestion of interference by the new prime minister, for which Anwar was duly grateful. He was released immediately, since he had already completed the sentence imposed for corruption. Here, however, the court refused to overturn the conviction. Anwar was a free man, but one without any political future.

So far Ahmad Badawi has a good track-record as prime minister. He has given more power to anti-corruption agencies and made it easier for the public to reveal corrupt practices to the authorities. With considerable public approval – reflected in his election victory in 2004 – Ahmad Badawi arrested several Mahathir-era cronies on charges of corruption. He also accepts Islam Hadhari, a doctrine according to which Islam and economic and technological development are not incompatible.

THE LEE DYNASTY

So much for Malaysia, but what happened to Singapore in the forty years following its expulsion from the federation in 1965? Even more than in Malaysia, the history of this period is tied up with the rule of a single man, Lee Kuan Yew, who established his uncompromising hold on Singapore long before Mahathir came to power in Malaysia. His style of government can best be judged by a statement he made to the *Financial Times* on 22 November 1982:

> Every time anybody starts anything which will unwind or unravel this orderly, organized, sensible, rational society, and make it irrational and emotional, I put a stop to it without hesitation.

By this time Lee had solved one major problem, the closing down of the British military bases on Singapore Island. The policy decision was made in London in 1967, with the deadline for departure of the British services set for 1972. Given the economic importance of the bases, Singapore was threatened with the loss of 20 per cent of its national income. Lee, however, saw only new opportunities. The land abandoned by the British would not only be available for housing and industry, but also for Changi Airport. The naval dockyard provided the site for a new dry-dock, as a basis for shipbuilding and repair. The time was favourable, since the US, still engaged in the Vietnam War, willingly made use of the new facilities. Singapore also became an important centre for oil exploration in neighbouring countries.

The price paid for all this was complete subordination of the people of Singapore to Lee's autocratic style of government. A new Industrial Relations Act curtailed the right to strike, allowing the government at the same time to appoint union leaders. The Employment Act laid down new rules governing hiring and firing of employees. Corporations were set up for new industries like armaments and shipbuilding, and foreign direct investment was encouraged.

On the political side, detention under the Internal Security Act of their leaders led opposition parties to boycott elections, leaving the way open for Lee's PAP to win all the seats in the elections of 1972, 1976 and 1980. The media were controlled and exploited by the government, to the point that all newspapers, in whatever language, became the property of a single company with directors nominated by the government. Students were banned from politics, and could be denied readmission at the beginning of the academic year if they had in any way broken the ban. All men were subject to two years of national service, which meant that Singapore had an army of 50,000 active soldiers, supplemented by 250,000 reservists. The armed services, with modern tanks, fighter aircraft and warships, were supported by advisers from Israel – much to the disgust of Singapore's two Islamic neighbours, Malaysia and Indonesia. All this was a lot of clout for a very small country.

In foreign policy Singapore had first to reckon with Malaysia, which supplied half its water, and whose airspace was essential for operations from Changi. Together with Indonesia, Malaysia controlled the sea-lanes essential for ships bound for Singapore. On the other hand a third of Malaysia's exports and up to a fifth of Indonesia's passed through Singapore. None of this helped Malaysians or Indonesians actually in Singapore. Malaysians, although some 20 per cent of the population, enjoyed less than half the average income, and security-sensitive positions, particularly in the armed services, were closed to them. Even so the level of discrimination was less than what Chinese had to put up with in Malaysia. The position of Indonesians, many of whom had come to Singapore in search of a better living, was even more difficult.

In spite of its problematic relations with Malaysia and Indonesia, in 1967 Singapore did join with them, together with Thailand and the Philippines, in creating the Association of Southeast Asian Nations (ASEAN). In its first years ASEAN did not make much impact, but it came into its own after the US withdrew from Vietnam and Cambodia in 1975. By then deciding to represent the interests of Cambodia in the aftermath of Pol Pot, ASEAN discovered that its voice – speaking for some 300,000,000 people – counted internationally, and particularly in Washington. By the end of the twentieth century ASEAN had expanded to include Brunei, Burma, Laos and Vietnam, with Cambodia as a prospective member. With its concerns now mainly economic, rather than political, ASEAN – representing some of the world's fastest-growing economies – stands up effectively against China and Japan, the EU and the US.

The state of Singapore, as bequeathed by Lee when he resigned as prime minister in 1993, threatens to be killed by its own success. In particular, Singapore, in common with many other states, failed to control its demographic profile, as it changed over the course of time. In the early days of the new republic the prospect of a population too large for the space available to it, whether in housing or employment, led to an official policy of encouraging family planning and discriminating against large families. Predictably it was the more highly educated that responded best, which in Singapore means the ethnic Chinese – not at all what Lee was looking for. Now graduates earn a $20,000 tax rebate with every child after the second. Even so, the citizens of Singapore are still growing too old, creating a labour shortage that only short-term immigrants can make good. The labour force now includes some 400,000 low-skilled workers from Bangladesh, India, Indonesia, Malaysia, Philippines, Sri Lanka and Thailand, whose presence is the cause of considerable social unrest.

In 1993 Lee handed over to his chosen successor, Goh Chok Tong, who held the prime minister's chair warm until Lee's son, Lee Hsien Loong, was ready to take over from him in 2004. Lee Kuan Yew's legacy to Singapore was remarkable, as he himself made clear in his autobiography, *From Third World to First: The Singapore Story: 1965–2000*.[9] While he preferred to attribute Singapore's achievements to Asian values shared with Taiwan, South Korea, Hong Kong, Malaysia and Thailand, they owed more to the introduction of Western values, including Western-style individualism. The question is whether Singapore has come to terms with the way that modern capitalism dilutes group values. The consequences are to be seen in a high crime rate in the face of extremely severe penalties. The new world requires education focused on creativity, but how far is this compatible with Singapore's authoritarian society, in which hundreds – not all of them members of Chinese secret societies – are still detained under the Internal Security Act?

The high tide of Lee Kuan Yew's PAP is long past, as can be seen from election results in the 1990s. The party hardly gained in credibility when it brought actions for defamation against opposition candidates – a strategy also favoured by Italy's Berlusconi. The new generation of PAP leaders are at heart managers with a technocratic cast of mind, and no particular concern for hard-needed political reform.

Lee's achievement was to make Singapore a state dominated by a majority of English-speaking ethnic Chinese, of whom some 20 per cent have become Christians. There is no doubt about Singapore's prosperity, nor of the opportunities it offers to entrepreneurs. There is, however, a considerable downside to its success. Just as in Malaysia there is large-scale drug abuse, which draconian penalties have failed to eradicate. Much-publicized executions of foreigners involved in drug-traffic have little affected Singapore's international standing, which depends as much on the high reputation of the national flag-carried Singapore Airlines, and its home base at Changi Airport. Both strategically and economically this small island republic is much too important world-wide, and much too successful in ordering its own affairs, for any other power to attempt to change its politics. Singapore's winning streak promises to continue for a long time.

10

The Philippines: corruption and democracy

THE AMERICAN YEARS

In 1898, the United States acquired the Philippines (see map on page xi) as, in the words of President McKinley, 'a gift from the gods'.[1] Although this was an incidental result of the American victory in the Spanish-American War, which was fought mainly to ensure that Spain would no longer have any empire in the Americas[2] – a final consummation of the Monroe doctrine – the possession of Manila, which was the Philippines' capital city and largest harbour, immensely strengthened the American presence in East and Southeast Asia.[3] In the colonial geography of the region, Spain, which since the seventeenth century could hardly be counted as a great power, was supplanted by the United States, which under McKinley, and his successor, Theodore Roosevelt, was becoming stronger every day. Given that London welcomed – indeed had facilitated – the American acquisition of the Philippines, this transfer of sovereignty foreshadowed the dominance of the English-speaking world in the Pacific in the second half of the twentieth century.

Given their location on the eastern side of the South China Sea the islands of the Philippines were undoubtedly important strategically, and on the main island of Luzon the United States retained its naval base at Subic Bay and its air-base Clark Field until 1992.

In many ways the Philippines were the most privileged of all American overseas territories, almost as if the islands were chosen to be a show-case of American enlightenment. The American takeover was far from straightforward, for although the Spanish had been defeated, an insurgent leader, Emilio Aguinaldo, who, with his followers, had been fighting for independence since 1896, was still active. It was only after the Americans had succeeded in capturing him in 1902[4] that peace was restored throughout the islands. Then, however, little time was lost in establishing what, according to American principles, would be an appropriate form of government, so that, in 1907 the Philippine Assembly became the first freely elected legislature in Asia. What is more, two members of the old ruling Spanish oligarchy, Manuel Quezon and Sergio Osmeña, founded the Nacionalista Party, which became the dominant force in Philippine politics. In 1913 Francis B. Harrison, liberal at heart, became governor and during his term of office ensured that the government bureaucracy was staffed by Filipinos. In 1922 Quezon, by defeating Osmeña in the election for president of the upper house of the legislature, became the dominant figure in Filipino politics. Trusted by the US Congress, he orchestrated the Tydings-McDuffie Act of 1934, which in 1935 re-constituted the Philippines as a commonwealth, with internal self-government, to be followed by full independence ten years later. Not surprisingly, Quezon was elected first president of the Commonwealth – with Osmeña as his vice-president. In two respects the newly reconstructed Philippines was unique in Asia: first, English was the official language, and second, Christianity (dominated by Roman Catholics) was the leading religion.

The Pacific War, which was traumatic for the Philippines, ensured that the way to independence was far from simple. Japanese carrier-based aircraft had bombed Manila on the same day as they had attacked Pearl Harbor, 7 December 1941, and their actual invasion forces landed at Manila on 2 January 1942 – a follow-up that Hawaii was spared. Quezon, trying to save his country, reacted by proposing surrender to the Japanese combined with neutralization. President Roosevelt would hear nothing of it, so the war continued with the Japanese troops steadily gaining territory in face of a bitter rearguard action by American troops in the Bataan peninsula, south of Manila. General Douglas MacArthur, commander-in-chief of US armed forces in the Far East, left the Philippines for Australia on 17 March 1942, promising the people 'I shall return'. He was followed on 9 April 1942 by Quezon and Osmeña, who set up a government in exile in the United States. When Corregidor, a massive fortress at the end of the Bataan peninsula, finally surrendered on 6 May, Japan controlled almost the whole of Southeast Asia. Only a small enclave around Port Moresby in New Guinea and some of the small islands off its coast remaining in allied hands.

When Quezon died in exile on 1 August 1944, American plans for invading the Philippines were far-advanced. On 20 October 1944 MacArthur kept his promise of 1942, and with soldiers of the US invasion force waded ashore on the island of Leyte. Osmeña, who had succeeded Quezon as president of the Philippines, accompanied him. It took nearly two months of hard fighting to capture the whole of Leyte, and that was just the beginning of the war to liberate the Philippines. Although the capital, Manila, was captured at the end of March 1945, Japanese guerrillas were still active in the mountains of northern Luzon when, on 6 August 1945, Hiroshima was destroyed by an atomic bomb.

By the end of the Pacific War the Philippines were utterly devastated, with many of the leading politicians such as José Laurel and Benigno Aquino Sr. in Japan, where they had served in a puppet government set up in Tokyo. At the same time, the members of the political, landed and business dynasties – known as the *ilustrados* – who had remained behind accommodated the Japanese occupation in much the same spirit as they had the Spanish and American. Although Roosevelt had demanded that traitors 'be removed from authority' and MacArthur had promised to 'run to earth every disloyal Filipino', Osmeña was faced with a considerable dilemma. The purge seemingly required by the United States would require him to govern without the support of the traditional elite, which included his own two sons, left behind in the Philippines when he went into exile. The task was not easy, and MacArthur, although never taken with Osmeña, was – as any conservative would be – sympathetic to the dilemma confronting him. A solution was, however, at hand.

MANUEL ROXAS AND PHILIPPINE INDEPENDENCE

MacArthur's eye lighted upon Manuel Roxas, who, already promoted colonel in the US Army before the war, joined in the defence of Corregidor in 1942, to escape just before its fall. The Japanese, however, captured Roxas, but saw in him an ideal puppet president. Pleading ill-health, he was able to decline the honour, and became instead the head of food distribution under the local administration set up by the Japanese. In April 1945 Roxas succeeded in reaching the American lines at Baguio in the mountainous north of Luzon. In much the same area the Americans finally captured General Tomoyuki Yamashita, the commander of the local Japanese forces.

MacArthur summoned his old friend, Roxas, promoting him to Brigadier-General, as a reward for his having been 'one of the prime factors in the guerrilla movement' and a source of 'vital intelligence'. Although official US Army investigators failed completely in their search for Roxas' 'connections with the underground' his rehabilitation was complete. In June 1945 Osmeña, prompted by MacArthur, summoned the Philippine legislature – most of whose members had collaborated with the Japanese – to meet in Manila, and Roxas was immediately chosen as president of the upper chamber. From this position he made MacArthur, 'one of the greatest soldiers of all time', an honorary Philippine citizen. In August 1945 MacArthur freed five thousand collaborators, in response to a 'well-organized propaganda campaign to persuade the world that all those who collaborated with the Japanese had done so only from the finest motives of patriotism, and that the nation should really be grateful to them' – the words are those of MacArthur's own counter-intelligence chief.[5]

MacArthur deflected criticism by having Yamashita, who had allowed his soldiers 'to commit brutal atrocities and other crimes', tried as a war-criminal. He was escorted to the court-martial through crowds of indignant Filipinos. He was convicted and sentenced to death by hanging.

Roxas, in the meantime, went from strength to strength. He founded a new Liberal Party to fight the presidential elections set by MacArthur for 23 April 1946. The press (much of which Roxas controlled) described Osmeña as 'old, decrepit and impotent', and referred to his Chinese origins and the support given him by communists (largely recruited from the Hukbalahap guerrillas who had fought the Japanese during the war). MacArthur, granting Roxas access to the US Army radio-network, made clear his support. Osmeña hardly campaigned, and when the election came, the Liberal Party were the winners with 54 per cent of some 3,000,000 votes cast. Quezon's Nacionalista Party, founded nearly forty years earlier, had been defeated for the first time in its history.

When Roxas was inaugurated as the first president of the independent Philippines on 4 July 1946 any number of intractable problems faced his administration. The first was the country's future relationship with the United States. In 1946, with Japan utterly defeated, its strategic importance was far less than before the Pacific War. General Eisenhower, then US Chief of Staff, doubted whether it was worthwhile maintaining bases in the Philippines at the cost of antagonizing the local population, while the US Navy would be quite content with bases on small, easy to defend islands such as Guam (a US possession since 1898, but occupied by Japan during the Pacific War) and Okinawa (occupied by the US after the defeat of Japan) – both of which were still operational at the beginning of the twenty-first century. Roxas shrewdly saw the undoubted economic advantage of US bases in the Philippines, and in March 1947, signed a treaty granting 99-year leases on twenty-two sites, of which the Clark Field air-base and the Subic Bay naval-base were much the most important. The US, following its long-established practice, retained extra-territorial jurisdiction over not only its own citizens, but also over the hundreds of Filipinos employed by the bases. Filipinos were not slow to notice that these terms were more onerous than those imposed on Japan – the defeated enemy – in regard to Okinawa and other US bases there. Not surprisingly the antagonism feared by Eisenhower became reality, and as such played a significant part in Filipino politics until the bases finally returned to the Philippines. At the same time the whole strategic situation changed radically, first in 1949, when Mao Zedong's revolution succeeded in China, then in 1950, when Kim Il Sung's forces invaded South Korea and finally in the years following the French defeat at Dien Bien Phu in 1954, when the forces commanded by Ho Chi Minh began to take over Vietnam – a process that would only end in 1975. Events such as these enormously increased the strategic importance of the US bases in the Philippines, so that Roxas, if he had but known, could have held out for much more favourable terms from the Americans. As it was, he was ready to grant all that the Americans asked for, assuring a sceptical legislature with the words, 'I find no dream of empire in America'.[6] If this did not quite convince all the legislators, they still gave the 1946 treaty the required two-thirds majority, if only because, in the words of one of them, 'we are flat broke, hungry, homeless and destitute'. This was much closer to the truth than any words of Roxas. What is more, the treaty also continued the economic ties enjoyed by the United States before the Pacific War, so that both the American export monopoly and unrestricted Filipino access to the US market were revived, with the peso pegged to the dollar. Critically Filipinos were still prohibited from selling any products that might 'come into substantial competition' with, in effect, US manufactured goods. Even more drastic was the so-called 'parity provision'[7] granting to Americans the same rights as Filipinos to the ownership of mines, forests and other natural resources. This required an amendment of the Philippines' constitution, but under pressure from the US Congress, this too was adopted. All this added up to a colossal sell-out, but then, as the great mass of Filipinos knew all too well, 'beggars can't be choosers'. Nonetheless, the country would have done better with leaders less self-seeking than Roxas and his cronies – an advantage which, in the years since Roxas, it has seldom enjoyed.

Apart from his dealings with the United States, Roxas faced armed insurrection on his own home-ground. One legacy of the war years was a guerrilla force eventually known as *Hukbalahap*,[8] which had fought effectively against the Japanese in the mountains of central Luzon – and that at a time when many of Roxas' political allies were collaborating with them. Its leader, Luis Taruc, was a genuine man of the people, and when the war ended, he lent his support to the new Democratic Alliance, a radical political party representing communists, socialists and peasant unions, formed to fight the 1946 elections. The party programme was anathema to the traditional power elite of businessmen and landowners, and an American officer helped their cause by describing the *Hukbalahap* as a 'subversive … radical organization [committed to] carnage, revenge, banditry and hijacking … never equalled in any page of the history of the Philippines'. Not surprisingly Luis Taruc was driven underground, announcing that he would be 'of more service to our country and our people … if I stay with the peasants'. Roxas saw this as a declaration of war, and promised to vanquish Taruc within sixty days. He failed completely. With the army against them much of the rural population joined Taruc's *Hukbalahap*. Roxas outlawed the movement, demanding unconditional surrender – at the same time pardoning all former collaborators with the Japanese. It was his last political act, for on 18 April 1948 he died suddenly while visiting Clark Field. Although Roxas' successor, the indecisive Elpidio Quirino, first tried to accommodate Taruc – even to the point of allowing him to take up his seat in the legislature – Taruc's demands were not met, and in August 1948 he fled back to the mountains to become leader, once more, of a guerrilla movement.

SALVATION UNDER MAGSAYSAY

Quirino was a disastrous president: returned to office in 1949 after a rigged election his administration was corrupt to the core, with government contracts, import licences, public jobs and immigration permits consistently sold to the highest bidders, or those with the best connections. The army dealt with the *Hukbalahap* by devastating villages across the countryside. In the opinion of Myron Cowen, the US Ambassador, the men in power in the Philippines were 'self-seeking and unscrupulous men' of whom the most 'evil' was the president himself 'who would prefer to see his country ruined rather than compromise with his own insatiable ego'.[9] At the same time Daniel Bell, leader of an economic mission sent by President Truman, reported that 'the profits of businessmen and the incomes of large landowners have risen very considerably [but] the standard of living of most people is lower than before the war'.[10] All this was in spite of American aid, adding up to more than $2,000,000,000, given to the Philippines following the favourable political stance taken by Roxas in 1946. Washington, only too aware of what its support for Jiang Jieshi had led to in China, was not disposed to support Quirino, who, like Jiang in the years before 1949, faced a communist insurrection in his own back-yard. The answer to this dilemma was to be found in a new charismatic leader, Ramón Magsaysay, whom the Americans could support.

Magsaysay was discovered by a USAF colonel called Edward Lansdale.[11] After Quirino Lansdale saw in Magsaysay, a man of relatively humble origins with a good war record of actually fighting the Japanese, as just the right man to combat the *Hukbalahap*. As Lansdale saw it, 'Communist hide among people ... if you win the people to your side, the Communist guerrillas have no place to hide. With no place to hide, you can find them'.[12] Magsaysay was just the man to win the people, and supported by Lansdale he became the Philippines' Secretary of Defence. Helped by $500,000,000 in American military and economic aid, he doubled the size of the army, promoted officers on merit, reduced corruption, so that all in all he had an unprecedentedly effective fighting force. At the same time he initiated projects to win the hearts of the peasants, even to the point of promising farms to rebels who surrendered. As almost inevitable in the Philippines, Magsaysay, for the most part, failed to deliver, but he did enough to become a folk-hero. In 1951, after assigning soldiers to watch over the polling-stations, the Philippines acquired a new legislature after a more or less fair election.

Later in the year the *Hukbalahap* were finally defeated. Although the official view was that this was the result of Magsaysay's 'aggressive'[13] policy and American aid, the *Hukbalahap* had operated without any outside help, and in the end their command in Manila was betrayed by an informer, and the whole operation collapsed. Lansdale then set his sights on having Magsaysay elected president in

1953: this was quite a problem since neither of the two main parties wanted him as their candidate. Since Quirino, still in office, insisted on standing again as a Liberal (foreclosing Magsaysay's chances in his own party), Lansdale wooed the Nacionalistas. The party's two main leaders, José Laurel and Claro Recto, who had both collaborated with the Japanese, grudgingly accepted Magsaysay. With massive American support – which only added to his popular appeal – Magsaysay was elected with nearly 70 per cent of the votes cast. A diplomat in Manila rightly attributed the victory to 'Colonel Landslide', but even so it was wildly popular among ordinary people.

A year later, a young reporter, Benigno Aquino Jr., after contacting the Hukbalahap leader, Luis Taruc, who was still at large, persuaded him to surrender. Taruc was tried and given three life-sentences (for which he ultimately served fourteen years), Aquino, recognized as a popular hero, set out on a tragic political career – a story told later in this chapter – and Lansdale left Manila for Saigon.[14]

In spite of his early successes, Magsaysay failed as president. Old style Filipino politics simply proved too much for him. He was in the end more popular in Washington than at home. In a critical period of foreign policy relating to Asia he backed every American enterprise, and on his own turf the CIA rewarded him by subverting his political opponents. Returning from a campaign tour of the Visaya islands on 16 March 1957 Magsaysay lost his life when his aeroplane crashed. A year later, a local CIA operative advised Washington, 'Find another Magsaysay'.

THE LOST YEARS OF GARCIA AND MACAPAGAL

It was not to be. Before looking, however, at the Philippines in the years after 1957, it is useful to consider the state of play as it was when Magsaysay died. In spite of twelve years as an independent state, enjoying considerable economic support from the United States, the Philippines in 1957 had solved none of its fundamental economic, social or political problems.

To start with geography dealt the country an almost impossible hand. Hundreds of islands, of varying sizes, scattered across a wide expanse of ocean, make establishing an efficient infrastructure both difficult and expensive. Traffic between the islands had always depended on countless poorly maintained and often over-crowded ferries, so that accidents at sea were frequent – as they still are. From a very early stage local airlines also played a part, although for most potential travellers they were unaffordable.

The economy of the Philippines was dominated by that of Luzon, the largest island and the only one with a rail-network. The capital, Manila, at the centre of Luzon, was also much the largest city. The other large islands, such as Leyte and Mindanao, have also developed local communications infrastructures, but almost all the islands, including Luzon, have large inaccessible areas of jungle and mountain, inhabited by primitive tribes.[15] All in all this was a topography that lent itself not so much to head-hunters as to guerrilla warfare, terrorism and piracy, all of which plagued the Philippines in the twentieth century.

As a result of both Spanish colonialism before 1900, and the various regimes imposed by the United States thereafter, the Philippines, as part of the world economy, concentrates on fishing and agriculture – with sugar, tobacco and rice as the main crops – and the exploitation of natural resources, such as tropical hardwood, oil and base metals. Plantation agriculture is the preserve of a *latifundista* mestizo oligarchy, which invests heavily and corruptly in politics, simply to preserve its own interests. This is supplemented by local peasant small-holdings, with production determined by the demands for subsistence and of local markets. Outside agriculture textiles and food-processing produce for the national market. Tourism is now a useful direct source of income from abroad, but much more important are remittances from Filipinos working overseas, which in 2001 exceeded $6,000,000,000 – not far short of $100 for every single one of the country's inhabitants.[16]

As for large-scale investment, the private economy is mainly the preserve of the Chinese minority, originally established, centuries ago, before any form of Western involvement in the islands. Although comprising only one per cent of the Philippine population of some 80,000,000, Chinese control the country's four airlines and almost all the banks, hotels and big conglomerates.[17]

The mix of the factors listed above produces a development economy in which the overwhelming majority of ethnic Filipinos live on less than $2 a day, with an increasing number forced to live in the barrios of the large cities, in particular Manila.

Although this is almost a prototype culture of poverty it is remarkable, at least in Southeast Asia, for its adherence to Rome for its religion and to the United States for language, education and constitutional and legal forms. Filipinos may be poor but for most of the twentieth century their votes counted, so much so that much of the money generated by political corruption is spent on American-style campaigning. Philippine politics are governed by the old principle of Tammany Hall in nineteenth-century New York, of 'money from the rich and votes from the poor'. This makes for a dangerous political life-style, characterized by intense rivalries between individual politicians.[18]

As for the Catholic Church, its position changed radically during the twentieth century. After 1900, the Spanish religious orders lost their power base as young American missionaries, mainly Jesuits, began to champion enlightened labour laws and land reform. Although to begin with they confronted a conservative local hierarchy, the bishops gradually began to support them, particularly after

Pope John XXIII's proclamation of the doctrine of *aggiornamento*. Today the Church in the Philippines, hardly tainted by political corruption, is definitely on the side of the angels. Until his retirement in 2004 it had, in Jaime Cardinal Sin, for thirty years a charismatic leader[19] – who will reappear later in this chapter – but the course of enlightenment was well set long before his time.

Returning to the succession, following the death of Magsaysay, the new president, Carlos Garcia, ensconced at the centre of the spider's web of Filipino politics, outdid all his predecessors in the game of corruption. In 1958, his first full year of office, he became $700,000,000 richer by fraudulently selling import licences, and by 1959 Filipino politics was 'an almost incomprehensible tangle of party splits, personal vendettas and rivalries within rivalries'.[20] There was a crying need for a new Magsaysay, particularly in the local office of the CIA. Their man in Manila even had a slush fund, but at $250,000, it was peanuts compared to the sums available to Garcia. Even so, the CIA's man, Diosdado Macapagal, was elected president in 1961 after campaigning with the slogan 'Honest Mac, the Poor Man's Best Friend'.[21]

Macapagal, for all his good intentions, failed completely: corrupt bureaucrats and politicians did not give him a chance. The murder rate in Manila, with only one-eighth of the population, was higher than that of New York. To court popularity he expelled several Chinese businessmen, many actually citizens of the country, and deported an American businessman worth $50,000,000, gained from a variety of business enterprises. They were all accused of corruption, and were no doubt guilty, but in the Philippines there is no other path to wealth. By 1965, when Honest Mac came up for re-election, his reforms had infuriated the wealthy, and their failure meant that he was hardly the poor man's best friend.

THE MARCOS KLEPTOCRACY

Opposing him was a noted rising star in Filipino politics, Ferdinand Marcos, whose wife, Imelda, had persuaded Fernando Lopez – a scion of one of the Philippines' richest families – to be candidate for vice-president. Marcos spent money on about the same scale as George W. Bush in the United States in the year 2000, and with even greater success. Not surprisingly the Chinese business community was particularly generous in making campaign donations but they were by no means alone. Marcos gained a majority of 600,000 out of some 8,000,000 votes cast – with only about 5 per cent estimated as rigged. This was the beginning of the most disastrous and long-lasting presidency in Filipino history. True to the style of Filipino politics, Marcos started off by claiming a 'mandate for greatness' coupled with a vow to end 'every form of waste or conspicuous consumption and extravagance' and to uphold 'the supremacy of the law'.[22] In fact twenty of Marcos's years in office – twelve more than the constitution allowed when he first came to power in 1965 – were characterized by unprecedented waste, conspicuous consumption and extravagance (particularly on the part of his wife, Imelda), only made possible by complete disregard of the law. When he finally left office Marcos's personal fortune was $6,000,000,000, and the 'crony capitalism', characteristic of his term of office, made rich men out of many key supporters.

Given the state of the Philippines in 1965 Marcos's election to the presidency was to be expected. His first term of office was blessed by some good fortune: with American aid new roads and bridges were built, and with new high-yielding strains the Philippines became a net exporter of rice. On the other hand only 3,000 tenants benefited from Marcos's land reforms, and violence – often politically inspired – was part of everyday life. Even so, Marcos's re-election in 1969 was assured.

As the 1973 presidential election approached Marcos knew only too well that the constitution barred him from seeking a third term of office. By this time a new factor had entered Filipino politics. On 26 December 1968, Mao Zedong's seventy-fifth birthday, a new communist party was founded in a remote corner of Luzon, and in March 1969 this led to the formation of the New People's Army, led by the renegade son of a rich land-owner and a former *Huk* guerrilla, to bring about a Maoist revolution in the Philippines. In the course of twenty years the rebellion, encouraged by Marcos's corruption and cronyism, spread throughout the country.

Marcos's chosen strategy was to proclaim martial law, for which the Maoist threat provided the necessary pretext. Given the Philippines' special relationship with the United States, some sort of support from Washington was essential. At Marcos's request, the American Ambassador Henry Byroade returned to Washington in August 1972. The moment was ill chosen: President Nixon was campaigning for re-election, the news of the Watergate burglary had just broken, and National Security Adviser Henry Kissinger was busy both negotiating a ceasefire in Vietnam and preparing the ground for a rapprochement with China. Byroade got nowhere, and the best he could do, on his own initiative, was to pledge 'support for the President of the Philippines in the event of a genuine Communist danger'.[23]

In September explosions occurred in downtown Manila, while another wrecked the sewage system in Quezon City. Marcos blamed the Maoists, but he could himself have orchestrated the explosions – as suggested by intelligence reaching the local CIA office. In any case Marcos had made his point. With criminals and racketeers profiting from the ensuing chaos, Marcos saw the Maoists moving toward 'open war'. He alone stood between anarchy and stability – a stance reluctantly accepted by Washington.

On 22 September 1972 Marcos formally decreed martial law, in order, as he said in a broadcast, to 'eliminate the threat of violent overthrow of the government'.[24] Within hours Benigno Aquino Jr., popularly known as 'Ninoy', who would have opposed Marcos's candidate in the 1973 presidential election, was arrested, and in the following weeks some six thousand others, identified as communists, or at least sympathizers, shared his fate. Most were released in due course but Aquino was kept in prison until 1980. Newspapers, radio and TV stations were closed, censorship imposed, airlines and utilities seized. Washington hardly reacted: in the final days of the Vietnam War the Pentagon could not miss the bases in the Philippines.

There was no presidential election in 1973; instead a new constitution dictated by Marcos allowed him to stay in office, and at the end of term, be re-elected. On the other hand, with Jimmy Carter becoming US President in January 1977, Marcos's position in Washington became much more problematic. Under a new pope, John Paul II, the Church also stepped up the pressure. Then, on 5 May 1980, Aquino, still in prison, had a heart attack, and the doctors recommended a coronary by-pass. Imelda Marcos, seeing that it would a public-relations disaster if Aquino died during surgery, persuaded her husband to let him go into exile in the United States. The operation was then carried out in Dallas.

THE CHARISMA OF CORY AQUINO AND THE END OF MARCOS

By 1982 Aquino seriously contemplated returning home from exile – for a number of reasons. A new coalition, the United Democratic Nationalist Organization, was forming in the Philippines. By becoming its leader Aquino could save it from the communists. At the same time Marcos had become so ill that he was eventually to need two kidney transplants. Aquino, fearing that Imelda Marcos, supported by an old family friend, General Fabian Ver, as chief of a military government, would take over the presidency, decided that this drastic scenario required his return to the Philippines. Aquino saw to it that he was accompanied by the press, and when the plane landed in Manila a welcoming crowd jammed the terminal. Three soldiers boarded the aircraft, and forced Aquino to disembark via a service stairway. As he stepped off at the bottom, shots rang out, and seconds later he was dead from a single shot through the back of his head. Next to him was the bullet-riddled body of a man in mechanic's overalls: this was Rolando Galman, a small-time criminal, who, according to a broadcast by Marcos the following day, was an agent of the communists.

This scenario convinced no one. It had clearly been set up by General Ver, who was present with the soldiers (although, predictably, he was acquitted when tried in early 1985). Imelda, on a visit to New York, had warned Aquino to delay his return until 'the area is sanitized', and once back home she told friends that if Aquino did return he would be dead in 'just one hour'.[25] It was not even a minute. This, however, was a political assassination that back-fired.

Aquino's funeral was conducted by Cardinal Sin, who condemned the 'oppression and corruption, fear and anguish' of the Marcos regime, while the widow, Cory Aquino, thanked the mourners for their 'love and devotion'. As a final farewell the cardinal said, 'May the martyrs welcome you'.[26] There were more than a million people in the funeral cortege, which took eleven hours to cover the twenty-odd miles to the cemetery. The coffin was covered with yellow chrysanthemums, and the crowd was also bedecked in yellow, the Aquinos' colour. For weeks afterwards parades, demonstrations and riots paralysed Manila, and yellow banners and ribbons were to be seen everywhere.

Marcos had at last forfeited the trust of his foreign supporters, and international bankers were getting worried about their money. The collapse of the economy encouraged the communist insurgents, leading the US Embassy in Manila, supported by visiting congressmen, to advise Washington that they be taken seriously, while the Defense Department considered new island bases on Guam and Tinian to replace those leased from the Philippines.

In spite of his ill-health, coupled with drastic loss of credibility, Marcos was still determined to hold on. He realized, however, that desperate measures were needed. By late 1984, and a year after the murder of Aquino, the communist insurrection had spread to sixty-two of the seventy-three provinces of the Philippines. The US Embassy in Manila found no trace of any outside support: that Marcos himself was the problem, not the solution, was the view of many at the top of the US administration, including Admiral William Crowe, commander of the Pacific Fleet. President Ronald Reagan, however, still backed him – so much so that at the end of 1984, when campaigning for re-election, he stated that 'to throw Marcos to the wolves would leave America facing a communist power in the Pacific'.[27]

In the event Marcos himself forced the pace by declaring, on 3 November 1985, a presidential election that would take place two years ahead of time. This was a colossal miscalculation. Following the murder of her husband, Ninoy, Cory Aquino enjoyed unprecedented popular support. When the election was announced, a priest advised her that she alone embodied the values of 'truth, freedom and justice' that could beat Marcos.[28]

The obvious establishment candidate to oppose Marcos was Salvador Laurel, the leader of United Democratic Nationalist Organization formed as a supporters' club for Ninoy Aquino in 1982. Like many a Filipino politician his reputation was dubious, and at earlier stage he had even worked with Marcos. On the other hand he had nothing of Cory Aquino's popularity, as became clear from a petition with more than a million signatures asking her to stand for president. Having consulted Cardinal Sin, she agreed to run, with Laurel as candidate for vice-president. The Cardinal persuaded Laurel with the words, 'Make the sacrifice, or Marcos will win', which, after dithering for some weeks, he then heeded.

Marcos nearly won anyway, mainly because he had the backing of President Reagan until almost the last minute. In the Philippines Cory Aquino enjoyed not only the support of the Church and the people, but that of much of the business community. The US Embassy, with the tacit support of Secretary of State George Schultz in Washington, also helped her. Leading politicians on both sides of the Congress supported her. On election day, 7 February 1986, ballot boxes were stolen, voters intimidated and some even killed, and it was clear to all except Reagan that Marcos was responsible. That US defence strategy was more of a concern than justice was made clear when he said, 'I don't know of anything more important than those bases'.[29]

On 15 February, after the votes had been counted, Marcos proclaimed victory, with the Soviet Ambassador among the first to congratulate him. While more than a hundred bishops condemned Marcos's 'fraudulent' election, Cory Aquino staged a huge rally to unseat Marcos. Philip Habib, a diplomat sent out by Schultz to assess the situation, advised that 'Cory had won the election and deserved our support'.[30] At the same time, Juan Ponce Enrile, who as Marcos's defence minister in 1972 had declared the critical state of emergency, organized a coup in support of Cory Aquino: although this was mismanaged in the early stages, in the evening of 22 February Enrile arrived at Camp Aguinaldo, a military stronghold and site of the defence ministry, and in a TV news conference recognized Cory Aquino as the winner in the elections, confessing that he had himself faked 400,000 votes in favour of Marcos. Within a few hours thousands of supporters, including many disaffected soldiers, gathered at the camp, while Cardinal Sin told Cory Aquino, 'This may be the miracle we've been expecting'.[31] It was.

While Manila filled with crowds demonstrating for Cory Aquino, a group of top men, summoned by Schultz in Washington, heard from the ambassador in Manila that 'Marcos will not draw the conclusion that he must leave unless President Reagan puts it to him directly. Go for a dignified transition out'.[32] It took another two days before a formula was found that was both acceptable to Reagan and sufficient to persuade Marcos to go into exile. On the afternoon of 25 February he finally left Manila with a retinue of sixty. In characteristic show-biz style Marcos and Imelda made a final appearance on the balcony of Malacanang, the presidential place, singing 'Because of You' to the crowd gathered beneath them.[33] A day later the Marcoses and their children were in exile in Hawaii. Once in America they confronted grand juries investigating their numerous crimes involving dealings in the United States, to say nothing of the civil suits filed against them. Even Reagan began to see the truth about his old friend, and shortly before his final term was up he signed a new interim bases agreement with Cory Aquino.

Predictably Cory Aquino's new administration did not mean that paradise was just round the corner. The economy, in the state left by Marcos, was in ruins, the country was bankrupt, socially divided and two insurgent groups were active.[34] On the other hand, no one doubted that it was Marcos's flagrant mismanagement and venality which had bankrupted the country, and Marcos was gone. At the same time Cory Aquino enjoyed the good will of both the Manila business community and the Catholic hierarchy.[35] She also strengthened her hand by appointing, first as Defence Chief of Staff, and then as minister, Fidel Ramos, a cousin of Marcos – and his chief of police – who had switched sides at the critical time when the Marcos regime was facing collapse.

In spite of a good start Cory Aquino's administration suffered from drift, disorder and doubt, coupled with criticism rather than support from the intellectuals, businessmen, clergy and soldiers who had helped her into power. Before long many would agree with the words of one of her closest political friends, the Jesuit Joaquin Bernas, 'the people are not getting the president they voted for'.[36] In 1989 this discontent was reflected in an unsuccessful *coup d'état*, when soldiers led by Colonel Gregorio Honasan – still active in Filipino politics[37] – tried to topple Aquino.

Shortage of money was the obstacle to any large-scale reform, particularly in the countryside. If land was to be distributed to those who farmed it, the landowners would require compensation, while the new independent farmers would need credit for seeds, equipment and above all training. There was also the need to service some $28,000,000,000 in foreign debt run up by Marcos. In the large cities, particularly Manila, the middle classes enjoyed unprecedented prosperity, but the Philippines returned to its characteristic endemic corruption, in which even the Aquino family was involved. In a country where the Church hierarchy denounced birth control as 'dehumanizing and immoral' the population increased at a rate that only exacerbated the endemic poverty.

Although Marcos's departure led to a significant loss of support for the communist New People's Army (partly because it had boycotted the presidential election that led to his downfall) it still remained active, and the measures taken to combat it led to widespread human rights abuses. In parts of the country where they were strong, the communists could even finance their operations by taking protection money from the landowners. With the fall of Soviet Russia, and China taking a new direction under Deng Xiaoping, the communists, deprived of outside support, became less of a danger to the government in the final years of Aquino's presidency. At this time the US also agreed to relinquish its bases in the Philippines, notably that of the navy at Subic and of the air force at Clark Field. In 1991, the departure of the US forces was hastened by the most shattering event in the Philippines' twentieth-century history: the eruption of the volcano, Pinatubo, on 15 June, which covered the bases, and the rich agricultural countryside around them, with a blanket of ash. This was the climax foreshadowed by a series of earthquakes afflicting the island of Luzon in the preceding eleven months, leading to both villages and farmland being lost to landslides.

Helped by the remaining US forces, the Philippine government evacuated some 60,000 people from the area in danger from the eruption, while another 18,000 left Clark Air Base – an exemplary operation in dealing with a major natural disaster.[38] This was not the end to the trials suffered in this part of Luzon. Volcanic ash from Pinatubo covered vast areas, which rain transformed into glutinous mud, known as 'lahar'. On 1 October 1995 Typhoon Mameng caused vast flows of *lahar* to bury whole communities, many of which had emerged as a result of resettlement following the eruption of Pinatubo in 1991. Mameng, however, was only the worst of the typhoons – characteristic of the Filipino climate – to cause such havoc, while at the same time new earthquakes, throughout the 1990s, also devastated areas reclaimed from landslides and settled by refugees from Pinatubo.

HALF-HEARTED REFORM FROM RAMOS TO ARROYO

Under Aquino the Philippines acquired a new constitution, limiting the president to one six-year term of office: this meant a new election in 1992, which Fidel Ramos, in a wide field, won with only 23.5 per cent of the votes cast – an unprecedentedly low plurality. The almost inevitable allegations of fraud did not stick, and Ramos was probably the most successful president in the post-Marcos era. His economic reforms – intended to open up the national economy, encourage private enterprise, invite more foreign and domestic investment, and reduce corruption – pleased the World Bank more than they did the Philippine voters, and nothing came of his attempts to have the constitution amended so as to allow him a second term of office. He had no chance, therefore, to implement his Philippines 2000 programme of radical economic reform. Instead he was accused of corruption on a massive scale, which led in the end to a World Bank inquiry. On the other hand, in 1996, he successfully reached a peace agreement between the government and the Moro National Liberation Front – which was at the centre of Muslim insurgency.

Ramos's worst failure was in the realm of 'law and order'. Half-way through his term of office, in September 1995, the Philippine Chamber of Commerce and Industry warned that persistence of 'the twin problems of kidnappings and bank robberies' undermines investor confidence and reinforces 'the perception that the government is helpless in alleviating the situation'.[39] Here the local Chinese business community – the most dynamic and successful in the country – provides frequent targets, with little hope of the police, often corrupted by the kidnapping gangs, taking any effective action.[40] Significantly there was a fivefold increase in reported kidnappings during Ramos's first four years in office – not much to be proud of for a man who had once headed the country's constabulary.

The impending departure of Ramos left the presidency up for grabs in an election in which the leading, and ultimately successful, contender was the country's most popular film-star, Joseph Estrada – a Filipino Arnold Schwarzenegger. When he became president in 1998 he had a long life in politics behind him, ending up with his being Ramos' vice-president. With a quite different social background, however, he espoused the cause of the poor, promising to redistribute the country's wealth. In fact he had plenty himself – otherwise he could never have afforded a presidential campaign. Once in office he was plagued by rumours not only of corruption and illegal business transactions, but also of the luxurious accommodation – provided at public expense – for his numerous mistresses. He was ousted by a coup, supported by the military, in 2001, to end up in a secure military hospital, while being tried for impeachment, following the offences allegedly committed by him during his three years in office. Like Marcos, if on a smaller scale, he was accused of accepting millions of dollars in pay-offs – largely by gambling operators.

While the trial – inevitably given Estrada's background – soon became a television spectacular, the Philippines acquired, for the rest of his term, a new president. With Gloria Arroyo – who had been his popularly elected vice-president – the office returned to the established ruling oligarchy: her own father was Diosdado Macapagal, who, as 'honest Mac', was president from 1961 to 1965. His daughter, if she was to succeed, certainly had to do better, but her term of office was beset by problems. In her first year – as related in Chapter 15 – the extremist Abu Sayyef group of Islamic extremists, in a wave of kidnapping, took hostages to be used in bargaining with the government. Then, on 1 May 2002, a large number of Estrada's supporters, who had remained loyal to him, stormed the presidential palace, demanding Arroyo's resignation. A year later, on 27 July 2003, some 300 soldiers – equally disenchanted with her regime – rigged a giant Manila shopping mall with explosives, and then barricaded themselves in a nearby hotel. Although both Arroyo's Secretary of Defence and her military intelligence chief had to resign, she held on to compete – successfully and in her own right – in the presidential election of 2004.

The new six-year term of office became almost immediately problematic following the discovery of a tape-recording of a conversation between Arroyo and an election commissioner at the time of the 2004 election. Although this was admittedly improper, the resulting storm of protest by opposition politicians was insufficient to remove Arroyo from office: the balance of power in Manila was just in her favour, if only because there was obviously no better game in town.

At the end of the day Filipino politics is always the same old story of 'gold, goons and guns – wealth and power'. The fact that traditional politicians, popularly known as 'trapos' – the Spanish for 'rags' – tells it all. All but a handful of elected representatives are millionaires, often because they come from large landowning families, who, by their very nature, can hardly be much interested in emancipating the millions of poor Filipinos. If, in theory, these could vote for 'virtuous, altruistic men and women who would champion their cause and create a more just society', in practice by doing so they elect men like the disastrous and self-seeking Estrada. In practice varying combinations of 'philanthropy, charisma and terror … keep most politicians in power, and as long as this system persists it is difficult to see how a fairer society can be created'.[41]

11

Indonesia: the long road to justice and reform

THE END OF DUTCH IMPERIALISM

When in May, 1940, Nazi Germany overran the Netherlands, the Dutch government escaped to London, where it continued to function throughout World War II. This meant that the considerable resources of the Netherlands East Indies would be available not to Germany, but to its enemies. The raw materials, such as petrol and rubber, produced there, were essential to the allied war effort.

In September 1940 (as related in Chapter 1) the Vichy government in France was forced to accept Japanese military bases in Indochina, and allow the country's resources to be appropriated for use by Japan in its war with China. The Dutch government, on the other hand, followed Britain and the US in freezing Japanese assets and blocking all exports to Japan, whose government was already planning to incorporate the whole Dutch Empire in Asia into their 'Great East Asia Co-Prosperity Sphere'.

The signs were ominous: the Dutch responded to the Japanese threat by increasing their military forces, in part by creating a 6,000-strong local Indonesian militia. In the event none of this helped. Within two weeks of Pearl Harbor Japan attacked Borneo, Celebes and the Molucca islands, although the invasion of Java, at the heart of the Netherlands East Indies, only began on 1 March 1942. By this time the situation was hopeless, and the Royal Netherlands East Indies Army, with 93,000 men, surrendered a week later, together with many allied soldiers. The Japanese had conquered almost the whole of an empire that had existed for more than three centuries. Few of its subject peoples regretted its demise, and such leaders as they had wanted only to establish an independent state. The Japanese occupation gave them the chance they had waited for.

The Dutch in Indonesia ran a very tight ship. Their administration, based on Batavia, provided the only essential unity, while local populations had very little access to the centre of power. Very few ever learnt Dutch, and although Malay might count as a lingua franca, there were any number of other indigenous languages spoken in the hundreds of islands comprising the East Indies. Nonetheless, Malay had flourished, and by World War II there were some 400 newspapers and periodicals, and any number of books, published in it – often by the official Dutch government printing house.

The success of Malay was such that Indonesian intellectuals had renamed it the Indonesian language, or 'Bahasa Indonesia' – which has been its status since the founding of the republic in 1948. Political activity among the new intellectuals was definitely not encouraged: many who engaged in it were imprisoned or exiled – a repressive policy that created a number of folk-heroes, such as Mohammad Hatta, Sutan Sjahrir (both educated partly in the Netherlands) and, above all, the charismatic Ahmed Sukarno.

As rulers of Indonesia the Japanese had a much more limited economic perspective than the Dutch. It hardly extended beyond oil and other raw materials essential to their war economy. Since Sumatra and Borneo were the main oil producers, this meant that the exchange economy of Java – home to more than half the Indonesian population – lost almost all its markets. By the last winter of the Pacific War, 1944–45, the whole of Indonesia, flooded with worthless Japanese currency, suffered inflation, shortages, profiteering, corruption, black markets and death on a massive scale.

In the course of 1942, the Japanese interned all Dutch civilians and appointed Indonesians to positions in government and the economy never open to them under the Dutch. Because the Japanese had proclaimed themselves as 'liberators' local political groups, suppressed by the Dutch, became active in the early days of the occupation. The Japanese, however, were anxious to avoid any disturbance, and so often suppressed such activity, preferring to follow the established Dutch policy of relying on traditional local leaders. In practice the Japanese faced much the same organizational problems as the Dutch had, but their mobilization of resources, including manpower, was much more heavy-handed – particularly after the tide of war had changed.

Japan allowed something of a free hand to top-level political activists who had been imprisoned or exiled by the Dutch. Nationalist leaders such as Sukarno and Hatta did collaborate, but only so far as it enabled them to pursue their own political agenda, which was focused upon complete independence for Indonesia. Incorporation into Japan's Great East Asia Co-Prosperity Sphere was never part of it.

On the other hand the more the war turned against the Japanese, the more they needed the support of the nationalist leaders – which the latter well appreciated. In November 1943 Sukarno and Hatta were even invited to Tokyo, to receive decorations from the emperor, but they left with little satisfaction after Tōjō, the prime minister, refused to concede the right to use nationalist symbols such as the new Indonesian flag.

Tokyo never fully realized that any new policy for Indonesia would only attract people such as Sukarno and Hatta if it could be turned to their own political advantage. Finally, in January 1944, Sukarno and Hatta did accept top positions in the new Java Service Association (*Jawa Hokokai*), which, although formally headed by the Japanese commander-in-chief (*Gunseikan*), allowed them considerable freedom of action, particularly when it came to travel. Sukarno, in particular, made good use of the opportunity to realize his own political agenda, and under the auspices of *Jawa Hokokai* became established as a popular leader right down to village level.

Japanese attempts to win support from Islamic leaders were equally heavy-handed. The Japanese failed in suppressing the use of Arabic or in requiring believers, who under Islam could only bow to Mecca, to bow to the emperor in Tokyo. They made more progress with the *kiais*, Islamic teachers at village level – who were offered special training courses, but this did little to offset the steadily increasing unpopularity of the occupying forces. For this there was any number of reasons: not least among them was the recruitment of 'volunteers' (*romusha*) for unskilled labour in any part of Southeast Asia. Of these only 70,000, fewer than half the number recruited, survived the war.

While Sukarno and Hatta maintained a high profile, Sutan Sjahrir, whose nationalist credentials were equal to theirs, operated underground. In Bandung and Jakarta educated young people demonstrated against the Japanese, and at the same time, in the countryside, there were local peasant revolts. 1944 was the year in which Japan, suffering one defeat after another, with considerable loss of territory, found it almost impossible to maintain an effective military presence in the areas, such as Indonesia, which it still controlled. In July 1944, the loss of the key Pacific island of Saipan led to the resignation of the prime minister Tōjō. On 7 September his successor, Koiso Kuniaki, in an attempt to gain support in Indonesia, promised independence at some future unspecified date, and allowed the Indonesian flag to fly at *Jawa Hokokai* offices.

At the same time, a senior Japanese officer, Vice-Admiral Takashi Maeda, began working with Sukarno and Hatta, and won the trust of many influential Indonesians, with their appointment as senior officials providing unprecedented opportunities for meeting together. This helped the cause of Indonesian nationalism more than it helped the Japanese. At a plenary meeting on 1 June 1945, Sukarno proclaimed the guiding fivefold principle of *Panchila*: belief in God, nationalism, humanitarianism, social justice and democracy. Since this was not acceptable to Islamic leaders a new compromise Jakarta Charter (Piagam Jakarta) was promulgated, adding after *God* the words, 'with the obligations of the adherents of Islam to carry out Islamic law' – a provision later giving rise to serious disagreements. On this basis a new constitution was drafted, providing for a new unitary state, to include Malaya and British Borneo.

In 1945 the Japanese, facing defeat, would do almost anything to prevent the restoration of the Dutch colonial government. At a meeting in Singapore, at the end of July, 1945, Java was promised independence in the coming September, with the other islands to follow later. On 11 August, the day after the devastation of Nagasaki by the second atomic bomb, the Japanese Commander-in-Chief, Field-Marshal Hisaichi Terauchi, promised Sukarno and Hatta independence for the whole of Indonesia, but not including the former British possessions.

Then on 14 August the Japanese Emperor announced his country's surrender. The result, in Indonesia, was a considerable political void: no allied troops arrived to take over the islands, and the thousands of Dutch internees, even if released, would be in no state to do so. The result was that the *Gunseikan* held the fort, as best he could, until the allies arrived.

SUKARNO'S DECLARATION OF INDEPENDENCE

At this stage Admiral Maeda wanted to hand over to older responsible Indonesians, while revolutionaries, supported by Sjahrir, wanted an immediate declaration of independence. Sukarno and Hatta, whose support was critical for any such action, found it expedient to work with the Japanese. With a view to forcing their hand, impatient young revolutionaries kidnapped them during the night of 15 August, and held them in a garrison of the Peta youth movement, an auxiliary force set up by the Japanese in 1943. Admiral Maeda was able to contact the garrison, and assured the kidnappers that if Sukarno and Hatta returned to Jakarta, the Japanese would look the other way if they declared independence. Sukarno and Hatta then spent the night of 16 August in Maeda's house, working on a draft declaration. This was ready on the morning of the 17 August, and Sukarno returned to his own house in Jakarta to read it to a small group of Indonesians who had assembled there.

Proclamation:

We the people of Indonesia hereby declare
The independence of Indonesia.
Matters concerning the transfer of power, etc., will be carried out
in a conscientious
manner as speedily as possible.

Jakarta, 17 August 1945.

In the name of the people of Indonesia,

[signed] Sukarno Hatta

Although it would be more than four years before the Republic of Indonesia achieved international recognition, the road to independence started with the proclamation of 17 August 1945 – a day since celebrated as Independence Day.

With the defeat of Japan the people of Indonesia demanded national unification and independence, while the Dutch simply wanted to restore their empire in the East Indies. Paradoxically only the Japanese had the power to maintain law and order, so they remained in control until allied military forces arrived to replace them.

In September 1945 the Japanese had to deal with massive youth demonstrations, which they had to suppress, if only for their own safety. By this time all they wanted was a degree of order sufficient to enable them to return home to Japan. Before the Japanese departed, it was clear that allied forces would have to be deployed at key points throughout the islands, if only as peacekeepers. Matters were not made easy for the indigenous populations, since the Japanese had disarmed the local nationalist militias, and destroyed their command structures. There was also the problem of liberating and rehabilitating the tens of thousands of European civilians interned by the Japanese, a process that could count on little local support.

From the middle of September, 1945, the allied military government,[1] under Admiral Mountbatten, began to restore order, with the larger cities in the eastern islands being assigned mainly to Australian troops, and those in Java and Sumatra to Indians. The Dutch, needless to say, hoped that Mountbatten would reconquer Indonesia for them, but his remit did not go further than accepting the surrender of local Japanese forces and releasing European internees.

In eastern Java, and the islands further east, allied troops did help the Dutch re-establish their authority, but in western Java and Sumatra, where nationalists were strong, the local British commander, Lt Gen Sir Philip Christison, kept the Dutch forces out. Instead he recognized, de facto, local representative bodies, where they existed. In the volatile interior of Java Christison had to negotiate a ceasefire with Sukarno, before he could rescue some 10,000 internees.

The reconstruction of Indonesia was far from peaceful. The worst violence occurred in Surabaya, a large harbour city in eastern Java, where the local Japanese commander, Vice-Admiral Yaichiro, while surrendering the city to the Dutch Navy on 3 October 1945, allowed his forces to hand over their weapons to local Indonesians who later formed the nucleus of the Indonesian Army.[2]

On 25 October some 6,000 Indian soldiers arrived in Surabaya to help evacuate internees. Within three days 10–20,000 Indonesian soldiers, supported by mobs ten times greater, attacked the Indian soldiers, both inflicting and suffering severe casualties. Once again only the intervention of Sukarno, on 30 October – at the invitation of the local British commander – could bring about a ceasefire. Even this did not hold, and the British had to bring in reinforcements before they could evacuate the internees. Supported by air and naval bombardment, the British finally cleared the city, leaving it devastated. This left the British government with little popular support for military intervention in Indonesia, although, in principle, it supported the rights of the Dutch to their former East Indian Empire. With the departure of General Christison, on 1 February 1946, the Dutch were effectively left on their own.[3]

The battle of Surabaya became a symbol for the revolution. The British were confirmed in their view that neutrality was the only possible policy in Indonesia,[4] and the Dutch realized, for the first time, the vast extent of popular support for an independent republic. On the other hand the nationalists were far from united: the fact that Sukarno was the leader of a secular party was one reason why he was so anxious to restore peace in Surabaya, where the uprising was declared a *jihad* by Islamic leaders.

Although the revolution reflected a common commitment to independence, it took place against a background of struggle between individuals and factions. More than anything else, it was the oppressive means adopted by the Dutch to restore their authority in the years following 1945 that welded Indonesia into a unitary republic.

The Indonesian nationalists held all the cards that counted. The Japanese occupation had destroyed the whole Dutch power structure, whether in government, economy or education. If up to 1941 some 100,000 Europeans were able to govern a thousand times that number of native inhabitants, this was only possible because of the vastness and diversity – religious, cultural and ethnic – of a territory comprising hundreds of islands, in which the Dutch were the only central authority. Only their language was spoken throughout Indonesia, and they did little to encourage their subject peoples to learn it.[5] It was a shrewd move on Sukarno's part to establish Bahasa Indonesia as the national language at a very early stage.

More than anything else, it was the numbers that counted. Beyond a certain critical threshold of support for the nationalist cause, the Dutch would never be able to restore their East Indian Empire. Already with Sukarno's proclamation of 17 August 1945 the writing on the wall was clear enough, but in spite of warnings from within their own camp[6] it was nearly four years after the end of the Pacific War before the Dutch got the message. Part of the problem faced by the Dutch was to be found in the general failure of law and order on the both sides of the Malacca Straits following the departure of the Japanese in 1945. Singapore was wide open to smuggling operations from both Sumatra and mainland Malaya: rice imports from Sumatra were critical for feeding its population, while at the time vast stocks of arms, left behind by the Japanese, or supplied to guerrillas in Malaya by allied air-drops, could be shipped in the other direction – so much so that they provided a substantial part of the arms needed by the Indonesian nationalists.[7]

The nationalists, after 1945, enjoyed considerable international support. When the case for Indonesia first came before the United Nations in January 1946 Australia and the Soviet Union already supported it. The United States and the United Kingdom would take the same line if the Netherlands failed to persuade the Indonesian nationalists to agree a new federal government recognizing Dutch interests. The Dutch, with no significant support in the outside world, spent some three years vainly trying to reach such an agreement. Their case was made even more difficult by the fact that British India, following the policy of the Labour government elected in 1945, would become independent in 1947, and once a member of the United Nations would certainly support the cause of Indonesian independence. The Netherlands – where voters consistently showed their support for government policy – stood alone. President Truman, in particular, once again made clear that the United States had not fought and won World War II to restore any European colonial empire.

As early as July 1947, the Netherlands, under UN pressure, had agreed a ceasefire with Sukarno. Within the Netherlands this was hardly a welcome move, given Sukarno's record of collaborating with the Japanese occupying forces. The help given by Sukarno to the British forces, in 1945, in establishing some sort of order, can be seen as an attempt to rehabilitate himself with the victorious allied forces. Even so the Dutch government could not countenance their acting governor-general, H.J. van Mook, negotiating the future of Indonesia with Sukarno. The Indonesian nationalists diplomatically appointed Sjahrir (who had never worked with the Japanese) as prime minister, so that he would negotiate with van Mook, and later represent the Indonesian cause at the United Nations. Sukarno and Hatta withdrew to the background after they had accepted the titular offices of president and vice-president.

Van Mook's policy was to set up a new federal Indonesia, in which the Netherlands, from the areas in which it had regained some control, would continue to rule, and so far as possible, extend and consolidate its power. On the other side the nationalist position was threatened by two key political factors, which did not relate directly to the Dutch presence in Indonesia. These were Islamic radicalism and international communism.

A radical Islamic movement, Darul Islam, led by the mystic S. M. Kartosuwirjo, was well-established in west Java. In spite of a strong Dutch presence in this area, the Indonesian General A. H. Nasution was also active there with a whole division under his command. In February 1948 he made a strategic withdrawal, leaving the Dutch to deal with Darul Islam. Nasution then re-deployed his forces in central Java, where they were confronted almost immediately by a popular uprising led by Musso, who in the 1920s had played a major part in setting up the Indonesian Communist Party (PKI). After a failed uprising in 1925 the party was suppressed by the Dutch, but Musso went into exile in the Soviet Union.

Returning from exile on 11 August 1948, he lost no time in resurrecting the PKI, at the same time encouraging strikes and the expropriation of land by the peasants who worked it. This led to a show-down when, on 18 September 1948, PKI supporters, including some thousands of soldiers, occupied strategic points around Madiun, in central Java.[8]

Sukarno, realizing that any sign of support for the PKI would antagonize the United States, denounced the Madiun rebels, and sent troops to suppress the uprising. The fighting lasted for about seven weeks, with appalling atrocities committed by both sides in the local villages. Musso and many others lost their lives. The Madiun incident established a tradition of hostility between the PKI and the army – dominated by Sukarno and Nasution – leading in turn to much closer ties between it and the government, in which Hatta was now the dominant figure. At this stage, also, the United States resolutely supported Sukarno's anti-communist stance.

Internationally the Dutch refusal to recognize the success of Sukarno's policy was fatal to their interests. On the contrary, on 18 December 1948, Dutch soldiers directed a 'police action' against Yogyakarta. In 1756 it had become the capital of the dominant sultanate of central Java, and in 1946 the Dutch had allowed the nationalist government to set up house there. Although by the end of 1948 Dutch forces controlled all the major towns of Java and Sumatra, the Yogyakarta police action was appallingly misconceived. Although the city was taken in one day, and the republican government made captive, this was a pyrrhic victory. The Dutch treated the UN headquarters with contempt and contrary to their expectations the Sultan of Yogyakarta refused all collaboration, as did the local civilian population. Nationalist guerrillas constantly harassed the Dutch garrison. In January 1949 the UN Security Council demanded the release of the Indonesia cabinet, with transfer of sovereignty to a new interim government before 1 July 1949. Already, in 1948, the US Congress had threatened to block aid to the Netherlands under the Marshall Plan if Indonesia's demands for independence were not met.

THE GRANT OF INDEPENDENCE

On 6 July 1949 the Indonesian government returned to Yogyakarta, and set up a conference to plan Indonesia's future as an independent state. It was agreed that the army would be the basis of new Republic of the United States of Indonesia (RUSI), with Sukarno as President and Hatta as Vice-President. On 1 August a ceasefire was agreed with the Dutch, to take effect almost immediately. From 23 August until 2 November the Dutch and Indonesians came together at a Round Table conference in the Hague. The Dutch accepted Indonesia's demand, made by Hatta, for formal transfer of sovereignty on 27 December. The Netherlands would retain Irian Jaya (the western half of New Guinea), and the republic would assume the Netherlands East Indies debt of f.4,300,000,000 (most of which had been incurred in the struggle to retain the colonial empire[9]).

In the new year, 1950, the republic still had to persuade a number of states, established as part of van Mook's failed attempt at federation, to accept its authority. By the end of March the majority had agreed to merge into a unitary state, but the Ambonese South Molucca Islands (where Christianity was strong) claimed that the constitution agreed at the Hague allowed it to retain its local autonomy. Resistance in the Moluccas was crushed by the armed forces of the new republic, and thousands of the islands' inhabitants fled to exile in the Netherlands.

On 17 August 1950 a new constitution, abolishing RUSI and creating a unitary Republic of Indonesia (see map on page ix), with Jakarta as its capital, was adopted. The new state was a non-federal, non-communist and non-Islamic, representative democracy – but even so it had many unresolved problems. Its new leaders were hardly men of the people. Elections, as provided for by the constitution, did not take place until 1955. In 1950 little had been done to restore the plantations and industry essential for Indonesia to compete in the world economy after the devastation wrought by the Japanese. At the same time the population – 77.2 million in 1950 – increased by 20 million in the next ten years, and was to double again in the next forty years. (It is now well over 200 million.) Land-holdings often became too small to support the traditional peasant cultivation of the staple rice, let alone produce a surplus for consumption by the growing non-agricultural population. Peasants became wage-labourers on plantations, or, in increasing measure, moved to the large cities.

The new government gave education high priority so that the adult literacy rate, which under the Dutch had been less than 10 per cent, was by 1960 not far short of 50 per cent, and the newly literate, who were mainly young, looked for jobs requiring their skills. This led to a vast increase in the bureaucracy, where former nationalist guerrillas claimed office jobs, almost as a matter of right. By 1960 the proportion of the population in government employment was nearly four times what it had been under the Dutch; inevitably the new bureaucrats were inefficient, poorly paid and open to corruption.

Inevitably also, major enterprises in oil, rubber, shipping and banking, all essential to the exchange economy of Indonesia, remained the preserve of foreigners, American, English, Dutch and, at local level, Chinese. The greatest problem, however, was to form a government from the parties represented in the first parliament under the 1950 constitution. The largest party, *Masyumi* – a sort of umbrella for diverse Islamic factions – held only 21 per cent of the seats. The three main secular parties, united only by a common desire for a secular state, between them held 29 per cent; of these nearly half were held by the communist PKI, which, after the disastrous Madiun incident of 1948, was making a come-back. Some 42 per cent of the seats were held by numerous small parties.

The result was a succession of weak governments, generally based on a coalition between *Masyumi* and the nationalist PNI, which was generally thought to enjoy the favour of Sukarno, who, as president, was above politics – in principle, if not in practice. Following the new constitution in 1950, one problem facing every successive coalition government was the excessive size of the armed forces – a legacy of the four years spent fighting for independence. An army of 200,000 was a heavy burden on the Indonesian economy. During the first year of the Korean War when prices of the two leading exports – rubber and oil – were high, it was just about supportable, but by the end of second year of the war, when prices were much lower, this was no longer the case. By the autumn of 1952, the Ministry of Defence, with General Nasution playing a leading role, proposed a centralization and demobilization scheme that would reduce the army to 100,000 soldiers. Significantly the PSI, the opposition socialist party led by Sjahrir, was seen as a power behind the scenes.

This was too much for regional commanders of the central army group based around the capital, Jakarta. On 17 October 1952 some 30,000 demonstrators, supported by tanks and artillery, gathered in front of the presidential palace. The crowd, seduced once again by the magic words of Sukarno, dispersed. The charismatic president then received an army delegation, and the soldiers returned home. The army was seriously weakened as a political force, but the cabinet was also discredited and Nasution suspended.

After the '17 October affair' the succession of weak governments was acceptable to no one, and in April 1953 parliament passed a bill providing for a general election not later than September 1955 – the month in which it actually took place. There would then be a second election in December 1955 for members of a Constituent Assembly to draft a permanent constitution. The politicians in Jakarta began to look for mass support.

TRIUMPH AT BANDUNG

Shortly before the 1955 election a coalition government led by Ali Sastroamidjojo (July 1953–July 1955) achieved a remarkable international success. In April–May 1954 the prime ministers of India, Pakistan, Ceylon, Burma and Indonesia met together in Colombo, the capital of Ceylon.[10] There Sastroamidjojo made a well-received proposal for a large conference of Afro-Asian states, and it was soon agreed that this would take place in the Indonesian city of Bandung in April 1955. The conference was a triumph for Indonesia. Twenty-nine states sent delegates, of whom many were heads of government. Indonesia could reasonably claim to be the leader of the world's non-aligned powers.

The presence of the Chinese prime minister Zhou Enlai at Bandung was particularly significant. In the first three years after its founding in 1949, the People's Republic had been hostile to the non-communist states of Asia, but its stance then became noticeably more open. Indonesia sent its first ambassador to Beijing in May 1953. At Bandung Indonesia and China signed a dual nationality treaty, which later would be critical to the position of the strong Chinese community in Indonesia.

China traditionally recognized all overseas Chinese as its own citizens. The new treaty obliged those residing in Indonesia to make a definitive choice, one way or the other. Its terms made it much more advantageous to opt for Chinese citizenship, which meant in effect that Indonesia would have to accept a large, well-established, local population of non-citizens. The local Chinese, counted in millions, were not only by far the largest expatriate group of residents, but also the one with fewest ties to its home country. Although successive Indonesian governments from the beginning of the 1950s had done everything possible to favour local Indonesian entrepreneurs, success was most likely to come to those who were a front for Chinese businessmen, who knew only too well how to be on the right side of notoriously corrupt politicians and bureaucrats.

In 1954, at the same time as the Sastroamidjojo government was dealing with the Chinese question, it also agreed a protocol with the Netherlands which would end – in the event, in 1956 – the formal relationship that van Mook had enshrined in the Netherlands–Indonesian Union. At the same time Indonesia claimed, not for the first time, the western half – Irian Jaya – of the island of New Guinea. The claim's only foundation was that this too had been part of the Dutch colonial empire.[11] Throughout the 1950s the Dutch consistently pointed out that Irian Jaya had never been governed from Batavia, but instead had its own administration. At no time in the history of the East Indies had any local sultanate shown any interest in New Guinea – a vast island, much larger than any other in the Indonesian archipelago, of which the eastern half, in any case, belonged to Australia. New Guinea, with next to no infra-structure, consisted largely of inaccessible mountain ranges, covered with rain-forest and inhabited by hundreds of different tribes, often at war with each other. A happy hunting-ground for anthropologists and missionaries, it would require massive outside investment if its natural resources were to be profitably exploited. Nonetheless, although in 1954 even the United Nations failed to support the claim to Irian Jaya, Indonesia persisted and in the end got what it wanted.

Although Bandung was the great success story of 1955, the election due in September was the critical event of the year. Two significant and far-reaching developments preceded it. First, under Sastroamidjojo the communist PKI was as free to operate as any other party – a major factor in improving relations with China. In the year leading up to the election its membership and wealth (based largely on contributions from the Chinese business community) increased spectacularly. Second, on 18 July 1955 *Nadhlatul Ulama* (NU), originally founded in 1926 as an orthodox Islamic party – its name means 'rise of the religious scholars' – decided to leave its shelter under the *Masyumi* umbrella, and set up, once again, on its own. The result was an end to Sastroamidjojo's government, which was succeeded by a weak Islamic-socialist coalition excluding the nationalist PNI.

Although the fact that more 90 per cent of all registered voters voted in the 1955 general election could be interpreted as a triumph for democracy, the actual results made the formation of a strong government almost impossible. The two Islamic parties, *Masyumi* and the NU, shared between them nearly 40 per cent of the votes cast, while the two most successful secular parties, the PNI and the PKI, were together only a percentage point behind.[12] The socialists (PSI) only received 2 per cent of the votes, while more than twenty splinter parties gained some 12 per cent – so becoming entitled, under the system of representation inherited from the Dutch, to a proportionate number of seats in the new parliament.

The distribution of the votes across the different islands showed a quite different pattern from the national results. In Java, much the most important island, the secular parties had a clear majority except in traditionally Islamic west Java, where *Masyumi* was the largest party. Except for Bali and the Christian islands, such as the Moluccas, *Masyumi* was by far the strongest party outside Java: in Sumatra, Aceh – always an Islamic stronghold – gave it three-quarters of all the votes cast.

With these results, the withdrawal of NU support for the coalition in January 1956 inevitably brought it to an end. In March Sastroamidjojo, determined to exclude the PKI from government, returned to power with a new PNI-*Masyumi*-NU coalition. Indonesia's first democratically elected government lasted for four years, but Sukarno, as president opening the new parliament, was lukewarm in his welcome, and soon began to talk about 'guided democracy'.

In its first year the new coalition gained some popularity by repudiating the unpaid balance of the Netherlands East Indies debt, assumed as part of the price to be paid for independence in 1949. This also defused the communist PKI claim that Indonesia still accepted a semi-colonial status. These populist moves solved nothing in a country with a steadily deteriorating economy. Particularly in the outer islands and the Islamic areas of Java, mobs attacked Chinese businesses, while regional commanders became involved in such activities as smuggling.

Hoping to restore law and order the government rehabilitated Nasution and appointed him army chief of staff. He in turn joined an alliance formed by

Sukarno and Sastroamidjojo, with the political support of the nationalist PNI. This then proceeded to transfer officers out of the regions where they had built up private business interests. Not surprisingly this policy split the officer corps: one group, consisting mainly of officers from outside Java, opposed Nasution, while another supported him. In late 1956, the former group, supported by officers of the elite Siliwangi Division, took advantage of Sukarno's absence from the country on a state visit to China, the Soviet Union and other communist states and attempted a *coup d'état*. It failed, and Nasution, by arresting or transferring the officers opposing him, established the Siliwangi Division as the most reliable in the armed forces.

Sukarno, returning from his foreign travels, spoke out against the party system of government, and on 30 October 1956 he introduced his idea of 'guided democracy'. Although some parties, such as PNI and NU, were attracted by Sukarno, none was happy with the prospect of liquidation. Only the communist PKI declared its support, but this was pure opportunism based on the hope that it would survive under the new regime.

There was once more resistance from the military: in Sumatra, the largest and richest of the islands, local commanders forced civilian governors to declare for independence from Java. Once again the crisis was dealt with by appointing new officers to local commands; at the same time Aceh, much the most troublesome area, was pacified by being recognized as a separate province with an ethnic Acehnese as its governor.

On 9 January 1957 *Masyumi* withdrew from Sastroamidjojo's coalition, so depriving it of its parliamentary majority. A number of local *Masyumi* leaders in the important islands of Kalimantan, Sulawesi and Maluku – where the party was always strong – then switched their support to recalcitrant local army officers.

SUKARNO'S GUIDED DEMOCRACY

This was too much for a minority government, and on 21 February 1957 Sukarno showed the nation what he meant by 'guided democracy'. Its basis would be mutual cooperation between the major parties, including the PKI (which never having been in power had no record of corruption), supported by a National Council of functional groups defined by various categories, such as students, workers, peasants and religions, rather than political parties. There was some talk of a new cabinet headed by Hatta (who had the advantage of coming from Sumatra), but then Sukarno refused to meet Hatta on 11 March 1957. Three days later the Sastroamidjojo cabinet resigned and Sukarno declared martial law. Such was the passing, or at least the eclipse, of parliamentary democracy in Indonesia; free elections had to wait until 1999, more than forty years later.

Sukarno was one of the twentieth century's most controversial national leaders. However unprincipled his willingness to deal with the Japanese during the Pacific War, it was essential to his long-term aims. Later, in the 1950s, many saw his acceptance of the communist PKI as a pact with the devil, but for Sukarno the end always justified the means. He was also a master of timing, always knowing when to wait and when to act, even though for most of his career he knew that he had the tide with him. Sukarno was still a great survivor and he, more than anyone else, established Indonesia as a single, essentially secular state, united by its own language, with power concentrated at the centre. *Guided democracy* was intended as the blue-print for the government of such a nation. The way its practical application, over a period of eight years (1957–65), proved to be disastrous for both Indonesia and the reputation of Sukarno, defines the next stage in the country's history.

In April 1957 Sukarno appointed a 'business cabinet', which was essentially a PNI (nationalist)-NU (orthodox Islamic) coalition. This was followed, in May 1957, by a National Council consisting of 41 'functional groups', precisely as envisaged by 'guided democracy'. Although the functional groups were in principle non-party, most political parties, including the communist PKI, had members in key positions. The same was true of the army, where Nasution was particularly successful in gaining control of the powerful veterans' league, where the PKI had been strong. Of the major parties, only the Islamic *Masyumi* was excluded.

In attempting to solve the crisis, the cabinet, National Council and army decreed, under martial law, the arrest of many opposition politicians for corruption. Although this did reduce the power of the old parties, and more particularly the PKI, in the outlying regions, their supporters were far from being won over to the new order. This became clear when, in provincial council elections held late in 1957, the number of votes cast for PKI – which had campaigned in favour of guided democracy – was higher than ever before. In central Java, the PKI was top of the poll, at the same time coming second in several other important provinces.

Following these results, Sukarno accepted that the PKI should be allowed to play a part in government. In September 1957 this led dissident army officers in Sumatra to put forward a programme with three objectives: first, a new president should be elected; second, Nasution should be replaced as commander-in-chief; and third, the PKI should be outlawed. Because Islam forbade communism, this objective was also proclaimed in the same month by an All-Indonesia Congress of Islamic Scholars, convened by *Masyumi*. At this stage the army high command held its hand, but then an unsuccessful attempt on the life of Sukarno on 30 November 1957 led Nasution to give up any hope of compromise with the dissident officers.

On the previous day, 29 November 1957, the UN failed once again to pass a resolution calling upon the Dutch to settle the west Irian question. Sukarno had long warned of the dire consequences that would then follow. They were not long in coming. On 3 December 1957 union activists – many belonging to the PKI, which was only too ready to attribute Indonesia's semi-colonial status to the Dutch in Irian – began appropriating Dutch-owned businesses. The first to be taken over was the Royal Mail Steam Packet Company (KPM), the major shipping line operating between the islands. This led many of the ships then at sea to leave Indonesian waters, with the consequent decline in services inevitably fuelling discontent in the outlying islands. If Royal Dutch Shell, a major oil producer, was not taken over, it hardly helped that 46,000 expatriate Dutch citizens were expelled from Indonesia. Nasution took the opportunity to give the army control of many of the expropriated enterprises, a move enormously increasing his own power in relation both to the government and to the regional commanders. In particular he set up a new oil company, Pertamina, entrusting its management to a trusted deputy, Colonel Ibnu Sotowo.

These developments inevitably produced a political reaction. On 10 February 1958, while Sukarno was abroad, dissident officers meeting in Sumatra combined with local socialist (PSI) and *Masyumi* leaders to call for the dissolution of the cabinet followed by new elections. Five days later a new Revolutionary Government of the Indonesian Republic (PRRI) was announced, and was reported to receive secret support from Americans concerned for their property in the Sumatran oil fields.

The three major oil companies had in fact accepted that their interests would be protected, and continued to pay the revenues due to Jakarta. Even so, given the government's ties to the communist PKI, there was little doubt about American sympathy for the rebel PRRI. For a time support for the rebels was condoned, but after an American B-26 bomber, with a civilian pilot, was shot down over Sumatra, the State Department – set on maintaining good relations with Jakarta – condemned such military intervention. On the other hand Singapore and Malaya – recently independent and separated from Sumatra only by the narrow Malacca Straits – were also a source of arms for the PRRI. While the Philippines, Taiwan and South Korea were also sympathetic, the Chinese community in Indonesia, knowing where its interests lay, was solid in its support of the PKI. The PRRI, however, never came near to success at national level.

The failure of PRRI rebellion strengthened the hand of Nasution, who was enabled to remove the dissident officers. Martial law had, however, made the army unpopular, particularly after new officers, mainly from Java, had been appointed to local commands in the outlying islands. Sukarno, seeing his own position threatened, looked to the communist PKI for support. Nasution banned *Masyumi* and the socialist PSI, following their support for PRRI. While Nasution looked for radical constitutional reform – even to the point of restoring the 1945 constitution which Sukarno had proclaimed from his house in Jakarta – Sukarno engaged in characteristic political rhetoric, finally coming up, in 1960, with the doctrine of *Nasakom*, based on the unity of nationalism, Islam and Marxism. This could only be realized by a coalition of the nationalist PNI, the orthodox Islamic NU and the communist PKI, all of which were based on Java. (Most of the other parties had been suppressed by Nasution.) While the army would not countenance PKI members of the cabinet, Sukarno was able to have lifted bans on the party made by regional commanders in Sumatra and Sulawesi (although they continued in Kalimantan for a whole year).

At this stage the fate of west Irian once again forced the pace of Indonesian politics. In August 1960 diplomatic relations with the Netherlands were broken off as a delayed result of an official Dutch announcement, made earlier in the year, of elections which would be the first step on the way to an independent state of Irian. The PKI took the opportunity to mobilize mass demonstrations in favour of military action. Already, in January 1960, Khrushchev, while on an official visit to Jakarta, had granted a loan of $250 million, and a year later, in January 1961, Nasution negotiated in Moscow a further loan of $450 million for the purchase of arms. Given the increasing communist strength in Vietnam – just the other side of the South China Sea – this was not a welcome development for the United States, and the new President, Jack Kennedy, decided to work for a negotiated settlement of the Irian question.

This was to take some time, and in December 1961 Sukarno set up, under his own command, a new Supreme Operations Command for the liberation of Irian. The actual fighting was to be directed by the recently promoted Major-General Achmad Suharto. The war began badly when, in January 1962, the Dutch defeated an Indonesian naval force off Irian. This provided Sukarno with the opportunity to restructure the top command, as a result of which Nasution, while still remaining Minister of Defence, lost the command of the forces fighting the Dutch.

The Irian campaign allowed the communist PKI (which was never in favour with Nasution) to increase its membership enormously, making it a political force to be reckoned with, particularly since the Soviet Union was bankrolling the purchase of arms. Finally, on 15 August 1962, the Dutch, yielding to American pressure, agreed to allow an interim UN administration to take over West Irian on 1 October 1962, followed by transfer to Indonesia on 1 May 1963. Both the United States and the International Monetary Fund (IMF) were then ready to grant financial assistance, provided first, that the PKI was kept out of the government, and second, that economic reforms were put in hand. These were absolutely essential: the state of the economy under Sukarno was desperate. In the years 1961 to 1964, the price paid for *guided democracy* was an annual rate of inflation of more than 100 per cent.

In the same period that the West Irian question was settled in favour of Indonesia (1961–63), the prospective independence of Malaya, Singapore and the three British territories in north Borneo – Sabah, Brunei and Sarawak – was also part of the American agenda. The result, agreeable to both the British and the Americans, was a new Federation of Malaysia, comprising all these territories.[13]

The developments in Malaysia were deeply resented in Indonesia. Jakarta, jealous of the economic success of Malaya and anxious about the Chinese strength in Singapore, had not forgotten the support given to the PRRI from the other side of the Malacca Straits. At the same time Jakarta regarded Malaysian membership of the British Commonwealth as acceptance of neo-colonial status, the more so since the United Kingdom would retain some of its bases in the new federation (just as the United States had done in the Philippines).

On 16 September 1963, its very first day, mass demonstrations against the new Malaysian federation, with communist PKI members in the vanguard, took place on the streets of Jakarta. The mob burnt down the British Embassy and attacked that of Malaysia, provoking in turn an attack on the Indonesian Embassy in Kuala Lumpur. On 17 September 1963 Malaysia broke off diplomatic relations, and within four days Indonesia severed its economic ties with Malaya and Singapore – between them the gateway to the outside world for more than half its exports. On 25 September 1963 Sukarno announced that he would 'gobble Malaysia raw',[14] a policy praised by both China and the Soviet Union – which otherwise were already following separate paths in international affairs. The strategic importance of Malaysia, at a time when China was gaining in strength and the communist threat in Vietnam was inexorably increasing, was such that the United States would never have allowed so unstable a nation as Indonesia to have any influence there. The new federation would not be 'gobbled'.

In the two years following Sukarno's announcement of 25 September 1963, Indonesia's descent into chaos continued inexorably, to end with a rate of inflation of 500 per cent, and nearly twice as much with the price of rice, the staple food of most of the population. Sukarno attempted to deal with increasing hostility from the armed forces by continually changing the command structure at the top – to frustrate, in particular, the ambitions of Nasution – and playing the different services off against each other. For Suharto, the most successful general in the Irian campaign, a new post was created in Jakarta, when he was put in charge of *Kostrad*, the new Army Strategic Reserve Command.[15] All in all, continual intrigues among senior officers – each group having its own agenda – were the inevitable result of Sukarno's chaotic policies, and the only question that mattered was which group would come out on top in the end.

At the same time the PKI leader, D.N. Aidit, returning from a long visit to both countries, chose to align his party with China against the Soviet Union. The

Soviet Union reacted by looking for support in the Indonesian Army, while the Americans gave clandestine support to PKI's opponents. The PKI in turn stepped up its campaign for land reform, and in areas where it was strong villagers began seizing land, including British-owned plantations – although here the army often stepped in to run them. There were violent clashes between the PKI and the orthodox Islamic NU, to which many dispossessed landlords belonged. In January 1964 Sukarno announced that the United States could 'go to hell' with its aid. In Borneo the army was fighting a losing battle against Malaysian and British forces, but even so, in August and September 1964 Indonesian forces landed on the Malay peninsular. By the end of the year the army pulled out of its hopeless confrontation with the British, and transferred its best troops to Suharto's *Kostrad*, where he made certain that they remained in Java.

China was only too ready to fish in the troubled waters of Indonesia, and even offered to explode a nuclear device there – a move calculated to attract support from the Indonesian Army, while at the same weakening the influence of the Soviet Union. No doubt with a view to strengthening the communist PKI, China also transferred the assets held by its central bank in Jakarta to the Indonesian government. In January 1965 Indonesia withdrew from the UN – from which the Chinese People's Republic was still barred by Washington's power of veto – as a protest against Malaysia being given a non-permanent seat on the Security Council. While this may have cemented the alliance with Beijing, it certainly weakened Indonesia's position as a leader of the non-aligned world of Africa and Asia.

These were all signs of a strategy, clearly accepted by Sukarno, to strengthen the PKI so as to counteract the army's involvement in politics. It was only partly successful. When in February 1965 newspapers in Jakarta and Medan opposing the PKI were suspended, the army began to publish its own newspapers. Although each side did its best to undermine the other, with the PKI trying to infiltrate the army, and *vice versa*, the two sides occasionally worked together. When, as a result of the bombing of North Vietnam, popular anti-American sentiment was at its height, trade unions, many affiliated to the PKI, seized American businesses, with the army then taking over their management. At the same time the Peace Corps was expelled and the three major American oil companies placed under government supervision. On the other side, high-level delegations from Beijing – one even led by Zhou Enlai – visited Jakarta.

Although Sukarno was clearly playing off the PKI against the army, his long-term strategy – if he had one – was unclear. The PKI went from strength to strength, to the point of claiming some 27 million Indonesians as members and supporters. On independence day, 17 August 1965, Sukarno, after having broken off with the IMF and the World Bank, proclaimed an anti-imperialist alliance linking together Jakarta, Phnom Penh, Hanoi, Beijing and Pyongyang, even though Indonesia's main trading partners were the United States, West Germany and Japan.

SUHARTO TAKES OVER

Although Indonesia was near to collapse, the majority of its citizens could hardly contemplate a country without Sukarno. Nonetheless, his deteriorating health, together with the chaotic state of the country, made the question of succession critical. The end could not be far off. On the night of 30 September 1965, after meeting together at the Halim air-base outside Jakarta, a group of senior officers, supported by three army battalions and local PKI activists, set off to eliminate the army's high command. Once in Jakarta they murdered three generals, including Achmad Yani, the chief-of-staff, and took three others prisoner. Nasution escaped, but his five-year-old daughter was shot: within a week the three captive generals were dead. Such was the beginning of the 'gestapu', an acronym for the 30 September Movement.

Some 2,000 soldiers, supporting the coup, occupied three sides of the Medan Merdeka, the great square in front of the presidential palace in Jakarta. On the fourth side stood the *Kostrad* HQ, where shortly before dawn Suharto – whose name was absent from the list of intended victims – arrived. With Yani and Nasution nowhere to be found, Suharto, with the consent of such surviving generals as could be contacted, took over command of the army, and ordered all soldiers to be confined to barracks. At the same time the leaders of the coup announced by radio that they had acted to foil an American CIA plot, supported by the army high command, to dethrone Sukarno. Although the part Sukarno himself had played has never been clear, his reaction to the news of the night's events was to summon the navy and police commanders, together with Johannes Leimena, a key supporter in the cabinet, to Halim. There he learnt not only the fate of the six generals, but also that Nasution had escaped.

Suharto, in the meantime, persuaded the soldiers at Medan Merdeka – who were hot, tired, hungry and thirsty – to give up the struggle. When, at 4pm on 1 October 1965, Sukarno let it be known that he had himself assumed command of the army, Suharto paid no attention. Instead, at 9pm he announced by radio that he was in command, would crush the *gestapu* and safeguard Sukarno. He was as good as his word. Although, for a few days, supporters of the movement continued to be active outside Jakarta, its defeat in Jakarta was decisive. Guided democracy was effectively at an end.

The thirty-odd years that then followed had one main theme: the rise and fall of Suharto. Although, in 1939, Suharto left his home in rural Java to become a soldier in the Dutch East Indies Army, as a native Indonesian he was able to maintain a low profile during the Japanese occupation. With the defeat of Japan he cast his lot with the nationalist rebels, and with his military background rose rapidly to the rank of lieutenant-colonel. On 1 March 1949 he commanded the troops that infiltrated Yogyakarta and attacked the Dutch garrison there. Although the city was retaken by the Dutch the same day, this incident became an important part of the Suharto image, which was greatly strengthened by his success as a general in the struggle for West Irian in 1962. By this time he had already discovered how to gain popularity with junior officers by rewarding them with opportunities for corruption, a practice for which he would later become notorious.

On 1 October 1965 the challenge to Suharto was to bring order and prosperity to a country ruined by the regime that he had, somewhat unexpectedly, overthrown. Although guided democracy was at an end, Suharto, realizing the popular reverence for Sukarno, allowed him to retain – but only as a figurehead – the supreme command of the army. Suharto took upon himself the task of restoring order and security, at the same time pinning the blame for the failed *gestapu* coup on the communist PKI.

The army arrested more than 10,000 PKI activists, and the leaders among them were shot. At the same time the general population – after years of chaos only too ready to go along with Suharto – was encouraged to take the law into its own hands. This led to scenes reminiscent of the *Kristallnacht* of October 1938 – when German mobs, egged on by their Nazi leaders, destroyed Jewish life and property – but this time, in Indonesia, a victim could be almost anyone linked to the PKI. In the vanguard were a spontaneous student movement, KAMI (Indonesian Students Action Front), and orthodox Islamic groups, who saw the fight against communism as a *jihad*. By the spring of 1966, when the main action had subsided, some 500,000 were dead; many of them had little connection with the PKI. The breakdown of law and order, to which Suharto turned a blind eye, was for many a pretext for settling old feuds – or for landlords to get rid of squatters. The dead were not the only legacy of Suharto's first months in power; at the end of the day some 100,000 were still imprisoned without trial.

Sukarno played no part in these terrible events. After the defeat of the *gestapu* he still praised the PKI role in the revolution, but his orders to ban KAMI and close the University of Indonesia were ignored. The army was already holding trials based on the premise that the PKI was behind the *gestapu*. Finally on 11 March 1966, Sukarno, learning, at the opening of a cabinet meeting, that his life was threatened by hostile students demonstrating on the streets outside, fled by helicopter to Bogor, a town some distance from Jakarta with a presidential palace inherited from the Dutch Governor-Generals. The same evening three generals loyal to Suharto arrived at Bogor with a document for Sukarno to sign. This, the so-called *Supersemar* (11 March letter of instruction), conferred upon

Suharto full authority to restore order, facilitate the functioning of government and protect the president in the name of the revolution. Sukarno, although still nominally president, was deprived of whatever power or influence he may have retained after the defeat of the *gestapu*.

Suharto lost no time in making use of his plenary powers. The PKI, together with organizations affiliated to it, were banned, eleven cabinet ministers whose loyalty to Suharto was uncertain were arrested and the army purged of officers loyal to Sukarno. This left the way open to a new cabinet appointed on 27 March 1966 in which the Sultan of Yogyakarta and a new figure, Adam Malik, would be Suharto's main lieutenants.

Malik, appointed foreign minister, set out to undo the work of his predecessors. Attacks on Chinese diplomatic staff and private property, condoned by the new government in the months following the defeat of the *gestapu* on 30 September 1965, foreshadowed the end of almost all ties with Beijing. In February 1966 the ambassador in Beijing was recalled, but he preferred to remain there and claim political asylum. In May Beijing recalled its ambassador in Jakarta, after closing the local branch of the Xinhua news-agency and the three Chinese consulates in Indonesia.

His diplomacy notwithstanding, in Indonesia Suharto still courted the top Chinese entrepreneurs, the so-called 'cukong'. These would then help the new generals with their own business enterprises, while at the same time helping Suharto with their capital resources, connections with the outside world and general business expertise. This was a shrewd strategy, since the unpopularity of the Chinese community – with its ties to Maoist China – made it a negligible political force in its own right. The Chinese community was then rewarded with protection from local hostility and any number of opportunities for graft – shared, needless to say, with Suharto's cronies in the officer corps.

Internationally Malik continued to follow a pro-Western course, so that in April 1966 Indonesia rejoined the UN, and later in the year, the IMF. In May 1966 Suharto sent a number of senior officers on a goodwill mission to Kuala Lumpur, and later in the month he himself met the deputy prime minister of Malaysia in Tokyo. Full diplomatic relations were not, however, restored until August 1967. This opened the way to Indonesia becoming a founder member of the new Association of Southeast Asian Nations (ASEAN), together with Malaysia, Singapore, Thailand and the Philippines. The idea was that ASEAN would function as a regional counterweight to Japan and the US. At the same time non-communist creditors formed the Inter-Governmental Group on Indonesia (IGGI) to coordinate financial dealings with Indonesia.

Inside Indonesia Suharto continued the process of discrediting and weakening Sukarno. After replacing supporters of Sukarno with his own men, Suharto allowed the nationalist and secular PNI party to continue to function as a counterweight to Islamic groups. After being dealt with in the same way, the Provincial People's Consultative Assembly (MPRS) convened in July 1966, and summoned Sukarno to appear before it to explain both the failed policies of guided democracy and his own role in the *gestapu*. (In January 1967 he finally denied any such involvement.) All this led, as planned, to Sukarno forfeiting his title of 'president for life', with loss of any right to issue presidential orders (as he had done earlier in the year). Finally on 12 March 1967, the MPRS reconvened to strip Sukarno of any remaining powers and nominate Suharto as acting president.[16]

While all this was happening those (including the PRRI rebels of 1958) arrested under Sukarno for opposing guided democracy were released, with the top men among them, just like Suharto's officer cronies, granted new business opportunities. On the other side of the fence new trials dealt with those involved in the *gestapu*, while officers not involved, but still loyal to Sukarno, were bought off with appointments to embassies abroad and other favours.

On the economic front Suharto came to rely on a number of Indonesian graduates from top American universities: these, the so-called Berkeley mafia, advised a regime of strict internal controls. Although Suharto, unashamedly, would claim exemption on behalf of himself, the *cukong* and his officer friends, the new policy went down well with the West. This enabled Indonesia's substantial foreign debts – a legacy from the Sukarno era – to be rescheduled, particularly after reforms proposed by the World Bank and the IMF were accepted. To encourage maximum economic growth foreign investment was encouraged, and American and British businesses confiscated under Sukarno returned to their owners. Drastic budget cuts extended even to defence, but this little affected the army since it was active in its own right in both oil and the cultivation of rice.

The drastic economic reforms, while benefiting the *cukong* and overseas investors, did little for small-scale local enterprise: the result was increased unemployment and widespread discontent, even among students belonging to KAMI. One result was an increase in religious adherence, which also had the advantage of effacing any history of past support for communism. This new turn of events did not so much help radical Islam – tainted by its role in the violence following the defeat of the *gestapu* in 1965 – as Christianity, Buddhism and Hinduism and even *Kebatinan*, a sort of traditional Javanese mysticism. While Christianity was particularly strong in the growing cities of Java, there was serious anti-Christian rioting in Makasar, Aceh and even some parts of Java. From 1967 Suharto had some success in using the military to enforce reconciliation and reduce violence, but religious forces were always to cause him trouble. On the political side parties such as the secular PNI and the Islamic NU were tolerated so long as they did not threaten Suharto, but power became increasingly centralized, with both provincial governors and heads of local authorities being appointed from the military. Finally, in March 1968, the MPRS reconvened to elect Suharto president for five years. His new government, including many technocrats and economists, was immediately popular with potential donors of aid in the Western world.

On 1 April 1969, the strength of the Indonesian economy, as a result of increased oil production, reduced inflation and foreign loans at an unprecedentedly high level, enabled the introduction of an optimistic new domestic development plan for agriculture, the infrastructure, and industries focused on exports and import-substitution. This success was so well-regarded in the West that US President Nixon, among many others, came on a visit (bringing with him $40 million in military aid).

In 1969, following rigged local elections (which nonetheless satisfied the UN), Irian was incorporated as 26th province – a move which later would lead to trouble with the Free Papua Organization (OPM). Slowly also, international pressure led to the release of the majority of political prisoners, but even low-category prisoners were not welcome back in society. On the other hand increasing centralization led to occasional purges of senior officers.

In the process of tightening his control of the country Suharto, in 1969, radically restructured representation in parliament to include a large number of appointed members. Another strategy was to establish *Golkar* – originally set up by the army in 1964 to promote cooperation between army and civilian bodies – as a party which all government employees were required to join. This move deprived the secular national PNI of a major constituency. Even though *Golkar* election candidates were screened for reliability, the party still won large-scale popular support as the only viable secular alternative to the Islamic parties.

By this time, however, Suharto's wife, brother and foster-brother were already becoming rich as the result of lucrative business sent their way by the government. In spite of student protest at mounting corruption, *Golkar*, in an election held in July 1971, got 61.8 per cent of the votes, giving the government 73 per cent of the seats in parliament with the remainder being held mainly by the Islamic minority parties. New regulations, from which *Golkar* was exempt, then limited the scope of the minority parties even further, and on this basis the assembly, in March 1973, elected Suharto to a second term as president, with the Sultan of Yogyakarta as vice-president.

The strength of the Western-oriented economy led to a substantial increase in both trade with Japan, and local investment by Japanese capital. By the end of 1973, 53 per cent of all exports, including 71 per cent of all oil produced, went to Japan, which was also the source of 29 per cent of all imports. Japanese companies operating in Indonesia were also perceived as competing unfairly with local enterprise. Matters came to a head when a visit by the Japanese prime minister, Kakuei Tanaka, in January 1974, led to the worst riots in Jakarta since the fall of Sukarno. At the height of this 'January disaster' (*Malapetake Januari*) hostile crowds, numbering tens of thousands of students and poor city-dwellers, surrounded both Tanaka's guest house and the presidential palace, while 800 cars and 100 buildings – many shops selling Japanese goods – were burnt down. Suharto, predictably, clamped down ruthlessly, but with few communists left preferred to blame activists from the former socialist PSI and Islamic *Masyumi* – both parties banned by his regime.

In October 1973 the Yom Kippur War between Israel on one side and Egypt and Syria on the other was followed by the majority of the world's major oil producers outside the United States setting up OPEC – the Organization of Petrol-Exporting Countries – which included Indonesia as a founding member. OPEC immediately adopted a policy of enforcing production quotas on its members, so as to increase prices in the world market for oil. In Indonesia the government's first reaction was to nationalize Pertamina, a consortium of oil producers set by the army in 1968, but heavily in debt after a shameful history of mismanagement. This was the beginning of a long period of prosperity based on high oil prices, which made Suharto's government, however corrupt, more acceptable to the people of Indonesia.

By this time the international political scene, particularly as it affected Indonesia, was changing radically. Nixon's visit to Beijing in 1972 – soon to be followed by the Chinese People's Republic being admitted to the UN as a permanent member of the Security Council – together with the impending withdrawal of US forces from Vietnam, gave Mao's China a new status in world politics, making Indonesia's pro-Western stance even more important for the US and its allies. This was enhanced in 1976 when a conference of the anti-communist ASEAN states was held in Bali.

In Aril 1974 another key event occurred on the other side of the world when Portugal's right-wing dictatorship, which had been in power for nearly fifty years, was toppled. As a result of events related in Chapter 12, this led to Indonesia first invading East Timor, Portugal's only surviving colony in the East Indies in December 1975, and then incorporating it as its 27th province in July 1976. For reasons of *realpolitik*, if no other, this was accepted by the rest of the world. Foreign aid continued to increase, with major investment by Japan, the Soviet Union and Shell.

THE *GOLKAR* CONSPIRACY

By 1976 the new order was firmly established, with the military, known as ABRI (short for 'Armed Forces of Republic of Indonesia') the dominant force in politics. *Golkar*, the only effective political party, controlled an economy run by technocrats. Oil was the key export, and the economy flourished so long as

OPEC was able to maintain high prices on the world market. By 1982, the year which this regime came to an end, Indonesia had become the world's largest producer of liquefied natural gas (LNG) – a particularly important factor in the long term, given that by the twenty-first century LNG had become world-wide the preferred fuel for power stations.

In spite of lower oil prices the Indonesian economy flourished until almost the end of the 1980s: Suharto had seen to it that he was re-elected president in 1977, 1982 and 1987. In a climate friendly to foreign investment both ABRI and the civil bureaucracy worked productively to increase the prosperity of the population at large. The drastic decline in rice production under Sukarno was reversed to the point that there was once again a surplus available for export. Tourism, encouraged by visa waivers, became increasingly important. Mass education expanded to the point that some 90 per cent of the population were at home in Bahasa Indonesia. Medical services, although lagging behind Malaysia, Thailand and the Philippines, also improved greatly, with an effective family planning programme lowering the birth-rate in a country whose population was approaching 200 million. As in many other developing countries population increase was concentrated in the large cities, with Jakarta approaching 10 million inhabitants.

Although *Golkar*'s dominant position was never seriously threatened political Islam continued to be strong with the NU still active (although Suharto did his best to neutralize its influence). Following pressure from US President Jimmy Carter in 1977, Suharto improved his human rights record by releasing the majority of the more than 50,000 political prisoners held since the beginning of his regime. The main problem was steadily increasing corruption, which led to some 30 per cent of the money received in foreign aid or for government contracts being siphoned off into the hands of Suharto's friends – mostly in ABRI – and his growing family. Occasional student protest demonstrations were always suppressed. In spite of criticism from the media, the two foreign powers that counted for most in Indonesia, the US and Australia, were reluctant to interfere in the domestic politics of a country that had clearly taken the right stance on both communism and radical Islam. Suharto himself actively promoted his international profile, making state visits to Washington and Tokyo in 1982, and receiving heads of state from India, Pakistan, and even communist Rumania, in Jakarta. The Japanese prime minister, Yasuhiro Nakasone, visited in 1983, promising an increase in aid and oil purchases. In October 1985 Suharto, at a meeting of the UN Food and Agriculture Organization (FAO) in Rome, was the spokesman for the South in a North–South dialogue, while François Mitterand spoke for the North. A year later, in 1986, US President Reagan visited Bali to meet Suharto and other ASEAN leaders, turning a blind eye to months of unrest and government abuse of civil rights.

Suharto's international policy was to maintain his profile as leader of the non-aligned world, while doing nothing to antagonize the West. At the end of 1978, however, Vietnam's invasion of Cambodia led him to take a position different from that of the other ASEAN states. In spite of Vietnam being a communist state Suharto – like Sukarno before him – had always supported it, if only because, like Indonesia, it had successfully fought for independence against a colonial power. At the same time Indonesia, by supporting Vietnam's presence in Cambodia in the UN General Assembly, gained Vietnam's support for its occupation of East Timor.

In 1988, after the defeat of the Khmer Rouge in Cambodia, Indonesia used its friendship with Vietnam to help settle the country's future. In 1989 it shared the chair with France at an international conference in Paris, which, in October 1991, led to a comprehensive agreement about the future of Cambodia. Indonesian troops then became part of the UN transitional authority. The whole chain of events greatly enhanced Indonesia's international standing – so much so that in 1991 it won the presidency of the non-aligned movement, in spite of its record in East Timor.

At home Suharto did not have everything his own way. Retired officers, including Nasution, protested at the widespread corruption but to little effect. The NU attracted attention by walking out of parliament in March 1980, but Suharto, reacting, was able to sidetrack it out of party politics, at the same time banning a leading Islamic newspaper. Then, in 1981, Islamic extremists hi-jacked an aeroplane from Garuda, the national airline. There were separatist movements active in West Irian, East Timor and Aceh, but these were suppressed, with extreme brutality, by special ABRI forces commanded by Major-General Prabowo Subianto, a son-in-law of Suharto. In the aftermath of these uprisings some 5,000 people were executed without trial.

Throughout the 1980s Suharto's secular government never quite succeeded in coming to terms with Islam. From the local branches of the State Institute for Islamic Studies (IAIN) came a steadily increasing number of committed educated Muslims, whose popular support led both ABRI and *Golkar* to be concerned about the stability of the country. Ten thousand new mosques opened during the 1980s, and by 1990, with some 87.2 per cent of the population professing Islam, Indonesia had become the world's largest Islamic state, even though there were also some 17.2 million Christians – living mainly in the large cities.

Although in 1984 the NU ceased to be a recognized political party, it still survived as a religious organization acknowledging Sukarno's principle of *pancasila*, and under the leadership of a moderate mystical figure, Abdurrahman Wahid, dealt successfully with rival Islamic factions.

More orthodox Muslims, particularly among the poor, became steadily more disgusted by the extravagance and corruption of the *cukong* and others close to Suharto. Finally, on 12 September 1984, after ABRI had fired on a crowd demonstrating against the government in Jakarta's Tanjung Priok port district – killing at least 28 people – discontent among Muslims led to a wave of violence. Before the end of the year mobs burnt down the Bank of Central Asia – the property of the richest of all Suharto's *cukong* cronies. In January 1985, Borobudur, the well-known Buddhist monument dating from the ninth century, was bombed, and in July a shopping mall in Jakarta's Chinatown was fired, with some sixty buildings in the city's business district sharing the same fate in September.

These incidents were followed by show trials of prominent Islamic figures out of the favour with Suharto, while critical Islamic publications were suppressed. The suppression of dissent also focused on former members of the communist PKI, leading to the execution of nine men who had spent years in prison. Some 2,000 oil workers were sacked for having been involved with the PKI twenty years before.

In 1986 the deposition of Ferdinand Marcos in the Philippines was a bad moment for Suharto and his friends. The two had too much in common. The result, in Indonesia, was increased ABRI vigilance, but the growing middle classes judged it prudent not to challenge *Golkar* and ABRI, seeing them as lesser evils to possible alternative bodies representing the millions of poor Indonesians. At this stage under Suharto there was in fact something for almost everyone – electricity, schools, clinics, more rice, better times ahead in both town and country, with new opportunities for the poor, particularly in such traditional sectors of the black economy as construction. There had been a steady increase in non-oil and manufacturing exports, agriculture accounted for less than half the work-force, and the economies of Sumatra and the eastern islands were catching up with Java. 1988, as generally expected, saw Suharto elected to a fifth 5-year term as president. Non-aligned Indonesia was appreciated by the West not only for the business opportunities it offered, but also for its record of controlling militant Islam.

In 1989 the tide turned for Indonesia. With the collapse of the Soviet Union and its European satellites the Western world became less interested in Indonesia's anti-communist stance. There was also concern for Indonesia's stability in the face of internal unrest. The middle classes were becoming less tolerant of flagrant corruption in high places, and after years of prosperity, economic crisis was threatening Southeast Asia. In June 1989, international condemnation of the brutal repression by the Chinese army of the student uprising in Beijing's Tiananmen Square could have been read as a warning to Suharto, but it is one he chose to ignore.

Local attacks on the regime were not long in coming. Also, in 1989, in Aceh in north Sumatra – for centuries a trouble spot for outsiders – the Independent

Aceh Movement (GAM), only formed in 1989, attacked a number of ABRI posts and captured weapons. As recorded in Chapter 12, there was even greater trouble for the regime in East Timor. To some degree Suharto, noticing the direction of events in his own back-yard, reacted with accommodation, as well as repression. In December 1990 he recognized the All-Indonesian Union of Muslim Intellectuals (ICMI), but this new organization, significantly, was led by a long-term protégé, Yusuf Habibie, who in the 1980s had emerged as a devout Muslim. Although the government conceived ICMI as the acceptable face of modernist Islam, its emergence represented, nonetheless, a profound political change.

Habibie, after a long and successful career in business and technology in Germany, was called back in 1974 to set up the Indonesian aircraft industry (IPTN). Once back home Habibie invested (and lost) government funds in hi-tech state enterprises in aviation, arms, electronics and shipbuilding. In spite of resentment on the part of ABRI, whose members had little liking for powerful civilians – particularly if they were Muslims – Habibie's ICMI, with its own newspaper (*Republika*) and think-tank (CIDES), flourished as a bridge between the state and moderate Islam. Wahid, still leading the NU, refused to join, however, condemning ICMI as an elitist and sectarian threat to a pluralist Indonesia. Suharto, in turn, made concessions to orthodox Islam, imposing further restrictions on women and giving more power to religious courts. A pilgrimage to Mecca in 1991 allowed him to add Haji to his name. Promotion in ABRI was also used to win Islamic friends. Suharto's motives, however, were almost entirely cynical: at the head of what had become world's most corrupt nation, with all six of his children multi-millionaires, and 70 per cent of all private business belonging to his *cukong* supporters, Suharto could also do with friends among the general population. Even so justice and the police dared not touch his rich and corrupt cronies.

In the 1990s Suharto's luck ran out. Although, in 1991, he once again presided over the non-aligned conference, foreign criticism was increasing, with reporters from the *International Herald Tribune* and the *New York Times* banned from Indonesia. Suharto's regime once more confronted the international media on 12 November 1991, when ABRI soldiers, facing a crowd in Dili, the capital of East Timor, demonstrating after a funeral procession, opened fire and – on ABRI's own admission – killed at least 19 people. A charismatic leader, Xanana Guzmão, captured by ABRI, was sentenced to life imprisonment (later commuted to 20 years). Aid from Canada, Denmark and the Netherlands was suspended, and that from the United States (under pressure from Catholic congressmen) was cut back. In 1992, when the Netherlands, holding the chair of the Inter-Governmental Group on Indonesia (IGGI), demanded that Indonesia improve its human rights record if aid was to continue, Suharto simply withdrew from the organization. Even so aid continued, indeed increased. In June 1992, in a new election *Golkar* still won 68.1 per cent of the votes, allowing Suharto to enter into his sixth five-year term of office in 1993. Significantly the Indonesian Democratic Party (PDI), a coalition of minor non-Islamic parties created in 1973 and tolerated by Suharto largely because it had so little popular appeal, achieved, under a new leader, Soerjadi, a record 14.9 per cent of the votes cast.

As ABRI's reaction to unrest in the early 1990s was increased repression, Suharto followed a more conciliatory course, allowing the NU under Wahid to set up new local enterprises, including a number of banks. Although ABRI, following the 1992 election, succeeded in getting its own man in as vice-president, it had to accept a new cabinet dominated by Habibie, together with the promotion of senior officers favourable to Suharto and the appointment of his brother-in-law, Arismunanda Wismoyo, as chief-of-staff.

In 1993 Suharto saw to it that Harmoko, a trusted supporter, became chairman of *Golkar*, while a daughter, Tutut, became vice-chair and a son, Bambang, treasurer. Faced with PDI's success in the 1992 election he blocked first, Soerjadi's re-election as chairman, and then that of Megawati Sukarnoputri, a new figure in Indonesian politics distinguished by the fact that she was Sukarno's daughter. When, in December 1993, PDI delegates voted once more to be led by her, Suharto found it prudent to accept this.

Although the economy had improved in 1993, Indonesia had to contend with a new American President, Bill Clinton, who required an assessment of its human rights record, before any new arms sales. By this time the level of foreign debt was so high that some 32.1 per cent of export earnings was needed to paid the interest due. This was the result of both Habibie's appalling mismanagement of state enterprises and the increased wealth of those close to Suharto, including his six children, as a result of breathtaking corruption.[17]

With all religions, not only Islam, gaining ground, new conservative leaders of ABRI, in an attempt to neutralize Wahib's orthodox supporters in the NU, courted Islam by portraying democracy as a Western threat. Organs of the press seen as hostile, and often satirical, were shut down in a move later ruled by the courts as illegal. Almost inevitably ICMI, led by Habibie, became the most powerful group within the bureaucracy, side-tracking Wahid, a champion of honesty, justice, ethnic and religious pluralism.

These were times of both labour unrest and religious conflict. In Kalimantan, head-hunting Dayaks – many deprived of their land by illegal logging carried out by Suharto's *cukong* friends – combined with local Malays to murder recent settlers from Madura, an over-populated island just off the northeast coast of Java. In east Java the people rioted against Christianity, and in East Timor against Islam. By 1996 even government supporters could no longer accept Suharto's favouritism and nepotism. His son Tommy orchestrated a notorious scam involving the importation of cars from South Korea, free of import duty – on the pretext that they were actually made in Indonesia. Challenged on this point, Tommy said he would arrange for Indonesians to work in the factory in Korea. Absurdly the name chosen for the car was 'Timor'. This brazen violation of the rules of international trade led both Japan and the US to protest to the World Trade Organization.

ABRI, concerned by Suharto's close ties to Habibie and the ICMI, found that he should step down. The leaders of four separate factions also declared their opposition to the government. One of these was Megawati Sukarnoputri, whose PDI was steadily gaining support from pro-democratic forces and the urban poor. The failure of a government supported plan to remove her from the chair of the party was followed, on 27 July 1996, by a mob attack on its headquarters in Jakarta. This led to two days of rioting. On the first day ABRI made around two hundred arrests, and many of their prisoners simply 'disappeared'. Given that soldiers out of uniform proved to be part of the mob, there is little doubt that the whole event was orchestrated by ABRI, although the government pinned the blame on a small left-wing student group – a move calculated to please orthodox Islamic organizations.

Whatever its moral justification, the ABRI strategy seriously weakened the PDI: Abdurrahman Wahid withdrew the NU's informal support for the party, so that in the 1997 election it lost some 80 per cent of its votes. The result was an unprecedented victory for *Golkar*, with 74.5 per cent of the votes, the highest level it ever achieved. *Golkar* was helped by a World Bank assessment, earlier in the year, that the Indonesian economy was fundamentally sound – overlooking the unprecedentedly high level of social and political unrest, which defined the background to the election.

In spite of *Golkar*'s success in the election, 1997 did not end well for Suharto. The Indonesia rupiah, hit hard by currency crisis that struck the whole of East and Southeast Asia, lost about 85 per cent of its value. Savings were eliminated; unemployment and the number of small business bankruptcies increased drastically. Finally in December, Suharto, 76 years old, suffered a minor stroke.

THE FALL OF SUHARTO AND THE RESTORATION OF DEMOCRACY

With the new year, 1998, Suharto, under pressure from Clinton, the German Chancellor Kohl and Japanese Prime Minister Hashimoto to accept drastic new proposals from the IMF, announced reforms, which including closing some sixteen banks. Of these, two, both belonging to members of the family, were allowed to reopen. Suharto went on to announce his candidature for a seventh term of office as president, and parliament duly elected him in March 1998. In the new administration Habibie was vice-president, but for the rest the cabinet was recruited from the usual suspects – Suharto's family and circle of business friends.

For Suharto and his new government there was little question of business as usual. Student demonstrations started almost immediately, leading to massive riots in Jakarta, Medan and Surakarta. On 12 May four students from the Trisakti University in Jakarta were shot by ABRI marksmen. In the following three days a thousand people died as rioters targeted businesses owned by Suharto's family and *cukong* cronies. The personnel of foreign embassies and businesses, together with many wealthy Chinese, fled Jakarta.

All this happened while Suharto was in Cairo, attending a meeting of top Islamic leaders. Returning to Jakarta he found that no cabinet would serve him, and on 21 May 1998, in front of the television cameras, he resigned. Habibie was immediately sworn in as the new president. The leaders of ABRI announced their support and promised protection for both the Suharto family and its accumulated wealth. Students who had occupied the parliament buildings left as national heroes.

Even before he took up office Habibie knew that he was heir to a regime crying out for radical reform. Almost everyone he had to work with had lived for years in a climate of corruption, an inevitable result of the way that Suharto had used his power to enrich both his own family and his closest supporters. The latter divided into two categories: political, with ABRI at the centre, and economic, with the *cukong* dominant.

Habibie's problems were compounded by economic disaster. In mid-1998 inflation was at 80 per cent, rice production had declined drastically as a result of storms caused by El Niño, the companies manufacturing cars and civil aircraft were bankrupt, the exchange rate for the Indonesian rupiah was at all-time low, 56 per cent of the population lived below the poverty line, with 40 per cent, unable even to afford basic foodstuffs, facing starvation.

It did not make things easier for Habibie that he owed his job to Suharto, the man mainly responsible for all the country's sorrows. In economic matters Habibie's own record was unimpressive: after all it was he who, in the 1970s, had set up Indonesia's hopelessly mismanaged aircraft industry – although the initiative had come from Suharto. One obvious solution to the economic problems was beyond Habibie's powers. When Suharto left office the wealth accumulated by his family was, by one estimate,[18] as high as £18.8 billion, and that of the two wealthiest *cukong* families was also counted in billions. Habibie's attempts to recover this vast wealth for the benefit of the economy got nowhere.

During Habibie's short term of office one major international problem was solved, although not in a way that brought much satisfaction to the people of Indonesia, or credit to their president. East Timor was on the agenda in Habibie's first month in office, and within a year Indonesia was involved in a civil war, which – as related in Chapter 12 – led to the loss of its 27th province.

While the problem of East Timor was resolved, there was ethnic and religious strife in many other parts of the country. In east and west Java hundreds died in a wave of mass hysteria directed against practitioners of black magic, while the NU urged its followers to protect themselves by frequently reading the Koran. In Ambon Muslims and Christians were at each other's throats, with the police often more inclined to participate in the violence rather than restrain it. Once again new settlers from Madura were being murdered in Kalimantan. The worst violence, however, was the result of active independence movements in the two extremes of the archipelago, Aceh and Irian Jaya, but neither case was open to a solution comparable to that in East Timor.

After being ruled by Suharto for more than thirty years Indonesia, on 7 June 1999, had its first free elections since 1955. Campaigning began three weeks earlier, with five new major parties competing for votes. (Even *Golkar* had recreated itself as '*New Golkar*'.) The run-up to the election was not peaceful. Demonstrations, often violent, were a daily event, and there religious riots in both the eastern islands and Java. Ambon came close to witnessing a *jihad* directed against Christians, and in Jakarta, after a mosque had been destroyed, mobs destroyed eleven churches and two Christian schools, while up to twenty Christians, mainly Ambonese, were burnt or lynched.

At the actual election only six parties crossed the critical 2 per cent threshold of votes cast that would allow them to participate in the election due in 2004. Although *New Golkar* won 66 per cent of the votes outside Java, Megawati Sukarnoputri's party (PDI-P) did best overall with 33.1 per cent of all votes cast. She was not, however, acceptable to parliament (with 200 out of 700 seats reserved for non-elected members) as president, so Abdurrahman Wahid, whose PKB party (successor to NU) had obtained only 11 per cent of the votes, took over, with Sukarnoputri as his vice-president.

President as a result of free elections, Wahid worked hard to undo the harm done by Suharto, but his poor health prevented him from being effective, and liberal schemes, such as allowing a referendum on the future of Aceh or giving new freedom to communist sympathisers, led to widespread demands for an end to his administration. Anti-Christian violence was worse than ever, and many parts of the country had to accept internal refugees. Wahid, like his predecessor, Habibie, was powerless to curb corruption, mob violence and inter-ethnic conflict: corruption in the police and judiciary made restoring the rule of law next to impossible. The result was chaos, and in July 2001 parliament, meeting in a special session, removed Wahid from the presidency. His successor was Megawati, who – with a much wider political base – became Indonesia's fifth president.

In a period of less than three years the country had had four presidents. The challenge to the last three was to repair the immeasurable damage done to the country by the first of them, Suharto. ABRI, much less powerful without Suharto, could not hinder progress towards democracy, although it still had a role in dealing with unrest in provinces such as Aceh and Irian Jaya. Habibie, although he assumed office as a protégé of Suharto, introduced significant reforms, but they had little success. Political prisoners were released, some after thirty years behind bars. Wahid, although becoming president after free elections, did no better.

Megawati, in her first three years of office, proved more effective than either Habibie or Wahid. A crucial test of her authority came with the terrorist bomb outrages, in 2002 and 2003, related in Chapter 15. This is a measure of just of one problem, religious extremism, that Megawati had to deal with. Then, in a series of elections in 2004, spread over six months, her regime had to justify itself to the voters, and was found wanting. Following the bomb attack on the Australian Embassy[19] only three weeks beforehand, Islamic extremism became a key factor in the final run-off, on 5 October, to the presidential election. This was won by a popular retired general: Susilo Bambang Yudhoyono – in short 'SBY' – became president, after a campaign in which he consistently promised to deal decisively with Indonesia's endemic corruption. His problem, after inauguration on 20 October, was that with his own Democrat Party holding only 57 out of 550 seats in parliament, he needed a coalition to govern effectively. Five parties, holding altogether 233 seats, then combined to form the *People's Coalition* to support him. Another five parties then formed the opposition *Nationhood Coalition*, which with 317 seats, had a parliamentary majority, including the two largest parties, *Golkar* and PDI-P; these were also those of the two defeated presidential candidates, Wiranto and Megawati. Then, on 19 December 2004, the *Golkar* party conference voted to remove its chairman, Akbar Tandjung, almost as a reprisal for his having allied the party with Megawati's PDI-P. The new chairman, Jusuf Kalla, was already vice-president of Indonesia as a result of the elections held earlier in the year. His success, inside the country's largest political party, makes him extremely powerful. What is more, his pledge to support SBY, means that the government coalition now has a parliamentary majority. The opportunity to put the country in order is too good to miss.

There is no doubt that politics in Indonesia have changed immeasurably – and mostly for the better – following the fall of Suharto, but the plethora of political parties represented in parliament casts doubt on the government's chances of governing effectively, for as Singapore's *Straits Times* commented, 'Indonesians cannot eat democracy'. Government is made even more difficult by the way power is divided between the president, parliament and the judiciary. The survey of Indonesia published by *The Economist* on 11 December 2004 is a long tale of woe. Compared to other countries in Southeast Asia it attracts little foreign direct investment, labour in unproductive and over-protected, the infrastructure is run down, and in spite of a new Corruption Eradication Commission, the police and justice system are still mired in corruption. In a country with enormous natural wealth almost half the population subsist at a level below the World Bank's poverty line. In 2002, only one province, East Kalimantan – rich in gas, oil and timber – had a GDP per person greater than $5,000, while in the three poorest provinces it was less than $1,000. On the other hand Indonesia is slowly recovering from the Asian economic crisis of 1998, and its vast economic potential – it is already the world's largest exporter of liquefied natural gas – offers hope for the future.

12

Timor Leste: a war of independence (1999)

THE INDONESIAN TAKEOVER

The twentieth century ended in the Pacific with the attention of the world focused on one its least-known islands, Timor.[1] The events of 1999 were, through several removes, a legacy of a colonial history going back to the end of the sixteenth century, when the dominant power in the East Indies was Portugal. The new republic of the Netherlands was, however, becoming a major challenge, and in the course of the seventeenth century the Dutch took over almost completely from the Portuguese in the Far East, leaving them little beyond the island of Macao, close to Hong Kong, off the south China coast. Portugal did, however, maintain a presence in the remote island of Timor, which, in the eighteenth century, was contested with the Dutch. (Both sides were interested in exploiting the natural stands of sandalwood, but by the end of the century, these were nearly exhausted.) Portuguese Timor, counting for next to nothing economically, was administered from Goa thousands of miles away, on the west coast of India. Finally, in 1859, after the Dutch, following the Napoleonic wars and the Treaty of Malacca of 1824, had reconstructed their empire in the East Indies, Portugal and the Netherlands agreed to divide Timor, roughly in two along a north–south line – with the east going to Portugal and the west to the Netherlands, as shown on Map 4 on p. ix. No great concessions were made by either side: the island had simply too little to offer, although on both sides cattle estates and plantations developed in the late nineteenth century.

Significantly the spread of Islam hardly reached the remote island of Timor: Dutch Protestantism was strong in the west, in part because converted Christians from the neighbouring islands of Savu and Rote had been encouraged to settle there. In East Timor, although Portuguese missions were active for nearly four hundred years, the indigenous population remained largely animist; even so, among converts to the world religions, there were many more Catholics than Muslims. Culturally, politically and economically, the whole island, as it entered the twentieth century, was completely marginal.

In the first months of the Pacific War, when the Japanese overran almost the whole of the East Indies they made no distinction between East and West Timor, disregarding the fact that they were not at war with Portugal. Japan simply occupied the whole island, but at considerable cost. Its rugged terrain was well-suited to guerrilla warfare, and the Timorese could be supplied with arms, and helped by military advisers, from Australia, some 500 kilometres away across the Timor Sea – a relatively small distance in that part of the world. The indigenous population made clear its capacity to fight for its own rights: at the end of the century Indonesia would have done well to have heeded the lesson taught to the Japanese.

Indonesia's leaders, in the successful struggle for independence (1945–49) following the end of the Pacific War, had their sights set on establishing a single state comprising the entire Dutch Empire in the East Indies. It made no difference that this empire had been acquired piece-meal over the course of hundreds of years, nor that such unity as it had was entirely the result of Dutch colonization. There was no ancient Indonesian Empire to be restored. East Timor, which had never been Dutch, was not part of the equation, so the new Indonesian republic was content for it to remain a Portuguese colony.

In 1974 events on the other side of the world in Europe directly involved the future of Indonesia. A successful and largely peaceful revolution in Portugal brought to an end a long-standing right-wing dictatorship dedicated to defending, maintaining and developing a colonial empire that had lasted nearly 500 years. The old men who ruled in Lisbon had outlived their time, and the cost of their colonial policy, in both men and money, was an intolerable burden for the younger generation. With the collapse of their oppressive and unpopular regime, the way was open to the Portuguese colonies to claim independence.

The result, in East Timor, was for three political parties to emerge, known by their acronyms, *Fretilin*, UDT and *Apodeti*.[2] Of these, the first, *Fretilin*, a radical left-wing party, claimed immediate independence from Portugal. The second, UDT – the party of the country's modest establishment, defined by those who had done well under the Portuguese – sought gradual independence. The third, and much the smallest, Apodeti, sought incorporation into Indonesia. To begin with *Fretilin* and the UDT, although representing quite different sections of the population, formed a coalition, but they were soon at loggerheads when *Fretilin* began to draw ahead in the countryside. Under some pressure from a clandestine intelligence operation[3] orchestrated by the Indonesian military, UDT staged a coup that *Fretilin*, helped by Portuguese troops still on the island, successfully resisted. After weeks of bitter fighting, leading to some 1,500 people dying on both sides,[4] *Fretilin* had driven many of its opponents over the border into West Timor. On 28 November 1975 *Fretilin*'s leaders proclaimed the independent state of East Timor, but the world was not listening.

Suharto, the Indonesian dictator, had no wish to tolerate an independent radical state of East Timor. On 30 November, his foreign secretary, Adam Malik, produced the Balibo declaration, in which UDT and other opposition leaders who had escaped from East Timor accepted that it was part of Indonesia: with this, according to Malik, 'diplomacy is finished. The solution for the East Timorese problem is now the front line of the battle'.[5] His words were prophetic, if not in the way he intended.

On 7 December 1975 Indonesian forces invaded East Timor, and in the face of fierce local resistance took it over, leaving a record of torture, rape and looting that horrified the world, particularly after five Australian journalists had died in the process of reporting it. Roger East, the last to leave, was, together with hundreds of local Timorese, executed by Indonesian soldiers on the jetty at Dili, the capital city, while waiting for a boat to take him off the island.[6]

The Indonesian occupation completely disregarded the fact that Portugal was still recognized by the UN as the administering power in East Timor. Suharto simply went ahead and in July 1976 East Timor was incorporated as Indonesia's 27th province, with some 30,000 troops to keep order.[7] While the rest of the world had little choice but to grant *de facto* recognition, only Australia granted it *de jure*. This was because Indonesia, but not Portugal, had shown itself ready to sign an agreement, favourable to Australia, regarding the exploitation of the sea-bed of the Timor Sea separating the two countries.[8] Given not only the circumstances of Roger East's death, but also the fact that as many as 80,000 Timorese – out of a population of less than a million – had lost their lives as a result of the invasion, the Australian stance was widely condemned. Nonetheless, Gough Whitlam's Labour government in Canberra held its ground, as did also, for some time, its successors in Malcolm Fraser's Liberal government.[9] Canberra was never ashamed of *realpolitik*.

In East Timor the Indonesian military administration never had an easy time. A hard core of *Fretilin* supporters, led by Xanana Guzmão,[10] organized a guerrilla force, *Falintil*,[11] in the inaccessible mountainous interior of the island. In the seven years following the incorporation of East Timor into Indonesia *Falintil* succeeded in killing up to 27,000 Indonesian soldiers.[12] Then in March, 1983, it accepted a ceasefire, which was broken by the Indonesian Army's Kraras massacre in August. Although this greatly reduced *Falintil*'s numerical strength, Guzmão escaped with sufficient forces to continue fighting. Then, in 1985, seeing the way the wind was blowing with international communism, he gave up his support for *Fretilin*'s Marxist programme, left the party, and proclaimed *Falintil* as an umbrella movement for all those committed to resisting the Indonesian government in East Timor.

THE FIGHT FOR INDEPENDENCE

As *Falintil* continued the armed struggle for independence the local Roman Catholic Church, guided by its charismatic leader, Bishop Carlos Belo, played a significant political role. During the Portuguese colonial period less than 30 per cent of the population was Catholic: in the years following the Indonesian invasion the figure rose to nearly 90 per cent[13] – demonstrating the people's rejection of Islam, the religion of the occupying forces. Then, in October 1989, Pope John Paul II visited East Timor, a move that once again showed that it counted on the world scene. Even though the visit provided the occasion for a mass-demonstration in Dili in favour of independence – whose brutal suppression was reported by the international media – Indonesia could still count on support from the international community. Two months later, in December, the treaty regulating the exploitation of the Timor Sea was finally signed by Australia.

Outside Indonesia, East-Timor activists, led by José Ramos-Horta, and supported by human rights organizations, did their best to influence the international community. In 1991 another pro-independence demonstration in Dili, born out of a funeral procession at the Santa Cruz cemetery, led Indonesia forces to open fire, killing at least fifty of the participants. The intensive media coverage finally gave Ramos-Horta the forum his cause needed. The world listened: Canada, Denmark, and the Netherlands suspended aid programmes in Indonesia, and in Washington a number of Catholic congressmen lobbied, successfully, for a reduction in US aid.

In November 1992 Indonesian forces claimed their greatest success by capturing Guzmão, who was tried and sentenced to life imprisonment, later commuted to twenty years. International recognition as a charismatic leader in the fight for independence may well have saved his life. When it came to his own future, Suharto could already read the writing on the wall. In September 1993 the US Senate required his government's human rights record to be assessed as a condition for further arms sales. The message became even clearer when in 1996 Belo and Ramos-Horta were awarded the Nobel Peace Prize, and when in July 1997, Nelson Mandela visited Guzmão in prison in Jakarta on a state visit to Indonesia.

By this time Suharto, who in June 1992 had been elected to his fifth term as president, could see that his long-standing regime was disintegrating, and on 20 May 1998 he resigned, to be succeeded by Dr B. J. Habibie, who had long been his protégé.

The future of dissident territories, bent on secession, was not the least of the new president's problems. In the case of East Timor, he promised, after a meeting with Bishop Belo in June 1998, an undefined special status, but many Timorese, led by Ramos-Horta, rejected this offer on the grounds that accepting it would be a recognition of the legality of the Indonesian regime. His local support proved overwhelming when EU ambassadors visited East Timor in June 1998, to witness ten of thousands demonstrating outside their hotel for a referendum offering the choice of independence. A similar demonstration by activists carrying *Fretilin* flags greeted the UN Special Envoy when he visit Dili in December.

In January 1999 Habibie's foreign secretary announced that if the Indonesian proposals should prove unacceptable, East Timor should be granted independence. Guzmão left prison for a secure house in Jakarta. By this time, however, Habibie's days were numbered; a date had already been set for a new general election, in which his major opponents made clear that they would not countenance an independent East Timor.

Notwithstanding Habibie's uncertain hold on Indonesia, on 5 May 1999 an agreement to hold a referendum was made in New York with UN Secretary-General Kofi Annan and the Portuguese foreign minister. The date set was 30 August. In the run-up, which included voter-registration in July, local Indonesian militias, mainly recruited from settlers from outside who had come in response to the national policy of *transmigration*, harassed pro-independence activists, in a way which Guzmão foresaw would lead to civil war. The actual referendum was peaceful, but when, contrary to official expectations, out of 446,953 votes cast (representing a turn-out of 98.6 per cent) 438,968 (78.5 per cent) were in favour of independence, all hell was let loose.

In the ensuing reign of terror the militias, supported by soldiers out of uniform, murdered pro-independence Timorese, targeting particularly priests and nuns. Buildings of every kind were destroyed, and not only in Dili. Guzmão, released on amnesty from prison in Jakarta, took refuge in the British Embassy rather than return to East Timor. Bishop Belo, whose home, full of refugees, was being attacked by the militias, fled to Australia, followed by the local UN staff. After Habibie, quite ineffectually, had declared martial law, he gave in to international pressure on 12 September, and agreed to accept an international peacekeeping force. On 15 September the UN Security Council mandated the International Force for East Timor (*Interfet*) and on 20 September the first of some 2,500 troops from Australia, New Zealand and Great Britain were on the scene, to restore law and order. The participation of Australia was particularly ironical, given that it had been the only country to recognize, *de jure*, the incorporation of East Timor into Indonesia. Once again this was pure *realpolitik*: the way the wind was going, the treaty regarding the oil and gas resources of the Timor Sea would in any case have to be renegotiated with an independent East Timor – as actually happened in 2001.

On 25 October 1999 Indonesia formally handed over its authority to Sergio Vieira de Mello,[14] who had been appointed special representative of the UN and head of the new Transitional Administration in East Timor (UNTAET). Two days later Guzmão returned and on 30 October the last Indonesian forces departed. To begin with Guzmão felt marginalized as a result of the powers granted to Vieira de Mello, resenting at the same time the UN's failure to protect the people of East Timor. Nonetheless, Guzmão and Vieira de Mello travelled all over the country in UN helicopters to explain the new regime, to prepare the ground for the transfer of power to the new state of Timor Leste. (UNTAET was also to help negotiate the critical new Timor Sea treaty with Australia.) In December 1999 a National Consultative Council was established, and on 28 February 2000 UNTAET took over from Interfet responsibility for security. *Falintil*, which had never given up the fight against Indonesia, had been disbanded on 1 February, with 650 of its members being recruited into the new East Timor Defence Force. July saw the establishment of a cabinet-style transitional administration, responsible for organizing the election, to be held of 30 August, of the 88 members of the Constituent Assembly, who would write the new constitution. Although, when the election was held, *Fretilin* came top of the poll, the number of votes it won fell short of the two-thirds majority that would allow it to proceed on its own without forming a coalition. Even so, it was possible to form an all-Timorese cabinet in September. Presidential elections held on 14 April 2002 were predictably won by Guzmão, and Timor Leste finally attained independence on 20 May and was admitted to the UN on 27 September.

At the same time the UN set up a Commission for Reception, Truth and Reconciliation, which, after spending some three years hearing some 8,000 witnesses, found that in the 24 years of subjection to Indonesia between 84,000 and 183,000 East Timorese were murdered, disappeared or died of directly related illness caused by deliberate contamination of food and water supplies by Indonesian forces. Although the Commission's report was ready in October 2005, it was suppressed at the request of Guzmão – who was concerned for good relations with Indonesia. Nonetheless, under pressure from human rights organizations,[15] it was presented to the UN on 20 January 2006. Earlier in the month East Timor and Australia agreed to divide billions of dollars in expected revenues from oil and gas deposits in the Timor Sea, but failed to settle the disputed maritime boundary.

13

The Russian Far East: the GULAG legacy

RUSSIAN PACIFIC

The effect of Russia's Pacific coastline – far longer than that of any other country – on the country at large is extremely problematic. The hardcore of Russia in Europe is thousands of kilometres from the Pacific. The country has eleven time-zones, so that midday in St Petersburg is nearly midnight in remote Chukotka, the autonomous region facing Alaska on the other side of the Bering Strait. Travelling by train from Moscow to Vladivostok, the harbour city at the other end of the Trans-Siberian Railway, takes over a week, with only a few towns along the way to relieve the monotony of a featureless countryside – covered in snow for much of the year – with hardly any human population. By any normal criteria the Russian Pacific is next to uninhabitable, because the winters are too long and too cold. Vladivostok, both the largest town and the one with the least severe climate, has a mean January temperature of –14°C making it, among cities with a population of more than 500,000, the seventeenth coldest in the world. The coldest of all is Khabarovsk with a mean January temperature of –22°C; this town is only 700 kilometres – a small distance in the Russian Far East – to the north of Vladivostok, but being inland, and separated from the Japan Sea by a range of mountains, it does not benefit from the warm air coming off the ocean.

Although Russians first began to explore the Far East in the sixteenth century, it was not until 1727 that the Danish explorer Vitus Bering was commissioned by Tsar Peter the Great to explore the coastline north from the Kamchatka peninsula, leading five years later, in 1732, to the discovery of Alaska, which was formally annexed in 1784. Although the vast lands stretching beyond the Ural mountains to the Pacific coast were home to a number of tribal peoples (including Inuit in the far north) they were regarded by the tsars as *terra nullius*, that is, as belonging to no one. It then followed that the first Christian state to occupy them gained a title recognized by international law.[1] The tsars, however, not only claimed title, but found it important to settle the new lands: it is estimated that in the 250 years up to 1800 new territory was occupied – with hunters and trappers in the vanguard of new settlement – at the rate of 35,000 square kilometres per year.

In the years 1858–60 a further 644,000 kilometre^2, north of the Amur River, was ceded to Russia by China, making possible, at the end of the nineteenth century, the construction of the Trans-Siberian Railway. In 1867 Alaska was sold to the United States.

In 1900 Moscow's concern to strengthen its hand in the Far East – in competition with both the Western powers and Japan – became clear with its active participation in the suppression of the Boxer Rebellion, as related in Chapter 1. Then, in the immediate aftermath, its main conflict of interest was with Japan, which disputed Russian claims to commercial privileges in Korea and Manchuria. In 1904 this led to the war described in Chapter 1, but the peace treaty imposed by US President Theodore Roosevelt never satisfied the Japanese. At the end of the 1930s, following the outbreak of war with China, Japan challenged Soviet interests, leading to outright war at Changkufeng in 1938 and Nomonhan in 1939 in the frontier area between Manchuria and the Soviet Union. The rest of the world, inevitably pre-occupied with the advance of Nazi Germany in Europe, hardly noticed what was happening. It should have paid more attention. The heavy Japanese losses at Nomonhan – without any territory being won – discredited the army high command, leaving the way open to the Japanese admirals to impose a policy in which the navy would call the shots in any further Japanese aggression. The end of the road, on 7 December 1941, was the attack on Pearl Harbor by Japanese carrier-based aircraft. The Soviet Union was not part of the equation, and vis-à-vis Japan remained neutral until almost the end of the Pacific War. By this time it was committed by the Yalta agreement, of February 1945, to joining the war against Japan. Soviet forces invaded and occupied Manchuria in a matter of days. As agreed at Yalta the Soviet Union was rewarded with the southern half of the island of Sakhalin, together with the Kuril Islands, which until 1945 had been part of Japan. After this acquisition of territory there has been no change in Russia's Far Eastern frontiers.

THE GULAG ECONOMY

In the nineteenth century, settlement of the Russian Far East took a new turn when convicts and exiles were sent to Siberia, a practice which in the Soviet Union, under Stalin, led to the founding of the notorious GULAGs. Although the greatest concentration was in European Russia, in the Far East there were a number of GULAGs just north of the Amur River and along the Pacific coast, including two on Sakhalin: in all these largely uninhabited areas the GULAG prisoners were a very substantial part of the population. This was, however, just one part of a process of economic development, ruthlessly implemented by Stalin from the early 1930s, by which vast new industrial cities were set up in the frigid wastes of Siberia and the Far East at a cost, both human and material, that represented a vast over-commitment of the resources of the Soviet Union.[2] Instructions, given by the Soviet National Council (Sovnarkom) to the secret police (OGPU) on 11 July 1929, envisaged 'colonizing these regions and exploiting their natural resources with the use of prisoners' labour'.[3] The GULAGs not only played an important part in this process, but after the end of the Pacific War got a new lease of life as a result of Stalin's ruthless tyranny as he confronted the Western world in the atomic era. Some half a million Japanese, taken prisoner in Manchuria in August 1945, were also held for up to ten years. When Stalin died in 1953 the total GULAG population was estimated at two and a half million; then, at last, the system did begin to wind down, but there were still 600,000 prisoners when Khrushchev ended it definitively in 1960.

In economic terms the location of the GULAGs was mainly determined by the need for labour to exploit natural resources. The problem can be simply stated. The wealth of Russia in natural resources, as of many another state, is commensurate with its area: if Russia's share of the world's natural resources, awaiting exploitation, then related to the area of its territory, seen as a fraction of the world's land-mass, the country, in absolute terms, would be extremely wealthy. Given Russia's relatively low population density, any individual Russian's share in this wealth should be even higher. Life, particularly in Russia, was never that simple and this potential wealth has never come close to realization. For many primary resources, particularly minerals, there is nothing in nature to relate their distribution to the suitability of different localities for human habitation. This then means that the more natural resources, of any category, are exploited, the more any further exploitation is likely to take place in parts of the world so barren and inaccessible as to discourage any, but very small-scale, permanent human settlement. This factor applies with even greater force in a country such as Russia in which a quite disproportionate part of the whole territory, from the time when modern extractive industries first emerged, had these negative attributes. The lesson to be learnt from Alaska or the Canadian north is that in a free economy, with the same attributes, they can only be overcome by massive infrastructural investment and a willingness to accept labour costs at a level several times higher than are incurred in more temperate climates. The GULAG system brutally suppressed the latter, drastically reducing factor costs on this side, but it still required an infrastructure. This then was its main legacy, at least in the long term.

THE GULAG LEGACY

In the short term, at the time the GULAG system was wound up, the demographics of the Soviet Far East still reflected, if on a reduced scale, the disastrous industrial policies initiated by Stalin. The result was that some 15–18 per cent of all Soviet industrial output came from Siberia and the Far East. The contribution of the Pacific coast was, however, relatively small, simply because of its remoteness from any market, combined with the poor state of an infrastructure with next to nothing in the way of roads or long-distance power lines. Even the electrification of the Trans-Siberian Railway was only completed in 2002, but this only helped the southern Primorski region, with the harbour cities of Vladivostok and Nakhodka. Thousands of kilometres to the north, Magadan is almost completely deprived of links to the outside world, although, with a population of nearly 100,000, it is the administrative centre of a vast region: even so one of the largest complexes of GULAGs was located in its immediate hinterland. The Kamchatka peninsula, totally reliant on electricity from local oil-fired stations, has the most expensive power in Russia. Food costs, although exceptionally high in Magadan and Kamchatka, are low in relation to Anadyr, the administrative centre of Chukotka, where they are more than twice those in Moscow: it is just as well that Anadyr's population hardly reaches 10,000.

The gradual reversal of Stalin's economic planning, which began in the Khrushchev era, led almost inevitably to a steady decline in population – a particular cause for concern in Moscow when it related to the regions bordering China. This accelerated after the collapse of the Soviet Union in 1991, so that in the years since 1991 the Chukotka region has lost nearly two-thirds of its population, and Magadan more than half. To the south Kamchatka and the island of Sakhalin have done better, but this is largely the result of developing new natural resources. This gives some indication as to how Pacific Russia would have developed in response to conventional market forces, free from the exigencies of a 'planned economy'. Historically, however, the Soviet Union's over-commitment to Siberia and the Far East was a major factor in the breakdown of its economy at the end of the 1980s, leading to final collapse in 1991. The hard truth is that 'the Soviet State was … its military industrial complex. There was no political object in the system other than to feed this…'[4]

Given this background strategic factors inevitably determined the whole character of the Soviet Far East. By 1980 some 25–30 per cent of the Soviet armed forces were east of the Ural mountains, with 30 per cent of the navy stationed in Pacific bases. Petropavlovsk Kamchatkiy, on the east coast of the Kamchatka peninsula, was the most important, mainly because it was the Pacific base not only of the Soviet submarine fleet – which by 1968 had become the largest in the world[5] – but also, after their arrival in 1979, of the ships of the Minsk carrier-group. (It was also the site of the four military airfields, but these, together with the numerous rocket-launching sites along the whole Pacific coastline, constituted a quite separate branch of Soviet defence.) Vladivostok was more important as a base for surface vessels. Together with other Pacific harbours, such as Nakhodka, it was also home to many of the large modern vessels constituting the Soviet fishing fleet, which was the world's largest – as is still true of modern Russia.

In spite of having the world's longest coastline, the Soviet Union's naval strategy was always subordinate to the demands of land-based forces and weapons systems. In the west any Russian Navy's access to the world's main shipping lanes is inevitably problematic, since it involves either sailing out through the Baltic or the Black Sea or round Norway's North Cape from a base on the Arctic Sea. If, in the east, ships from Pacific bases have direct access to the ocean, great distances still separate them from major shipping lanes.

Soviet naval strategy in the Pacific had two objectives: the first was 'sea denial'[6] within the internationally recognized 200-mile limit from the shore – a principle also extended to air-space. Here the underlying mind-cast was reactive and defensive. This reflected the small volume of freight traffic from Vladivostok and Nakhodka, the only two commercial harbours in the Russian Far East. Significantly the merchant ships carrying supplies from the Soviet Union to North Vietnam in the years before 1975 sailed, without any naval escort, from European ports, passing either through the Suez Canal or round the Cape of Good Hope. (Washington wisely held back from attacking them en route, or in harbour when they reached their destination: on the other side the Soviet Pacific Fleet was never assigned a combat role in the Vietnam War – no doubt out of respect for the much superior strength of the US Seventh Fleet in the South China Sea.) Although the second objective, intelligence gathering, had a much wider compass – extending as far as Hawaii and New Zealand, its main focus was on American naval operations in the seas off the coasts of China and Korea: the close shadowing of US naval units even led to a collision, on 10 May 1967, between the *Besledniy*, a Soviet destroyer, and the USS *Walker* – an incident, with minimal damage to both sides, nicknamed 'Sea Chicken'.[7]

In 1979, when China and Vietnam were at war, the Soviet Union dispatched a large carrier-group to the Pacific: the Minsk-group entered through the Straits of Malacca on 18 June on course to Vladivostok, engaging in exercises in the East China sea *en route*. This was clearly a demonstration of support for Vietnam, but once again there was no question of combat. Japan, which had signed a peace treaty with China in 1978, recognized an increased military threat, but was unconcerned so long as the US did not reduce the strength of the Seventh Fleet.

The nuclear deterrent, which was critical to Soviet strategy, dominated the defensive systems of the Far East. Long-range ballistic missiles, ready for instant retaliation, were deployed at a large number of different launching sites inland from the Pacific coastline. Protecting these sites from US air reconnaissance was essential to Soviet security, as was shown when a ground-to-air missile brought down the Korean KAL 007 commercial flight from Anchorage to Seoul – off course over Kamchatka on 1 September 1983 – as related in Chapter 5. From 1987 the Soviet Navy also disposed of the Typhoon class of nuclear powered submarines – at 26,000 tons the largest ever made – to launch long-range nuclear missiles from underwater.[8] Although these were designed for operating from under the Arctic ice, they could also have been based at Petropavlovsk Kamchatkiy, together with other older, smaller and less powerful submarines with similar capabilities.[9]

Moscow, from the early 1960s, was also preoccupied by the need to defend Soviet territory against attack by China. The logistical problem was acute. Whereas the Chinese in Manchuria, south of the Amur River, enjoyed good communications with their own heartland, the Soviet forces, north of the river, had to rely on tenuous supply lines leading from the other end of Russia, which was also their main source of manpower. This was another aspect of the problems arising out of the vast distances separating the Pacific Far East from the rest of the Soviet Union.

Following the collapse of the Soviet Union in 1991, demographic and economic factors tipped the balance of power across the Amur River even more decisively in favour of China.[10] Nonetheless, today's Russia has political concerns, closer to its own heartland, much more serious than any possible problems with China.

DEMILITARIZATION AND DEVELOPMENT

In the Far East the focus is on demilitarization coupled with economic development. The natural resources waiting to be exploited are considerable. Moreover, the rapid economic growth of China offers a vast new market provided Russia develops the necessary infrastructure. The best immediate prospects are for oil, coal and natural gas. Significantly some 80 per cent of all foreign direct investment is in energy. Sakhalin Island is rich in oil and natural gas, with the possibility of transport by pipeline not only to the mainland – and on to China – but also to Japan, with fierce rivalry between the two. In 2004 both countries had to deal with the American oil giant, Exxon Mobil, the lead investor in the project, and the owner of 30 per cent, with Japanese companies owning an equal share. Exxon Mobil, in 2005, then agreed to sell 'the total volume' to the China Natural Gas Public Corporation, via a pipeline to the Russian mainland and then on to Manchuria.

The reasons for this preference were purely commercial. The pipeline through Russia and China is planned to be ready in 2008, whereas the Japanese dragged their feet rather than commit themselves to a 930-mile undersea pipeline linking Sakhalin to Japan. In part this was because the Tokyo Electric Power Company, already Japan's biggest buyer of LNG, was reluctant to buy piped gas on the scale demanded by Exxon Mobil. Politics lie behind the whole chain of events. Tokyo is much more sensitive to popular pressure than either Moscow or Beijing, and Japanese fishermen – a very powerful lobby – demanded advance compensation for potential losses following from laying the pipeline. This is far from the end of the story. Exxon Mobil is ready to pipe gas down to Progorodnoye, at the southern end of Sakhalin, where a local energy consortium is building a liquefaction plant for LNG. This would suit Japan, which has more than half the world's LNG terminals – and fishermen cannot complain about LNG tankers. In 2005 the total investment in these projects had already reached $22 billion, which gives some idea of the economic potential of this remote – and mainly peaceful – corner of Russia.[11]

In September 2006 the prospects of a parallel project, led by Royal Dutch Shell, became uncertain when Russian regulators withdrew an environmental permit for a $20 billion oil and natural gas development. This could well be no more than a pretext for renegotiating the terms of the project, with a view to including Gazprom, the Russian natural gas monopoly, in the consortium. Under existing terms, the Sakhalin projects of Shell and of Exxon Mobil are projected to provide $85 billion in taxes and royalties to Russia by 2050. Moscow may be right in thinking it can do better.

Essentially new Russian enterprise in the Far East has to come to terms with a past in which successive Soviet governments, until well into the 1980s, developed the whole area in a way that gave priority to strategic factors that make little sense in today's world. The economic and demographic consequences still cast a shadow over development, not least because many still retain the mind-cast of the Soviet era. The story of the exploitation of Sakhalin's oil and natural gas confirms, however, an enormous potential for creating new wealth. This is just the beginning. If the Russian Far East can learn from Alaska and the Far North of Canada how to exploit natural resources in an Arctic environment, with all that this involves for infrastructure and the right facilities for labour, then its economy will contribute substantially to the welfare of the rest of the country. First, however, the harm caused by Soviet economic planning must be undone, and second, the Soviet obsession with strategic factors must be abandoned. Watch this space.

14

Migration: gains and losses

BEFORE THE PACIFIC WAR: RESTRICTION AND ETHNICITY

Human migration is one of the oldest, most fundamental and certainly most complex themes in history. Its Pacific dimension, even in a history focused on the twentieth century, has ancient antecedents that must be taken into account. There are always two sides to migration. First, there is the actual process of human populations, of varying sizes, moving home, whether to establish new immigrant communities, or add to ones already existing. Second, there is the changing character of the new communities that arise as a result of this process. Throughout the Asia-Pacific region there is any number of established immigrant communities.

Although the Asia-Pacific world, as it was transformed in the course of the nineteenth century, defines the essential background to its immigrant communities, it is their development during the second half of the twentieth century that defines their standing in the countries where they are established. There are two perspectives, one relating to the old world, and the other to the new. The old world of the Pacific, already defined in Chapter 1, consisted essentially of China, Japan, Korea, Thailand, Vietnam and Cambodia, all ancient empires with an autochthonous, literate culture, together with a number of historically more recent sultanates belonging to what are now the modern states of Malaysia and Indonesia. Common to all these different states was a well-entrenched policy of exclusion; each one, in varying degrees, was a law unto itself. In practice the success of this policy was always qualified, if only because immigrant communities, mainly Chinese, were essential, for local economic reasons. Long before the twentieth century, Chinese communities – almost all originating from the coastal provinces of southern China, notably Kwangtung and Fukien – were established along the coasts of all the kingdoms and sultanates of Southeast Asia, a vast area known as 'Nanyang',[1] a name loaded with significance in Chinese.[2] The mainly urban Chinese in Nanyang, sometimes welcome and sometimes barely tolerated, were in any case indispensable for both their specialist skills and their commercial ties. This was also true of the Philippines, a Spanish colony since the sixteenth century with, as the mainstay of its economy, a long-established commerce with mainland China.

During the nineteenth century, the Chinese communities extended to the new world, as a result both of Chinese initiative and of the increasing demand for the essential human capital that they represented. At the beginning of the century, the Pacific coast of the Americas was the domain of Spain and Russia, and neither empire had done much to develop its territory or exploit its resources. Australia was firmly British, but it counted for little – not surprising, seeing that the British had only come at the end of the eighteenth century. Australia had already been chosen as a destination of both free immigrants and convicted criminals, so possible rival claims by other European powers were unlikely – the more so given the state of the game in Europe after the defeat of Napoleon.

The Asia-Pacific new world changed radically throughout the nineteenth century. The Louisiana Purchase of 1803, followed by the Lewis and Clark expedition in 1805–06, ensured that the United States would have a Pacific coastline. In 1818 the 49th parallel was agreed as the boundary between Canada and the continental United States west of the Great Lakes. Victory in war against Mexico led to the United States acquiring California under the terms of the Treaty of Guadalupe Hidalgo in 1848, which established a long Pacific coastline between Mexico and Canada: this is now shared between three states, California, Oregon and Washington. The treaty also left the United States with a considerable Hispanic population, now increased several times over by immigration from Latin America in the years since 1848. In 1867, the American presence on the Pacific was vastly extended by the purchase of Alaska, which left Russia without any territory in North America. Finally, in 1898 Hawaii and the Philippines became part of the US Pacific empire.

The westward expansion of the United States opened up a vast territory ripe for settlement, which, following the Mexican War, was not long in coming. The discovery of gold in California in 1848 attracted thousands of prospectors. The same happened in Australia, when gold was discovered in Victoria in 1851. In both cases this involved internal migration on a massive scale, with many of those seeking their fortune recent immigrants from Europe. At the same time the demand for low-paid unskilled labour was met by coolies brought from China – so that Melbourne's Chinatown is now the oldest in the new world.

In nineteenth-century China the opportunities for emigration were vastly increased as a result of the treaty ports established by the Western powers – where necessary by armed force – to open up China to trade. This process had also greatly weakened the authority of the emperor. At the same time, the change from sail to steam in international shipping, which went back to the beginning of the century, meant that unprecedented numbers of passengers could cross the ocean – particularly if they were packed together in the holds of the new steamships. In many parts of the Pacific, economic development, particularly of mines and plantations requiring large unskilled labour forces, depended on the transport, under harsh conditions, of Chinese immigrants. In many cases, such as on the Hawaiian sugar plantations, they were followed by Japanese, for Japan also had become open to the West following the arrival in 1853 of the American Commodore Perry, with his steam-powered iron-clad battleships. On the American west coast there was a new demand for Chinese labour, when, following the end of the Civil War in 1865, new railroads were built across the continent.

The position in Southeast Asia was somewhat different because by the end of the nineteenth century the recruitment of immigrant labour was subject to the local jurisdiction of the colonial powers – the Dutch, and marginally the British, in the East Indies, the British in Malaya, the French in Indochina, and, as a result of victory in the Spanish-American war (1898), the Americans in the Philippines. In every case but the last, the colonial power preferred to exploit its own imperial resources in labour, to meet the demands of a local economy. For the tin-mines of Malaya and the sugar-plantations of Fiji, therefore, the British recruited labour from India, as the Dutch also did when it suited them. Chinese, once again, were almost always available: their welcome, however, was qualified by the fear, often well-founded, that local Chinese communities were becoming too powerful. The Philippines were something of an exceptional case, because the Americans soon came to see the islands as a source of cheap unskilled labour that could take the place of the immigrants recruited from China and Japan in the nineteenth century. Within a generation the fact that English, with strong American support, had replaced Spanish as the official language of the Philippines made Filipinos particularly useful as immigrant labour. The result is that no country in the world has so many of its citizens working overseas, and remitting part of their earnings to their families left behind. (Hospital patients, not only in the US, now take it for granted that Filipino nurses will care for them; international maritime trade depends on ships crewed by Filipinos.) The figures speak for themselves: in 1990, $7 billion dollars was sent home by some 7 million Filipinos working abroad.[3] Their life is not always easy: many are recruited by unscrupulous agents to work for abusive employers, and have little redress for the maltreatment suffered.

Well before the end of the nineteenth century there was considerable local backlash, notably in Australia and on the American west coast, against the Chinese, and later Japanese immigrant communities whose origins went back to the time – in the middle of the century – when cheap labour was required for mining and railroad construction. When this labour was first recruited not much thought was given to an exit strategy once the mines were worked out or the railroads completed. Events soon showed that Chinese immigrants, except in very small numbers, would not then want to return home to an old empire collapsing amid war and local insurrection. The regions they had left were in any case poor and neglected – which is one reason why so many were ready to seek their fortune in the outside world.

Events also showed that Chinese immigrants, once they were no longer tied to mines or railroads – and later plantations – were only too intent on broadening their economic base, particularly by going into business on their own. The Chinese laundry is proverbial, but there were any number of other businesses in which the Chinese proved to be successful entrepreneurs, as the Japanese would also, at a somewhat later stage. What is more, even in the field of wage labour, immigrants proved to be unusually adaptable and hard-working, while, at the same time, they maintained a high level of mutual support. This was particularly true in many a typical immigrant community, the majority of whose members came from the same local region in China, and spoke the same Chinese dialect. Once again much the same pattern was to be found among Japanese immigrants.

The almost inevitable result was for government, responding to strong political pressure, to put the breaks on immigration. The Chinese Exclusion Act of 1884, barring the entry of Chinese labourers into the US for ten years, was only finally repealed – after several extensions – by the Chinese Act of 1943 (which also made possible the naturalization of Chinese residents). Following the acquisition of Hawaii in 1898, the Organic Act of 1900, by extending the application of US laws to the new overseas territory, effectively restricted the admission of both Chinese and Japanese, although women were still allowed in to become wives of those already there – an essential provision for the emergence of a viable immigrant community. Although the demand for immigrant labour was then met by Filipinos, they never came in sufficient numbers for their community to be as large as that of the Chinese and Japanese. Quite simply, changing economic factors meant that the demand for plantation labour was much less than it had been a generation earlier. Finally, the Johnson-Reed Immigration Act of 1924 effectively ended immigration to the US from the Far East, except from the Philippines.

However drastic the restrictions on immigration imposed by the US, those enacted by the Commonwealth of Australia immediately following its creation in 1901 were much more severe in their actual operation. For ten years the Australian Labour Party, founded in 1891, had been concerned by the threat to the labour market by potential immigrants belonging to 'inferior races'[4] – for which the Chinese were exemplary. Given the growing economic power of the Chinese immigrant communities already established, this concern, however prejudiced, was hardly surprising. Its result was the Immigration Restriction Act of 1901 which provided the legal foundation for the notorious White Australia policy, which so effectively restricted new immigration to those of European descent that by 1947 Australia's non-European population was no more than 0.25 per cent of the total.[5]

Australia was concerned not only to keep out non-European immigrants, but also to build up, as rapidly as possible, a substantial population of British descent. Although the original settlement of Australia owed much to the transportation of convicted criminals from the United Kingdom, there were always free immigrants, and in the course of time convicts also obtained their freedom, to remain as settlers. Even so, it was becoming clear at the beginning of the nineteenth century that the population must substantially increase if Australia's resources were to be fully exploited. Although the country was then wide open to immigrants from almost anywhere, the vast distance separating it from Europe meant that those seeking a new life in the new world were much more likely to prefer the US or Canada, or, if coming from southern Europe, Uruguay, Argentina and Chile.

The solution found to this problem, provision for assisted passages, was first adopted in 1831 and, remarkably, continued until 1982, more than 160 years later. Originally only British subjects qualified for assistance, but in 1947 assisted passages were extended to non-British subjects as a result of an international agreement, and in fact the largest number, 875,000, came during the 1960s, by which time British immigrants were no longer a majority. (They are now no more than 10 per cent of new settlers.)

AFTER THE PACIFIC WAR: A TIME OF LIBERALIZATION

World War II, and its aftermath, radically changed both the pattern of the immigration, and the character of immigrant communities, throughout the Pacific. In the US one result of the Japanese attack on Pearl Harbor on 7 December 1941 was an immediate backlash against Japanese-Americans. Given the restrictions on new immigration in the early twentieth century, most of these were 'nisei', or second-generation Japanese. The *nisei*, being born in the US, were American citizens, with the largest number in California. Even so, the largely self-contained Japanese communities had kept their own culture and language, and in the popular climate born out of the Japanese 'act of ignominy' – as President Roosevelt described the attack on Pearl Harbor – an executive order was signed at the beginning of 1942, relocating some 110,000 west-coast Japanese in remote internment camps. Neither the fact that some two-thirds of these were citizens, nor the fact that no credible intelligence implicated any of them in involvement in imperial Japan's advance preparations for Pearl Harbor, was sufficient to protect them; on the contrary, in 1944 the US Supreme Court ruled that military necessity justified the executive order.[6] The losses suffered as a result of internment were considerable, for many of those deported were agricultural small-holders or small businessmen, whose property was simply appropriated by those who had clamoured for their internment.

Somewhat paradoxically the Japanese in Hawaii, the actual location of Pearl Harbor, were not included in Roosevelt's executive order. The result of doing so would have been drastic: the Japanese, in 1941, constituted some 40 per cent of the Hawaiian population. At a time when the Hawaiian Islands together constituted the most important military base in the Pacific, the contribution of the Japanese in Hawaii to the US war effort was indispensable – as the US high command came to accept long before the end of the Pacific War. By this time also there was little doubt about the loyalty of Japanese Americans to their adopted country. Young men, both from the mainland internment camps and from Hawaii, were allowed to enlist in the US armed forces, and for one unit, the 442nd Combat Team, the number of casualties suffered and medals won was unprecedented in American history. The 25,000 who served during the Pacific War were welcomed home as heroes, and in 1988 the US government granted each of the 60,000 surviving internees $20,000 in restitution for the losses suffered during the war. By this time Japanese Americans, in common with other immigrant communities originating in East and Southeast Asia, were more prosperous and well-educated than average Americans, with little question of racial or ethnic discrimination. One result of Pearl Harbor, which imperial Japan had certainly not envisaged, was that Japanese Americans chose quite deliberately for assimilation, even in spite of internment. Ties with their home villages in Japan were broken. Families that had always spoken Japanese at home switched to English and abandoned traditional domestic ritual. Long before the end of the twentieth century only the very old still spoke Japanese as a matter of course, and when they did so, they used the antiquated language of Meiji Japan.

The rehabilitation of the Japanese Americans was only one part of the immigrant scene in the Pacific as it took shape after the end of the Pacific War. Other cataclysmic events in the aftermath of the war, notably the flood of refugees escaping from China after Mao Zedong's defeat of the Guomindang at the end of the 1940s and of displaced persons arising from the partition of Europe according to the Yalta agreement of 1945, left millions seeking a new home in the Western world.

As to the former, the Guomindang, with its leader, Jiang Jieshi, escaped to Taiwan in the face of Mao's revolutionary forces. Tens of thousands of Guomindang supporters, mainly soldiers, accompanied them, and until 1972 the legitimacy of the government in exile in Taiwan was still recognized internationally, which meant that it occupied China's place in the UN Security Council. This was entirely the result of US pressure, which, following Chinese involvement first in the Korean War, 1950–53, and then in Vietnam, was unlikely to let up. Mao, from the very beginning, always insisted that the Chinese in Taiwan were citizens of the People's Republic: in practice they had little choice but to support the Guomindang government, even though this left little room for native-born Taiwanese. With the forces brought from the mainland, and the command structure established by Jiang, the Taiwanese themselves had little say in choosing their own government – a position that would not begin to change until the 1980s. If the immigrant community constituted by refugees from the mainland is still not completely absorbed into the general Taiwanese population, it has certainly lost its dominant position in the island's politics.

As for the European refugees of the 1940s and 1950s, Canada, the US and Australia all came to the rescue; between 1954 and 1959 the US admitted 200,000 refugees from communist persecution, though only a minority came to the Pacific coast. At the same time a high proportion of Australian assisted passages went to displaced persons from Eastern Europe, who – together with Turkish and Spanish immigrants – were also a welcome addition to the manual labour force, at a time when British and north-European immigrants, even when assisted, looked for something better.

The fall of the European colonial empires in Southeast Asia in the aftermath of the Pacific War also had important consequences for immigration. The Dutch case was the simplest. The founding of the new republic of Indonesia in 1949 was fatal to the interests and security of the well-established Dutch expatriate community. Until 1941, some 100,000 Dutch citizens maintained a flourishing European enclave in the East Indies, with its own newspapers, learned professions, universities, and, above all, soldiers. Its well-being was entirely dependent on the services of tens of millions of subordinate local inhabitants, but this privileged position could not survive the wartime internment, by the Japanese, of almost the whole Dutch community – men, women and children.

With the coming of the new republic, Indonesians had little time for their old masters. Most of the Dutch, therefore, had to return to the Netherlands, whence many of them – heeding the government policy of encouraging emigration – went on to settle in the new world, including, notably, Australia and New Zealand. The departure of the Dutch, needless to say, radically changed the character of the life of their former colonial subjects, not all of whom were to find that the change was for the better. In particular, many inhabitants of the Molucca Islands had reason to fear persecution. In a country dominated by Islam many were Christians, and in the time of the Dutch had readily volunteered to serve them as soldiers. Some tens of thousands were therefore allowed to emigrate, as refugees, to the Netherlands, where their community still cherishes the vain hope of returning to an independent Moluccan republic in the East Indies. This is one of the more unlikely scenarios of the twenty-first century.

The case of the French in Indonchina was more involved, since they were better able to withstand the pressure to leave the country. Even so, in 1954, with defeat in the battle of Dien Bien Phu in the war against the communist Viet

Minh, the French had to abandon North Vietnam completely, at the same time entrusting the South to a Vietnamese government that could only survive with US support. The writing on the wall was clear: the French, with no future in Vietnam, nor for that matter in Laos or Cambodia, had no choice but to go home. In contrast, however, to the Dutch in Indonesia there was no single government in a position to succeed the French in Indochina. Their former colony was to be fought over for more than twenty years after the French departed. When peace finally came, in 1975, it left Vietnam entirely in the hands of the Viet Minh. But with the south of the country being involved for more than twenty years in a war against the north, there were hundreds of thousands left in the south who feared rightly for their fate. Inevitably there was a flood of refugees trying to escape, either across the frontier separating Thailand and Cambodia, or by sea, to any destination their boats could reach. The result was that hundreds of thousands[7] ended up in different parts of Southeast Asia. Many, because of old colonial ties, ended up in France, but once again the new world offered a haven, so that from 1975 new immigrant communities of Vietnamese were established, with the goodwill of the respective governments, in such countries as Canada, the US and later Australia. There was no question of repatriation, except in Hong Kong, a relatively accessible destination for boats escaping from Vietnamese waters. Given both the general overcrowding of Hong Kong, and its special relationship with China, the thousands of Vietnamese refugees were not welcome. The great majority were detained in special camps, while the Hong Kong government negotiated their return to Vietnam, a policy which became a bitterly contested human rights issue.[8]

After the end of the Pacific War the British colonies in Southeast Asia, all of which had been occupied by the Japanese, were set on the path to independence, which was finally granted in 1957. For the British the aftermath of the Pacific War was far less traumatic than it proved to be for the Dutch and the French. Nonetheless, over a long period, starting in 1947, the British had to deal with the so-called emergency arising out of the decision by the Malayan Communist Party (MCP) to fight 'a war of national liberation' against the government of Malaya. Although the British, by the mid-1950s, had succeeded to the point that the communist guerrillas were no longer a serious military threat,[9] the fact that the key MCP strategy was to take over the political leadership of the Chinese in Malaya inevitably affected the standing of the Chinese community as a whole. The MCP strategy failed, but if it had succeeded – as seemed quite possible at the end of the 1940s – then the next step would have been to extend the party's rule to the indigenous Malay population.

There had always been a conflict of interest between the Malays and the Chinese – although neither side was particularly homogeneous – and this was exacerbated by the way local populations reacted to the Japanese occupation of 1942–45. The Malays, who always saw themselves as constituting the true indigenous population, accommodated the Japanese, who in turn favoured them as against the substantial and economically more powerful Chinese immigrant population. The Chinese, on the other hand, never lost their loyalty to China, which for many years had been at war with Japan. They were not only harshly treated during the occupation, but also offered serious and often effective resistance to the Japanese – which is one reason why the MCP guerrillas were so long able to challenge the government. It also explains why the indigenous Malays were so ready to join the fight against them.

In 1957 Malaya became independent with a constitution designed to give a privileged status to the language, culture and religion of the indigenous Malays, even though they had hardly constituted a majority of the population. Singapore was also moving towards independence, and although its Chinese population was far greater than that of the Malays, its political leaders still favoured union with Malaya, largely because of the common British heritage. Leaders on both sides had been to the same schools and spoke the same language, English. In economic terms the proposed union also made sense.

Union would, however, jeopardize all the privileges provided for indigenous Malays by the 1957 constitution. Together Singapore and Malaya would contain more Chinese than Malays. The solution found to the problem was to establish a new Federation of Malaysia, incorporating not only Malaya and Singapore, but also Sarawak, Brunei and Sabah, which together occupied the north of Borneo, with the rest of this large island constituting the Indonesian province of Kalimantan. The large Malay and indigenous populations of north Borneo would then set off the Chinese majority in Singapore. Even so, Singapore had to agree to under-representation in the Federal Parliament.

The federation was finally constituted in 1963 but it lasted only two years. There are a number of reasons for its failure, but at the heart of things the demographics never added up. The end was hastened by the aggressive political leadership of the Chinese Lee Kuan Yew in Singapore. Lee was held by many to be responsible for race riots between Chinese and Malays that broke out there in 1964. The government in Kuala Lumpur faced the choice of arresting Lee or expelling Singapore from the federation. London made clear that the first option was not open, so in August 1965 Singapore became an independent nation. For the first time in history the overseas Chinese had their own state to govern, even though it was one containing several ethnic minorities, including numerous Malays[10]: in the forty-odd years since 1965, as described in Chapter 9, they have showed quite spectacularly what they could achieve.

In spite of losing Singapore, Malaysia also developed into a second-rank Asian tiger, with an economy increasingly dependent upon immigrant labour – so that in the course of the 1980s it became a net importer of labour. In the year 2000[11] there were 850,000 registered foreign workers, to say nothing of several hundred thousand who were undocumented. Nearly two-thirds were Indonesians, who had the advantage of being close to home, speaking the same language and sharing the same religion. In the island states of Sabah and Sarawak both the plantations and the informal economy would have been lost without immigrant labour, much of which came from the Philippines. The question of immigrant labour is highly politicized: agriculture and construction demanded more foreign workers, while the trade unions saw them as a threat to jobs and wages. The Chinese were concerned that labour from Indonesia would strengthen political Islam, while on all sides many feared for health and public order.

For the Chinese in Indonesia, just across the Malacca Straits from Singapore, 1965 was a disastrous year. In September, as related in Chapter 11, came the final reckoning with the chaotic administration of Ahmed Sukarno, the charismatic and mercurial demagogue who had ruled the country since the grant of independence in 1949 – significantly the same year as Mao Zedong's victory in China. Sukarno, in his attempts to establish himself as a world leader of the developing countries uncommitted to either side in the Cold War, had flirted with Beijing – little concerned about the loss of American goodwill. This was a policy calculated to attract the support both of the PKI (the Indonesian communist party) and of the local Chinese communities, whose members' loyalty was to China – whatever government was in power – rather than to communism. Beijing, following the old tradition of imperial China, regarded all Chinese as citizens, wherever they happened to be, and in 1959, free repatriation was offered to any who wanted to return home from overseas. In Indonesia some hundred thousand responded to this offer, and ships were sent to bring them back to China. The majority, which was counted in millions, chose to remain.

Sukarno, by relying too much on the support of the PKI and the local Chinese, failed to take into account the very considerable power of the Indonesian armed forces. The military leaders had their own political agenda – focused largely on enriching themselves – and in September 1965 the collapse of Sukarno's regime brought to power a new leader, General Achmad Suharto. Tens of thousands of Chinese were among the victims of his harsh regime. Their fate depended largely on where they lived. The worst case was in western Kalimantan, where Chinese villagers were suspected of supporting communist guerrillas supplied from Sarawak, which was part of Malaysia. The death of innocent villagers hardly concerned the Indonesian provincial governor, in whose judgement all Chinese were 'hand in glove with Mao Zedong and a part of his plan to take over Asia'. The military's reaction was to clear the jungle villages, so as to cut off the guerrillas' supply lines, leaving thousands of Chinese to be resettled in camps on the coast. Few, however, chose to return to China, which was then on the threshold of the cultural revolution. At all events, by May 1966 Indonesia no longer had any diplomatic relations with China, while, on the other side, relations were being restored with both the West and international agencies.

Suharto, in spite of turning a blind eye to the persecution of the Chinese in the months after September 1965, soon realized that the Chinese trading community could be induced to collaborate with his unashamed kleptocracy. The Chinese, in effect, were offered both protection from local hostility and a share in the spoils, in exchange for their overseas connections and general business expertise.

By this time the migration of Indonesians within their own country had become equally important. There were two sides, one common to developing countries world-wide and the other specific to Indonesia. The former was defined by urbanization. In 1949 the new republic took over an essentially rural economy; the Dutch, concerned not to lose the East Indies as a market for Dutch industry and commerce, did little to develop industry, and were content with an infrastructure mainly focused on the export of primary commodities – plantation crops, oil and minerals. Indonesia, on the other hand, was intent on developing a mixed economy, and during the Suharto years over-invested in industry, often as a cover for syphoning money into inherently unprofitable businesses owned by Suharto's family and cronies. One result was an enormous increase in the urban labour force, not only in the new plants but in the supporting services. In the twenty years from 1971 to 1990 the number of city dwellers increased from 17.3 to 30.9 per cent[12] of the population, while the number of those living in Jakarta, the capital and largest city, went up from 4.5 to 8.3 million.

If all this repeated a familiar pattern of internal migration, Indonesia's policy of transmigration was quite distinctive. The basic principle was to increase the relative populations of the outer islands at the expense of Java, a relatively small island[13] which even today is the home of some 60 per cent of all Indonesians. The policy, which went back to colonial times (when the Dutch with some success recruited Javanese labour for the Sumatra sugar plantations), was never very successful, and such success as it had was bought at a price. Transmigrant Javanese have been a major factor in religious conflict in southern Sulawesi, and, much more seriously, the rights granted by Jakarta set Javanese transmigrants at odds with the native populations of the two provinces, Irian Jaya and Timor Leste, acquired after independence. In both cases there was armed conflict with local peoples who, historically, had no connection with the rest of the Indies, and in that of Timor, UN intervention in 1999, as related in Chapter 12, led to this old Portuguese colony becoming an independent state – at the price of considerable bloodshed.

In the years since 1965 national immigration policy in the Pacific new world changed radically in favour of admitting non-Europeans. In the US this was the result of the Immigration and Nationality Act of 1965; in Australia of a change in policy adopted by Harold Holt's Liberal Government in 1966. The result in both cases was to encourage a stream of Asian immigrants to cross the Pacific in one direction or another – a process greatly helped by the development of air travel. Following the end of the war in Vietnam in 1975 some 60,000 came as political refugees. Although many more went to the US than Australia, the change in the composition of the Australian immigrant community was much more radical. At the same time there were countless legitimate migrants across the Pacific, most of them seeking a share in booming local economies on the other side of the ocean. As a result of the Alaska oil boom, the Samoan community in Anchorage numbers several hundred, and that in a city where 93 languages are spoken in the school system.[14]

ASYLUM SEEKERS AND THE ETHNIC BACKLASH

In Australia the result of diversification was quite considerable white backlash, which during the 1980s began to impact on politics. In the general election of 1983, the right-wing Liberal Party, having lost its leader, Malcolm Fraser, was defeated. The new Australian Labour Party (ALP) government, which then came to power was continuously confronted with immigration problems, very largely as the result of citizens from countries subject to civil disorder – notably Sri Lanka, Lebanon and, in the aftermath of Tiananmen in 1989, China – seeking admission on humanitarian grounds; for these, by the end of the 1980s, official quotas were laid down.

In 1990 asylum seekers, outside any official quota, were beginning to arrive by boat – many originating in Cambodia. In 1991, following an increase in numbers, mandatory detention was decreed for all members of this class, and the Port Hedland detention centre was opened. This, somewhat extreme reaction – given the relatively small number of such arrivals – was followed, in the course of the 1990s, by the opening of camps in new desert and Pacific island locations, such as Woomera (once the site of a nuclear testing range) and Nauru.

This was in part a political response to new proposals made by the Liberal Party, which, although still out of office – as it would be until 1996 – was being challenged by extremists who played the race card. Although not the first of these in point of time, the popular and charismatic Pauline Hanson was much the most successful. At the same time, John Howard, the present Liberal prime minister, had captured the centre of his party by adopting a conservative stance on immigration questions. On the other hand, after the Liberal Party victory in the 1996 general election, he showed his moderation by withdrawing his endorsement of Pauline Hanson even though she had won, as a Liberal candidate, a normally safe ALP seat in Queensland. This move was the result of Pauline Hanson's maiden speech in Parliament which stated what she claimed to be views 'typical of mainstream Australians'. In her own words, 'we are in danger of being swamped by Asians ... They have their own culture and religion, form ghettoes and do not assimilate ... I should have a right to say who comes into my country'.

With Pauline Hanson cast out of the Liberal Party, the new One Nation Party was created in 1997 to advance her policies. The success it soon won at the polls shocked the major parties. In 1998 it gained, first, 23 per cent of the votes in the Queensland state election, and then, later in the year, around a million votes in each of the commonwealth elections for the Senate and House of Representatives. This was in fact the high-water mark. In the new century One Nation's votes were way down, as so often happens with single-issue populist parties. Even so, in the whole of Australian history, no party had ever been so successful campaigning on a programme of limiting immigration. Its success tempted the other parties to pander to its prejudices, while at the same constructive immigration policy was put on the back-burner.

Then, at the end of August 2001, the whole question took a new turn with the *Tampa* crisis. Some time early in the month people-smugglers packed some 460 asylum seekers, mainly Afghan, into the Palapa, a 20-metre-long wooden fishing boat, to take them from Indonesia to Australia. This was only the last in a succession of boats illegally carrying asylum seekers to Australia. On 24 August the Palapa stranded about 75 nautical miles north of Christmas Island, an Australian possession in the Indian Ocean, which was its probable destination. Two days later the Australian Rescue Co-ordination Service, learning of the Palapa's distress, sent out a call to all ships in the area to come to its rescue. The *Tampa*, a Norwegian freighter bound for Singapore, rescued the asylum seekers, but when they learnt that the captain, Arne Rinnan, planned to take them back to Indonesia – the correct procedure under international law – they threatened to jump overboard or according to some reports, throw their children overboard.

Captain Rinnan, confronted by hundreds of unruly Afghans, many of whom were sick, set sail for Christmas Island, only to be refused permission to enter Australian territorial waters. The Australian government would go no further than provide medical assistance and food, and to this end sent military personnel to Christmas Island. Captain Rinnan declared a state of emergency, and defying the Australians, went ahead on course for the island. Once the *Tampa* was inside Australian territorial waters, 35 SAS Commandos boarded the ship, to prevent it reaching Christmas Island: Captain Rinnan had no choice but to anchor some four nautical miles offshore. Although confronted by the SAS he refused to return to international waters until the asylum seekers were off-loaded.

In spite of being pressed by the Australian government, neither Indonesia nor Norway would accept the *Tampa*'s unwanted passengers: the incident became a diplomatic disaster for Australia, with the UN and other international organizations becoming involved on the side of Norway. While Norway awarded Captain Rinnan its highest civil honour, and the companies shipping cargo on the *Tampa* congratulated him on his handling of the crisis, Australia threatened him with prosecution as a 'people-smuggler'.

In the end the government did not go this far, but late on the night of 29 August the prime minister John Howard introduced an emergency bill which, if enacted, would not only legitimize all and any of the kind of actions taken against the *Tampa*, but would do so from the morning of the same day – so that it would effectively be retroactive. The Australian Senate, however, rejected the bill after it had been passed by the House of Representatives, which meant that it had to be shelved. On the other hand the government, with opposition support, was able to exclude Christmas Island, together with a large number of other offshore islands, regarded as 'magnets for people-smugglers', from the migration zone from which illegal immigrants could apply for refugee status.

As for the refugees, Australia was forced to accept responsibility: there was simply no alternative. Following successful diplomacy, the *Manoora*, a ship of the Australian Navy, was able to transport some 300 to the small inhospitable island of Nauru and 150 to New Zealand, where they were later granted asylum with the further prospect of citizenship. Australia did finally grant three-year temporary protection visas to those left in Nauru who were found to be genuine refugees, but this meant that their position, once in Australia, was extremely precarious.

In this whole story it is the political dimension that counts. John Howard's coalition faced an election before the end of 2001, and given the success of One Nation at the end of the 1990s, a hard line on immigration was almost certain to attract votes – even more so when 9/11 in New York came less than two weeks after the *Tampa* crisis. John Howard's statement 'we decide who comes into this country and the circumstances in which they come' proved to be the slogan which won the election for the Liberal Party. At the same time the issue proved to be divisive for the ALP, which lost many votes to the Liberals on one side and 'Greens' on the other.

From an international perspective, Australia's political reaction, not only to the *Tampa* crisis, but to the whole question of illegal immigration, seems to be exaggerated. In the end it had involved at least six other sovereign states – Afghanistan, Indonesia, Nauru, New Zealand, Norway, Singapore – in one way or another, to say nothing of the United Nations.

The whole problem, for geographical reasons if nothing else, is much more severe for EU countries. Today almost all the home countries of asylum seekers – many of which are in Africa – are much closer to Europe than to Australia. Moreover, the fact that Australia can only be reached after a difficult sea voyage, to be made, in almost all cases, at the end of a very long trek across much of Asia, makes it an inherently unattractive destination both for people-smugglers and their human cargo – as the statistics clearly show. In an average year, the UK, for example, must deal with about five times the total number of unwanted immigrants that Australia has so far been forced to accept. Nonetheless, Australia continues to maintain its hard-line policy, although the notorious Woomera detention centre was closed after riots in 2001.There may have been some softening at the edges, in response to criticism by human rights activists, but even so immigration to Australia is very tightly controlled; all new arrivals, except from New Zealand, now require a visa.

In contrast to the unwanted immigrants there is another class, that of students – often from countries whose citizens would otherwise be unwelcome – which Australia, together with any number of countries in Europe and North America, is only too eager to welcome. This policy often extends to opening the door to students, at the end of their study, to stay on as permanent immigrants with the prospect of naturalization. The underlying rationale has several aspects. First, because of restricted public funding for higher education, overseas students, with no right to government support, effectively pay fees at a level that represents a profit for the institutes where they study: this provides extra money for universities at the same time as it lessens the burden on public funds. (In Australia local students have complained that the poor command of English of those coming from overseas slows the pace of instruction: after all the opportunity to become proficient in English is often the main reason for overseas students coming in the first place.) Second, the professional and academic qualifications of graduates make it unlikely that they will claim any sort of welfare support; on the contrary, the chances are that they will contribute substantially to the wealth of whatever country they reside in. This explains why Australia makes it easy for students to stay, particularly since their youth and general good health is also on their side. Third, graduates, when they do return home, are more than likely to be good ambassadors for the countries which have welcomed them as students. It is not for nothing that universities work hard to keep in touch with foreign alumni, who often end up as people of wealth, power and influence in their own countries.

15

Crime: piracy, smuggling and terrorism

THE ASIA-PACIFIC DIMENSION

Crime may be much the same the world over, but even so crime in Asia-Pacific is distinctive, particularly when it has an international dimension. Geography and economy, culture and religion, together account for this. These factors need to be looked at before going on to specific types of crime, such as piracy and smuggling.

As for geography, international communications overland count for little in the Pacific. With so many island states it could hardly be otherwise, but even where there are land frontiers, there is often little traffic across them. The main international commerce of Thailand, a country bordering four others in Southeast Asia – Burma, Laos, Cambodia and Malaysia – is for goods, by sea and for people, by air. Significantly, when it comes to crime, Thailand's land frontiers become much more important: for one thing the so-called 'Golden Triangle', notorious for the cultivation of opium poppies, lies just beyond them. Smugglers, who now traffic in people (as witness the story of the *Tampa* told in Chapter 14) as well as goods, are relatively frequent among travellers coming into Thailand from Burma, Laos and Cambodia.

When it comes to the human dimension of geography, and its relation to crime, the factor that counts, more than any other, is the considerable differences in wealth between neighbouring countries. As for wealth, Thailand, once again, is a very long way ahead of Burma, Laos and Cambodia, though not of Malaysia. (It is no coincidence that communists, in one guise or another, while governing the first three countries named, failed in their attempts to take over Malaysia.) Economically Australia is a different world from Indonesia, the other side of the Timor Sea. Crime, in its way, redresses the balance between rich and poor, however high its social costs. This is the 'Robin Hood effect'.

Culture determines both the distinctive character of criminal organizations, and of the way they are accepted in society. The *Triads* could only be Chinese, and the *Yakuza* only Japanese, and in both cases society tolerates, and sometimes even supports, the criminal fraternity. This will be particularly so in an immigrant community, such as that of the Chinese anywhere outside China. Local police are often hamstrung in dealing with crime within an ethnic community.

Religion generally goes with culture, but adds a dimension conceived of as altruistic by its practitioners. This is a major factor in Islamic terrorism: a suicide bomber acts, *a fortiori*, on behalf of others, at least in the perception of his co-religionists. (A cynical outsider may see his sacrifice as no more than an ego-trip leading to over-kill.) The statement made by idealistic suicide is mainly political, as witness the immolation of Buddhist monks protesting against the Diem government in Vietnam in 1963. (The most extreme case is that of the Japanese *kamikaze* pilots operating in the final days of the Pacific War: they can hardly be classed as terrorists, let alone criminals.) Note, at the same time, however, that terrorists are well able to explode bombs without losing their own lives: this was the case with Bali bombings of October 2002 and the attack on the Australian Embassy in Jakarta of September 2004.

PIRACY IN A CHANGING WORLD

Piracy is a crime committed at sea.[1] In almost all cases the motives of pirates taking over a ship by force are purely economic – once again, the Robin Hood effect. Any injuries, including death, inflicted upon officers and crew are incidental to the main object of the crime. This, in the first place, is likely to be any money on board, which, if a large sum, such as pirates go for, will be in the ship's safe. Officers and crew, together with passengers, if any, will also have their money taken from them. The amount of money on board, according to circumstances, can be considerable, and pirates generally know which boats to look for. In many cases an act of piracy may add up to no more than a quick raid, providing a large haul of cash. Everything is over in a matter of minutes.

The advantage of this sort of operation, to those carrying it out, is its relative simplicity. All that is needed is a small fast boat with crew members trained to get aboard larger vessels with built-in defences against raiders. The pirates must overcome these defences and outwit the crew of the target vessel, who in principle – though all too often not in practice – should be trained to combat them. With surprise the key to success, pirates learn how to approach a ship from a blind side, at a time when light, or more often its absence, is in their favour. Weather also counts. It helps the pirates also to operate from safe harbours, where local law enforcement is weak. A long indented coastline, with many small harbours, hidden by mangrove swamps, is ideal. All these circumstances are to be found along the Indonesian coasts of the Straits of Malacca, which, with about a quarter of the world's maritime trade – equivalent to some 50,000 ships – passing through each year, is the world's busiest shipping lane.[2] It is also the scene of about a third of all pirate operations. Both Sumatra, on the opposite side of the straits to Malaya, and the numerous islands offshore from Singapore, provide well-established bases for pirates. These are recruited from the local maritime communities, which make a relatively poor living from fishing, their normal means of subsistence – so once again it is the Robin Hood effect. Many a fisherman in these waters doubles as a pirate, profiting from detailed knowledge of winds, currents and underwater hazards, gained in the course of his working life – and that of his forbears.

The Malacca Straits are not the only home to pirates: fishermen – mainly from Thailand – doubling as pirates, operated in the South China Sea in the aftermath of the war in Vietnam. The numerous small boats carrying Cambodian and Vietnamese refugees were a very soft target, the more so given that the refugees got little beyond sympathy in the way of outside support. For a country like Australia anything that discouraged them could only reduce the numbers demanding asylum, however cruel a fate it was for the refugees themselves to lose everything they had to pirates. The hard truth, as always, is that crime tends to be opportunistic. When the flow of refugees ceased, the Thai pirates returned to fishing.

Not every pirate is content with a few thousand dollars, or whatever, taken from a ship's safe or, as in the case of the Vietnamese boat people, simply stolen from its passengers. Ships carry cargoes valued in millions, but here the problems to be overcome are much greater. Taking an entire cargo requires considerable advance planning, for it must either be trans-shipped at sea – a difficult and time-consuming operation, open to counter-action by the forces of law and order – or the ship brought to a safe anchorage, where off-loading its cargo can proceed undisturbed. A typical pirates' home-base, in a small fishing village sheltered by mangrove swamps, will not be sufficient. Because an anchorage safe from unwelcome attention must also, in the circumstances of the case, offer space to move around in, it will not be all that safe. Many a large-scale trans-shipment has been left half-complete, when those involved in it have to flee in face of a naval patrol boat. The Indonesian Navy is relatively strong in ships specially designed and equipped to combat piracy, although poor strategy and a corrupt command structure often prevent their effective use. Malaysia, and even more Singapore, could do much better, at least if Indonesia, waiving its rights under international law, permitted their ships to operate in Indonesian territorial waters. Indonesia, up to now, refuses to grant such permission – an instance of how international law is only too often on the side of pirates. Law enforcement is helped by the fact that many ships are provided with devices which enable them to track, continuously, on radar screens, but even so, the time that the window of opportunity for effective counter-action is open may be counted in minutes.

In the most extreme cases a whole ship is stolen. In such cases (which are often fatal for the officers and crew) not only must the cargo be off-loaded, but all signs of the ship's ownership – such as its name and home-port painted on the stern and the owner's logo on the funnel – must be effaced, and new ones substituted to give it a new identity. This process relies on taking advantage of all the complexities involved in the international registration of shipping, but this is well within the capabilities of the crime-syndicates behind piracy at this level.

Finally, pirates may take over a ship to kidnap the captain and demand a ransom for his release. This is a new version of piracy, first reported in the year 2000 when the Filipino captain Simon Perera of m/t *Tirta Niaga IV* was kidnapped, after anchoring his ship, which had developed engine trouble, just off the coast of Sumatra. The charterers in Singapore paid a ransom of $30,000 for his release.[3] Events were soon to show how such an operation could fund terrorists: later in 2000, members of the Islamic separatist free Aceh movement[4] – which was then at war with the Indonesian Army in northern Sumatra – held the crew of another ship, the *Ocean Silver* for ransom.

What is the historical dimension? What is new in all this? Piracy goes back to the earliest days of sea-faring, so what changes? Politics combined with technology provides the answer. The change from sail to steam in the nineteenth century made life much more difficult for pirates, but it greatly increased the value of the prizes to be won. Significantly, however, the change took place at a time when every country in Southeast Asia was a European colony, while in East Asia almost all the powers, European and American, involved in trading with China and Japan, maintained a strong naval presence to protect their subjects. To take, as an example, a typical colonial case, that of the Dutch in the East Indies, there was no question of the colonial government turning a blind eye to piracy. On the contrary, the Dutch squadrons in the Indies had a long history – going back to the days of sail – of dealing with pirates and giving them no quarter. In the comfortable days before 1940 piracy was hardly a problem for any of the colonial powers – Britain, France, the Netherlands and the US – in Southeast Asia.

Almost everything changed after the end of the Pacific War. As one country after another won the struggle for independence, the old colonial restraints on piracy were no longer effective. One result of Indonesia's war against the Dutch at the end of the 1940s was a climate in which wealth acquired, by whatever means, at the expense of the old colonial powers, was seen as part of the spoils of victory. When in Indonesia after 1965 General Suharto and his cronies were becoming multi-millionaires by milking foreign aid funds, they could hardly complain about the activities of 'fishermen' at the other end of the socio-economic spectrum. On the contrary one and the same network of corruption facilitated the depredations of both classes. At the same time there were changes in the character of international shipping, with passenger lines disappearing, to be replaced by containers – a very difficult target, incidentally, for pirates. If on the other side pirates work with better and faster boats, the same is true of the forces of law and order, which, on balance, gain more advantage from advances in technology. At the end of the day, the fight against piracy is a matter of political will, informed, in cases like that of Indonesia, by the knowledge that victory pays dividends. The Indonesian Navy, with the need to patrol an archipelago of some 17,000 islands, has too few ships available to combat piracy; even so, used effectively, and above all in cooperation with Malaysia and Singapore, they could go a long way towards winning the battle.

Internationally, the main concern is terrorism rather than straight piracy. In June 2004, Tony Tan, Singapore's deputy prime minister, pointed out that a ship sunk offshore, at the right point, 'could cripple world trade'.[5] Sceptics, pointing out the difficulties of sinking a ship at a precise point, see the danger as theoretical rather than real. Even so the US has asked for, but so far been refused, permission to patrol the territorial waters of the coastal states of the Malacca Straits.

KIDNAP AND TERRORISM

Where the straits are a happy hunting ground for Indonesian pirates, the South China Sea is the scene of action for Filipino kidnappers. Like Indonesia the Philippines is a country with thousands of islands, characterized by extreme ethnic, political and religious diversity. In a process that still continues, and attracts massive investment, these have been developed as a tourist paradise; beautiful and largely unspoilt, in a low-cost country wide-open to visitors, with English as its official language and Catholicism as its dominant religion, the islands have everything going for them. Too much it may be said, since sex-tourism, exploiting both boys and girls from impoverished families, is part of the available package – although recently the governments of both the Philippines and the tourists' home countries have been collaborating in clamping down on this traffic. However this may be, countless small islands, with isolated resorts attracting Western tourists, offer endless opportunities for kidnappers, operating from inaccessible mountain encampments, or like pirates in Indonesia, from secluded fishing villages.

If it were just a question of crime – as it often is – the kidnappers are out for ransom, which once paid, buys the release of their victims. The danger then comes when armed intervention by the forces of law and order leads to a shoot-out, which, whatever the fate of the kidnappers, may cost the lives of the hostages. At the same time, the areas of highest risk are often those – such as western Mindanao, Palawan or the Sulu Islands – with a substantial Islamic population. Even so, the small but very active Abu Sayyef group (ASG) has also operated in urban centres, such as Manila and Cebu.

The significance of ASG is that it claims to be an Islamic separatist movement, fighting for independence. The main Muslim separatist group, the Moro Islamic Liberation Front, denies all responsibility for kidnapping, contending, at the same time, that the ASG makes an industry out of it. Its Islamic ties would then be little more than a pretext justifying its activities among local Muslim populations, with the object of making them less likely to cooperate with government forces. This put the Philippines government in a quandary: the better it could present the ASG as no more than a gang of bandits, the more likely it was to win local support in counter-acting it. On the other hand, by linking ASG to international terrorism, the Philippines gained financial, technical and strategic international support.

The ASG emerged in the mid-1980s in the 1,700 square kilometres of mountain jungles of the Basilan Islands with the declared objective of creating a separate *Pure Islamic Bangsamoro Homeland*. Its original leader, Ustadz Abdurajak Janjalani, trained with the Mujahiddeen in Afghanistan, where he came in contact with Osama bin Laden, who supported his plan to make the Philippines a major operational hub of Al Qaeda. For a period of nine years from 1988, Janjalani was assisted by bin Laden's brother-in-law, Mohammad Jamal Khalifa. The *Moro Islamic Liberation Front* was also involved. The ASG, however, only started to operate outside the Basilan and Sulu Islands towards the end of the 1990s. The government response was to increase the scale of its operations, and Janjalani was killed in a shoot-out with the police in December 1998; his main lieutenant was arrested a month later.

Despite this setback, in April 2000 the ASG staged its first operation outside the Philippines, when it kidnapped 21 people, including ten foreigners, from the Malaysian island resort of Pulau Sipadan, just offshore from Sabah. Hardly a year later, on 27 May 2001, the kidnapping of 21 people at the Dos Palmas resort in Palawan attracted world-wide attention, in part because an American Christian missionary, Martin Burnham and his wife Gracia were among the victims. Although three of the hostages were released immediately, President Gloria Arroyo reacted by unleashing a massive military operation. The ASG, returning to its base in Basilan, went on to take several more hostages, including Deborah Yap, a Filipina nurse, at a hospital, and a few days later, another 15 at a rubber plantation. On 12 June the kidnappers announced the execution of an American hostage as an Independence Day gift to the Arroyo government. Other executions followed, but increasing military pressure resulted in several escapes, rescues and releases until, finally only the Burnhams and nurse Yap were still held hostage. The end came with a shoot-out, which only Gracia Burnham, of the three hostages, survived. Although the course of events that then ended gained the most attention from the media, it was only a part of the clashes between government forces and the ASG. By the end of 2001, 82 government troops had been killed, with 229 wounded, with civilian casualties on the same scale. On the other hand 249 ASG members were killed, with another 67 taken captive.

Following 9/11, and noting the Philippines' *Al Qaeda* connections, the US sent special forces to support the Arroyo government's operations against ASG. Although the Philippines' constitution bans the use of foreign troops in direct combat, US forces have accompanied the Philippine troops engaged operationally. In addition the US has given some $100 million in military aid, including a C-130 transport, eight helicopters, night-vision devices, and 30,000 M16 rifles. US carrier-based aircraft, equipped with heat-sensing and electronic monitoring devices, have also helped with reconnaissance.

According to official claims, the campaign against the ASG, although involving casualties on both sides, succeeded in reducing it to a kidnapping-for-ransom operation, even though its leadership continues to maintain an Islamist political stance. The sophisticated US equipment allows Filipino troops to operate much more effectively in the Basilan mountain jungles, a process helped by the US paying $5-million rewards for capturing ASG's top leaders. Tighter immigration controls have not only made it more difficult for ASG members to move freely between the Philippines and Malaysia, Singapore and Indonesia, but have also led to some hundred arrests. In spite of all these measures, ASG, early in 2004, still claimed responsibility for a bomb attack on a ferry in Manila bay.

By launching its three-year A$5 million Philippines counter-terrorism assistance initiative in April 2004, Australia joined the US in supporting the fight against terrorism. This involved funding an 18-month port security building project, so enabling the Philippines to comply with the International Maritime Organization's international ship and port facility security code (ISPS), which forms part of a new global security regime for international shipping. A further $3.65 million went to a counter-terrorism project, which will provide the Philippines' Bureau of Immigration with document fraud detection equipment and training to strengthen security in the southern Philippines.

If, in the Philippines, the distinction between kidnapping and terrorism, or crime and Islamic *jihad*, is blurred, in Indonesia terrorism is the weapon of Islamic fundamentalism, and almost always means destruction of life and property – often on a very large scale. At a local level, such as the ongoing conflict between Christians and Muslims in southern Sulawesi, each side is vulnerable to terrorist attacks by the other. Here the conflict is between Indonesians, but in the twenty-first century acts of terrorism aimed at foreigners – mainly Australians – have changed the whole scenario.

On 12 October 2002, terrorist bombs destroyed two clubs in the Balinese resort Kuta, killing more than two hundred people. This was an international incident. The great majority of casualties were foreign tourists, mainly from Australia, whose prime minister, John Howard, came a few days later to visit the scene of the outrage. Three Islamic extremists were tried, convicted and sentenced to death for murder, but many believe that others were ultimately responsible. With few tourists daring to visit Bali after the incident, the economy paid a high price. A year later, on 5 August 2003, a related group detonated a bomb outside the Marriott Hotel in Jakarta, killing 12 people, mainly Indonesians, and injuring 147 others. Then, on 12 September 2004, a bomb exploded in front of the Australian Embassy in Jakarta and devastated a wide area, although only 8 people died.

In all these cases government security services, not only in Indonesia, but also in Malaysia, Singapore, Australia and the US, attributed the attacks to *Jema'ah Islamiyah* (JI), an Islamic extremist organization, whose members had received operational training in secret camps in the southern Philippines, where one of their leaders, Abu Bakar Ba-asyir, had proclaimed a *fatwa* said to come from Osama bin Laden.

The Indonesian government not only condemned all these attacks, but took every possible measure to find the culprits: some of those responsible for the Bali bombing, including Ba-asyir, have already been tried and convicted. (Although the sentences have been reversed, in part, on legal grounds, these will not be valid if those responsible for the Jakarta bombing are brought to trial.) At the same time, very few Indonesians actually support Islamic extremism, let alone terrorist acts carried out in its name. The 2004 elections made this clear beyond any doubt. Also, after two major incidents involving Australia, the question why this country is targeted by JI must be answered.

To begin with, Australia, with an extremely proactive stance in Asia-Pacific politics, has a very high profile in every country in the region. While the massive city-centre office blocks built to house Australian embassies are part of the picture, ubiquitous Australian tourists, often young, noisy and with money to throw around, are another. Such phenomena are not confined to Indonesia, but they are felt there more keenly. Moreover, Australian interventions in Asia-Pacific, such as the action taken against the *Tampa* in 2001 or the military operations carried out in East Timor in 1999 (described in Chapter 12) are not calculated to win friends in Indonesia. On the other hand, Australia's contribution to the Indonesian economy is indispensable, and not only because of the money spent by tourists.

In the early 2000s, small-scale acts of terrorism occurred almost every week in Thailand's three southern provinces, close to Malaya, which have a substantial Muslim population with its own language, Yawi. Active terrorists – some belonging to the self-styled Pattani United Liberation Front – then call upon support from across the frontier, for Malaysia is an Islamic state. The situation is a thorn in the flesh for Bangkok, and not only because of the threat to law and order. The three Muslim provinces are at the southern end of the narrow

Kra isthmus, separating the Indian Ocean from the South China Sea. A Thai government plan, published in 2004, contemplates the construction of a 'land bridge',[6] with oil and container terminals on either side, that would bypass the sea-route round Singapore. Moreover, the coast along the Indian Ocean, at the northern end of the isthmus developed as a major tourist area – devastated by the *tsunami* of 26 December 2004. Not surprisingly, any terrorists apprehended are treated with a heavy hand – so much so that what they go through once taken into custody gives human rights activists much to complain about. (In October 2004, the death by suffocation of 78 captured insurgents, while being transported in a Thai army truck, led to angry reactions from the Muslim world.) The terrorists exploit the common Muslim grievance, that in Buddhist Thailand they are treated as second-class citizens.[7] Their position, therefore, is comparable to that of their co-religionists in the Christian Philippines, but in the Thai case – where there is no *Al Qaeda* presence – the government has not needed to call on US support.

More than any act of terrorism in the Philippines or Indonesia, horror was caused on the Tokyo metro in 1995, when the extremist religious cult Aum Shinrikyo released the deadly gas *sarin*, in one of the busiest stations, killing 11 people and sending a wave of fear felt far outside Japan. While the 'supreme truth' proclaimed by the cult-leader, Asahara Shoko, never took any hold on the public at large, it nevertheless led a hard-core of devotees – many university graduates – to bring death and sickness to the heart of the capital city. The activities of this bizarre cult – which included the assassination of back-sliders – were known for some time before this incident, but no effective action was taken. The arrest of Asahara Shoko and his conviction for murder set the minds of most Japanese at rest. Somewhat disconcertingly the sect he founded still survives under a new name, Aleph: although its members have disowned the crimes Asahara committed in the 1990s, they now revere his daughter, Arahari. It must be said, however, that bizarre cults set on the path to self-destruction are also to be found outside Japan.

SMUGGLING: PEOPLE AND DRUGS

Smuggling, although by definition an international crime, has many different facets, whose character is largely determined by that of the goods being trafficked. In the classic case, what makes smuggling pay is the difference in taxes or duties charged by two neighbouring states. This automatically puts a premium on goods subject to the lower rates, but this has to be set off against the costs of the smuggling operation. In a developing country, such as Indonesia, where costs in terms of human capital are relatively low, and of law enforcement relatively high, goods with a high value to weight ratio, such as tobacco and *batik*, are inherently attractive to small-scale smugglers. The result is a high volume of traffic in such goods across the Malacca Straits to Malaya, where both duties and overhead costs are much higher. A fishing-boat, sailing out of a small harbour on the coast of Sumatra, can easily find a market in Malaya for contraband. The same factors as encourage pirates are equally favourable to smugglers, and not surprisingly, the two classes overlap. At this level law enforcement consists simply of making the risks involved unacceptable to the smugglers: the confiscation of both contraband, and the boat transporting it, particularly where accompanied by a substantial fine, should, in principle, make smuggling a game not worth playing – the more so if possible penalties include long terms of imprisonment or even capital punishment. An alternative is simply to open up more rewarding ways of earning a living – an example of a policy, widely favoured by international agencies, of alternative development. In practice, at the penny-ante level of the small-scale smuggling across the Malacca Straits, there is little alternative to low-level law enforcement. Too high a commitment just does not pay, particularly given the level of petty corruption, at local level, in countries such as Indonesia or the Philippines. Even so, the two approaches, law enforcement and alternative development, are often combined – with circumstances deciding the balance in any given situation.

The case becomes quite different where the traffic itself, quite apart from its fiscal consequences, is illegal both nationally and internationally. Two cases are salient here: people and drugs. People come into the hands of smugglers when they are destitute, persecuted, uprooted and traumatized by war. With no life worth living in their own country, they are desperate to find a new home abroad. This was the state of the 460 passengers on the Palapa who, in August 2001, were rescued off the coast of Indonesia by the m/v *Tampa*. They were mainly from Afghanistan, and although few doubted the awful fate awaiting them if they returned there, no other state would receive them – unless international law required it. The smugglers failed to honour their side of the bargain, which was to get the people they trafficked in ashore.

The Pacific has not been a happy-hunting ground for people-smugglers. Transport overland is at the heart of this traffic, and the geography of the Pacific determines that international travel is mainly by sea or air. Surveying the whole Pacific Rim, then, in terms of pure numbers, people-smuggling across the land-frontier between Mexico and the US is much the largest operation of this kind. The problem of unwanted immigrants is at its most acute in the US and the EU, and in both cases, the seas to be crossed, if any, are not part of the Pacific.

It need hardly be said that the hardcore of smuggling, as developed in the half-century-odd since the end of the Pacific War, is defined by drugs. Although the production, sale and use of drugs constitute a challenge to law enforcement, world-wide, the modern history of Thailand, in one way or another, and better than that of almost any other state – at least in the Pacific – illustrates the changing nature of the problems involved, and the solutions adopted to resolve them.

Because the focus must then be on opium, and its derivative, heroin, something must be said about production and distribution. Raw opium is essentially the latex produced from the seed capsules – approximately the size of a walnut – of one particular species of poppy. Opium poppies can easily be cultivated, on a small scale, in areas little suited for other agriculture. These areas, generally remote and inaccessible, are often inhabited by ethnic minorities, whose members are marginal, both socially and economically, in a nation reluctant to recognize them as citizens. Some two to three months after poppy seed is sown broadcast on the ground prepared for it, the distinctive red flowers are fully grown and ready for harvest. The opium latex, extracted ten days after the petals have fallen off the flowers, is then rolled into balls and wrapped in leaves or paper. The result is a product that is easy to transport in small quantities. Given its high value to weight ratio, both manufacture and distribution are extremely rewarding, particularly for the marginal members of society involved in these operations. This is much more so with heroin, a refined opiate that retains the essential morphine, but not the other alkaloids contained in raw opium. Since opium loses both its distinctive smell and some 90 per cent of its volume in the refining process, heroin is much easier to smuggle. Because of the relatively advanced skills and equipment required, the costs of production, however, are substantially higher.

In the nineteenth century the Western world had, essentially, only one China policy, which was to open up that country to trade, and, in particular, the import of opium. It is not for nothing that two armed conflicts between China and the West, arising as a result of this policy, are known as the Opium Wars. In 1858 the Chinese imperial government, bound by the treaty that ended the second Opium War, legalized the sale of opium. The background to Western intervention in China was purely commercial: the opium to be sold there was produced in countries such as India, Burma and Laos, which were part of European colonial empires. As the demand for opium within China increased, farmers in remote inland provinces, along the frontiers of Laos and Burma, began to cultivate the poppies from which it is made, so much so that by the end of the nineteenth century China produced twice as much opium as it was importing.[8] Constant fighting between rival warlords in these remote areas led many cultivators, almost all non-Chinese ethnic minorities, to move south, first into Laos and Burma, and then into Thailand. No matter which country was chosen for settlement, the extensive and inaccessible mountainous terrain was uniform throughout the whole wide area – and there was little question of any frontier-control. In northern Thailand, two groups originating in China, the Hmong and the Mien, knowing that opium poppies thrived at elevations above 1,000 metres, started

– quite legally – cultivating areas not claimed by any other population. As such they differed little from other 'hill tribes' in Burma and Laos. At the same time, having settled in Thailand, they soon found new markets among the ethnic Chinese populations in the large cities that developed in Southeast Asia in the late 1800s. Not least of these was Bangkok, the Thai capital.

The hill cultivators, however, faced a problem. Although the Kingdom of Siam, under British diplomatic pressure,[9] had legalized the cultivation of opium poppies in 1855, it had immediately imposed a royal monopoly of opium, according to which selected growers were licensed to sell to the government at low prices. The government monopoly then sold on at high prices, with the difference going to the state treasury.[10] The hill peoples, to stay in business, were left to smuggle opium to the thriving Bangkok black market. This meant that they became small-holders skilled in the clandestine production of opium, and its transport to urban markets. Inevitably an alternative informal infrastructure emerged alongside the supply-chain of the royal monopoly.

During the Pacific War, in which the whole of Southeast Asia was occupied by the Japanese, the vast highland area shared between southern China, Burma, Laos and northern Thailand, was a no-go area for any forces of law and order. Such policing as Britain and France had maintained in Burma and Laos – which between them stood between China and Thailand – counted for nothing, whereas the only Japanese concern was to build a railway linking Thailand to Burma. Apart from defending the line of rail the Japanese had little or no presence in the rest of the highland area: it was wide open, therefore, for the production of and traffic in opium. The only people with links throughout the area, and indeed beyond it into the lowlands of Burma, Laos and Thailand, were Chinese, who took full advantage of the opportunity to develop a flourishing opium-based informal economy.

This was the state of the game at the end of 1945. Then, in 1949, one of the first moves of Mao Zedong's new government in China was to suppress the use of opium. The policy was strictly enforced and by the mid-1950s poppy cultivation had ceased.[11] Given the demands of the world market, this was an incentive to increase production in what, in the 1970s, came to be called the 'Golden Triangle' – the name given, by an American diplomat in 1971,[12] to the mountainous frontier areas shared between Thailand, Laos and Burma. Then, in 1956, a Thai government proclamation banned all production, sale and use of opiates, although, to allow time to make good the prospective loss of revenue from the royal monopoly, the enabling legislation did not take effect until 1959 – but this was by no means the end of the supply network built up by the Chinese during the war. The result was in fact to increase the consumption of heroin at the expense of opium in the lowland areas, particularly in Bangkok. Then, with the escalation of the war in Vietnam after 1965, vast numbers of US troops came to Thailand. This led to a much-increased demand for drugs, particularly among men who came to the beach-resorts along the South China Sea to recuperate from the war. The economic incentive to cultivate opium poppies in the hill areas, or to smuggle opium in from Laos or Burma – where many of the hill tribes were closely related to the Hmong and Mien – was greater than ever. So also was the incentive to refine it into heroin, so much so that this became part of the operation among the hill tribes. These developments could only increase the determination, by both Washington and Bangkok, to suppress the whole operation.

The first step was to survey the areas in which opium was cultivated. In 1962 a team from Thailand's Public Welfare Department went into the hills, interviewed growers – of whom many were Hmong – and inspected fields of poppies. According to its findings, an individual cultivator could earn $1,000 per annum, by producing only a few kilograms of raw opium – a vast sum for an impoverished peasant population. What is more, the total production for the whole country then worked out at about 145 tons, a figure which horrified Bangkok.[13]

In 1976, the establishment of the Office of the Narcotics Control Board (ONCB) opened the way both to much more intensive and sophisticated surveys, and to ever more ingenious ways of concealing the cultivation of poppies, at the same time increasing their yield. By 1985 ONCB could claim the destruction, every year, of about half the total production. By the end of the century its task was still not complete, even after the introduction of such hi-tech gizmos as satellite imaging. The relative success of the ONCB operations had a number of consequences: first, scarcity led Thailand to become a net importer of opium. The street-price of opium increased fivefold, making not only heroin, in increasing measure, the drug of user-choice, but also encouraging the use of alternatives, such as amphetamines, which had to be smuggled in from outside.

Bangkok's narcotics policy has two other dimensions: alternative development and law enforcement, both of which have attracted enormous investment since the 1960s. The former involves four inter-linked projects: building new roads to open up remote areas, of mainly forest and hills; providing extension services to marginal populations so that they can profitably grow cash crops, often fruit and vegetables, for the national market, while at the same settling in one place; building schools and health centres in the villages emerging as a result of resettlement; and exploiting natural forest products such as tropical hardwood.

All these projects come with a price, but they were set up at a time when Thailand's economy was booming, and foreign aid available from any number of sources – from UN and foreign government agencies to private funds from charities working internationally – and for any number of reasons, both strategic (in the case of the US) and economic. In the background, King Bhumibol

Adulyadej proclaimed opium poppy replacement as a national priority. The policy has had considerable success with raw opium, but much less with heroin – probably because of the demands of addicts.

As for law enforcement, the much-extended communications infrastructure has made surveillance in the frontier regions much more effective. On the other hand, by making long-distance travel, generally by bus, so much easier, tens of thousands of people are in a position to carry small quantities of drugs, from the economic periphery to the centre. Inevitably some are intercepted, but not enough to put an end to the traffic. The alternative is to concentrate police operations on the centre. This means effectively Bangkok with its substantial middle-class drug-scene, which is based as much on amphetamines as on heroin. Here the police target both users and suppliers, which under prime minister Thaksin led to substantial human rights abuses – often following violent shoot-outs between the police and drug dealers. Much is at stake: long sentences await those convicted of drug offences, as quite a number of Europeans have discovered – often after being arrested directly after arriving with contraband drugs at Bangkok's Don Muang Airport.

ENVIRONMENTAL CRIME

Environmental crime, far more than any other category, threatens the destruction of the habitat and livelihood of countless people in Southeast Asia. The land most at risk is tropical rainforests, where natural stands of hardwood are being devastated by illegal logging. The gravity of the situation was highlighted by US secretary of state Colin Powell, speaking on Earth Day, 22 April 2003:

> Illegal logging and bad environmental management equate to billions of dollars each year in lost revenue – billions of dollars that, instead, could be used by governments to build schools, to get rid of debt, or to lift millions out of misery and poverty.

Kalimantan, the part of the island of Borneo belonging to Indonesia, illustrates the gravity of the situation. Hundreds of canals – excavated by local people and illegal loggers as transportation infrastructure – have been used to transport illegally felled trees to sawmills. Some 433,250 have been discovered in just one province, West Kalimantan – most being operated without any official permission or documentation from relevant authorities. From the sawmills the wood is smuggled out of the country, to Malaysia, Singapore, China, Japan, Taiwan and above all the US.

Much of the vast forest area of Kalimantan is home to tribes ethnically distinct from all other Indonesian populations, but who, in the last quarter of the twentieth century, confronted new immigrants – mainly from Java – coming to their island under the official transmigration policy described in Chapter 14. Although the tribesmen remained beyond the normal reach of government, they were only too ready to earn money by felling natural hardwood trees. The logs are then bought by mainstream Indonesian middlemen, who can then sell them on to the sawmills at a profit of at least 200 per cent. The whole operation, which is illegal from start to finish, flourishes as a result of the government's lack of political will to enforce its own regulations for controlling the exploitation of the forests. The local police and military are simply bought off by the illegal loggers.

The consequences have been appalling. Not only is an irreplaceable natural resource being squandered, but intensive logging, by radically altering the forest environment, has led, on one side, to unprecedented flooding – which in 2002 led to the destruction of thousands of homes and the devastation of rice-paddies on the same scale[14] – and on the other, to vast forest fires, with clouds of smoke extending far beyond the island of Borneo. Ironically some have even crossed the South China Sea to reach Malaysia, one of the major importers from Kalimantan.

Kalimantan does not stand alone: in Indonesia the lowland tropical forests of Sulawesi and Sumatra have already been cleared by loggers, in a process that lost the whole country some 10 million hectares – equivalent to some 40 per cent of its forest cover – in the last half of the twentieth century. The market background is simple: the level of legal supplies of wood fibre is a third of that of demand.

Indonesia is not, however, the worst case: the Philippines has now lost all but 700,000 hectares of an original 16 million hectares of natural forest. In this case, however, clearing ground for agriculture, to satisfy the demands of a rapidly increasing rural population, has played a major part. The process, however, goes hand in hand with the depredations of illegal loggers. Apart from the two island states of Indonesia and the Philippines, on the mainland these extend from Russia (a major supplier to China), through China, to all the countries of Southeast Asia.

As in Indonesia's domestic market, the problem is simply the market's demand for timber. The world's major industrial countries account for some three-quarters of all imported timber and timber products, most of which originates in countries where illegal tree felling is rampant. It has been estimated that of some $500 million dollars worth imported from Indonesia every year by the US, about 70 per cent could represent $330 million worth of timber from illegal sources. Japan, with a construction industry that relies on timber, imports from Indonesia on the same scale – a trade that would be quite impossible if Indonesia enforced its own regulations as effectively as Japan has for centuries. The difference is palpable: Japan still retains the greater part of its historic forests.[15] Now China, with its booming construction industry, is outrunning Japan, and is even less scrupulous about the source of its imported hardwood.

In his first term of office, President George W. Bush took a much-publicized initiative to prevent illegal logs from crossing international borders, which if effectively implemented would provide a significant historical case of a poacher turned game-keeper. The strategy proposed was to provide for certification of legally felled timber under existing international agreements, such as the Convention on International Trade in Endangered Species of wild fauna and flora (CITES). The underlying principle was that if importers would only accept certified timber, then illegal felling would lose its market. Certification, however, is only possible at source, which means effective cooperation by local officials in countries such as Indonesia. This could be helped by providing, on one side, effective monitoring systems, and on the other, an alternative means of livelihood for those who actually cut down the trees. This adds up to the sort of policy – described earlier in this chapter – adopted with some success by Thailand to control the supply of drugs. Given the market factors outlined above the chances of success are problematic, even though at government level, as had already been recognized in China, the services that forests provide, such as flood control, can be worth far more than the lumber they contain.

In the search for an effective policy there has been no want of trying. A south Asia ministerial conference on forest law enforcement and governance was held in Bali in 2001. To develop legally sourced forest products Washington has facilitated partnerships under USAID's sustainable forest products global alliance funding projects, while using the International Tropical Timber Organization (ITTO) to improve tropical timber export and import data. On the face of it, all this adds up to words rather than deeds: time will tell.

16

The American west coast and the US Pacific empire

PEACE AND RECONSTRUCTION

The end of the Pacific War brought hard times to the millions attracted to California by the wartime economy's demands for labour. Wartime industrial production peaked in 1944, when it became clear that production threatened to exceed the demands for shipping and aircraft: the Japanese surrender in 1945 not only ended the whole programme, but also left a vast fleet of ships and aircraft for which there was little use, while hundreds of thousands of those who had worked on their construction faced unemployment. Members of minorities who had come to the west coast to find war work were particularly hard hit, being left to depend on welfare payments in poor suburbs of the large cities.

Watts in Los Angeles was one of these new urban ghettoes, where seething discontent took hold among the black population in the post-war years. This was exacerbated in 1964 when Californians, by voting for Proposition 14, blocked the fair housing provisions of President Lyndon Johnson's Civil Rights Act. Then, on 11 August 1965, a routine traffic control sparked off riots that lasted for six days, leaving 34 dead, more than a thousand injured and hundreds of buildings destroyed. Worse was to come in 1992 – by which time much of the population was Hispanic rather than black – after a chance observer had recorded white police beating a black motorist. At a time when almost 40 per cent of the Watts residents lived below the poverty line, 58 people died and $1 billion worth of property was destroyed. According to a 2005 survey,[1] on any measure the blacks in Los Angeles still fall behind Latinos, whites and Asians. Part of their problem is demographic: with less than 10 per cent of the population they are now the smallest of the city's four major ethnic groups.

In the first post-war decade, west-coast politics reacted not so much to the sorrows of the poorest citizens as to the intransigence of the Soviet Union under Joseph Stalin, and even more to Mao Zedong's successful revolution in China. This was particularly the case in California, where there was some very dirty play.

In the 1946 congressional election, Richard M. Nixon, using innuendo to taint the incumbent Democratic congressman, Jerry Voorhis – a model of integrity

– with alleged communist associations, won California's 12th District for the Republicans. In 1948, by using the same strategy in the Senate race Nixon became one of California's two US Senators. The other Senator, William F. Knowland – also a Republican – became so notorious for his support for Jiang Jieshi's nationalist government set up in Taiwan after Jiang's defeat by Mao on the mainland, that he was often referred to as 'the Senator from Formosa'.

Nixon became Vice-President to Dwight Eisenhower in 1953, while Knowland became leader of the Republican Party in the Senate. Both, apparently ill-fated, went on to lose the race to become state governor – Knowland in 1958 and Nixon in 1962, after losing the 1960 presidential race to John F. Kennedy. Knowland's star then faded, and he ended his own life in 1974. Nixon, notoriously, went on to succeed Lyndon Johnson as president in 1969, to end his second term of office, prematurely, in 1974 as the result of threatened impeachment following the Watergate scandal. During his whole term in the White House, Ronald Reagan, who had been an active supporter in the 1960 presidential campaign, was Governor of California – going on to be, in the period 1981–89, the third president from the state.

Any one-sided view of west-coast politics, born out of this train of events, would be mistaken. Politics, both in the three west-coast states and in British Columbia, are polarized and extremely volatile – as witness the way Arnold Schwarzenegger became Republican Governor of California on 8 October 2003 – but then George W. Bush failed to carry any of the three west-coast states in the two presidential elections so far in the twenty-first century. All are strongholds of liberal rather than conservative politics: Oregon's laws on social issues, such as abortion and marriage between homosexuals, are continually targeted by the Christian right – and in California, San Francisco is not far behind.

In the sixty or so years following the Pacific War it is the economic history of the west coast that really counts. Events soon mitigated the post-war depression described above, whatever its long-term legacy in places like Watts. With Mao's victory in China in 1949, and even more the outbreak of the Korean War in 1950, the west coast was once more in the frontline – as it continued to be, in the field of international conflict, at least until the end of the Vietnam War in 1975. If in the early post-war years the Pacific, with East and Southeast Asia devastated by the war, offered few commercial opportunities, the position was transformed by spectacular economic growth throughout the area from the mid-1950s onwards.

THE HI-TECH REVOLUTION

Critically, US defence-based industries were never allowed to run down; indeed new weapons research brought prosperity to many west-coast areas. Some 100 kilometres inland from San Francisco, the *Lawrence Livermore National Laboratory*, set up in 1952 and managed by the University of California, was from the very beginning the research centre for developing thermonuclear weapons. This was largely the initiative of Edward Teller, its director from 1958 to 1960, who later, in the 1980s, sold President Ronald Reagan his Strategic Defense Initiative, otherwise known as the 'Star Wars' programme – revived, incidentally, under the presidency of George W. Bush. In fact *Lawrence Livermore* prefers to focus its research on peace rather than war, so that nuclear fusion, for the generation of electricity, became part of its remit in the 1980s. Whats more, it is but one of the six national laboratories on the west coast, along with, for instance, the *Joint Genome Institute* at Walnut Creek close by, whose remit is strictly peaceful and earthbound. The national laboratories are only part of the hi-tech complex: just think of Silicon Valley developed in the 1950s on land made available by Stanford University, itself a world-ranking research institution. At the same time the RAND Corporation, set up in Santa Monica – the home of Douglas Aircraft – as a think-tank for the US Air Force, should not be overlooked: its strategic thinking over the forty-odd years of the Cold War complemented Teller's nuclear weapons research at Lawrence Livermore.[2]

In the nearby Santa Clara valley, in 1975, Steve Jobs and Steve Wozniak set up *Apple Computers*, which with all its ups and downs is still a name to be reckoned with. Bigger if not better than all the competition is Bill Gates' *Microsoft Corporation*, founded in the same year, which belongs not to California, but – since 1986 – to Redmond, Washington. If this were not enough for the greater Seattle area, Renton, the home to Boeing, is also there. What is more Seattle is, next to Los Angeles, the largest harbour on the west coast.

INFRASTRUCTURE: THE SOCIOLOGY OF TRANSFORMATION

From 1950 onwards the west coast, more than any other part of the US, was transformed by the revolution in road, air and sea transport. On land the *Highway Act* of 1956 established, for its time, the world's largest public works project, that of the US *Interstate Highways*. The initiative came from President Eisenhower, who, in 1919, had been one of the officers on the *Truck Train Convoy*, the US Army's first ever organized motorized convoy across the US. Its route, called 'The Lincoln Highway', was compounded of short stretches of mainly unsurfaced local state highways. Although the convoy left Washington with instructions to 'proceed … to San Francisco without delay' the journey still took 62 days, to complete the final stage by ferry from Oakland, accompanied by two US Navy destroyers. It is no wonder that Eisenhower felt that he could do better, particularly after he had seen for himself – as the Allied Commander-in-Chief at the end of World War II – the military usefulness of the German autobahns.

There had of course been considerable progress since 1919, with the completion of Route 66 in 1938 as a landmark event, but even so, when Eisenhower took office in 1953, the entire length nation-wide of the interstate network was barely 10,000 kilometres – quite insufficient to cope with any new traffic. By 1974, the term set by the 1956 *Highway Act*, the aggregated length of the 'interstates' was some 65,000 kilometres, consisting entirely of limited access four-lane highways, or better.

There were three main routes across the continent to the west coast, terminating at Los Angeles (I-40), San Francisco (I-80) and Seattle (I-90) – echoing the development of the railroads in the nineteenth century. The west-coast cities were also linked by their own interstate, I-5,[3] stretching from the Canadian to the Mexican frontiers. Needless to say, the system continued to expand after 1974, but not at the same rate – the last link, in Los Angeles, only opened in 1993. Eisenhower's claim, made in 1963,[4] that 'more than any single action by the government since the end of the war, this one would change the face of America', proved to be correct – nowhere more so than on the west coast.

The problem – particularly acute in and around Los Angeles – was that the Interstate Highway had encouraged the development of suburbanization and sprawl. Although never planned by Eisenhower, the interstates reached right into the major US cities, bringing problems of congestion, smog, automobile dependency, drop in densities of urban areas and the decline of mass transit. The urban freeway systems built to solve these problems often exacerbated them. Nation-wide the Los Angeles and San Francisco-Oakland areas come first and fifth in the level of traffic congestion. Since the mid-1950s the easy accessibility of the west coast by road is a major factor in attracting new residents, whose presence only increases the need for more highways. Right down the west coast, both of Canada and the US, populations, as well as the number of private cars, have increased faster than in any other part of North America.

With sea transport the west coast is more than ever dominated by its major harbours – Los Angeles, San Francisco/Oakland, Portland, Seattle and Vancouver – trans-shipping containers, oil and LNG. While, at the beginning of the twentieth century, the orientation of the coast was largely inland, at its end it was the lands beyond the western horizon, over the Pacific. The transformation can best be seen in the acceptance into local society of Chinese, Japanese, Koreans, Vietnamese, Filipinos – many as a result of war first in Korea, and then in Indochina (which sent hundreds of thousands of refugees to the US and Canada, most going no further than the west coast). These minority groups are mainly urban – as witness, for instance, Vancouver, where more than ten per cent of the population is ethnic Chinese. California, always the most popular destination, now has a minority white population. Here the Hispanics, representing nearly a third of the population, are fast catching up, with one of their number, Antonio Villaraigosa, elected mayor of Los Angeles in 2005. The Asian minority – about a tenth of the population – has been, however, economically far more successful. Its contribution has been indispensable to the hi-tech industries in Silicon Valley and elsewhere. Relatively few African Americans, however, came after the war-time rush to defence industries – hardly surprising given the way that those who remained after the Pacific War fared in places like Watts.

With the rate of population growth notably higher on the west coast of the US and Canada – and a lower average age – one is left asking why this part of the world is so attractive. There is for one thing a climate of success. The big names in west-coast history are those of entrepreneurs: in addition to those mentioned in this book – Donald Douglas and Robert Boeing in aircraft, Steven Jobs and Bill Gates in computing – there are many others, such as the Hearsts in newspapers or the Gettys in oil, to say nothing of all the Hollywood moguls.

Those in government on the other hand had their hands tied, often as a result of constitutional and legal provisions directed precisely to this end. The result is politics based on personalities rather than programmes, so that movie-stars, like Ronald Reagan and Arnold Schwarzenegger, do well – at least as long as they recognize who are their most powerful backers. The public at large must be content with the power to vote, *ad hoc*, for popular initiatives such as those that reduce property taxes or curb immigrant rights to welfare payments.

Nature also counts for much, as can be seen by the way that the whole North American west coast attracts visitors – ready, it seems, to accept the risk of volcanic eruptions, earthquakes, forest fires, floods and other natural disasters – to say nothing of man-made trials such as smog, highway congestion and power-cuts. At least in popular perception the balance is still in favour of the good life, even though for many – such as Native Americans, right down the coast, and African Americans in Los Angeles – it is far out of reach.

This chapter now turns, on one side, to Alaska and Hawaii, which have been states of the union since 1959, and on the other, to the Panama Canal Zone, where the US surrendered its treaty rights to the independent state of Panama in 1999. All played a significant part in Asia-Pacific history in the years following the end of the Pacific War.

ALASKA

Alaska – organized as a US overseas territory in 1912 – came into its own in the Pacific War, during which it actually lost territory, in the form of two remote and very small islands, Attu and Kiska, to Japanese forces – an attribute shared with no other of the present fifty states of the union. With the end of the war, the political climate in the US was favourable to the claims made by Alaska's residents for their territory to become a state of the union. As had happened in the past with the admission of new states, there were concerns in the US Congress about changes in the balance of power, which explains why Alaska had to wait until 3 January 1959 to join the US as the 49th state.

As a state of the union Alaska is in every way exceptional, perhaps even more so than Hawaii, which became the fiftieth state later in the same year. With nearly one-sixth of the total area of the US, but with just over 0.2 per cent of the population, Alaska has, by a very wide margin, the lowest population density. The vast inland area, although rich in natural resources and spectacular scenery,[5] is virtually unpopulated. Almost all residents of Alaska live along its coasts, which comprise a shoreline with twice the length of that of all other states combined. Anchorage, whose international airport is familiar to many globe-trotters, is the only city with more than 100,000 inhabitants, and nearly half the state population of some 600,000 live there or in the surrounding urban area.

The Alaskan coastline extends along three large distinct marine ecosystems, those of the Gulf of Alaska, the Eastern Bering Sea, and the Arctic Ocean. This means, effectively, that the northern Pacific Ocean is enclosed between Russia and the United States – a matter of great strategic importance during the Cold War. Alaska's economy is inevitably tied to the sea: while its commercial fisheries produce roughly half the seafood landed in the US, giant tankers and LNG carriers transport the vast quantities of oil and natural gas produced by the state. Cruise ships help support a flourishing tourist industry. There are considerable mineral resources, as witness the gold bonanza at the turn of the twentieth century immortalized by Charlie Chaplin in *The Gold Rush*. Because the exploitation of natural resources, which is the mainstay of the state economy, is almost entirely directed to the US internal market, Alaska, as seen from the other Asia-Pacific countries, always had a low profile. Even so, it is well placed to supply oil and LNG to East Asia, if there is ever a surplus after meeting the demands of the US. Japan, in particular, promises to become a good market for Alaskan LNG, but even so this must always take second place to the transmission of Alaska's natural gas by pipeline to the American market.

The history, then, of Alaska, is simply that of the systemic exploitation of its natural resources, a process in which the state much prefers to go its own way, without interference from Washington. The lesson had been learnt the hard way before the grant of statehood in 1959. Since then, state policy has been crowned by success, with a consistent budget surplus available to be shared out among its residents. The biggest disaster occurred on 24 March 1989 when a giant tanker, *Exxon Valdez*, 300 metres long and carrying more than a million barrels of crude oil, grounded on a reef in Prince William Sound shortly after midnight. So began one of the biggest environmental disasters in American history.

This occurred only because the ship, with a drunk captain, had deviated from authorized shipping lanes, and the investigations that followed sought to explain in detail why this happened – with the tanker owners, the Exxon Shipping Company, doing everything possible to limit their liability for the extensive damage caused by spilt oil along the coast of the Gulf of Alaska. In the event Exxon was fined $150 million for environmental crime, of which $125 million was forgiven because of its cooperation in the clean-up operation. An additional $100 million was agreed for damage to fish, wildlife and public lands. Beyond all this a civil settlement of $900 million, in ten annual instalments, was agreed with the state government, with the final payment being made in 2001, but individual claims are still before the courts. Many fish and wildlife species injured by the spill have yet to recover, and not all the oil has been cleared. Sport-fishing and tourism have, however, largely recovered, although some residents of Prince William Sound are still concerned about oil residues. Any number of new regulations and procedures for shipping in Prince William Sound were introduced as a result of the *Exxon Valdez* disaster, so that it is almost impossible that anything like it will occur again – at least in that part of the world. There is also an extensive bibliography relating to the whole sad history. Even so, all this did no more than close the stable door after the horse had bolted.

HAWAII

Although the Hawaiian Islands were first discovered by British Captain Cook in 1778, it was clear from early in the nineteenth century that both strategically and economically they were much more important for America than for Britain. From 1810 until 1893 Hawaii was an independent kingdom, but long before the latter date native Hawaiians had become a minority in their own homeland. Americans had not only invested heavily in sugar and pineapple plantations, for which the islands were well suited, but had also recruited foreign labour to work on them. The fact that many immigrant labourers were Japanese provided every reason for Japan to be concerned about the welfare of its citizens.

Pearl Harbor, on the island of Oahu close to Honolulu, the capital city, was, after the end of the American Civil War in 1865, an obvious strategic prize for the US Navy. In 1887 a treaty granted the US the exclusive use of this fine natural harbour. On the Hawaiian side this was the result of the new *Reform Party* (which had not a single native Hawaiian member) forcing the hand of King Kalakaua. For Hawaii this was an ominous sign that the days of their independent kingdom were numbered, and in 1893, with the forced abdication of Queen Lili'uokalani, the kingdom became a republic, with an American, Sanford P. Dole – a name that irresistibly recalls President Rufus T. Firefly in the Marx Brothers' *Duck Soup* – as its first and, as events proved, only president.

Many Americans took this to be the first step on the road to full annexation, but until 1897, this lacked the crucial support of the Democratic President, Grover Cleveland. With the election of a Republican President, William McKinley, in 1896, the political climate changed, but annexation had to await the settlement of a dispute with Japan, arising out of the Hawaiian republic's refusal to admit a thousand Japanese 'free labourers'. In early July 1898, Japan, which had stationed two warships off Oahu, was finally bought off for $75,000. On 6 July a joint resolution of both Houses of the US Congress provided for annexation, and the next day, President McKinley, with his Puritan conscience much troubled, signed it into law. In 1900 Hawaii was formally constituted as an overseas territory of the United States.

The history of Hawaii in the first half of the twentieth century was tied, at every stage, to the process by which, in 1959, it became the fiftieth state of the Union. The period of fifty-nine years between annexation and statehood was one of radical transformation: the main impulse was the Pacific War – which, with the Japanese attack on Pearl Harbor on 7 December 1941, started in Hawaii. The process had many dimensions, economic, demographic, strategic and, above all, political.

The annexation of Hawaii in 1900 was followed almost inevitably from the demands of the local American minority that dominated the plantation economy for political control of the islands, supported by Washington's concern for their strategic importance – particularly after the acquisition of Pearl Harbor in 1887. This was also about the last year in which native Hawaiians still constituted a majority of the population, which was then well under 100,000. By 1900, when the total population had risen above 150,000, they were less than 25 per cent, but the American population, numbering about 10,000, was barely 7 per cent: the greater part of the white population – known in Hawaii as 'haole' – then consisted of recent immigrants from Portugal, recruited for low-level management posts on the plantations. More than half the population consisted of ethnic Chinese and Japanese, who provided the backbone of the agricultural labour force. In 1900 they were hardly a political force to be reckoned with.

Following annexation Hawaii was overseen by a governor appointed by Washington, supported by a territorial legislature. Although in 1901 this was dominated by native Hawaiians, a variety of measures restricting the franchise, coupled with adverse demographic factors, soon ensured that the *haoles* were in control. The legislature was dominated by conservative Republicans, whose unashamed policy was to run the islands in the way that best suited American economic and strategic interests. Even though ethnic minorities counted for little, the territorial government did everything possible to reduce the threat they represented. Supported by Washington new restrictions were imposed on immigrants from China and Japan, to the point that in 1924 the door was completely closed to them.[6] The loss of potential labour was made good by granting privileged entry to Filipinos, who, by 1959, constituted more than 10 per cent of the population.

From a very early stage there were plans to admit Hawaii as a state of the Union: the first petition to the US Congress was made in 1903. It had little chance of success. The problem was simple: any constitution for the new state that satisfied the US constitutional provisions for universal franchise was certain drastically to reduce the entrenched powers of *haole* voters. The political weight of conservative southern Democrats in the US Senate at the beginning of the twentieth century made approval of any such constitution almost inconceivable – the more so given the predominance of officers from southern states in the US armed forces, which already had a strong presence in Hawaii. The result, at least until the beginning of the Pacific War in 1941, was that Hawaii had a colonial-style government, but then, with the coming war, the whole territory was overtaken by events in a way that neither local *haole* Republicans nor white southern Democrats could withstand.

With the overall population three times as great as in 1900, the *haole* population had increased disproportionately, to constitute nearly a quarter of all residents, while native Hawaiians were only about a sixth. The difference was made up by ethnic Asians, particularly Japanese, who were approaching 40 per cent of the population. By this point also, they were no longer just plantation workers, with few economic or social rights, but also tradesmen and craftsmen active and often remarkably prosperous in the local micro-economy – and at the same time ready to enter politics.

With the coming of the war there were inevitably doubts about Japanese allegiance, just as there were on the mainland. Even so there was little question of mass internment. Not only would this have been unworkable for some 40 per cent of the population, but given the strategic importance of Hawaii in the frontline Japanese labour was indispensable to the war-economy. What is more, thousands of Hawaiian Japanese enlisted in the US armed forces and served, in many different theatres, with exceptional distinction. By 1945 there was no longer any doubt about their standing as US citizens, and they returned home as heroes, to a booming economy, enjoying at the same time a claim to higher education as provided for by the *GI Bill of Rights*.[7] The status of civilian Japanese was enhanced in step with that of the returning servicemen. What was true of the Japanese held equally for all other ethnic groups, such as the Chinese, Koreans and Filipinos, who never suffered the taint of collaborating with the enemy. Even so the Japanese were in the ethnic vanguard, with such leaders as Daniel Inouye, who after losing an arm fighting the Germans in Italy embarked on a political career that led him to serve as a US Senator for nearly fifty years. Given the dominant role of the local Republican Party in the territorial government, Japanese Hawaiians adopted the Democratic Party as the vehicle for their political agenda.

This proved to be something of a handicap during the 1950s when it was clear that the grant of statehood could not long be postponed. In the old-style party in Hawaii trade unions, particularly that of the longshoremen,[8] were strongly represented, while at the same time communist links – fatal in the American political climate of the 1950s – were alleged. Finally, in 1959, Hawaii was admitted as the fiftieth state, but only after the US Congress had left it with a state constitution containing any number of safeguards against communist influences. At the end of the day this made little difference, since it was the Japanese and not the longshoremen who took over in Hawaiian politics: to this day the Democratic Party is as strong in Hawaii as in almost any other state.

The political transformation of Hawaii, leading up to and beyond statehood, had a significant cultural dimension. English took over as the dominant language among all ethnic groups, particularly that of the Japanese. At the same time intermarriage, generally with *haoles*, has led to a considerable population of mixed ethnic background. This is even more the case with native Hawaiians, so that those of pure Hawaiian descent now number less than 10,000, while those of mixed descent are 20 or 30 times that number. One result is that the Hawaiian language has almost died out, although projects led by the state university are having some success in reviving it. In the melting pot of Hawaii ethnic groups from the Islamic world are the smallest component, although there is a mosque in Honolulu. Overall, the great civilizations of East Asia, China, Japan and Korea enjoy the highest profile in contemporary Hawaii.[9]

The first fifteen years of statehood were a time of exceptional economic growth, which only slowed down in the late 1970s, largely as a result of the world oil crisis. In the 1960s, the introduction of wide-bodied jet passenger aircraft, accompanied by cheap-fare offers, made Hawaii accessible to millions, particularly after Japanese citizens were no longer subject to foreign-currency restrictions. The result is that tourism is the prime growth factor in the Hawaiian economy, the more so since the islands are a popular destination for visitors from such prosperous countries as Australia, Singapore, Thailand, China, Korea and Japan, to say nothing of the continental US.

Defence is also critical to the Hawaiian economy: Pearl Harbor continues to be the main Pacific naval base, while, at the same time, both the army and air-force of the US maintain a considerable presence for obvious strategic reasons. If the Soviet threat is no more a factor, the US withdrawal – whether in whole or in part – from bases closer to or even on the Asian mainland, in the Philippines, Japan and Korea, has enhanced the importance of Hawaii. Next to some 50,000 uniformed personnel – a large number in a state with barely a million inhabitants – there are as many local residents employed in defence-related occupations.

All in all Hawaii was one of the great winners in the Pacific of the twentieth century, and continues to be so. In almost every possible respect it has stayed ahead of the game. The location of the islands counts for almost everything, as it has since they were first discovered by Captain Cook in 1776. This, however, is what brought the US Navy to Pearl Harbor in 1878, and led the Japanese Navy to attack it in 1941 – putting Hawaii at the centre of the most destructive war in world history. Even so, the accessibility of Hawaii, from almost any direction, coupled with an exceptionally benign climate and remarkable ethnic harmony, outweighs the trauma of 7 December 1941 by a very large margin. Paradoxically, after that dreadful day Hawaii had no further experience of direct enemy action: any unrest since then has been generated by purely local stresses.

PANAMA: CANAL POLITICS

The history of Panama and its canal in the twentieth century exemplifies almost every aspect of American imperialism. At the turn of the century the isthmus of Panama – which was then part of Colombia – had been for nearly 400 years the shortest route from the Atlantic to the Pacific ocean. Following the invention of the steamship at the beginning of the nineteenth century the course of navigation at sea was no longer determined by currents and prevailing winds, while boats could pass along inland waterways under their own power. At the same time, the powerful machinery developed in the course of the industrial revolution – which by the end of the century could be driven by electricity – allowed for the construction of canals, with power-driven lock-gates, on a scale never before possible. Here, a canal across the isthmus of Panama was the ultimate challenge.

When, following victory in the Spanish-American War, President McKinley's administration turned to the construction of this canal, Panama itself was a province of Colombia. In a political show-down, orchestrated by Washington, it became an independent state, but one tied to granting the United States all rights relating to the construction and operation of the prospective canal. By a treaty that came into force on 26 February 1904 the United States was granted tenure of the canal in perpetuity, together with the exclusive right to commercial development and jurisdiction over a ten-mile-wide zone straddling the canal and the two cities at either end of it; in exchange Panama would be paid an immediate $10,000,000 and an annual payment of $250,000.

The construction plan was simple: at Gatún, on the Atlantic side of Panama, three gigantic locks would be built to rise above the Rio Chagres close to the point where it reached the sea. The new Gatún Lake, which would then be created behind the locks, would extend almost to the Pacific. The way to the Pacific side would be through the single Pedro Miguel lock and the double Miraflores lock. On both sides of the isthmus special waterways would then be dug to connect the locks to the sea. The result of all this would then be that for ships passing through the canal the greater part of their transit would be across the Gatún Lake, reached on both sides through three locks. The canal was finally open to traffic just two weeks after the beginning of World War I. The United States was always obsessive in its defence of its rights both to the canal and to the Canal Zone. It was administered as an 'unorganized' territory, to be ruled by a governor from the US Navy, enjoying the authority of a naval command. Federal laws and the fundamental provisions of the US Constitution (including the Bill of Rights) did not apply to it.[10]

Before World War II Washington regarded the Panama Canal as essential for transferring the warships of the United States and its allies between the Atlantic and Pacific Oceans, while denying this possibility to their enemies. Seen in this light the Panama Canal was a keystone in the arch of American security.[11] In principle Panama's position vis-à-vis the United States had been changed by treaty in 1936, whereby Washington – in accordance with President Roosevelt's 'Good Neighbor Policy' – renounced the formal American protectorate, but in practice the United States retained, indeed strengthened its hold over the Canal Zone.

At the beginning of the Pacific War the canal was considered to be so important that a number of plans were made to both extend its capacity and make it less vulnerable to enemy attack. One major factor was that warships already on the drawing-board would simply be too large to pass through. In the course of time this led to any number of proposals for the construction of a new sea-level canal. All such ideas were totally misconceived. The Americans had already decided, in 1940, to work with a two-ocean navy, which meant that fewer warships would need to pass between the Atlantic and the Pacific. As for the need to strengthen the canal defences, Germany, following its invasion of Russia in the summer of 1941, was no longer a threat, and nor was Japan, following the American victory at the naval battle of Midway a year later. Even so the US maintained a very tight hold on the canal throughout the war, which, even after its end in 1945, it showed little interest in relaxing. With the coming of peace, however, the political line-up in Panama – unstable though it was – made certain that the US would be forced to renegotiate its rights to the canal

The defeat of Japan in 1945 led many to see the canal in a new perspective. In the view of Admiral Daniel Gallery USN, as expressed in 1947,[12] it was not essential to American national security, so that its strategic importance was founded mainly on its economic value to American commercial shipping. Although by 1949 this was also the view of the Joint Chiefs of Staff, the security of the Canal was jealously guarded, and the main task of the American Ambassador in Panama was still to ensure that local politics did not get out of hand in a way threatening to American interests.

Following the intensive use of the canal during World War II, coupled with a vast increase in the number of American residents with money to spend, Panama ended up in 1945 with a vast budget surplus. This did not, however, reconcile its citizens to the status quo. When, therefore, in 1947, an agreement relating to the defence of the American bases in Panama was proposed by the United States, the Panamanian foreign secretary, speaking at the United Nations on 21 November, announced that his country would protest if the American bases were not promptly evacuated.[13] On 22 December, the Panamanian National Assembly voted unanimously to reject the proposed new treaty. Washington was furious, but even so it was becoming clear that the financial importance of the bases to Panama was greater than their military importance to the United States.

A presidential election held in 1948 found the republic's politics in turmoil, largely because Domingo Diaz, the candidate supported by the American Ambassador, Frank Hines, had practically no popular support. He was, nonetheless, in Hines' words, 'successfully railroaded ... into office', although on the day of his inauguration, 1 October 1948, he only just survived a bomb attack orchestrated by the opposition. This was led by Arnulfo Arias, who had returned to Panama from wartime exile in Argentina. A year later, after Diaz had died in office, he had the satisfaction of seeing the Electoral Jury that had confirmed the election of Diaz reverse its decision and pronounce him as president.

Arias, although only reluctantly recognized by Washington, lost little time in asking for American support for the construction of the Panamanian section of the new Inter-American Highway. He also requested a $30,000,000 loan from the Export-Import Bank – contemplating that repayment would later be waived 'as a friendly act to Panama'.[14] In the changed post-war climate, characterized by Marshall Aid to Europe and President Truman's Point Four Plan, Panama got much of what it was asking for: the American Ambassador supported a 'constructive program' to combat both Panamanian nationalism and 'Communist-influenced subversive elements'.[15] Whatever the justification for American support it was in fact sound policy: Panama still suffered from excessive dependence on the canal, and the new road network would encourage the development of the rest of the country.

Although with the Korean War, 1950–53, the canal was important for supplying the UN forces, Washington, in contrast to its stance during World War II, saw no need to militarize the Canal Zone – a view not necessarily shared by the Congress. President Arias was required, however, to ban ships registered in Panama – of which there were nearly a thousand – from trading, even indirectly, with communist China or North Korea.

The American hold over the canal was significantly reduced by a new treaty agreed in January 1955 between the United States and Panama. Although Washington did not abandon its fundamental position, the new treaty reflected the decline in the canal's strategic importance. In the words of a leading authority,

> Marginalized by the two-ocean Navy, dwarfed by the super-carrier, and defenseless against a nuclear strike, the waterway had become no more than a monument to the era when Washington first stepped decisively on to the international stage ... with the onset of the cold war, and the break-up of Europe's overseas empires, American preoccupations were nothing short of global and immensely more demanding than the effort to reconcile the competing claims of Atlantic and Pacific through the medium of Panama. The canal remained an impressive emblem of American power, but it would never again be its mainstay.[16]

The twentieth century ended with the transfer of all American interests in the canal to Panama. The process leading up to this was long drawn out. Essentially sentiment in Washington was always opposed to the surrender of all that had been so carefully constructed in the first half of the century. Colonel Nasser's expropriation of the Suez Canal in July 1956 was a set-back to Panama, which President Eisenhower accused of having 'connived with Nasser'. Even so the president was more liberal than the Congress, which saw concessions proposed by the White House – such as allowing the Panamanian flag to fly in certain specified locations in the Canal Zone – as 'the beginning of the end of exclusive US control over the Panama Canal'.[17] Washington was also concerned that Fidel Castro's success in Cuba would excite unrest in Panama.

In the early 1960s Washington once again contemplated the construction of a new sea-level canal, to be excavated by nuclear explosions – an idea favoured by Edward Teller, the 'father of the hydrogen bomb' – and completed by 1980. Given the declining strategic importance of the existing canal the whole line of thought was completely irrational. At all events, the acceptance by the United States, on 23 July 1963, of the Limited Test-Ban Treaty then made it impossible for the Atomic Energy Commission to develop 'cratering' technology to the point where it would be both safe and cost-effective.

Washington's failure to make any substantial concessions was met by increasing unrest in Panama, where the under-privileged masses of the cities at either end of the canal lived next door to the affluent American community in the Canal

Zone. In January 1964 riots in the two cities left twenty-two dead, including three Americans. Once peace was restored, President Lyndon Johnson sent a special representative, Robert Anderson, to report on the situation in Panama. In face of the official view, Anderson advised that the American sovereign rights in the Canal Zone, granted in perpetuity by the 1903 Treaty, would have to go.

Anderson accordingly worked on a set of three new treaties, at the time taking into account, as realistically as possible, objections likely to be made by Congress. Three new treaties, supplanting the 1903 convention, together with treaties agreed in 1936 and 1955, were initialled in July 1967, and in support of them former President Dwight Eisenhower cited, paradoxically, some wise words of Theodore Roosevelt:

> No treaties, whether between civilized nations or not, can ever be regarded as binding in perpetuity; with changing conditions, circumstances may arise which render it not only expedient, but imperative and honorable, to abrogate them.

The circumstances may have been right, but the 1967 treaties were rejected both by President Richard Nixon (who succeeded Johnson in the White House in 1969) and by a new president of Panama, Omar Torrijos, in 1970. Then, in 1973, Torrijos succeeded in upstaging Nixon in a way that placed Panama's case in a world forum. In March 1973 the UN Security Council met in Panama City, and a resolution was presented demanding 'a just and fair [treaty] to fulfill Panama's legitimate aspirations and guarantee Panama's effective sovereignty over all of its territory'.[18]

Although the United States predictably vetoed the resolution, Nixon did read the writing on the wall. The result was a new agreement, signed in 1974 by Secretary of State Henry Kissinger. Significantly there was no mention of a new sea-level canal – a big setback to the Pentagon. Otherwise the terms were much the same as in the agreements rejected in 1967. Once again the treaty was killed by Congress, and it did not help that Ronald Reagan, who was contending for nomination as Republican presidential candidate in 1976, was vehemently opposed to it. Also contending for the nomination, the incumbent president, Gerald Ford – Nixon's successor – wisely kept a low profile on this issue. He got the nomination, but lost the presidency.

The new Democratic president, Jimmy Carter, although reluctant to grasp the nettle, was persuaded, by both his Secretary of State Cyrus Vance, and his National Security Adviser Zbigniew Brzezinski, not to let the treaty go. With Torrijos still in office in Panama, there was a real threat of violence directed against Americans, for as Torrijos himself had said, 'the only thing I have against Christ is that he died without fighting',[19] to which one senior American officer responded by noting, 'the last thing in the world we want now is to be ordered to start shooting into a crowd of Panamanians'.[20]

New negotiations, which began on 15 February 1977, provided for two treaties, one to guarantee the neutrality of the canal into the indefinite future, and the other to provide for the eventual transfer of the Canal Zone, and its defence, to Panama. The final and complete transfer was set for 31 December 1999, but after a brief transition period following ratification of the treaty large tracts of the Canal Zone would be transferred without waiting until 1999, and American civilians become subject to Panamanian law. A commission, with five American and four Panamanian members, would run the canal in the interim period, 1979–99. At the same time the income that Panama would gain from the canal was increased to a level of some $53,000,000 a year[21]: for the first time this included a share in the transit tolls paid by shipping, long demanded by Panama, but never granted.

After a number of concessions made to secure the votes of one or two recalcitrant senators, on 16 March 1979 the neutrality treaty gained the necessary two-thirds majority in the US Senate, with one vote to spare. The Canal Zone treaty passed with the same margin on 18 April. Torrijos reacted by commenting in a media interview[22] that 'today the canal was placed within two votes of being destroyed', and as he told his friend, the novelist, Graham Greene (who later wrote a book about him), 'Blow a hole in the Gatún Dam and the Canal will drain into the Atlantic. It would take only a few days to mend the dam, but it would take three years of rain to fill the Canal'.

The battle in Congress was not quite over, since implementing the legislation required the support of the House of Representatives. In the end only one wrecking amendment[23] was accepted by the House; this provided for the suspension of payments to Panama due under the treaty if Panama was 'interfering with the internal affairs of any other state'. It was a reaction to reports that Torrijos was supporting the Sandinista rebels in Nicaragua. Since, even without his help, the Sandinistas were victorious, the amendment effectively became a dead letter, as Torrijos had correctly foreseen.

With the treaties taking effect on 1 October 1979, the Canal Zone, after 76 years, ceased to exist, to the great sorrow of many Americans. The last word was had by one of those resident in the Canal Zone: 'the past is dead, Teddy Roosevelt is in the ground'.[24] The future, however, is bright for Panama: in October 2006, the people, in a special referendum, voted to widen the canal sufficiently to allow the world's largest vessels – such as the giant oil-tankers and container-ships[25] – to pass through it. The project is expected to generate 40,000 new construction jobs, and when completed will bring a fourfold increase – from $1.6 billion to $6 billion – in the revenue earned from tolls. Where the necessary capital – estimated at $10 billion – will come from is a question yet to be answered. President Martin Torrijos is not worried: after all, it was under the presidency of his father, Omar Torrijos, that his country retrieved the canal from the Americans.

17

Australia

MENZIES' AUSTRALIA

From its experiences in the Pacific War Australia (see map on page viii) learnt that it was well-placed to adopt a much higher profile, internationally, than ever had been contemplated in pre-war days. Just before the end of the war, its foreign minister Herbert Evatt led a strong Australian delegation at the San Francisco conference convened to establish the United Nations Organization. This was held in the early summer of 1945, with the British Dominions being admitted as independent states. Evatt as a member the committee that produced the final draft of the UN Charter, succeeded in strengthening the powers of the General Assembly at the cost of the Security Council. Committed to the preservation of White Australia Evatt also insisted on an amendment banning the UN 'from forcible intervening in any matter considered to be essentially within the jurisdiction of a sovereign state'[1] – a provision which, in the following sixty years, left the door open for human rights abuses in many different parts of the world. Evatt's concern was the same as that of Billy Hughes, who represented Australia at Versailles in 1919 – the preservation of white Australia.

In 1948 Australia went on to play a key role in ending Dutch colonialism in Indonesia, an issue in which, at that time, neither Britain nor the US wished to be involved.[2] In an international conference convened by India 'Ways and Means of dealing with the Indonesia issue', Evatt instructed the Australian delegates to support the republican cause. This led to Australia becoming a member of a UN committee which recommended 'a speedy transfer of sovereignty in the Dutch East Indies to a United States of Indonesia' – a result finally achieved on 27 November 1949.

This was the end of Evatt's appearance on the world stage, for in December 1949 the Labour government, of which he was a member, was defeated in Parliament. This was the result of a series of unpopular measures, but by this time also, Robert Menzies, who had largely failed as prime minister in the first two years of World War II, had got his act together. The *United Australia Party* (UAP), which had brought him to office in 1939, reflected the fact that each

Australian state had preserved its own distinctive political line-up – a legacy from the days before federation. At national level almost every UAP politician had a dual loyalty, first to his state and only second to the nation at large. Many a politician who was strong in his own state made no impact at national level. During his eight years (1941–49) in the wilderness, Robert Menzies succeeded in overcoming this limitation. His successful strategy was to persuade various state parties, opposed to Labour, to unite in a new federal Liberal Party, insisting that 'Election policy must be propounded by the Federal Leader in consultation with his Parliamentary colleagues'.[3] This was a winning formula: Robert Menzies was to remain in office for seventeen years – although this was only made possible by a Liberal–Country Party coalition, an essential combination in Australia for any conservative government.

Menzies, in opposition, had promised a Bill declaring the Communist Party 'unconstitutional and illegal' – a popular measure, which once enacted, was declared unconstitutional by the High Court. Nonetheless, it divided the Labour opposition – mainly along sectarian lines. Communism, in any form, was anathema to the many Catholic MPs, as it was also to their spiritual leader, Cardinal Mannix of Melbourne.[4]

With the outbreak of the Korean War in June 1950, Menzies' stance on communism served him well. He immediately committed Australia to sending troops to Korea, where, together with those from Britain and New Zealand, they became part of the British Commonwealth Division. By this time the strategic importance of Australia, at last recognized in Washington, led to the *Australia, New Zealand and United States* (ANZUS) agreement of 1951, which meant, in effect, that the US assumed the defensive role that Britain had before World War II. To Menzies, as much as any Australian prime minister, a defensive alliance with the US was essential to the security of Australia – the more so given the emergence of new, independent states in Southeast Asia. As a price for ANZUS Menzies had to accept a 'soft' treaty for Japan, which had become an indispensable forward base in the Korean War – an unwelcome development to the many Australians who still saw Japan as *the* enemy. The Australian foreign minister, Percy Spender, did, however, insist on 'adequate assurances that Australia would be protected against Japanese aggression'.[5]

In April 1951 Menzies' position as prime minister was greatly strengthened when his coalition won a solid majority in a general election. The fifteen years under his leadership that then followed were the last of 'old world' Australia. Menzies himself was inordinately attached to British institutions, and to judge from the enthusiastic welcome given to Queen Elizabeth II in 1954 – the most successful of all royal visits to Australia – he had the country with him. Even so Australia still came first, as can be seen by the protectionist legislation introduced by his government.

At the same time as he was negotiating the ANZUS treaty Spender realized that Australia also had important interests in its own Asian backyard. In 1950 he produced the first draft of the Colombo Plan, which although at first a Commonwealth initiative, was later subscribed to by Japan and the US, and finally, in 1956, by Burma, Indonesia, Nepal, the Philippines, Thailand, Cambodia, Laos and South Vietnam. The underlying principle was the provision of the maximum possible aid to new democratic governments, in order to protect them against 'opportunist, disruptive and subversive elements'.[6] In addition there was a specific commitment to offer higher education to Asian students at a time when many were tempted to accept the free education offered by the Soviet Union. By the end of the 1950s this had brought thousands of young Asians to white Australia, where accommodating them meant that long-entrenched attitudes had to change.

The paramount issue in Asia was the status of communist China. While Britain's Labour government recognized Mao Zedong's regime in 1950, the US continued to support Jiang Jieshi, who with his Guomindang supporters, had retreated to the island of Taiwan. Menzies and Spender, fearing that China was ready to start World War III, sided with America.[7] There was soon a price to pay.

Following the treaty agreed in June 1954 for ending the war in Vietnam after the decisive defeat of the French Army at Dien Bien Phu in early May,[8] a second conference was convened in Manila in September, to agree the *Southeast Asia Collective Defense Treaty*. Since the main thrust of the *Southeast Asia Treaty Organization* (SEATO), set up to implement the treaty, was defence against communism, both India and Indonesia refused to join it. This left the US, Britain, France, Australia, New Zealand, the Philippines and Thailand, as the actual members. The result, for Australia, was unequivocal alignment with the US. As stated by a spokesman for the Department of External Affairs the consequences for Australia's international standing were quite categorical: 'We start our good neighbour policy with two handicaps: SEATO; which connotes intervention in the affairs of Asia and "provocation"; ANZUS: which connotes accord with US foreign policy in Asia towards Peking, Jiang Jieshi and the Geneva agreement'.[9]

Until the end of the 1950s relations with Japan were still problematic: Australians, more than any of their allies in the Pacific War, refused to forget the suffering inflicted upon many of their compatriots under the Japanese. Although Australia, bound to the US, could not escape the 1952 Peace Treaty, this did not end its legal restrictions on trade with Japan. Although, economically, they could only be counter-productive, they were tolerable so long as the volume of trade remained low, and with little prospect of growth. On the other hand, as the Japanese economy took off in the 1950s it had an almost insatiable demand for raw materials, for which Australia was an obvious source. When, in 1958, vast deposits of high-grade iron ore were discovered in the Pilbara hills of Western Australia – leading to the development of the biggest open-cast mine in the world – the Japanese market could hardly be ignored, particularly since Japan had become full member of GATT in 1956. There was, however, a problem. In 1938 the Nippon Mining Company had quite legally started mining ore on Koolan, an Australian offshore island in the Timor Sea.[10] Canberra, concerned, for strategic reasons, about a Japanese foothold in Australia, imposed an embargo on the export of iron ore, giving as its reasons, the needs of Australia's own manufacturing industry.

This was enough to freeze off the Japanese in 1938, but the ban continued even after World War II, when for many years it critically discouraged prospecting and investment in iron-mining. By the mid-1950s it was already clear that reserves far exceeded the demand by local industry, so that their exploitation could contribute substantially to Australia's export economy. The way was opened to trade with Japan by the Commerce Agreement of 1957, followed, in 1960, by the lifting of the export ban. Whatever feelings Australians may have had about Japan, they could not complain about the extremely favourable balance of trade, with exports including wool and grain as well as minerals and fossil fuels.

While the key to good relations with Japan was for Australia to forget its wounded pride, the problem posed by the new republic of Indonesia was much more complex – almost entirely as a result of ill-considered policies of President Sukarno relating to the new state of Malaysia, where Australian forces, already engaged in Borneo, were critical to the defence against Indonesian invasion. The problem was actually solved inside Indonesia, in 1965, when Suharto took over from Sukarno, to set Indonesia on a course much less threatening to the ANZUS powers. Australia could overlook the fact that the events that brought Suharto to power cost the lives of some half-million people: most, after all, were communist sympathizers, and many, Chinese. That this was not quite the end to what the Indonesians called 'konfrontasi' became clear when Australians, at the end of 1999, found themselves as peacekeepers in Timor Leste after its people had voted overwhelmingly for independence from Indonesia in a referendum supervised by the UN.[11]

Australia's double commitment to defence against communist aggression and close alliance with the US was put the test by the war in Vietnam. Early in 1964, as the political situation there deteriorated, the US President, Lyndon Johnson, made clear that America would 'expend every effort and mobilize every resource to get Vietnam strong enough to be independent and feared by any aggressor'. In each of eleven capital cities of countries recognized as American allies, the US ambassador was instructed to prepare an 'adequate program' for participation in the projected escalation of war in Vietnam. In Europe the ambassadors failed completely, but in Asia Thailand and South Korea both accepted programmes written by Washington. This was no more than self-interest: both countries derived very considerable economic and political advantages from supporting the US in Vietnam.

Australia, following the US response to the Gulf on Tonkin incident of August 1964, pledged its support with the broad agreement of all the major political parties. This related in part to the confrontation with Indonesia in Borneo, but, however that may be, a public announcement, in Menzies' name, declared that 'The takeover of South Vietnam would be a direct military threat to Australia and all the countries of South and Southeast Asia'. In fact the real threat to Australia was seen as coming from Communist China.

Following President Lyndon Johnson's decision, announced on 7 April 1965, to send US ground troops to fight alongside the South Vietnamese, Australia stood by his side. First one combat battalion, and then two more, were sent to Vietnam, where they came under American command. With some 8,000 Australian soldiers being out-numbered 50 to 1 by the US forces, their contribution's military value was small: even so, they won a significant two-day battle at Long Tan in August 1966.

CHANGE OF DIRECTION

By this time Menzies had finally retired as prime minister. John Holt, his successor – and a much less effective leader – did not hesitate to outdo Menzies when it came to the Chinese and their support of communism. He welcomed the fact that the new Indonesian leader, Suharto, had 'knocked off ... 500,000 to 1,000,000 communist sympathizers' – many of whom were Chinese. China, in Holt's view, was 'implacably committed to its goal of a communist-dominated world', while Australians were fighting for 'free peoples everywhere'.[12] On the other hand, in 1966 Holt's Liberal government radically revised Australia's immigration laws, so that for the first time in the history of the Commonwealth immigration was possible, and to a degree even encouraged, from outside Europe. In the 1970s the success of the communist steam-roller in Vietnam and Cambodia meant that many of Australia's new immigrants came as refugees from those two countries.

Australia's Vietnam policy reflected the declining power of Britain in the Far East, as shown by Prime Minister Harold Wilson's decision, in 1967, to withdraw all forces east of Suez, leaving only the US to defend the Pacific. Support for the US in Vietnam was part of a policy designed to ensure that Australia would be a key part of American Pacific strategy. Although Lyndon Johnson visited Australia in October 1966, and found that it had many of the virtues of Texas, but on an even larger scale,[13] Australia was – over the long term – poorly rewarded for its support of the US, as it still is. As for Vietnam, Australia, while sharing in the humiliation of the American defeat of 1975, suffered proportionately fewer losses of men and material.

In the seven years following Menzies' retirement (1966–72), Holt was the first of three inadequate Liberal prime ministers: the last of them, William McMahon, was caught on the wrong foot by a radical change in US foreign policy. Following secret negotiations carried out by Henry Kissinger in Beijing, President Richard Nixon achieved a radical change in US policy towards China, which became known world-wide in February 1973. Recognition of the People's Republic in place of the Jiang Jieshi's regime in Taiwan would then follow: its position, internationally, as a member of the UN Security Council, would be transformed, as Nixon and Kissinger had foreseen. The opening came as a result of a stand-off between China and the Soviet Union, which from early 1969 had led to armed clashes between their armed forces along the Ussuri River – part of their common frontier. These, as reported by US intelligence, led Kissinger to conclude 'that the Soviet Union and China were more afraid of each other than they were of the United States'[14] so that, effectively, the US had little to fear from the two acting together on the international stage.

In Australia, Gough Whitlam, leader of the opposition Labour Party – perhaps because he had seen the way the wind was blowing – arranged a meeting with the Chinese prime minister, Zhou Enlai, to 'discuss terms on which your country is interested in having trade and diplomatic relations with Australia'.[15] McMahon presented this as a betrayal of Australia, with 'Chou [playing] Whitlam as a fisherman plays a trout'. Three days after making this comment, McMahon learnt – to his humiliation – of Kissinger's secret negotiations in Beijing: Australia had been betrayed not by Whitlam, but by its closest ally. Its government's Chinese policy was untenable. A general election held in December 1972 was won by Whitlam, who became the first Labour Party prime minister in 23 years.

Whitlam moved fast in carrying out his Asia policy. His government ended conscription, withdrawing all Australian troops from Vietnam, and went on to recognize the People's Republic of China. An amendment to the immigration law ruled out discrimination on the grounds of race, colour or nationality: after Holt had taken the first step in 1966, even the opposition had come to appreciate the low costs of skilled Asian labour. For all his energy, Whitlam came to office at an inauspicious time. His first year was that of the international oil crisis, following the Yom Kippur War of 1973 between Israel and its Arab neighbours. The result, for Australia as for much of the rest of the world, was financial chaos – with inflation at 17 per cent[16] – exacerbated by a whole chain of corruption and scandal, particularly in New South Wales.

All this led to the Whitlam government coming to an end in a way that is still bitterly contested in Australia. In both 1974 and 1975 the Senate, flouting convention but justified by the letter of the law, refused to pass the supply bills sent to it by the House of Representatives. The resulting deadlock blocked the government's power to raise funds to carry on its business. In 1975, Sir John Kerr, recently appointed governor-general – after being nominated by Whitlam – used a power reserved to him by the constitution to dismiss the government, at the same asking Malcolm Fraser, Liberal leader of the opposition coalition, to form a new one. The many who were outraged by this turn of events put forward all kinds of conspiracy theory to explain it, but Whitlam's government, at a time of crisis, was both corrupt and incompetent. This was also the view of the electorate: Fraser's coalition, having called an election, decisively defeated Labour.

THE PNG DILEMMA

During the political turbulence of the 1970s successive Australian governments had to contend not only with the international oil crisis – which was its principal cause – but also with two other critical problems arising outside the country. The first of these concerned the future of Papua-New Guinea (PNG) – that half of the island of New Guinea governed from Canberra as a 'territory'. The origins of the crisis went back to the 1960s when PNG was granted a Legislative Council following a critical UN report. In 1966 the council asked whether it could become a new state of the Commonwealth of Australia, following the principle already agreed for the future of the Northern Territories. The prospect of incorporating some two million new non-white citizens, most of whom belonged to remote tribes only recently in contact with modern civilization, horrified Canberra. Although in the context of Australian politics it was an absolute non-starter, the problem of PNG's future would not go away.

Canberra first responded to the PNG request by establishing a limited form of representative government, and in 1971 the Liberal prime minister William McMahon announced a five-year plan for internal self-government. On 1 December 1973 the impetuous new Labour prime minister, Gough Whitlam announced that PNG would become self-governing within three years: less than two years were needed and on 6 September 1975 it became an independent nation.

This development, although welcomed by almost every politician in Canberra – if only because it resolved the citizenship problem – led almost immediately to chaos in PNG. Its capital, Port Moresby, was notoriously a violent and disturbed community. The most serious crisis occurred not in the island of New Guinea, but in Bougainville, an island off the north coast, which had become part of PNG following dismemberment of the German Pacific colonies after World War I. If the accident of history had made Port Moresby responsible for Bougainville the local populations hardly related to each other.

Bougainville was critically important to the PNG economy because it was the site of a vast copper-mine,[17] which, although earning millions of dollars in revenue, devastated much of the island. It was little consolation to its inhabitants that the mining company – an Australian subsidiary of the London-based Rio Tinto Zinc – had provided new housing, hospitals, schools and roads, to say nothing of the chance of paid employment. Although, in 1974, the PNG government negotiated an increased share of the mining revenue for public funds, this was poor compensation for Bougainville. Local landowners, who had lost out to the mining company, reacted with such violence that the whole island was drawn into civil war, leading finally to the closure of the mine in 1989.[18] Port Moresby was powerless to control events, and Australians who had comfortably assumed that the grant of independence had 'wiped the slate clean, making PNG just another underdeveloped country'[19] were bitterly disillusioned. It took more than twenty years to settle the civil war, and even then this was the result of intervention by New Zealand – a country with a far better record of dealing fairly with indigenous local populations.

EUROPEAN CONFRONTATION

The second problem facing Australia in the 1970s – and afterwards – was coming to terms with British membership of the EEC. This had long been foreshadowed, but during the 1960s was blocked by President de Gaulle of France. For Australia the main consequence of Britain's membership – which had finally become definite as the result of a referendum held in 1975 – was the loss of imperial preference for its agricultural exports. Worse still, the agricultural regime of the EEC allowed for exports to be subsidized out of the common fund. Before joining the EEC Britain tried hard, but without success, to win concessions for Australia – although some were made for New Zealand. Later, in the 1980s, the position of both countries became even more difficult as a result of Washington's decision to counter the EEC subsidies with its own Export Enhancement Program.[20]

Except for Gough Whitlam's ill-fated Labour administration (1972–75) the Liberal-led coalition remained in office until 1983, with, for its last eight years, a much more effective leader, Malcolm Fraser. Long before it lost office – largely as a result of failure to cure the economic problems inherited from the 1970s – it was clear that Australia must develop a distinctive and independent role in the community of nations, recognizing that its remaining ties with Britain were based mainly on sentiment. The problem was acute for an economy based on the export of raw materials, with at the same time a weak manufacturing sector, made uncompetitive by high labour costs. When Labour returned to power in 1983, effective government was not helped by the ambitious and dynamic Paul Keating's challenge to its leader, Bob Hawke, from within the party. After eight years of acrimonious infighting, Keating finally succeeded Hawke as prime minister in 1991. Although this was a time of rising unemployment and increasing trade deficits, Keating's unmistakable personal mandate enabled him to remain in office until 1996. He was greatly helped by the indecisiveness of the opposition coalition, whose leaders were almost equally prone to bitter infighting.

THE HARD LINE AT HOME AND ABROAD

As to the Pacific, Hawke, in 1989, set up an organization for *Asia-Pacific Economic Co-operation* (APEC), with its management entrusted to Keating – a very important initiative. This was a difficult horse to ride, simply because of the extreme diversity of the countries which became members – many of whom were not natural trading parties. Within this framework, however, Australia did develop its markets in Asia. By the 1990s the corner had been turned, and with high prices for its raw material exports Australia entered into the longest period of continuous growth in its history, for which successive governments – Labour until 1996 and John Howard's Liberal coalition since then – have all claimed credit.

Also in the 1990s Australia, still loyal to the United States, played an important part in the Gulf War, as it did also in the war in Iraq from 2003. In 1999 its intervention in Timor Leste was crucial in establishing peace. For the Australian public John Howard's most controversial stand was taken on immigration: in 2001 his policy came into sharp focus as a result of the way he dealt with the Norwegian freighter, *Tampa*, after it had rescued at sea hundreds of Afghan would-be immigrants to Australia. This long and sad story,[21] which in the eyes of the world and of many, also, in Australia, did little credit to Howard, still won him votes in two successive general elections. After the liberalizing measures of the 1960s and 1970s a hard line on immigration still goes down well with the broad mass of Australians.

Historically the same is true when it comes to the country's own aboriginal inhabitants. If little account is given of them in this chapter, it is because from the earliest days they were completely marginalized in the development of the country, and had hardly any recognition outside it. Although for most Australians it was a question of 'out of sight, out of mind', the 'black fellas' have had their champions, such as notably, at the present time, Germaine Greer.[22] By the 1960s the tide was at last turning in favour of the aboriginals: in 1966 South Australia's Aboriginal Lands Trust Act allowed them the ownership of land and a year later, in May 1967, the Commonwealth voted overwhelmingly for a referendum in favour of granting them citizens' rights. In June 1992 a Torres Strait islander won a specific claim to land on the basis of his family's 'continuous association' going back to the original white settlement. Although the Torres Straits Islands differ in any number of ways from the Australian mainland – where most aborigines have always lived – the principle of 'native title', as recognized by the court, was applicable throughout the Commonwealth. Nonetheless Paul Keating, in his successful 1993 campaign for re-election, rightly judged the mood of the electorate when he assured voters that 'the decision would only have a very restricted impact'.[23]

Traditional attitudes, to both non-European immigrants and native aboriginals, reflect a deep-seated concern, perhaps tinged with guilt, that Australians' hold on their land, or even their right to be there at all, is essentially precarious. To quote the Australian novelist, Thomas Keneally,[24]

> The Australians ... believe that Asia – the Chinese, the Indonesians, the Japanese – will swamp them. Some welcome the idea, some fear it, but all expect it. The Australians are a young race who think like an old one.

18

The new Asia-Pacific: hope and despair

LOOKING AT THE BOTTOM LINE

If, when it comes to Asia-Pacific, there can be no doubting the radical changes – social, political, economic and even geographical – throughout the whole region, they still ask for a historical value judgement. In what ways, and for which peoples, has life, as a result of all these changes, become better in the sixty-odd years since the end of the Pacific War? To what extent is it possible to generalize, by seeing, for instance, as progress, the results of the end of European colonialism? In Indonesia, for example, no serious politician would dispute this, but then what about the Christian minorities in the Molucca Islands, the remote hill tribes of western Papua or even the Chinese communities in the large cities? Of course the question whether such groups would have been better off if the Dutch had been able to hold on to their empire in the East Indies is purely hypothetical. In this case it is better to accept that the end of European colonialism after the Pacific War was not only essential to the emergence of the former colonies as independent states but also a critical factor in the whole modern history of the Asia-Pacific region. Just read Chapter 7 on Vietnam.

Looking back on the war in Vietnam, and considering that it ended more than thirty years ago, we can see that Asia-Pacific is now enjoying the longest period of peace in modern times. True there was a small bitter war in Timor Leste in 1999, and radical Islam still disturbs the Philippines and Thailand, but the impact of such events is essentially local.

The long-term prospects are, however, threatened in East Asia – more specifically in North Korea and Taiwan. As to the former, lasting peace requires no more than that Kim Jong Il gives up his attempt to make the country he rules a nuclear power – although the rockets launched in the summer of 2006 suggest that this is no part of his strategy. Even so, with the right incentives this unpredictable man might just change course: South Korea, Japan, China, Russia and the US, ideally with UN support, must continue working for a diplomatic solution. There is no alternative. Resorting to the force of arms would be disastrous, particularly for the people of North Korea – who have long been sunk in the misery imposed upon them by their eccentric and intractable ruler.

In the North Korean stand-off a leading role is that played by China, the only foreign state trusted, if somewhat equivocally, by Kim Jong Il. As to Taiwan, the whole dispute revolves around this island's status as part of the People's Republic. In the short term the answer, for both sides, is to maintain the status quo, with Taiwan enjoying a booming economy made possible by its de facto political independence of mainland China. Once again the prospect of any but a diplomatic solution is quite horrifying. Almost everything depends upon the way the People's Republic develops, both politically and economically, in future years. In particular, if the people of Hong Kong, following its return to China in 1997, continue to prosper and enjoy, in sufficient measure, the freedoms to which they feel entitled, then, eventually, Taiwan could well accept a similar status. This, however, remains very problematic.

Much less threatening – but still extremely worrying – are continuing acts of radical Islamic terrorism. On one side there are states such as Thailand and Philippines where adherents of Islam are relatively few in number and largely confined to remote and marginal areas. The problem, in both cases, is the support, both moral and material, that terrorists receive from outside: Thailand has a land frontier with Muslim Malaysia, which, in turn, is only separated by a short sea crossing from the southern islands of the Philippines. Indonesia, an essentially secular state with a majority Muslim population, is always in the background, and has its own problems with religious extremists. Most acute is the situation in Aceh, the northern province of Sumatra devastated by the *tsunami* on 26 December 2004. At the same time other regions, far from the centre, such as Maluku and Sulawesi, suffer local armed conflict between Muslims and Christians – an unfortunate legacy of successful proselytizing by nineteenth-century Dutch protestant missionaries. Worst of all – at least for Indonesia's image world-wide – are terrorist attacks in places with a large number of foreign visitors, such as embassies and hotels in Jakarta or tourists spots in Bali.

Finally there is the scourge of the illegal drug trade, which is bound to flourish in areas such as Southeast Asia, where, on the one hand, the sources of supply are close by, while, on the other, considerable local poverty exists side by side with numerous, and extremely heterogeneous, visitors from overseas. The local response is tight security, particularly in airports and harbours, combined with draconian penalties: Thailand, Malaysia, Singapore and Indonesia have no qualms about exacting the death penalty for serious drug offences – with no quarter given to visitors from Europe or Australia.

The drug trade is essentially an epiphenomenon of the socio-economic matrix of states with more or less open economies characterized by extremes of wealth and high levels of both internal and external migration. Increased volume of traffic is at the same time an almost inevitable result of vastly extended communications, particularly by air – to say nothing of access to the internet and mobile telephones. None of these factors is reversible, however much conservative forces – often very strong locally – would like to turn the clock back. Even the remotest tribal areas – which, although almost everywhere in decline, still survive – are involved, whether as a source of contraband, labour for the exploitation of natural resources, or immigrants to the new mega-cities. In the long run this mix of different factors could be as great a threat to peace, almost anywhere in Asia-Pacific, as any armed stand-off involving China or North Korea.

The drug trade, as many other forms of crime, such as illegal logging, thrives on corruption at every level of government. This is the greatest scourge of the countries of Asia-Pacific, where a career in politics still provides an unequalled opportunity for acquiring wealth. Vast fortunes are still being made, particularly at the top, as witness the success of Prime Minister Thaksin of Thailand – whose party, Thai Rak Thai, gained a majority for the third time in the 2006 elections. Thaksin, however, is only the last in a long line, going back to Park in Korea, Marcos in the Philippines and Suharto in Indonesia. These are only the top men in their national kleptocracies. The worst of it is that for almost all of them service in the armed forces or the police was an essential stage along the route to power.

Once again the unequal division of wealth is at the heart of the problem. Taxation revenues, often reduced as a result of fraudulent accounting overlooked by corrupt inspectors, are essential for maintaining a vast bureaucracy of poorly paid officials, who have every interest in making the system they administer as complex as possible, so that bribery is accepted as normal for anyone dealing with them – otherwise nothing would ever be done. The same is true of those belonging to the forces of law and order, which, by definition, have the means as well as the incentive[1] to shake down almost anyone. The fact that smugglers, pirates and traffickers in illegal immigrants know well what price to pay, and to whom, explains why their activities continue to earn them a better income than they would find elsewhere.

The East Asian giants have also been involved in high-level corruption; indeed, they still are. In 1989 the Recruit Cosmos scandal in Japan brought down not only the government of Prime Minister Takeshita, but also involved at least two of his predecessors, Nakasone[2] and Tanaka,[3] to say nothing of numerous top members of the governing LDP. Much more recently, in September 2005, four accountants of the staff of Chuo-Aoyama – the Japanese operation of the international firm Pricewaterhouse Coopers, were arrested for their part in falsifying the accounts of the textile giant, Kanebo, over a period going back to the 1970s.

The level of business fraud is almost certainly even higher in China, but tight press control means that less is known to the outside world. Even so the official reports of the trial, which opened in September 2000, of more than a hundred officials in Fujian province for their involvement in smuggling through the port city of Xiamen, confirm the existence of corruption at the level of millions of dollars. This case became notorious for the involvement of families of some of China's senior leaders, as is confirmed by reports relating to those who lost their jobs. Death sentences, often arbitrarily imposed and carried out more frequently in China than anywhere else, are seen as appropriate in serious cases of corruption. Given the bureaucratic structure of government in the People's Republic, resulting in the need for official permits for any business enterprise, corruption is almost inevitable – and very few reach the top with clean hands. Much more than elsewhere government service is an essential stage on the way to business success.[4]

If the same is true in Russia, corruption as it affects the Pacific coastal areas is inevitably rooted at the centre in Moscow at the other end of the country. Even so, the vast new developments in oil and natural gas in Kamchatka and Sakhalin leave wide scope for corrupt dealings all along the line. There is, however, no distinctive Pacific dimension.

THE SLOW DECLINE OF TYRANNY

Life on both sides of the Pacific has changed for the better as, one after another, strong and ruthless leaders have died, or at least been forced out of office. The process started in the Soviet Union with the death of Stalin in 1953 – which opened the way to ending the Korean War – and continued with that of the Viet Minh leader, Ho Chi Minh in 1969 and of Mao Zedong in China in 1976. In the case of Ho Chi Minh – who died at a critical point in the war in Vietnam – his regime survived his death to continue, with final success in 1975, the policies associated with his name. Much the same happened when Kim Jong Il in North Korea, became the country's leader on the death of his father Kim Il Sung, in 1994.

Outside the communist states, the murder of Park Chung Hee in 1979 was an important step on the way to making democracy actually work in South Korea – a result finally achieved at the end of the 1980s. Significantly, perhaps, in the non-communist states popular discontent was in the end sufficient to force the strong men out of office, as happened to Marcos in the Philippines in 1986 and Suharto in Indonesia in 1998. In each of these three cases, the fall of the leader led to a significant change for the better in the everyday life of the country. In other cases, such as those of the retirement of Lee Kuan Yew in Singapore in 1993 and Mohamad Mahathir in Malaysia in 2003, the departing leaders managed to ensure a successor ready to continue their policies. This process required the show trial of Anwar Ibrahim – who represented the main threat to Mahathir – following his arrest in 1998. But then the softer line followed by Mahathir's successor, Abdullah Badawi, which brought an end to the judicial persecution of Anwar Ibrahim, is a sign of real progress towards a state no longer dominated by Mahathir's *Asian values*. These may still resonate with Hun Sen in Cambodia, but by allowing Sam Rainsy, in 2006, to return home from exile to challenge the government once more, he showed a welcome respect for democratic institutions. In Thailand a *coup d'état* in September 2006 finally cost Thaksin his office.

BOOM-TIMES

As for Pacific economies, that of China, with its remarkable and sustained rate of growth, now not only overshadows all others in the developing world, but has also led to its challenging the dominance of Japan.[5] Worldwide, one country after another is losing long-standing markets to low-cost Chinese enterprise.[6] To a degree this process echoes that already manifest in the economies of the *Asian Tigers* – Thailand, Korea, Taiwan, Malaysia and Singapore – but the difference in scale made possible by China having the world's largest population should radically change its character.

The enormously increased demand for natural resources is a key factor, and one extremely advantageous to major producers, such as Australia with its vast reserves of coal and metal ores. Shortage of oil, as in the rest of the world, is the greatest problem, particularly given the need for imports from outside the Pacific region – as witness the giant tankers passing day and night through the Malacca Straits. For East Asia the Russian share of the market is bound to increase, as may also local supplies from Indonesia and Malaysia, to say nothing of new oil-fields to be tapped offshore. Natural gas, particularly when shipped as LNG, should not only reduce the demand for oil, but also contribute substantially to the national economies – notably those of Indonesia and Russia – enjoying substantial reserves.

The problem, however, with a developing country such as Indonesia, is that however profitable the export of LNG may be for the national economy, the whole operation is capital rather than labour intensive. At the same time the actual location of rigs and terminals is largely determined by geo-physical rather than demographic factors, so that they are only too likely to be situated far from population centres. For management this may matter little, since the main requirement is for a small skilled labour force which can be recruited from almost anywhere, at least if the right conditions of employment – including, above all, generous remuneration – are offered. The result is to create small remote enclave communities relating little to local cultures and contributing only marginally to local economies – which, if based on agriculture, may well suffer rather than benefit from the presence of new hi-tech enterprise.

This phenomenon is certainly not confined to oil and LNG. A case in point is the vast American-owned Grasberg gold- and copper-mine[7] in Indonesian Papua forced to close in February 2006 as a result of attacks by local tribesmen – many former miners – who were denied the right to work the mining waste for gold residue. The actual mining had for years disrupted the traditional subsistence economy based on the cultivation of taro. All this was nothing compared to what happened in Bougainville, as island belonging to PNG, in 1989, when the local inhabitants turned on an Australian-owned copper-mine which, if it brought vast profits to the country of which they were citizens, brought them next to nothing – and any number of similar instances could be cited. Australia has less trouble with its domestic operations, such as mining bauxite in northern Queensland, where the open-cast Comalco mine is the third largest in the world. Here, as with most large-scale mining in Australia, there is no local indigenous population to mount a protest.

When it comes to degradation of the environment open-cast mining, on however large a scale, is nothing compared to illegal logging – the scourge of many different countries. The worst cases are in Indonesia, and above all, the Philippines, where, in February 2006, the loss of natural forest cover lay behind a massive mudslide that, on the island of Leyte, buried the village of Guinsaugon with the loss of hundreds of lives. Here also population pressure played a key part in a Catholic country where the hierarchy condemns artificial birth control. A largely rural peasant economy requires land to be cleared for new cultivation with little regard for environmental consequences. In the years since the Pacific War the Philippines has lost almost all of the rich natural forests that once covered the whole country. Cultivation, mainly of rice, is no alternative when it comes to restoring the balance of nature. In the long run it will not even feed the local populations engaged in it: in that case the only choice left is migration to the large cities. Metropolitan Manila,[8] with a population of more than ten million – already one of the twenty largest metropolitan areas world-wide – is still growing. The same is true of Jakarta, capital of Indonesia, where the population, recently estimated to be more than 13 million, is even larger.[9] On the other side of the Pacific the only rival is Los Angeles County in the US.

It is, however, on the coasts of East Asia that the growth of cities is most spectacular, with China – which claims Shanghai as the world's largest city – having some seventy cities with a population of more than a million. Given that China, with some 1.3 billion inhabitants, is the world's most populous state, this is not too surprising: the problem comes, as in Southeast Asia, with the enormous growth of the cities in relation to a relatively impoverished countryside. This relates to the economic boom which took off in the 1980s, with the vast investment in infrastructural projects – such as that of the Three Gorges Dam of the Yangze – which characterize it. By 2005 this had already displaced more than a million people, with minimal regard to compensation and adequate resettlement, to say nothing of spiralling costs and widespread corruption. At the same time the power consumption, whether industrial, infrastructural or domestic, makes almost impossible demands for fossil fuels.[10] The pollution caused by their use leaves one wondering how the athletes competing in the 2008 Olympic Games in Beijing will be able to breathe.

ENVIRONMENTAL FAILURE

More generally, the Pacific has not done well, internationally, in collaborating on plans to reduce atmospheric pollution. Two of its main industrial powers, Australia and the US, had consistently refused to ratify the Kyoto Protocol when it went into effect in 2005.[11] Instead they played a major part in promoting an alternative agreement, the *Asia-Pacific Partnership on Clean Development and Climate*, which was announced on 28 July 2005, and includes four other countries, China, India, South Korea and Japan.

This so-called 'AP6' line-up is significant, for the countries comprised in it have between them about half the world's population.[12] All six are heavy users of coal, and led by Australia's Industry Minister, Ian Macfarlane – notorious for his denials of climate change – they produced a classic stitch-up, funded by a miserably small budget. It is no wonder that the whole scheme was slated by the media,[13] particularly in Australia, for which coal is a major export. The best it could offer for combating climate change was an untried technology known as the *integrated gasification combined cycle*, which is designed to divert underground – at enormous cost – CO_2 emissions from power stations.

ASIA-PACIFIC INTERNATIONAL

The AP6, although far from being the only international institution focused on the Pacific, is typical for the whole region in its being confined to only a handful of different states, with but a single area of responsibility. The organization for Asia-Pacific Economic Cooperation (APEC), with twenty-one states as members, is much more comprehensive, but even so not a single island state of Oceania belongs to it and in Latin America only Mexico, Peru and Chile. On the other hand on the western Pacific Rim only Cambodia and North Korea are excluded, while next to China both Hong Kong and Taiwan have separate representation. Asia-Pacific (which comprises all but four of the member states) therefore defines the hard core of APEC, and the question is whether the organization actually adds up to anything important: the top men, such as US President George W. Bush, who attend its annual conferences could be mainly posturing.

Table 2: APEC Country Statistics

Member Economy and Year Joined	Area (000 sq. km)	Population (millions)	GDP (US $bn)	GDP per capita (US $)	Exports (US $m)	Imports (US $m)
Australia (1989)	7,692	20.2	692.4	33,629	86,551	103,863
Brunei (1989)	6	0.4	5.7	15,764	4,713	1,638
Canada (1989)	9,971	32.0	1,084.1	33,648	315,858	271,869
Chile (1994)	757	15.4	105.8	6,807	32,548	24,769
China (1991)	9,561	1,299.8	1,851.2	1,416	593,647	560,811
Hong Kong (1991)	1	6.9	174.0	25,006	265,763	273,361
Indonesia (1989)	1,905	223.8	280.9	1,237	71,585	46,525
Japan (1989)	378	127.3	4,694.3	36,841	566,191	455,661
Korea (1989)	99	48.2	819.2	16,897	253,845	224,463
Malaysia (1989)	330	25.5	129.4	4,989	125,857	105,297
Mexico (1993)	1,958	105.0	734.9	6,920	177,095	171,714
New Zealand (1989)	271	4.1	108.7	26,373	20,334	21,716
Papua-New Guinea (1993)	463	5.9	3.5	585	4,321	1,463
Peru (1998)	1,285	27.5	78.2	2,798	12,111	8,872
Philippines (1989)	300	86.2	95.6	1,088	39,585	40,297
Russia (1998)	17,075	144.0	719.2	5,015	171,431	86,593
Singapore (1989)	1	4.2	116.3	27,180	179,755	163,982
Chinese Taipei (1991)	36	22.5	335.2	14,857	174,350	168,715
Thailand (1989)	513	64.6	178.1	2,736	97,098	95,197
United States (1989)	9,364	293.0	12,365.9	41,825	818,775	1,489,704
Vietnam (1998)	332	82.6	51.0	610	26,061	32,734

The problem is that the Pacific as a whole is not a natural trading area. Nonetheless, the APEC countries account for more than half the world's GDP, and nearly half of total world trade. The fact that APEC operates with no more than a small secretariat in Singapore, to which the member states together contribute less than $4 million a year, leaves one doubting how significant it is.[14] As Table 2 above shows, vast disparities in key economic and demographic indicators – much greater than are to be found within the EU – define APEC's most salient characteristic. A flow diagram, relating to any aspect of international commerce and comprising all twenty-one APEC member-states, would reveal any number of clusters containing little or no mutual relationships between the states belonging to them. With other clusters, however, the level of mutual involvement

– whether political, economic or cultural – would be almost overwhelming. There is scope for endless analysis here, but when all was said and done the conclusions reached would be hardly surprising, and confirm the history and prophecy contained in my book. Asia-Pacific is dominated by the big actors, and the trend is almost certain to continue along an Australasia-East Asia-North America axis defined by Australia, China, Korea, Japan, Canada and the United States, with Hong Kong, Singapore and Taiwan playing important supporting roles and countries such as Thailand, Vietnam, Malaysia, the Philippines and Indonesia working hard – and with varying success – to join the club.

Essentially it is the regional clusters, and the organizations that represent them, such as NAFTA[15] or ASEAN, that count, and even at this level differences between states often count for more than similarities, as can be seen, say, by comparing Thailand with Malaysia, Indonesia with the Philippines.

One can easily discover that Asia-Pacific is not one world but many, and that the ocean shared by the countries in the region defines remarkably few common interests. If one thing holds it together, it is the English language: the end of Asian colonialism following the Pacific War was fatal for the continued use of other European languages – notably French and Dutch. If there is a twenty-first-century rival to English it is Chinese, but outside the People's Republic this is mainly heard spoken – in a wide variety of dialects – in the immigrant communities to be found in almost every corner of Asia-Pacific. The men at the top still talk to each other in English.

Asia-Pacific is also distinctive for avoiding problems that plague much of the rest of the world. Africa, with all the horrors of Darfur, Rwanda, Sierra Leone and Liberia – to mention no more than current instances – has no Pacific littoral. Nor has the Middle East, which for Asia-Pacific is pre-eminently a source of oil – and for some of its states, employment.[16] In Latin America, such problems as the traffic in drugs from Colombia have no Pacific dimension. The Caribbean to the north of the continent, which is also involved, is an Atlantic,[17] not a Pacific sea. Even the poorest and least tranquil states of Asia-Pacific are better placed to solve their own problems, particularly with the help of outside aid. From Vancouver to Sydney, from Los Angeles to Vladivostok, the weather is set mainly fair for Asia-Pacific. How this came about – along many a trail of sorrows – is the story of my book.

Notes

Notes to Chapter 1: Introduction: the world of Asia-Pacific

1 Penguin, 2006.
2 Quoted *New York Review of Books*, 2 November 2006, p. 25.
3 Compare the countries around the Atlantic, which, for more than 90 per cent of their aggregate population, get by with four related European languages, English, French, Portuguese and Spanish.
4 English and Russian are, however, both Indo-European, and Japanese and Korean, Altaic.
5 While the spoken languages, somewhat remarkably, belonged to quite different language families, their written forms tended to share one or two common origins in, notably, China or India.
6 It is on the face of it paradoxical that the western Pacific is enclosed by East Asia, while the eastern Pacific ends at the western coastline of the Americas. At least in the northern hemisphere, the international date line can be taken as a convenient boundary between the two. In principle this problem should not arise with the southern Pacific, but in fact one or two groups of islands included in it are just north of the equator.
7 This is important, since Korea, as related in Chapter 4, was for thirty-five years (1910–45) subject to Japan. This book recognizes that it now consists of two separate UN-member states.
8 For a short history see Preston, D., *The Boxer Rebellion*, Constable Robinson, 2002.
9 Remarkably a street and a metro-station are named after him in Amsterdam.
10 Then better known outside China as Chiang Kaishek.
11 See Chang, J. and Halliday, J., *Mao: The Unknown Story*, Alfred A. Knopf, 2005. In the three years (1931–34) of the Jiangshi Soviet Republic Mao drove the peasant very hard: ibid., p. 106.
12 Black, C., *Franklin Delano Roosevelt: Champion of Freedom*, Weidenfelt & Nicolson, 2003, p. 425.
13 Tuchman, B., *Sand against the Wind: Stilwell and the American Experience in China 1911–45*, Macmillan, 1981, p. 226.
14 This, the code-name for a mission led by US Vice-President Henry Wallace, was chosen because of its significance, at the time of the American Civil War (1861–65), as designating the rebellious southern states: ibid., pp. 591–93.
15 Large, S., *Emperor Hirohito and Shōwa Japan: A Political Biography*, Routledge, 1992, p. 51.
16 Ibid., p. 98.
17 Mme Jiang only died in 2003, aged 105.

18   See Crump, T., *The Death of an Emperor: Japan at the Crossroads*, Constable, 1989 and OUP, 1990, pp. 137f, for the source of these quotations from Tuchman, op. cit.

19   His full name was Luang Phibunsongkhram.

20   Churchill, W.S., *Grand Alliance*, Houghton Mifflin, 1951, bk 2, Chapters 11 and 12.

21   This was particularly true of the Dutch in the East Indies.

22   This must be extended to include the adjacent territories leased from China in the mid-nineteenth century.

23   See Map 5 on page x.

24   In alphabetical order Chile, Colombia, Costa Rica, Ecuador, El Salvador, Guatemala, Honduras, Mexico, Nicaragua, Panama, Peru.

25   The others were South and West Australia and the separate island of Tasmania.

26   Diamond, J., *Guns, Germs and Steel: The Fates of Human Societies*, Allen Lane, 1997.

27   Diamond, J., *Collapse: How Societies Choose to Fail or Survive*, Allen Lane, 2005, p. 389.

28   Partly as a result of the influence of authors such as Germaine Greer.

29   Welsh, F., *Great Southern Land: A New History of Australia*, Allen Lane, 2004, pp. 380–81.

30   Ibid., p. 422.

31   Ibid., p. 439.

Notes to Chapter 2: Revolutionary China

1   Chang, J. and Halliday, J., *Mao: The Unknown Story*, Alfred A. Knopf, 2005, p. 284.

2   In 1964 Mao told a visiting delegation from the Japanese Socialist Party that 'if the Japanese imperial army had not occupied half of China's territory, the Chinese people would not have united in their struggle, and our People's Republic would not have come into existence'; cited Leys, S., *Broken Images: Essays on Chinese Culture and Politics*, Allison & Busby, 1979, p. 54.

3   See *The Pacific Islands: an encyclopedia*, University of Hawaii Press, pp. 53f.

4   Fairbank, J.J., *China: A New History*, Belknap Press, 1992, p. 337.

5   Also known as Quemoy and Matsu. Nine years later, in 1958, when Mao once again planned military operations, a combination of US carriers and Soviet pressure caused him to back off from the bombardment and blockade of Jinmen.

6   Lynch, M., *Mao*, Routledge, 2004, p. 144.

7   See pp. 6 to 7.

8   This is the official name of the army of the PRC.

9   Chang and Halliday, op. cit., p. 352.

10   Ibid., p. 354.

11   The full story is told in chapter 4.

12   Lynch, op. cit., p. 150: I find the alternative account of Chang and Halliday (op. cit., pp. 358f), according to which it was Mao, rather than Stalin, who first promised to support Kim Il Sung's proposed invasion of South Korea, unconvincing. Their sources are, for one thing, almost impossible to check.

13   The complete text of the telegram sent to Stalin is given in Goncharov, S.N., Lewis, J.W. and Xue, L., *Stalin, Mao and the Korean War*, Stanford University Press, 1993, p. 275.

14   Lynch, op. cit., p. 152.

15 According to Gaddis, J.L., *The Cold War: A New History*, New York, Penguin Press, 2005, p. 45, Stalin was ready to accept MacArthur's advance to the Yalu river. It was Mao who, overriding own advisers, decided to intervene.

16 See p. 87.

17 See Chapter 6.

18 Lynch, op. cit., p. 166.

19 Taubman, W., *Khrushchev: The Man and his Era*, Free Press, 2003, p. 391. Much of the conversation took place in the swimming-pool of Mao's villa outside Beijing. The whole time Mao, a strong swimmer, was talking through an interpreter, while Khrushchev, who never learnt to swim, ended up sitting in the edge of the pool with his feet in the water. The whole set-up was Mao's revenge for being assigned a dacha without a pool during his visit to Moscow.

20 Yan Mingfu, quoted, ibid., p. 394.

21 Ibid., p. 471.

22 Lynch, op. cit., p. 175.

23 Its immediate rationale was to justify the Soviet invasion of Czechoslovakia in August 1968.

24 Lynch, op. cit., p. 197.

25 Tsang, S., *A Modern History of Hong Kong*, I.B. Tauris, 2004, p. 184.

26 Ibid., p. 178.

27 Ibid., p. 196.

28 Kissinger, H., *The White House Years*, Weidenfeld & Nicolson, 1979, p. 747.

29 Nixon, R.M., *The Memoirs of Richard M. Nixon*, Grosset & Dunlop, 1978, p. 580.

30 Cited Steinberg, D.J., *In Search of Southeast Asia*, Sydney, Allen & Unwin, 1987, p. 27.

31 The party congresses, which are held every five years, are followed by a series of full meetings of the Central Committee, which can provide the occasion for deciding major shifts in policy. It was at the third such 'plenum' (in December 1978) of the eleventh congress (held in August 1977) that Deng introduced the radical changes that effectively ended the Maoist era in China. At the fourth plenum, in September 1979, party vice-chairman Ye Jianying declared the Cultural Revolution 'an appalling catastrophe' and 'the most severe setback to [the] socialist cause since [1949]'.

32 Ho died in 1969.

33 Ramses Amer.

34 Skidelsky, R., *The World after Communism: A Polemic for our Times*, Macmillan, 1995, p. 14 notes the Soviet Union's existing commitments to communist regimes in Africa, Central America and Laos, at the time of its invasion of Afghanistan, foreshadowing their part in its final collapse.

35 Möller, K., China's Foreign Relations 1978–1999: Unleashed, the Tiger Feels Lonely, in Draguhn, W. and Goodman, D.S.G. (eds.), *China's Communist Revolutions: Fifty Years of the People's Republic of China*, Routledge Curzon, 2002, pp. 208–49, p. 210.

36 Ibid., p. 215. When, in 1982, Deng had insisted to Margaret Thatcher on the return of Hong Kong in 1997, she was surprised at his willingness to risk jeopardizing the economic advantages of Hong Kong remaining independent: ibid., p. 220.

37 See www.time.com/time/asia/features/heroes/zhao.html

38 Wan, M., *Human Rights in Chinese Foreign Relations: Defining and Defending National Interests*, University of Pennsylvania Press, 2001, p. 111.

39 'Most favoured' means in practice
    'normal': Patten, C., *East and West*, Pan
    Books, 1999, p. 299.
40 Kim, D.H., *The Korean Peninsula in
    Transition*, Macmillan, 1997, p. 248.
41 Möller, op. cit., p. 214.
42 As Patten, op. cit., p. 293, notes,
    'its arsenal is not even sufficiently
    menacing to take out Taiwan'.
43 Porch, D., The Taiwan Strait Crisis of
    1996: Strategic Implications for the
    United States Navy: www.nwc.navy.
    mil/press/Review/1999/ summer/
    frame_33.htm
44 Patten, op. cit., p. 29 suggests that
    Deng always had Taiwan in mind
    when devising this formula. It was
    also applied to the takeover of the
    Portuguese colony of Macao in 1999.
45 Tsang, op. cit., pp. 134–38 tells the full
    story.
46 Ibid., p. 142.
47 Goncharov et al., op. cit., p. 40.
48 The actual dates of the Berlin airlift
    were 24 June 1948 to 12 May 1949.
49 Defence White Paper, cited Tsang, op.
    cit., p. 155.
50 Ibid., p. 171.
51 This was established in its present
    form in 1986 by the consolidation of
    four local exchanges.
52 First introduced in 1964.
53 The first through train service between
    Hong Kong and Guangdong opened in
    1979.
54 Patten, op. cit., pp. 91f.
55 By section 1(1) of the Hong Kong
    Act, 1985, 'As from 1st July 1997
    Her Majesty shall no longer have
    sovereignty or jurisdiction over any
    part of Hong Kong'. Subsection (2)
    then provided that the Act would
    take effect with ratification of the
    Joint Declaration by both Beijing and

    London, which was also completed in
    1985.
56 Tsang, op. cit., p. 224.
57 Patten, op. cit., p. 58.
58 Tsang, op. cit., p. 230.
59 Patten, op. cit., p. 51.
60 Tsang, op. cit., p. 233.
61 Patten, op. cit., p. 83.
62 Ibid., p. 348.
63 Tsang, op. cit., p. 267.
64 Deng, who had died early in the year,
    did not live to see it.
65 Tsang, op. cit., p. 273.
66 Patten, op. cit., p. 305. One should
    also note what Wei wrote in *The New
    York Times* after an earlier release from
    prison in 1993:
    Is it really likely that Americans would
    abandon an opportunity to make
    money just to protect the human
    rights of those they have befriended?
    Is it really likely that the American
    people's determinations of right
    and wrong could ever influence the
    judgment of the US government? …
    It looks as if the Communist Party
    has answered these questions in the
    negative. So even though it may have
    realized that its own conduct might
    have been in error, it still firmly
    pursues a strategy of brinkmanship,
    giving ground only when absolutely
    necessary and always in the last five
    minutes …
    The Chinese people's understanding of
    the new direction of US policy toward
    China leads them to believe that the
    party was right all these years in saying
    that the American government is
    controlled by rich capitalists. All you
    have to do is offer them a chance to
    make money and anything goes. Their
    consciences never stopped them from
    making money.

67   See note 24 above.

Notes to Chapter 3: The restoration of Japan

1   The acronym SCAP refers, according to context, to either the command or its commander.

2   The Shōguns were the traditional Japanese commanders in chief who actually ruled the country from 1600 to 1868.

3   The leading text is Wolferen, K. van, *The Enigma of Japanese Power*, Alfred A. Knopf, 1989.

4   Although this was the name by which he was known to the outside world, it was hardly ever used in Japan, where he was, like his predecessors, referred to simply as 'Tennō' or 'Tennō Heika', best translated as 'His Majesty the Emperor'. At the beginning of his reign he chose the name 'Shōwa' to refer to his era as emperor, and following his death he became simply 'Shōwa Tennō' – in Japan itself the name Hirohito, bestowed at birth, is completely superseded.

5   See previous note.

6   See Crump, T., *The Death of an Emperor: Japan at the Crossroads*, Constable, 1989, Chapter 8.

7   Large, S., *Emperor Hirohito and Shōwa Japan: A Political Biography*, Routledge, 1992, p. 216.

8   Crump, op. cit., p. 154.

9   Large, op. cit., p. 143.

10   An English version of the full text is given in Crump, op. cit., pp. 69–70.

11   Ibid., p. 163.

12   Ibid., p. 182.

13   Ibid., p. 183.

14   Bix, H.P., *Hirohito and the Making of Modern Japan*, Harper Collins, 2000,

pp. 418f exculpates Konoye, but his case is very one-sided, and certainly few would have been persuaded by it in 1945.

15   Large, op. cit., p. 150.

16   This public holiday was abolished by SCAP, but revived by Prime Minister Shigeru Yoshida in 1953: Large, op. cit., p. 159.

17   Schoppa, L.J., *Education Reform in Japan: A Case of Immobilist Politics*, Routledge, 1991, p. 39.

18   Large, op. cit., p. 155.

19   Buckley, R., *The United States in the Asia-Pacific since 1945*, Cambridge University Press, 2002, p. 23.

20   Ibid., p. 184.

21   The *Jimintō* emerged in 1955 as a result of a merger of the parties that had belonged to Yoshida's coalition government.

22   Buckley, op. cit., p. 187.

23   A federal court case, *US v. Ushi Shiroma* (123 F. Supp. 145) decided that a taxpayer from Okinawa was still an alien, and as such obliged to inform the Internal Revenue Service of any address change.

24   Large, op. cit., p. 181.

25   Toyota's most recent plans (1906) include setting up a plant in Michigan, to take advantage of the labour force shed by the giant American manufacturers – at the same time creating goodwill in the Democratic Party.

26   Hsu, R.H. (ed.), *The MIT Encyclopedia of the Japanese Economy* (2nd edn), MIT Press, 1999, p. 17.

27   Henderson, C., *Asia Falling: Making Sense of the Asian Crisis and its Aftermath*, McGraw Hill, 1998, p. 49.

28   A report in 2005 showed that 55 per cent of Japanese household savings

were held in cash and bank deposits: *Economist*, 2 April 2005, p. 67.

29 Hsu, op. cit., p. 79.

30 A comparable incident in Europe was the unsuccessful coup staged by a Spanish officer, Antonio Tejera, in Madrid on 23 February 1981.

31 Full details are given by Crump, op. cit., p. 197.

32 The Japanese title was *Hagakure Nyûmon*.

33 In 1987 I observed a notice board in front of a building under construction stating that completion would be in Shōwa 65, i.e. 1990, but in fact the Shōwa Emperor died in 1989, so that 1990 immediately became Heisei 2, according to the era of his successor, the present emperor.

34 Op. cit.

35 *The Economist*, 11 June 2005, p. 54.

36 The name comes from the Hotel in New York where the accord was negotiated.

37 The political arm of the *Soka Gakkai* sect.

38 Table 11.3, Trends in Exports and Imports by Country/Region.

39 *The Economist*, 26 March 2005, p. 24; 16 April 2005, p. 12.

40 *The Economist*, 26 February 2005, p. 53.

Notes to Chapter 4: Korea: a country divided by war (1945–53)

1 Eliot Kang, C.S., 'North Korea's International Relations: The Successful Failure', in S.S. Kim (ed.), *The International Relations of Northeast Asia*, Rowman and Littlefield, 2004, pp. 281–99, 281.

2 Sandler, S., *The Korean War: No Victors, No Vanquished*, UCL Press, 1999, p. 20.

3 Oberdorfer, D., *The Two Koreas: A Contemporary History*, Little Brown & Co, 1997, p. 6.

4 Lankov, A., *From Stalin to Kim Il Sung: The Formation of North Korea 1945–1960*, Hurst & Company, 2002, p. 59.

5 Soviet support for Kim after 1945 may well have exceeded that given to Mao: Goncharov, S.N., Lewis, J.W. and Xue, L., *Stalin, Mao and the Korean War*, Stanford University Press, 1993, p. 133.

6 Sandler, op. cit., p. 38.

7 Goncharov et el., op. cit., p. 135.

8 Sandler, op. cit., p. 29.

9 Ibid., p. 41.

10 Ibid., p. 30.

11 Lowe, P., *The Korea War*, Macmillan Press, 2000, p. 28.

12 Sandler, op. cit., p. 99.

13 Ibid., p. 99.

14 Buckley, R., *The United States in the Asia-Pacific since 1945*, Cambridge University Press, 2002, p. 57.

15 Sandler, op. cit.

16 Ibid., p. 136.

17 Ibid., p. 127.

18 Ibid., p. 144.

19 Ibid., p. 145.

20 Ibid., p. 146.

21 Ibid., p. 241.

22 Ibid., p. 242.

23 Ibid., p. 247.

24 Ibid., p. 53.

25 The literature is considerable and highly controversial: see particularly Nikolai Tolstoy's *Victims of Yalta*, Hodder & Stoughton, 1977; and *Secret Betrayal*, Scribner, 1978.

26 Sandler, op. cit., p. 249.

27 Myers, R.J., *Korea in the Cross Currents: A Century of Struggle and the Crisis of Reunification*, Palgrave, 2001, p. 94.

28 Ibid., p. 258.

29 Ibid., p. 261.

30 Buckley, op. cit., p. 49.

31 Myers, op. cit., p. 94.

Notes to Chapter 5: Korea: North and South (1953–2006)

1 Oberdorfer, D., *The Two Koreas: A Contemporary History*, Little Brown & Co, 1997, p. 32.

2 Kang, D.C., *Crony Capitalism: Corruption and Development in South Korea and the Philippines*, Cambridge University Press, 2002, p. 53.

3 Myers, R.J., *Korea in the Cross Currents: A Century of Struggle and the Crisis of Reunification*, Palgrave, 2001, Chapter 7, 'The Bumblebee Economy'.

4 Emery, R.F., *Korean Economic Reform: Before and since the 1997 Crisis*, Ashgate, 2001, p. 1.

5 Kang, op. cit., p. 102.

6 Ibid., p. 106.

7 Cornell, E., *North Korea under Communism: Report of an Envoy to Paradise*, Routledge Curzon, 2000, p. 135 gives a good analysis of KPDR diplomacy at this stage.

8 Oberdorfer, op. cit., p. 112.

9 Ibid., p. 121.

10 Ibid., p. 131.

11 Myers, op. cit., p. 162.

12 Oberdorfer, op. cit., p. 141.

13 Ibid., p. 133.

14 Eliot Kang, C.S., 'North Korea's International Relations: The Successful Failure', in S.S. Kim (ed.) *The International Relations of Northeast Asia*, Rowman and Littlefield, 2004, pp. 281–99, p. 284.

15 Oberdorfer, op. cit., p. 157.

16 Ibid., p. 158.

17 Ibid., p. 160 and Cornell, op. cit., p. 103.

18 Oberdorfer, op. cit., p. 201.

19 Ibid., p. 204.

20 Eliot Kang, op. cit., p. 284.

21 Moon, C. and Kim, T., 'South Korea's International Relations: Challenges to Developmental Realism', in S.S. Kim (ed.) *The International Relations of Northeast Asia*, Rowman and Littlefield, 2004, pp. 251–80, p. 261.

22 Eliot Kang, op. cit., p. 284.

23 Oberdorfer, op. cit., p. 230.

24 Cornell, op. cit., p. 121.

25 Moon and Kim, op. cit., p. 260.

26 Oberdorfer, op. cit., p. 229.

27 Eliot Kang, op. cit., p. 286.

28 Oberdorfer, op. cit., p. 371.

29 Eliot Kang, op. cit., p. 287.

30 Eliot Kang, op. cit., p. 286.

31 Oberdorfer, op. cit., p. 224.

32 Cornell, op. cit., p. 126.

33 Tributyl phosphate.

34 The most powerful of these, the Taepodong-2, failed, crashing into the ocean soon after launching.

35 Moon and Kim, op. cit., p. 252.

36 Ogle, G.E., *South Korea: Dissent within the Economic Miracle*, Zed Books, 1990, p. 163.

37 Moon and Kim, op. cit., p. 265.

38 Eliot Kang, op. cit., p. 230.

39 Ibid., p. 234.

40 Emery, op. cit., p. 60.

41 Myers, op. cit., p. 3.

42 Emery, op. cit., p. 150.

43 Eliot Kang, op. cit., p. 237.

44 Moon and Kim, op. cit., p. 266.

45 Myers, op. cit., p. 3.

46 Moon and Kim, op. cit., p. 251.

Notes to Chapter 6: Thailand: a history of success

1 Muscat, R.J., *The Fifth Tiger: A Study of Thai Development Policy*, UN University Press, 1994, p. 24.

2 Ibid., p. 75.
3 Ibid., p. 120.
4 Wyatt, D.K., *Thailand: A Short History*, Yale University Press, 1984, p. 284.
5 Ibid., p. 290.
6 Muscat, op. cit., p. 103.
7 Wyatt, op. cit., p. 298.
8 Kang, D.C., *Crony Capitalism: Corruption and Development in South Korea and the Philippines*, Cambridge University Press, 2002, p. 175.
9 Vladimir Putin and Silvio Berlusconi are other possible role models, not acknowledged by Thaksin.
10 See Chapter 15, pp. 304–6.
11 Muscat, op. cit., p. 5.
12 G. Coedès, cited Galland, X., *Histoire de la Thailande*, Presses Universitaires de France, 1998, p. 125.
13 Neher, C.D., Thailand in 1987; Semi-Successful Semi-Democracy, *Asian Survey* (1988) vol. 28, p. 2.

Notes to Chapter 7: The battle for Indochina

1 Kratoska, P. and Batson, B., Nationalism and Modern Reform, in N. Tarling (ed.), *The Cambridge History of Southeast Asia*, vol. 2, pt. 1, pp. 245–320, p. 272.
2 Ellsberg, D., *Secrets: A Memoir of Vietnam and the Pentagon Papers*, Viking, 2002, p. 250.
3 Ibid., p. 251.
4 Kissinger, H., *Ending the Vietnam War: A History of America's Involvement in and Extrication from the Vietnam War*, Simon & Schuster, 2003, p. 16.
5 Ibid., p. 17.
6 Anderson, D.L., *Trapped by Success: The Eisenhower Administration and Vietnam, 1953–1961*, Columbia University Press, 1991, p. 17.
7 McNamara, R.S., *In Retrospect: The Tragedy and Lessons of Vietnam*, Random House, 1995, p. 31; see also Kissinger, op. cit., p. 18. The underlying argument had long been part of British Southeast Asian diplomacy, particularly in Thailand: Tarling, N., *Britain, Southeast Asia and the Impact of the Korean War*, Singapore University Press, 2005, pp. 34 and 55.
8 See Chapter 11.
9 Buckley, R., *The United States in the Asia-Pacific since 1945*, Cambridge University Press, 2002, p. 129.
10 Kissinger, op. cit., p. 21.
11 Ibid., p. 18.
12 Ibid., p. 26.
13 Ibid., p. 16.
14 Ibid., p. 154.
15 Ibid., p. 159.
16 Ellsberg, op. cit., p. 115.
17 Kissinger, op. cit., p. 26.
18 *Encyclopedia of Social and Cultural Anthropology* (ed. A. Barnard and J. Spencer), Routledge, 1996.
19 Eisenhower, D.D., *Waging Peace: The White House Years, 1956–61*, Doubleday, 1965, p. 610.
20 Kissinger, op. cit., p. 33.
21 Buckley, op. cit., p. 126.
22 Kissinger, op. cit., p. 35.
23 Buckley, op. cit., p. 133.
24 McNamara, op. cit., p. 129.
25 Ellsberg, op. cit., p. 13.
26 McNamara, op. cit., p. 131.
27 Ellsberg, op. cit., p. 8.
28 Ibid., p. 12.
29 McNamara, op. cit., pp. 135–36
30 Ibid., p. 167.
31 Ibid., p. 170.
32 Ibid., p. 171.
33 Buckley, op. cit., p. 138.
34 Ibid., p. 139.

35 Kissinger, op. cit., p. 223.
36 Ibid., p. 46.
37 Buckley, op. cit., p. 145.
38 Kissinger, op. cit., p. 47.
39 Ibid., p. 49.
40 Buckley, op. cit., p. 143.
41 Kissinger, op. cit., p. 83.
42 Dobrynin, A., *In Confidence*, Random House, 1995, p. 198.
43 Ibid., p. 247.
44 Ibid., p. 246.
45 Ibid., p. 241.
46 Kissinger, op. cit., p. 347.
47 Government of Vietnam.
48 Kissinger, op. cit., p. 352.
49 Ibid., p. 378.
50 Ibid., p. 424.
51 Ibid., p. 454.
52 Ibid., p. 464.
53 Ibid., p. 469.
54 Ibid., p. 499.
55 Ibid., p. 544.
56 Turnbull, C.M., 'Regionalism and Nationalism', in N. Tarling (ed.) *The Cambridge History of Southeast Asia*, vol. 2, pt. 2, pp. 257–318, p. 300.
57 Council for Mutual Economic Assistance.
58 Turnbull, op. cit., p. 304.
59 Owen, N.G., 'Economic and Social Change', in N. Tarling (ed.), *The Cambridge History of Southeast Asia*, vol. 2, pt. 2, pp. 139–200, p. 177.
60 In the early 1960s some 10 per cent of the population of South Vietnam were Catholics, while some 30–40 per cent counted as strong adherents to Mahayana Buddhism: Stange, P., 'Religious Change in Contemporary Southeast Asia' in N. Tarling (ed.), *The Cambridge History of Southeast Asia*, vol. 2, pt. 2, pp. 201–56, p. 236.
61 Private trade was nationalized in March 1983: Turnbull, op. cit., p. 303.
62 See for a general summary, McKenzie, S., 'Vietnam's Boat People: 25 Years of Fears, Hopes and Dreams', CNN Interactive, no date.
63 Harvie, C. and Hoa, T.V., *Vietnam's Reforms and Economic Growth*, Macmillan, 1997, p. 40.
64 Ibid., p. 55.
65 Ibid., pp. 5, 31.
66 Significantly the last time the *New York Review of Books* reviewed books relating to Vietnam was in 1995, and these all referred back to the war that ended in 1975.
67 Harvie and Hoa, op. cit., pp. 12–13.
68 See 'Six Countries Covet the Tiny Spratly Islands', *Economist*, 20 May 2004.
69 Which, as No. 2, was overtaken by Vietnam in 2001. See also 'Trade Wars over Shrimp, a Very Big Row over Very Small Creatures', *Economist*, 8 July 2004.
70 Specially designed standard size TEU containers are loaded on the plantation ready for shipment overseas.
71 Compare 'Goodnight, Vietnam: Vietnam Was Meant to Be the Next Asian Phenomenon. But This Tiger Never Roared', *Economist*, 6 January 2000 with 'Vietnam's Good Economic Performance: Vietnam Has Become One of the Fastest-Growing Countries in Asia', *Economist*, 6 May 2004.

Notes to Chapter 8: Cambodia: a kingdom upside down

1 Cambodia's principal language.
2 See Crump, T., *The Anthropology of Numbers*, Cambridge University Press, 1990, pp.

3   Chandler, D.P., *The Tragedy of Cambodian History: Politics, War, and Revolution since 1945*, Yale University Press, 1991.
4   See Chapter 6, p. 119.
5   Chandler, op. cit., p. 43.
6   Ibid., p. 58.
7   Ibid., p. 63.
8   Ibid., p. 65.
9   Ibid., p. 68.
10 Ibid., p. 70.
11 Ibid., p. 5.
12 Ibid., p. 70.
13 Cambodia's new flag included a picture of Angkor Wat.
14 It was reported that a hundred of these votes were cast in a village close to the frontier with Vietnam, after it had fallen temporarily into the hands of the Viet Minh.
15 Chandler, op. cit., p. 77.
16 Ibid., p. 86.
17 Ibid., p. 88.
18 Ibid., p. 118.
19 See Chapter 7, pp. 144.
20 The final and definitive break only came in April 1965.
21 aka. National Liberation Front (NLF).
22 Kissinger, H., *The White House Years*, Weidenfeld & Nicolson, 1979, p. 127.
23 Ibid., pp. 471–2.
24 Ibid., p. 171.
25 Ibid., p. 173.
26 Chandler, op. cit., p. 325.
27 Ibid., p. 228.
28 Ibid., p. 228.
29 Kissinger, op. cit., p. 485, but note that the reference to May should be to June.
30 Chandler, op. cit., p. 239.
31 Taken from the title of the film *The Killing Fields*.
32 Chandler, op. cit., p. 241.
33 Thion, S., *Watching Cambodia: Ten Paths to Enter the Cambodian Tangle*, White Lotus, 1993.
34 Ibid., p. 46.
35 Ibid., p. 53.
36 Ibid., p. 145.
37 An acronym for *Front uni national pour un Cambodge indépendant, neutre, pacifique et cooperative*.
38 Roberts, D.W., *Political Transition in Cambodia 1991–99: Power, Elitism and Democracy*, Curzon, 2001, p. 15.
39 Peou, S., *Intervention and Change in Cambodia: Towards Democracy*, Singapore, Institute of Southeast Asian Studies, 2000.
40 In Thailand.
41 Peou, op. cit., p. 250.
42 Ibid., p. 252.
43 Roberts, op. cit., p. 104.
44 Ibid., p. 115.
45 Peou, op. cit., p. 254.
46 Roberts, op. cit., Chapter V.
47 Ibid., p. 132.
48 Ibid., p. 136 citing 1997 Government White Paper.
49 Peou, op. cit., p. 328.

Notes to Chapter 9: Malaysia and Singapore: invention of Asian values

1   Firth, R., *Malay Fishermen: Their Peasant Economy*, Routledge & Kegan Paul, 1946.
2   Lennox Mills, cited Baker, J., *Crossroads: A Popular History of Malaya and Singapore*, Times Books International, 1999, p. 195.
3   New legislation in 1914 provided for exclusively Malayan rural reservations, usable only for traditional crops.
4   'The Indian National Army (INA) was formed during World War II by Indian nationalists and prisoners

of war dedicated to winning India's independence from the British Empire. Supported by the Japanese army and led by Subhas Chandra Bose, the INA established its own provisional government and initiated an attack against the British in India': Britannica On Line, 2005.

5   Kissinger, H., *Ending the Vietnam War: A History of America's Involvement in and Extrication from the Vietnam War*, Simon & Schuster, 2003, p. 33.

6   Baker, op. cit., p. 336.

7   Baker, op. cit., p. 355.

8   The record held for just six years: in 2003 Taipei 101, in Taiwan, became the world's tallest building.

9   Harper Collins, 2000.

Notes to Chapter 10: The Philippines: corruption and democracy

1   Cited Preston, D., *The Boxer Rebellion*, Constable Robinson, 2002, p. xxiv.

2   Spain, defeated in 1898, lost both Cuba and Puerto Rico.

3   Remarkably, in 1869, King Leopold II of Belgium, who was set on making his kingdom a colonial power, offered to buy the Philippines, after he had failed to acquire Sarawak in 1860. In the event Spain would have done well to have accepted the offer. Given the Philippines' role in the Pacific War history would have been quite different if they had then belonged to Belgium. Leopold II's colonial ambitions were finally satisfied by his acquisition of the Congo in 1885.

4   Karnow, S., *In Our Image: America's Empire in the Philippines*, Random House, 1989, p. 182.

5   Ibid., p. 328.

6   Ibid., p. 335.

7   Ibid., p. 334.

8   Short for *Hukbong Malagalayang Bayan*, or The People's Liberation Army': ibid., p. 341.

9   Ibid., pp. 345–46.

10 Ibid., p. 345.

11 Later the model for the all too innocent Ernie Pyle in Graham Greene's novel, *The Quiet American*.

12 Ibid., p. 348.

13 Ibid., p. 352.

14 There he tried unsuccessfully to make President Ngo Dinh Diem (who had little of Magsaysay's charisma) a popular figure in South Vietnam.

15 Their character can be judged by the books anthropologists write about them, such as M. Rosaldo's *Knowledge and Passion*, describing the head-hunting Ilongot of northern Luzon (Cambridge University Press, 1980).

16 World-wide only Mexico and India, both with much larger populations, receive more; in relation to population more Filipinos work in the United States than any other nationality.

17 Chua, A., 'Vengeful Majorities', in *Prospect*, December 2003, pp. 26–32.

18 It is not for nothing that a notice next to the entrance to the Philippine legislature reads 'NO FIREARM IS ALLOWED INSIDE THE SESSION HALL'.

19 Cardinal Sin died on 21 June 2005.

20 Karnow, op. cit., p. 363.

21 Ibid., p. 364.

22 Ibid., p. 365.

23 Ibid., p. 358.

24 Ibid., p. 359.

25 Ibid., p. 402.

26 Ibid., p. 405.

27 Ibid., p. 408.

28 Ibid., p. 411.

29 Ibid., p. 414.

30   Ibid., p. 415.
31   Ibid., p. 417.
32   Ibid., p. 421.
33   Ibid., p. 428.
34   Ibid., p. 360.
35   Ibid., p. 366.
36   Ibid., p. 424.
37   Once Ramos became president in 1992, Honasan turned to legitimate politics, to be elected to the Senate in 1995.
38   In the twentieth century, the eruption – ten times larger than the eruption of Mount St Helens in 1980 – was second in size only to an eruption in Katmai, Alaska, in 1912.
39   Hutchcroft, P.D., *The Philippines at the Crossroads: Sustaining Economic and Political Reform*, Asia Society, 1996.
40   Chua, op. cit., pp. 26–32.
41   The words quoted in this paragraph come from Pye-Smith, C., *The Philippines: In Search of Justice*, OXFAM, 1997, p. 60.

Notes to Chapter 11: Indonesia: the long road to justice and reform

1   Part of the British Southeast Asia Command.
2   Yong, M.C., *The Indonesian Revolution and the Singapore Connection, 1945–1949*, Leiden, KITLV Press, 2003, p. 14.
3   Buckley, R. *The United States in the Asia-Pacific since 1945*, Cambridge University Press, 2002, p. 40.
4   Tarling, N., *Britain, Southeast Asia and the Impact of the Korean War*, Singapore University Press, 2005, p. 440.
5   Groenboer, K., *Gateway to the West: The Dutch Language in Colonial Indonesia 1600–1950: A History*

of Language Policy, Amsterdam University Press, 1998, p. 1.
6   Such as that given by the young Marxist scholar, W.F. Wertheim, who had been imprisoned by the Japanese.
7   Yong, op. cit., Chapter VI, 'Clandestine Activities'.
8   Ricklefs, M.C., *A History of Modern Indonesia since c. 1200* (3rd edn), Stanford University Press, 2001, p. 280.
9   Ibid., p. 284.
10   Now Sri Lanka.
11   See Tarling, op. cit., pp. 77–97.
12   Ricklefs, op. cit., p. 304, contains a table with full details.
13   See Chapter 9.
14   Ricklefts, op. cit., p. 330.
15   Ibid., p. 331.
16   Sukarno retired to Bogor where he died in June 1970.
17   The death of Suharto's wife in 1996 was believed by many to be an unintended result of a shoot-out, over money, between two of the children.
18   *Financial Times*, 11 November 2004, p. 6.
19   Related in Chapter 15.

Notes to Chapter 12: Timor Leste: a war of independence (1999)

1   The Molucca Islands separate Timor from the main body of the Pacific.
2   Translated into English their full names were respectively Revolutionary Front of Independent East Timor, Timor Democratic Union and Timorese Popular Democratic Association.
3   Cristalis, I., *Bitter Dawn: A People's Story*, Zed Books, 2002, p. 35.
4   Ibid., p. 37.
5   Ibid., p. 38.
6   Ibid., p. 30.

7   Ricklefs, M.C., *A History of Modern Indonesia since c. 1200* (3rd edn), Stanford University Press, 2001, p. 364.

8   Welsh, J.M. (ed.), *Humanitarian Intervention and International Relations*, Oxford University Press, 2004, p. 511.

9   Ibid., pp. 509–10.

10 *Gusmão* is a common alternative spelling.

11 A Portuguese acronym meaning *Armed Forces for the Liberation of East Timor.*

12 Cristalis, op. cit., p. 116.

13 Ricklefs, op. cit., p. 390.

14 Murdered by insurgents in Iraq in 2003.

15 Supplied with the report by *The Australian*, a newspaper which had a leaked copy.

Notes to Chapter 13: The Russian Far East: the GULAG legacy

1   The same principle founded the British claims to Rupertsland in the west of Canada and the whole of Australia.

2   Hill, F. and Gaddy, C., *The Siberian Curse: How Communist Planners Left Russia out in the Cold*, Brookings Institution Press, 2003, pp. 80f.

3   Ivanova, G.M., *Labor Camp Socialism: The Gulag in the Soviet Totalitarian System*, M.E. Sharpe, 2000, cited Hill and Gaddy, op. cit., p. 83.

4   Skidelsky, R., *The World after Communism: A Polemic for our Times*, Macmillan, 1995, p. 110.

5   Mitchell, D.W., *A History of Russian and Soviet Sea Power*, André Deutsch, 1969, p. 524.

6   Jordan, J., *Soviet Warships: The Soviet Surface Fleet, 1960 to the Present*, Arms and Armour Press, 1983, p. 7.

7   Ibid., p. 135.

8   Hervey, J., *Submarines*, Brassey's (UK), 1994, p. 28.

9   Watson, B.W., *Red Navy at Sea: Soviet Naval Operations on the High Seas, 1956–1980*, Westview Press, 1982, p. 133.

10 Hill and Gaddy, op. cit., p. 171.

11 See map at the top of p. x.

Notes to Chapter 14: Migration: gains and losses

1   Now the name of a university in Singapore.

2   Connoting both 'south' and 'foreign'.

3   Castles, S., *The Age of Migration: International Population Movements in the Modern World*, Macmillan, 1993, p. 168.

4   Jupp, J., *From White Australia to Woomera: The Story of Australian Immigration*, Cambridge University Press, 2002, p. 8.

5   Ibid., p. 9.

6   See *Korematsu v. US*, 323 U.S. 214 (1944).

7   Jupp, op. cit., gives 130,000 as the number who fled Vietnam after the fall of Saigon on 30 April 1975, but this figure relates only to the first year.

8   See also Chapter 7.

9   Baker, J., *Crossroads: A Popular History of Malaya and Singapore*, Times Books International, 1999, p. 248.

10 Malay is still an official language in Singapore.

11 Castles, op. cit., p. 166.

12 Ricklefs, M.C., *A History of Modern Indonesia since c. 1200* (3rd edn), Stanford University Press, 2001, pp. 345, 371.

13 With 7% of total area of Indonesia.

14 *The Economist*, 23 October 2004, p. 44.

Notes to Chapter 15: Crime: piracy, smuggling and terrorism

1 Air-piracy, or hijacking, has no specific Asia-Pacific dimension, rather the opposite. In 1948, however, four Chinese took over a Cathay Pacific flight from Macao to Hong Kong, and crashed the aircraft into the sea.

2 See *The Economist*, 12 June 2004, p. 53.

3 Burnett, J.S. *Dangerous Waters: Modern Piracy and Terror on the High Seas*, New York, Penguin, 2002, p. 324.

4 This gained world-wide attention following the tsunami of 26 December 2004.

5 *The Economist*, 12 June 2004, p. 53.

6 This would be considerably cheaper than a canal: ibid.

7 This is examined in detail in Gilquin, M., *The Muslims of Thailand*, IRASEC, 2005, pp. 129–36.

8 Renard, R.D., *Opium Reduction in Thailand: A Thirty-Year Journey*, UN International Drug Control Program, 2001, p. 1.

9 This was the work of a British Ambassador in Bangkok, John Bowring, whose remit was to increase the quantities available for sale to China.

10 This was the same policy as that of a number of states of the US in relation to alcohol.

11 Renard, op. cit., p. 3.

12 Ibid., p. 8.

13 Compare the figures for Laos in the same year, 126 tons, and for Burma, 1,500 tons: ibid., p. 35.

14 See the *Earth Policy Institute* press release of 21 May 2002.

15 See Diamond, J., *Collapse: How Societies Choose to Fail or Survive*, Allen Lane, 2005, pp. 300–4.

Notes to Chapter 16: The American west coast and the US Pacific empire

1 *The Economist*, 23 July 2005, p. 43.

2 See Menand, L., 'Fat Man: Herman Kahn and the Nuclear Age', *New Yorker*, 27 June 2005, pp. 92–98.

3 The low odd number indicates a north–south highway in the western US: somewhat paradoxically I-1 and I-3 are in Hawaii. East–west routes have even numbers, starting from the north, with those divisible by 10 indicating the most important highways.

4 In his *Mandate for Change* 1953–1956.

5 Which includes Mount McKinley, at 6,194 metres, the highest mountain in the US.

6 See Chapter 14.

7 This provided for free college education for veterans of World War II.

8 *The International Longshoremen's and Warehousemen's Union* (ILWU), established on the American west coast in the 1930s, with Harry Bridges as its charismatic leader, was from very early days strong in the docks in Hawaii and later, despite the concerted opposition of the employers, the military and most of the political establishment, among sugar and pineapple workers there. The ILWU's work changed the political climate in Hawaii, breaking the hold on power that the white landed elite had exercised for half a century.

9 As witness many recent buildings, such as a beautiful Buddhist temple copied from that of Byodo-in just outside Kyoto, to commemorate the first centenary of Japanese immigration.

10 The same status as President George
W. Bush claimed for Guantanamo Bay
in Cuba in 2001.

11 Major, J., *Prize Possession: The
United States and the Panama Canal,
1903–1979*, Cambridge University
Press, 1993, p. 190, note 1.

12 Ibid., p. 190.

13 This led President Truman to ask,
off the record, 'Why don't we get out
of Panama gracefully, before we are
kicked out?', ibid., p. 317.

14 Ibid., p. 272.

15 Ibid., p. 273.

16 Ibid., p. 325.

17 Rep. Daniel Flood, ibid., p. 332.

18 Ibid., p. 342.

19 Gudeman, S., *The Demise of a
Rural Economy: From Subsistence to
Capitalism in a Latin American Village*,
Routledge & Kegan Paul, 1978, p. 161.

20 Major, op. cit., p. 346.

21 Ibid., p. 348.

22 Ibid., p. 354.

23 Submitted by Rep. John Murphy.

24 Major, op. cit., p. 357.

25 In 2006 27 per cent of the world's
container-ships exceeded the PanMax
limit of 8,000 containers that would
allow them to pass through the canal.
These figures can only increase in
coming years.

Notes to Chapter 17: Australia

1 Welsh, F., *Greath Southern Land: A New
History of Australia*, Allen Lane, 2004.

2 Ibid., p. 449.

3 Ibid., p. 451.

4 Before World War II, he had described
Mussolini as 'the greatest man living'
– with Franco not far behind: ibid.,
p. 441.

5 Ibid., p. 456.

6 Ibid., p. 459.

7 Ibid., p. 460.

8 See Chapter 7.

9 Welsh, op. cit., p. 461.

10 West, R., *River of Tears: The Rise of the
Rio Tinto-Zinc Mining Corporation*,
Earth Island Limited, 1972, p. 91.

11 See Chapter 12, p. 267.

12 Welsh, op. cit., p. 485.

13 Ibid., p. 486.

14 Kissinger, H., *Diplomacy*, Simon &
Schuster, 1994, p. 722.

15 Welsh, op. cit., p. 500.

16 Ibid., p. 514.

17 In 1971 the reserves were estimated at
900 million tons: West, op. cit., p. 109.

18 See ibid., p. 119.

19 Welsh, op. cit., p. 529.

20 Ibid., p. 544.

21 See Chapter 14, p. 289.

22 Whose original contribution to
Australian culture is commemorated
by a giant bronze medallion set into
the pavement of Sydney's Circular
Quay.

23 Welsh, op. cit., p. 542.

24 *A Family Madness*, Penguin 1987, p. 64.
Keneally also wrote *Schindler's List*.

Notes to Chapter 18: The new Asia-Pacific: hope and despair

1 According to a recent press report
the monthly salary of an Indonesian
major-general is only $250: no one
reaching this rank expects to live on
such a meagre income, particularly
given the cost of buying promotion.

2 Prime minister 1982–87.

3 Prime minister 1972–74, Tanaka was
also forced out of office as a result of
corrupt dealings, and later in the 1970s
became notorious for his involvement
in the Lockheed Scandal.

4   As it did for Prime Minister Thaksin of Thailand, who first made his career in the police.

5   Calder, K.E., 'China and Japan's Simmering Rivalry', *Foreign Affairs*, March/April 2006, pp. 129–48.

6   See, for a recent study, the Special Report: Italian textiles and China in *The Economist*, 25 Feburary 2006.

7   The actual owners are Freeport-McMoran Copper & Gold Inc.

8   This contains the capital, Manila, as well as 16 surrounding cities and municipalities.

9   UN Population Estimate Revision 2003.

10 China is a major producer of coal, but its mines have an appalling safety record. Almost all its oil has to be imported.

11 The only two others were Liechtenstein and Monaco.

12 Flannery, T., 'The Ominous New Pact', in *New York Review of Books*, 2006, vol. LIII, no. 3, p. 24.

13 See the *Sydney Morning Herald*, 13 January 2006.

14 Information from the official website, www.apec.com

15 *North-American Free Trade Association.*

16 Notably the Philippines, many of whose nationals work in the states around the Persian Gulf.

17 No island in the Pacific suffers from trials equal to those of Haiti in the Caribbean.

Bibliography

Anderson, D.L., *Trapped by Success: The Eisenhower Administration and Vietnam, 1953–1961*, Columbia University Press, 1991.

Baker, J., *Crossroads: A Popular History of Malaya and Singapore*, Times Books International, 1999.

Bix, H.P., *Hirohito and the Making of Modern Japan*, Harper Collins, 2000.

Black, C., *Franklin Delano Roosevelt: Champion of Freedom*, Weidenfelt & Nicolson, 2003.

Buckley, R., *The United States in the Asia-Pacific since 1945*, Cambridge University Press, 2002.

Burnett, J.S., *Dangerous Waters: Modern Piracy and Terror on the High Seas*, New York, Penguin, 2002.

Calder, K.E., 'China and Japan's Simmering Rivalry', in *Foreign Affairs*, March/April 2006, pp. 129–48.

Castles, S., *The Age of Migration: International Population Movements in the Modern World*, Macmillan, 1993.

Chandler, D.P., *The Tragedy of Cambodian History: Politics, War, and Revolution since 1945*, Yale University Press, 1991.

Chang, J. and Halliday, J., *Mao: The Unknown Story*, Alfred A. Knopf, 2005.

Chua, A., 'Vengeful Majorities', in *Prospect*, December 2003, pp. 26–32.

Churchill, W.S., *Grand Alliance*, Houghton Mifflin, 1951.

Cornell, E., *North Korea under Communism: Report of an Envoy to Paradise*, Routledge Curzon, 2000.

Cristalis, I., *Bitter Dawn: A People's Story*, Zed Books, 2002.

Crump, T., *The Death of an Emperor: Japan at the Crossroads*, Constable, 1989, OUP, 1990.

Crump, T., *The Anthropology of Numbers*, Cambridge University Press, 1990.

Diamond, J., *Collapse: How Societies Choose to Fail or Survive*, Allen Lane, 2005.

Diamond, J., *Guns, Germs and Steel: The Fates of Human Societies*, Allen Lane, 1997.

Dobrynin, A., *In Confidence*, Random House, 1995.

Eisenhower, D.D., *Waging Peace: The White House Years, 1956–61*, Doubleday, 1965.

Eliot Kang, C.S., 'North Korea's International Relations: The Successful Failure', in S.S. Kim (ed.), *The International Relations of Northeast Asia*, Rowman and Littlefield, 2004.

Ellsberg, D., *Secrets: A Memoir of Vietnam and the Pentagon Papers*, Viking, 2002.

Emery, R.F., *Korean Economic Reform: Before and since the 1997 Crisis*, Ashgate, 2001, p. 1.

Encyclopedia of Social and Cultural Anthropology (ed. A. Barnard and J. Spencer), Routledge, 1996.

Fairbank, J.J., *China: A New History*, Belknap Press, 1992.

Ferguson, N., *The Way of the World: Twentieth-Century Conflict and the Descent of the West*, Penguin, 2006.

Firth, R., *Malay Fishermen: Their Peasant Economy*, Routledge & Kegan Paul, 1946.

Flannery, T., 'The Ominous New Pact', in *New York Review of Books*, 2006, vol. LIII, no. 3, p. 24.

Gaddis, J.L., *The Cold War: A New History*, New York, Penguin Press, 2005.

Galland, X., *Histoire de la Thailande*, Presses Universitaires de France, 1998.

Gilquin, M., *The Muslims of Thailand*, IRASEC 2005.

Goncharov, S.N., Lewis, J.W. and Xue, L., *Stalin, Mao and the Korean War*, Stanford University Press, 1993.

Greene, G., *The Quiet American*, Penguin Twentieth Century Classics, 2003.

Groenboer, K., *Gateway to the West: The Dutch Language in Colonial Indonesia 1600–1950: A History of Language Policy*, Amsterdam University Press, 1998, p. 1.

Gudeman, S., *The Demise of a Rural Economy: From Subsistence to Capitalism in a Latin American Village*, Routledge & Kegan Paul, 1978.

Gilquin, M., *The Muslims of Thailand*, IRASEC, 2005, pp. 129–36.

Harvie, C. and Hoa, T.V., *Vietnam's Reforms and Economic Growth*, Macmillan, 1997.

Henderson, C., *Asia Falling: Making Sense of the Asian Crisis and its Aftermath*, McGraw Hill, 1998.

Hervey, J., *Submarines*, Brassey's (UK), 1994.

Hill, F. and Gaddy, C., *The Siberian Curse: How Communist Planners Left Russia out in the Cold*, Brookings Institution Press, 2003.

Hsu, R.H. (ed.), *The MIT Encyclopedia of the Japanese Economy* (2nd edn), MIT Press, 1999.

Hutchcroft, P.D., *The Philippines at the Crossroads: Sustaining Economic and Political Reform*, Asia Society, 1996.

Ivanova, G.M., *Labor Camp Socialism: The Gulag in the Soviet Totalitarian System*, M.E. Sharpe, 2000.

Jordan, J., *Soviet Warships: The Soviet Surface Fleet, 1960 to the Present*, Arms and Armour Press, 1983.

Jupp, J., *From White Australia to Woomera: The Story of Australian Immigration*, Cambridge University Press, 2002.

Kang, D.C., *Crony Capitalism: Corruption and Development in South Korea and the Philippines*, Cambridge University Press, 2002.

Karnow, S., *In Our Image: America's Empire in the Philippines*, Random House, 1989.

Keneally, T., *A Family Madness*, Penguin, 1987.

Kim, D.H., *The Korean Peninsula in Transition*, Macmillan, 1997.

Kissinger, H., *The White House Years*, Weidenfeld & Nicolson, 1979.

Kissinger, H., *Diplomacy*, Simon & Schuster, 1994.

Kissinger, H., *Ending the Vietnam War: A History of America's Involvement in and Extrication from the Vietnam War*, Simon & Schuster, 2003.

Kratoska, P. and Batson, B., 'Nationalism and Modern Reform' in N. Tarling (ed.), *The Cambridge History of Southeast Asia*, vol. 2, pt. 1, pp. 245–320.

Lankov, A., *From Stalin to Kim Il Sung: The Formation of North Korea 1945–1960*, Hurst & Company, 2002.

Large, S., *Emperor Hirohito and Shōwa Japan: A Political Biography*, Routledge, 1992.

Lee, K.Y., *From Third World to First: The Singapore Story: 1965–2000*, Harper Collins, 2000.

Leys, S., *Broken Images: Essays on Chinese Culture and Politics*, Allison & Busby, 1979.

Lowe, P., *The Korea War*, Macmillan Press, 2000.

Lynch, M., *Mao*, Routledge, 2004.

McKenzie, S., 'Vietnam's Boat People: 25 Years of Fears, Hopes and Dreams', CNN Interactive, no date.

McNamara, R.S., *In Retrospect: The Tragedy and Lessons of Vietnam*, Random House, 1995.

Major, J., *Prize Possession: The United States and the Panama Canal, 1903–1979*, Cambridge University Press, 1993.

Menand, L., 'Fat Man: Herman Kahn and the Nuclear Age', *New Yorker*, 27 June 2005, pp. 92–98.

Mitchell, D.W., *A History of Russian and Soviet Sea Power*, André Deutsch, 1969, p. 524.

Möller, K., 'China's Foreign Relations 1978–1999: Unleashed, the Tiger Feels Lonely', in W. Draguhn and D.S.G. Goodman (eds.), *China's Communist Revolutions: Fifty Years of the People's Republic of China*, Routledge Curzon, 2002.

Moon, C. and Kim, T., 'South Korea's International Relations: Challenges to Developmental Realism', in S.S. Kim (ed.), *The International Relations of Northeast Asia*, Rowman and Littlefield, 2004.

Muscat, R.J., *The Fifth Tiger: A Study of Thai Development Policy*, UN University Press, 1994.

Myers, R.J., *Korea in the Cross Currents: A Century of Struggle and the Crisis of Reunification*, Palgrave, 2001.

Neher, C.D., 'Thailand in 1987: Semi-Successful Semi-Democracy', in *Asian Survey*, 1988, vol. 28.

Nixon, R.M., *The Memoirs of Richard M. Nixon*, Grosset & Dunlop, 1978.

Oberdorfer, D., *The Two Koreas: A Contemporary History*, Little Brown & Co, 1997.

Ogle, G.E., *South Korea: Dissent within the Economic Miracle*, Zed Books, 1990.

Owen, N.G., 'Economic and Social Change', in N. Tarling (ed.), *The Cambridge History of Southeast Asia*, vol. 2, pt. 2, pp 139–200.

Patten, C., *East and West*, Pan Books, 1999.

Peou, S., *Intervention and Change in Cambodia: Towards Democracy*, Singapore, Institute of Southeast Asian Studies, 2000.

Porch, D., 'The Taiwan Strait Crisis of 1996: Strategic Implications for the United States Navy', www.nwc.navy.mil/press/Review/1999/ summer/frame_33.htm

Preston, D., *The Boxer Rebellion*, Constable Robinson, 2002.

Pye-Smith, C., *The Philippines: In Search of Justice*, OXFAM, 1997.

Renard, R.D., *Opium Reduction in Thailand: A Thirty-Year Journey*, UN International Drug Control Program, 2001.

Ricklefs, M.C., *A History of Modern Indonesia since c. 1200* (3rd edn), Stanford University Press, 2001.

Roberts, D.W., *Political Transition in Cambodia 1991–99: Power, Elitism and Democracy*, Curzon, 2001.

Rosaldo, M., *Knowledge and Passion*, Cambridge University Press, 1980.

Sandler, S., *The Korean War: No Victors, No Vanquished*, UCL Press, 1999.

Schoppa, L.J., *Education Reform in Japan: A Case of Immobilist Politics*, Routledge, 1991, p. 39.

Skidelsky, R., *The World after Communism: A Polemic for our Times*, Macmillan, 1995.

Stange, P., 'Religious Change in Contemporary Southeast Asia', in N. Tarling (ed.), *The Cambridge History of Southeast Asia*, vol. 2, pt. 2, pp. 201–56.

Steinberg, D.J., *In Search of Southeast Asia*, Sydney, Allen & Unwin, 1987.

Tarling, N., *Britain, Southeast Asia and the Onset of the Cold War, 1945–1950*, Cambridge University Press, 1998.

Tarling, N., *Britain, Southeast Asia and the Impact of the Korean War*, Singapore University Press, 2005.

Taubman, W., *Khrushchev: The Man and his Era*, Free Press, 2003.

The Pacific Islands: An Encyclopedia, University of Hawaii Press.

Thion, S., *Watching Cambodia: Ten Paths to Enter the Cambodian Tangle*, White Lotus, 1993.

Tolstoy, N., *Victims of Yalta*, Hodder & Stoughton, 1977.

Tolstoy, N., *Secret Betrayal*, Scribner, 1978.

Tsang, S., *A Modern History of Hong Kong*, I.B. Tauris, 2004.

Tuchman, B., *Sand against the Wind: Stilwell and the American Experience in China 1911–45*, Macmillan, 1981.

Turnbull, C.M., 'Regionalism and Nationalism', in N. Tarling (ed.), *The Cambridge History of Southeast Asia*, vol. 2, pt. 2, pp. 257–318.

Wan, M., *Human Rights in Chinese Foreign Relations: Defining and Defending National Interests*, University of Pennsylvania Press, 2001.

Watson, B.W., *Red Navy at Sea: Soviet Naval Operations on the High Seas, 1956–1980*, Westview Press, 1982.

Welsh, F., *Great Southern Land: A New History of Australia*, Allen Lane, 2004.

Welsh, J.M. (ed.), *Humanitarian Intervention and International Relations*, Oxford University Press, 2004.

West, R., *River of Tears: The Rise of the Rio Tinto-Zinc Mining Corporation*, Earth Island Limited, 1972.

Wolferen, K. van, *The Enigma of Japanese Power*, Alfred A. Knopf, 1989.

Wyatt, D.K., *Thailand: A Short History*, Yale University Press, 1984.

Yong, M.C., *The Indonesian Revolution and the Singapore Connection, 1945–1949*, Leiden, KITLV Press, 2003.

Index